MW00643318

Hope you
READ Best,
George
11/9/21

COTTON FIELDS TO SUMMITS

THE VIEW FROM CONTESTED GROUND

A MEMOIR

GEORGE KENNEDY

SETAF Publishing   Oro Valley, Arizona

Copyright © 2017 by G. Alfred Kennedy

All rights reserved. No part of this book may be reproduced or transmitted in any form or by any means, electronic or mechanical, including photocopying, recording, or by any information storage and retrieval system, without permission in writing from the author.

To contact the author or order
additional copies of this book
write to us at:
P.O. Box 68053
Oro Valley, Arizona 85737

This edition was prepared for publication by
Ghost River Images
5350 East Fourth Street
Tucson, Arizona 85711
www.ghostriverimages.com

Cover design and page design by
Grigory Lutsenko

ISBN: 978-0-9989059-0-7

Library of Congress Control Number: 2017905907

Printed in the United States of America

First Printing: May, 2017

Author's Note

"Cotton Fields to Summits" is a personal memoir written initially for family and a select few friends familiar with my story. It was only after I had completed the first draft that my perspective on this project began to evolve. I prevailed upon several close friends and a mentor to review the draft since I had never undertaken a writing project of this scope and magnitude before. They suggested my story might be of interest to a broader readership – something I had never contemplated. When I demurred, each of them said, "George, you've got a great story... tell it!" And so I have.

I faced the immediate problem of selection. My memory was too vast and there would be neither time nor space to share all of the choices, events, and outcomes that shaped my journey from the cotton fields of South Carolina at the tender age of eight to the summitry of international diplomacy in many of Europe's iconic capital cities. As I began to write, it was obvious my life was about embracing change and the attendant challenges. My life as it evolved was about choices and decisions, hopefully that would not lead to regrets but more a life of my own design. By focusing on key personal and career decisions, I imposed a discipline on my writing and thus avoided that cumbersome book your family and friends might get around to one day while it collected dust on a shelf or misplaced in a box somewhere in the garage.

If my story has a foundational theme, it would be the power – and consequences – of choices I made while struggling for balance between my head and my heart that affected the precarious fault line between life and family, and, naturally, my Foreign Service career. Choices are the essence of life and they are not always easy. They do, however, define us; they speak to our values. Choices I made shaped who I was to those who loved and supported me. Choices I made regarding my career also projected who I was to those who temporarily impeded my progress and, on occasion, conspired to bring me down.

With the clarity and wisdom of hindsight, there are choices I might have weighed more deeply or, perhaps, avoided e.g., to marry or not; the battles I chose to fight. We don't get "do overs" - just outcomes and, hopefully, opportunities to make other, more informed, choices.

Somewhere I read you're supposed to have a strategy when you write a book. I did not have one. My sole purpose was to tell a story – my story; an unlikely story I felt might serve as inspiration to those generations of nieces and nephews behind me with big dreams that rivaled, perhaps exceeded my own. And then there would be that generation far removed from my own that might raise the questions about me that my siblings and I raised about our great-grandparents: "Who was Uncle Al?" This memoir is also for them.

Therefore, my greatest hope in writing this book is that some aspect of my background, my experiences, or my personal development, may be of value to those whose journeys have begun but direction remains uncertain; or, those still full of hope contemplating the mysteries of life and the road ahead as I did so many years before.

If my story inspires just one family member, a friend, or anyone, to a career in international diplomacy, to reach for a higher rung on their chosen career ladder, or to lean their career ladder against a different wall of opportunity, I would feel gratified, even enriched.

That I was able to write this book is a tribute to many people who had a tremendous impact on the evolution and the direction of my life and, for this American child, an interesting journey of discovery in much of the world to do something different, to be something different. My success, as modest as it was in the larger realm of human endeavor, I willingly share with those whose love, wise counsel, and a willingness to share part of my journey, smoothed out many a rough spot when what appeared to be the end of the road was just a bend in the road.

The first and highest tribute goes to my mother, Emma Eleanor Kennedy, without whose love, encouragement, and support, I would not have dared to dream the really big dreams that were my constant companions. It was those dreams that lifted my spirits and gave buoyancy to the vivid imagination of a young Black child mystified by the graphics of the rigid racial segregation of Batesburg, South Carolina the summer of 1948 while visiting with distant relatives; that same child listening to the sounds of the wind and the rain through the trees in his backyard, or to the gravel beneath his feet on the hot, dusty, unpaved, and unlit roads of Mizpah, New Jersey in the late 1940s. It was while delivering messages from my mother to her friends in the vastness of our rural community; going to the distant country grocery store, or picking up the mail from an even more distant post office, that my dreams would whisper in my ear, "This is but the beginning." To what, I did not know. But, I was always hopeful.

This book describes other important people whom I encountered on my journey from a small community in southern New Jersey decades ago through life in Italy, Germany, France, Belgium, the Philippines and South Korea to the leadership of an important American diplomatic mission in Toronto, Canada decades later. Subsequent visits to Japan, Hong Kong, Mexico, Saudi Arabia, Singapore, and the rest of Western Europe extended the horizons of the curious kid from Mizpah. My journey of discovery did not end when I retired. Shortly thereafter, I made two trips to China – the first with a group of travel writers and the second with my wife, Anna. And then there was the life-altering trip to Uganda – a trip that connected me emotionally to those whose unknown names, faces, and experiences became part of my ancestry.

In my book, I refer to the important figures in my life as my chorus of angels, something each of us needs in our travels. Each journey, although deeply personal, is infinitely more arduous without our angels. Their collective contribution to my efforts is chronicled in the following chapters. An important aspect of my involvement with them however is not adequately conveyed because it is so deeply personal. That aspect is my profound appreciation to each of them and collectively for believing in me and demonstrating that belief in a material way at various points in my life when their support was critical to my continued success.

When I began writing this book, the only title that made sense to me was "Cotton Fields to Summits" My reasoning was simple: Daily life in the rural outback of Mizpah, New Jersey, slightly less harsh than that summer's experience of modern-day slavery in South Carolina, shocked the sensibilities of the eight-year-old that I was when we arrived there in late summer 1948 – a world away from the relative tranquility of Woodbury, my birthplace, slightly more than an hour's drive at that time. Life's responsibilities, in the absence of my father, imposed the discipline required of someone considerably older and experienced than my older brother and I were at the time. The bleak isolation of Mizpah, however, offered a level of solitude into which my fertile imagination flowed and thrived and I was along for the ride.

Mizpah, therefore, was my launchpad to wherever my choices would subsequently take me. Italy - the land of art, history, style, unimaginable cuisine, and love - the world I was exposed to at a critical point in my life that captured my interest, that fueled my wanderlust at the age of 19, one in which I felt I could best utilize my talents, energy, and imagination, was international diplomacy. That future beckoned.

This, then, is my story. It will be different than that of many of its readers. Irrespective of the differences in the stories of those who momentarily share this journey with me, it is my fervent desire to impart a message that transcends those differences. The message lies in the value of perseverance, focus, discipline, integrity, and most of all – Hope.

EPIGRAPH

"If someone be self-controlled, truthful, wise, and resolute, is there aught that can stay out of reach of such a person?"

Panchatantra

Contents

PART FIVE

CHAPTER 1

GENESIS OF A DREAM: THE EARLY YEARS

It was June of 1996 and I was exhausted, but uplifted by the events of the previous three years. Professionally, Toronto had been good for me. My principal policy objective was to build Canadian support for the North American Free Trade Agreement (NAFTA). Ambassador Chamberlin, from the embassy in Ottawa, and I made a good team and, together, we had effected a positive shift in public opinion on NAFTA. Canadians in Ontario understood that the agreement would not leave them odd man out with Mexico as the preferred partner. My tenure as the American Consul General in Toronto was now over and my successor would be arriving in late summer. The post was in the capable hands of my deputy. I had said farewell to many friends, colleagues at the consulate, supporters within the civic and business communities in Toronto and the Province of Ontario, and my Consular Corps counterparts. This was the most emotionally demanding part of the farewell and it was a struggle at times to keep my composure. My household staff and I had had dinner the night before at the residence and I thanked them for being part of my extended family and supporting me in the manner they had. I preferred entertaining at home and the demands on them were considerable. I would miss them because they had been family.

Following a leisurely breakfast – the car was already packed – I headed south to the border en-route to Washington, D.C. and home. The eleven-hour drive was pleasant; the weather was warm and, if I recall, there was not much traffic on the American side once I got outside Buffalo. I was again alone with my thoughts, something I enjoyed. For years, I listened to former colleagues speak of their transition into retirement and I often wondered how I would react when that became the next chapter in my life. Well, here it was! Yes, I was exhausted but I did not feel uncertain about the future, a sentiment expressed frequently by former colleagues. In a few days, I would begin the 30-day retirement seminar. This was touted as the best seminar of its type in the Executive Branch and I looked forward to it. I had not developed a resume in more than 20 years and I needed the practice.

During the drive home, I reviewed my career: the highs and lows, the friends, the unique experiences, the myriad opportunities to travel, and those occasions when I did gain respect for my ideas. By the time I arrived home, what had been the pinnacle of a life's achievement was comfortably receding into the past. That drive really helped! I felt a sense of satisfying relief. It was over and I knew the sooner I could close that chapter, the better it would be for me. Now, I knew how it felt to be a "former." On Monday, it was back in the classroom. I had the weekend ahead and calls to make.

The journey from "Cotton Fields to Summits" had been one helluva' ride! Several times during that long drive from Toronto, I chuckled to myself as events and people flashed through my head. It was an unlikely 35-year journey, a journey that had its genesis more than four decades earlier in the cotton fields of Batesburg, South Carolina; around the family dinner table, and in a small country church in Mizpah, New Jersey, a speck of a place between Mays Landing and Vineland in that part of the state that gives it its name – The Garden State.

The historical figures who most fueled my imagination and stoked my lifelong quest for knowledge as a child growing up in the 1940s and 50s were those history calls its pathfinders: Lewis and Clark, Christopher Columbus, Marco Polo and Magellan, to name a few. They dared to venture into the unknown; they charted a course for others to follow. Although I was not a boyscout, I understood the significance of their accomplishments. I suppose I admired them because they were different, adventurous; perhaps because they sailed against the prevailing tides of opinion. And then, there were the pathfinders in the realm of ideas, the men and women who saw life's imperfections and its injustices, who believed that an idea whose time had come could prevail against the odds. I speak here of giants of color: A. Philip Randolph, founder and president of the Brotherhood of Sleeping Car Porters; Clifton R. Wharton, Sr., the first African-American to enter the Foreign Service of the United States; Ralph J. Bunche, the first African-American to win the Nobel Peace Prize in 1950; and, Fannie Lou Hamer, a founder of the Mississippi Freedom Democratic Party (MFDP).

The world these giants chose to shape had immediate relevance for me because I did not have to reach across centuries of time and space to embrace their achievements. My maternal grandparents and my mother spoke of them and others across the dinner table and in polite conversation. Since books, newspapers, and magazines were central features in my cloistered life, these names were there; they made the news. I even met Fannie Lou Hamer years later in Washington, D.C. And my most vivid recollection of that meeting was the aura that seemed to surround her. I was moved by her quiet strength, the steel in her voice, and her passion. It was palpable as she spoke of her struggle for justice and equality and the necessity for truth in defining the African-American experience during the decades of the 1940s, 50s and 60s in the Mississippi Delta. Mrs. Hamer spoke with a clarity and conviction that mesmerized all of us under the sound of her voice in the conference room at the Federal City College that day.

The great equalizer, the qualities that leveled the playing field for all of these pathfinders was their passion for the quest and an ability to lead. I wanted to step into their shoes. I knew I was different, but the big question was, how was I different? Let's stop for a moment; I am getting ahead of the story.

It is true that my own quest for something greater than – even different from – events I saw playing themselves out daily with family and friends began with my love of ideas and the ability of an idea to transform a life; to transport someone from the confines of home and community to life on a larger, and as-yet, undefined stage. Call it a dream, a child's curiosity about the world over the hill, around the corner, and across psychological bridges I was admonished not to cross. "Be the best at what you do" my mother would say but implicit in that note of encouragement, I came to learn, was her desire that I not venture too far from this side of the "bridge." It was more her comfort zone than my own.

My retreat then was to the ever-expanding universe of my dreams about what lay beyond the hill and round the corner. I fantasized about the world I saw over the horizon and my place in it. My intellectual salvation came from the printed matter my mother could afford and a set of pre-World War 1 encyclopedias my father brought home from one of his road trips. My father was a long-haul trucker which meant he was away frequently – too frequently. On occasion, he would return home bearing presents. On one occasion, the present was the carton containing the encyclopedias. I could hardly contain myself. Although my three siblings were not that interested, I certainly was. I would rather spend time thumbing through the pages than finish my homework.

I was possessed of a powerful imagination fueled by historical and contemporary events; an imagination in which I could be anything I chose to be. Why not? I was a child and children are supposed to dream, even little Black kids of the 1940s. I do not recall any visible manifestations of this private side but others apparently did because as my career in the Foreign Service evolved, former high school classmates professed a complete lack of surprise about the life I had chosen. In fact, several of them said they always expected I would transcend the bounds that seemed to ensnare so many others. A child and an idea are often a force difficult to thwart and I remember vividly the day, the event, the location I refer to as the genesis of a dream; my dream to explore beyond the bridge.

My journey from "Cotton Fields to Summits" began on a hot and humid Sunday afternoon during the month of August in a small country church in Mizpah, New Jersey. The year was 1950 and I was ten years of age. Sitting in the back of that church near our house with the other kids on that hot Sunday afternoon, I was looking out the window with my left arm on the window sill day dreaming, oblivious to the pastor's sermon, and wishing I were elsewhere. My behavior in that moment was not abnormal for the average ten year old in this small community of African-Americans because Sunday was the only free day in the week for me. The humidity was high and I did not have a fan to cool myself. I recall sticking my head out the window slightly and looking along the length of the building. My mind drifted for a moment and the building's shape reminded me of a ship or plane en-route to some far flung destination with me on board as its most eager and excited passenger. The destination did not matter to me. It was only important that I was among the imaginary passengers. In that memorable moment, I felt that I was destined to live in a large universe. The details were unclear and the "hows" and "whys" I thought, would come later. Somehow, I instinctively knew my time would come.

I was born the second of four children of Bernard and Emma Kennedy at 11:45 pm on Tuesday, June 25, 1940 at 38 Bellevue Avenue, the home of my maternal grandparents in Woodbury, New Jersey. Mother told me years later I was a fragile child whose entry into the world was a very difficult process for her. My health was extremely delicate and my life did hang in the balance for a while. My earliest memories were of our life in Woodbury. We lived in a large, three-story house at 83 Carpenter Street, a stone's throw from my grandparents. In fact, everything in my universe could be seen from our house. My best friend, Maurice (I called him "Reecie") lived across the street, my school was a block away, the church was diagonally across the street from it, and my maternal grandparents' house could be seen from my bedroom window. We had our own play area in a large porch on the side of the house on the first floor. Life was good!

I remember myself as a quiet kid; shy, unassuming and possessed with natural athletic abilities. I loved to run. In fact, I rarely ever walked, even in the house. My demon was a speech impediment – I stammered. Mother said my father did also. I was also an insomniac, but that had its rewards. Between the ages of five and seven, my mother worked until late in the evening. Because I couldn't sleep, I would usually be awake when she came home. She would enter my bedroom quietly and call me to share some ice cream with her. That was special! On other occasions, she would even take me to a local carnival while my three siblings slept---completely unaware of the fun I was having. Of course, our baby sitter, who lived across the street, was sworn to secrecy. I cherished those special times with my mother. She would say, "don't tell the other kids...this is our little secret." She need not have feared that because I would never tell. In fact, I have not until now.

I thought life was just grand during my early years in Woodbury. I attended Carpenter Street School, the alma mater of my mother, her sister and brother, and most of my mother's friends. Although the school had been designated for Woodbury's African-American community since the 1900s, I never attached any importance to the fact that all of my classmates were African-Americans even though I knew that white children lived no more than a block from our school. I thought that was just the way things were. At eight years of age, I admit to a certain lack of sociological depth.

In 1948, my world was turned upside down. Several days after the school year ended, mother told my older brother Bernard and me she and my father planned to send us on a vacation to South Carolina. The operative word there was "vacation." My maternal grandmother's oldest brother, Clarence, had agreed to let the two of us spend part of the summer with him and his wife, Aunt Mattie, on their farm some distance outside Batesburg. Bernard and I were excited. My younger brother Michael was really upset that he would not be going with us. He was just barely five years old. My sister Jolene was unconcerned because she would have everything to herself. I turned eight that June and Bernard was approaching his 10th birthday.

What made this adventure so cool was we would be traveling alone. We would depart from Philadelphia's famed 30th Street Station on the Silver Meteor. Mother had everything under control: we wore tags around our necks with identifying information including our destination and who was to meet us. The conductors would keep an eye on us and we had firm instructions regarding our behavior on the train. Imagine two kids on the adventure of their young lives! We roamed the train from one end to the other, always under the watchful eye of the conductors. They knew who we were and the only thing they said was to be respectful of the other passengers and to not get in the way. Mother had packed a large lunch box to sustain us on the trip, otherwise, we would have been in the dining car every few hours. Of course, sleeping in our Pullman car was another first. We talked practically all night.

The next day, Uncle Clarence met us in Batesburg and the fun began. We were curious about everything. You would have thought our heads were on a swivel as we tried to take in everything. As the three of us walked through the train station, Bernard and I noticed our first "Colored" and "Whites" signs on restrooms, water fountains and waiting rooms. On the drive out to the farm, we asked about that. What did they mean? Why was it necessary? Was the water different? Our lives were about to be changed forever.

Arriving at the farm in Uncle Clarence's delightful truck (I think it was held together by bailing wire), he took us around to the kitchen door to meet Aunt Mattie. She was sitting close to the door and her first words to us were "Have a seat and shell peas," not, hello, how was your trip? Are you boys tired, hungry? She was shelling peas and she put us to work immediately. The pace with her was unyielding. Aunt Mattie was just plain mean-spirited and rarely spoke a kind word to either of us. Uncle Clarence, for the most part, said nothing and did not interfere. He whipped Bernard regularly because of an intermittent bed-wetting problem.

To Aunt Mattie, we were two extra field hands and we worked from dawn until well after dark six days a week. We would rise around 5 am for breakfast to arrive at the cotton fields just before daybreak. It is cold in South Carolina in the morning and Bernard and I were not allowed to dress for the weather. We wore short pants and T-shirts while Aunt Mattie was so heavily layered, her movements were slow and awkward. Picking cotton is hard, arduous labor and more often than not, it is done under the blazing midday sun. Cotton bushes were prickly and we did not know what we were doing. We learned quickly because Aunt Mattie was never more than a few feet away. Her impatience and bad temper were always on display and, when that did not suffice, she would hit us with switches. The noon break was taken under a shade tree at the edge of the field. Aunt Mattie would bring a full plate for herself but never more than a sandwich for my brother and me. In fact, we were always hungry!

At the end of the second week, Bernard and I were ready to go home. Mother said this was to be a vacation, but Aunt Mattie apparently had other ideas. She and Uncle Clarence did have a telephone but we were not allowed to use it. Moreover, Aunt Mattie censored our mail to ensure we did not include any comments about how we were being treated and that we wanted to come home. We were trapped!

When we were not picking cotton, we worked days in the corn fields. At night, bathing in aluminum tubs out in the yard, the bathwater contained dozens of corn bugs. Then, of course, there were the chickens, the hogs, and the cows that needed to be fed, milked, and stalls cleaned. Occasionally, we worked around huge, razor-sharp rotating saws at a lumber mill with Uncle Clarence. This was 1948 and safety equipment such as goggles and prohibitions against child labor in dangerous work conditions were non-existent or, most likely, ignored. We were frightened by that huge saw and refused to go within six feet of it. That refusal meant a whipping when we got home and probably no dinner. Well, both punishments were preferable to being hurt or possibly even killed. Just the high-pitched whine of that saw terrified us. Watching it cut through lumber conjured up images of that happening to us. No thank you, Uncle Clarence! We were kids but we were not stupid.

As punishment for unnamed transgressions, Aunt Mattie would send us out into the dark of night with a razor-sharp axe to cut wood for the kitchen stove. We knew it had to be done so we asked if we could do it during daylight hours. She, of course, said no. She sent us out into the night and closed the window shade to hide any light visible from the kitchen window. Well, here we were in a huge woodpile with an axe and no light to see what we were doing. I split my little toe with the axe when I missed the piece of wood I was trying to cut, and my brother almost hit me in the head with the axe when I got too close. Our combined effort produced one small piece of kindling for the stove: another night without dinner. Field hands brought in to help Uncle Clarence were fed better than we were.

I recall encountering a bobcat or some animal one evening while retrieving a head scarf Aunt Mattie had left in the field close to the house. I carefully made my way to the field along a path because it was dark and visibility was poor. There was also a briar patch I wanted to avoid. Miraculously, I found the scarf she had left and turned to head back when I think I saw two eyes and heard something. I bolted and ran screaming in a straight line toward the house a little more than a hundred yards away. The next morning, we discovered I had run through that briar patch. I never knew it. Aunt Mattie questioned the veracity of my claim that I had seen something but, I was in that field; I know what I saw and heard. The next day, Bernard and I did go back and we did see paw prints in the soft sand.

Uncle Clarence took us into Batesburg on several occasions and we saw first hand what race segregation meant, and how African-Americans had to comport themselves around whites. It was dehumanizing! Bernard and I would talk about what we had seen on those occasions in hushed tones at night or when we were not in earshot of Uncle Clarence or Aunt Mattie. They had lived in the South all of their lives, since before the turn of the 20th Century, and we were afraid of offending them by our remarks. As kids, we vowed to never live in the South or allow anyone to treat us in a similar fashion. It just was not right!

Until the eve of our departure for home, we performed every conceivable category of farm labor possible. Our enthusiasm for life in general had waned considerably. We now understood trauma, real fear, loathing, and contemporary slavery. Mother was horrified as my brother and I recounted every detail of our experience, as was my grandmother. Clarence, however, was my grandmother's oldest sibling and I am not sure if our concerns were ever expressed to him. We later learned that his wife had been one of his teachers and she was known to be mean-spirited. Bernard, I am convinced, never fully recovered from the psychological impact of the brutal whippings. The unfairness of racial segregation and the harshness of racial injustice tore at my soul and I vowed to confront this evil whenever and wherever I was able to.

The second life-altering event concerned by parents' decision to move from our house in Woodbury and away from everything that offered stability and continuity in our lives. The impact of this decision weighed even more heavily on my brother and me given recent events that summer. My father wanted to move the family to Mizpah to be closer to his employer, Charles Molinelli Trucking Company, located a short distance away in Vineland. Although Mizpah was only 36 miles from Woodbury, it was a far cry from anything I had experienced regarding a permanent change in lifestyle. Mizpah was a speck of a destination astride Route 40, a secondary highway leading to Atlantic City. If one were looking for Mizpah for the first time, you would have to drive slowly and be extremely alert, otherwise you would easily miss Mizpah's most prominent landmark: Mizpah Bar & Grill. Earlier, it was called the Mizpah Hotel. An inter-county bus actually picked up and discharged passengers there. If you missed the building, next to it was an enormous oak tree, itself at least 75 years old. Friends visiting for the first time were advised never to pass that massive tree.

A contemporary casual observer might perceive Mizpah in more idyllic terms. This was the late 1940s and there was no crime and no palpable social tensions. The only school was integrated but located in the predominantly white part of town. There was one paved, or blacktop road; no electricity and indoor plumbing in many homes on our side of the tracks, and outhouses were standard even for homes with electricity. In every kitchen was a hand pump with a pitcher of water beside it to "prime" it in the morning. The water was ice cold and delicious; some of the best water I would ever taste. This was rural America. There were several thousand African-Americans and second-generation Italian Americans. In varying capacities, all of Mizpah's residents earned their living from the commercial farms in the neighboring communities of Richland, Millville, and Vineland stretching down into Atlantic County. You worked on the farm and graduated to driving the interstate trucks hauling produce the entire length of the Atlantic Seaboard. Essentially, the residents of these small communities represented a large plantation-style labor pool, dependent almost completely on the good will of the plantation (farm) owners. Puerto Ricans were imported to live on many farms and African-Americans augmented their labor pool. Whites drove the vehicles on the farm, supervised the workforce, and worked in the warehouses processing the produce for shipment.

Aesthetically, Mizpah was dismal. Our new house (although the house was not a new construction) was a small, two-bedroom cottage with no electricity, running water or indoor toilet facilities. It was surrounded by 36 acres of woodland to which we had complete access; the acreage came with the house. Beyond that was an endless expanse of woods. Your only access to our house was a seemingly endless gravel road which produced dust storms whenever a car would pass the house. Local hunters hunted deer in our backyard in full view from the bedroom window. We were not allowed beyond the yard during hunting season. Directly across the road from the house did a widow and her precocious daughter operate a summer camp. I remember my first morning at the new house. I came out the front door and was immediately struck by the ubiquity of the forest around us. Looking at the summer camp across the road, I wondered why anyone would come to a place like Mizpah and then travel deep into this isolated community amid all these trees for a vacation. I thought it should be just the reverse. Initially, I felt lost, as though kidnapped in the dark of night and dumped into a place that might not even be a part of civilization, certainly not civilization as I knew it. My summer in South Carolina had been but an interlude, albeit harsh; this was permanent!

The most limiting aspect of living in Mizpah was the absence of intellectual stimulation. At eight years of age, I was an avid reader, a dreamer, and I loved the written word. In this place, there was not even a community library; the kids did not like school and they were no fun to talk to. My only intellectual stimulation came from pouring over the volumes of a pre-World War 1 set of encyclopedias my father had brought home from one of his frequent road trips. I memorized Aesop's Fables, saw photographs of Sicily's Mount Etna, the Huang Po River running through Shanghai, and learned that some thought there was a lost City of Atlantis. When I saw the photograph of Mount Etna, I promised myself I would go there one day. At some point, I began to understand the dimensions of a world much larger than the unmarked boundaries of Mizpah. Those encyclopedias stretched my imagination in ways I would appreciate later in life. Intellectually, my journey to the summits of international diplomacy had taken its first fledgling steps.

My father was completely immersed in his lifelong passion for trucks and therefore was not a ubiquitous presence. He left me with a few indelible impressions, the stuff of about 3-5 minutes of memories. The rest of the story, I learned from my mother. As she said, "he loved his trucks" - which he drove for over 50 years - and "he loved his freedom." My father spent his early years in West Philadelphia around Haverford Avenue. It was most unlikely that he and mother would have traveled the same social circuit had my father not formed a gospel group with one member from Woodbury. Their group performed at our family church in Woodbury and, according to my mother, she took one look at him and the rest is history. That was in 1936. They married in 1937 when she was 16 and he was 22.

The towering figure in my life during my formative years was my mother. Born on March 8, 1921 in Philadelphia, Pennsylvania, my mother, Emma, like many of her generation of African-American women, had few to no opportunities for self-expression outside the home. Although armed with nothing more than a primary education, my mother did not look the part. Mother was wise beyond her 27 years in 1948 and committed to giving each of her children the intellectual foundation and the values to prosper in a world she knew would be hostile to us. She was tall, beautiful, and extremely intelligent. Moreover, she had an uncanny ability to sense if any one of her children was lying to her. She was guided through her life by her faith in God, which never wavered.

She was a homemaker, friend to her children, confidant, advisor to many; strong willed, focussed and a stern disciplinarian, although basically a fair person. She was a towering presence to be ignored at one's peril. Mother did not live in a world of ambiguity; she simply could not afford to. Her message was always clear. She established rules and the consequences for disobeying them. If we broke the rules, as we inevitably did, we knew the punishment. You always had a choice with her. Mother was the demanding parent because my father was rarely at home. My father's frequent absences were to have unforeseen consequences in just a few short years.

Dinner conversations in my house were fun, but they often required advance preparation because Mother would often ask questions of my three siblings and me. Most of the questions related to appropriate behavior in certain circumstances, or school topics. "I don't know" was never an acceptable response to any question unless it was followed by "but, I will find out." Mother dominated all aspects of our lives as children. She assiduously checked all of our homework and knew all of our teachers, yet we did not have a telephone or a car. Mother would send notes to our teachers and it never occurred to any of us not to deliver the note or the teacher's response. She kept up with the latest slang among the children in the community, and insisted that we never use it. She was fond of saying that no matter how much we learned, how smart we became, "failure to communicate effectively would be the same as being stupid." "God was to be the guiding force in our lives" she said and that "you children must live and work as a team while we lived under her roof." Under her tutelage, we learned real survival skills which carried throughout our lives, certainly mine. My greatest fear was that of letting my mother down, not living up to her expectations of me, as formidable as they were. I wanted her to know that her investment in me was going to reap dividends some day. I was convinced of that, even as a child.

The balance of my first summer in Mizpah following our move from Woodbury was spent exploring life in my wilderness community and becoming familiar with my new surroundings. We rented our house from a Mr. Seidenstern who lived in New York City but had considerable property holdings in Mizpah. I cannot count the nights I lay awake listening to the sounds of the woods and wondered what was out there. By the end of that summer in 1948, I was ready to begin school. I was eager to return to the classroom. After all, I was in the third grade now. There, I could be exposed to many new things, learn of the world outside, and make new friends. I saw school as my salvation. The start of school also brought new responsibilities. We used wood stoves to cook and heat the rear of the house and the fireplace heated the front living room and my parents bedroom. My brother and I learned to cut wood early on. We got up early in the morning and went into the woods to chop down trees for firewood. After dragging them home, several under each arm, we would chop the trees and stack the wood on the back porch within easy reach of the door. After school, the whole process was repeated again. On Saturday, we spent the entire day in the woods and an hour or two at the end of the day cutting the trees into shorter lengths for the wood stove or the fireplace. Every family did this and the object was to find a patch of oak or pine unknown to other households. This did not last long because it was easy to follow the tracks created by dragging trees under your arm. As we got older and stronger, you could use the axe handle as leverage and carry two or three trees on your shoulder. Life's necessities required a daily regimen.

One of the more pleasant aspects of life in Mizpah in the late 40s and early 50s for me was riding the bus to school. As a third-grader the Fall term of 1948, I attended a two-room elementary school several miles from home. If you missed the school bus in the morning, you simply did not arrive at school in time, at least not for the first bell. Life on the school bus was an adventure. The 20-minute ride, when it did not snow, was replete with on-board romances, quiet arguments, silence for the newcomers like me, or, eventually, a brief opportunity to talk about an upcoming test, homework, or that favorite topic, who was rumored to like whom. My brother Bernard was a fifth-grader so he got to ride the bus to Mays Landing, about seven miles from Mizpah School.

The community Post Office was several hundred yards from the school and several times a week, my brother or I had to pick up the mail. Sometimes we also had to stop by Mr. Ausby's grocery store (on our side of the tracks) to pick up something for the house, then walk the two miles through the woods and down the long dirt road home. This was time to be along with one's thoughts, and, on occasion, fight off at least one of the community bullies who thought that I was too studious, did too well on my tests, loved English and somehow just generally did not fit. However, I always arrived home in time to complete my chores, even during the shortened days of winter. As far as I was concerned, even the walk home was being timed.

Midway through the third grade, I had become accustomed to my new surroundings and began to yearn for the promotion to the next grade. That would mean a longer bus ride to a larger school in Mays Landing. To me, this meant that when the bus stopped at Mizpah School to discharge my sister Jolene and younger brother Michael, I would remain on the bus with my older brother for the ride beyond the limits of

Mizpah and this two-room school. This would represent an important step beyond an important boundary. Each day, I would wonder what my older brother did and saw on the bus when it turned left at the top of the rise in the road and disappeared from sight.

When I received my certificate from Mizpah School, I could hardly contain myself. Now, I, too would be headed for Mays Landing. Mays Landing School was a regional school that encompassed grades four through eight. With the exception of those students from the City of Mays Landing, all of the students were from communities a considerable distance away. If you did not ride a school bus, no student, of whatever race, could attend that school. Parents worked and could not transport their children to school via the family automobile. At three o'clock every day, there were at least ten school buses parked on two sides of the school. I had never seen so many school buses in one place in my life. At my previous school in Woodbury, everyone walked to school. School buses did not have the social stigma they would later come to have in the 1960s. "Busing" was not a pejorative term at that time. In Mizpah and other rural counties in southern New Jersey, school buses were a fact of life; they were an essential mode of transportation. To their human cargo, a school bus for older students was a place to talk to that special person on whom you had a crush, a place of high energy with twenty simultaneous conversations all at decibel levels that only young ears could endure. For me, it was a place to be alone before arriving at Mizpah School to pick up the mail, go to the grocery store, fight one of the community bullies, and change from my school clothes to those more suitable for cutting enough wood to last until the next morning.

I quickly learned that life at Mays Landing School was about managing relationships with both African-American and white students for the first time. It was about dealing with more than one teacher during the day and managing expectations each of them had of me because I was quiet, bright, studious, and thrived on English, history, math, and geography. I also learned from my wise older brother that there was a darker side to Mays Landing: no African-Americans could live there at that time and none did. A new phase of my education had begun. I saw this in South Carolina but now here it was at home. Race and its pernicious effects was now part of my life away from what I had seen earlier in the summer. On the surface, this social construct did not generate any discernible tension between African-Americans and whites. Given my mother's abiding concern about fairness, I felt sure it was difficult for her to accept the fact that she was powerless to change this aspect of life. Naturally, she would have preferred that her family live closer to school and the amenities that Mays Landing offered. Her constant refrain was "be the best student in the class, and learn all that you can from whatever resource is available to you." I was in my element.

I felt at ease in Mays Landing's integrated school environment. I gravitated toward the challenges generated by each of my teachers. In the sixth grade, I met my first refugee from post-World War 11 Germany and a very attractive classmate from the former Soviet Union. There were Italian Americans, Irish, and Jewish students in all of my classes. I discovered that I loved the complexities of English grammar, but feared speaking in class because I stammered. My most horrific moments came when I would score the highest grade in the class on an English test and be singled out by my English teacher, Mr. Davies, as an example for the rest of the class. What went through my mind was who I may have to fight later in the day. Equally terrifying was the class requirement to memorize ten-to-fifteen poems and recite them in front of the class. To have a speech defect under those circumstances was a fate worse than death. Failing a test, or trying to relax in the social comfort of the "gentlemanly C" was not an option for me because the alternative to being singled out for distinction by Mr. Davies was facing my mother at home. Just the thought of uselessly attempting to explain a "C" grade motivated me to overcome my fear of being singled out in class and learn to appreciate speaking in front of it.

Mother recognized, more so than we did, how important it was for her children to be enriched by activities beyond the classroom and was determined to do what she could to fill the gaps in our social development – even in a barren place like Mizpah. I always enjoyed music, especially the piano, and Mother saw that as a natural place to begin my social enrichment. She arranged for a kindly old music teacher from Atlantic City to give me piano lessons even though we did not own one anymore. We had to leave ours in Woodbury when we moved. A close neighbor, about a mile down that dusty road, offered the hospitality of theirs. Financially, it was a bit of a stretch because we could only afford a few lessons. Mother and the teacher agreed that I had a good ear for the piano. I did enjoy the few lessons we could afford and well appreciate the sound of a great piano to this day.

The church was central to our lives and that of the community for more than spiritual nourishment. If you wanted to know what was going on in the community, including activities for youth, as few as they were, you had to be involved in the church – as we were. Mr. Bixby, one of the deacons and a proprietor of a small store nearby, was organizing a youth baseball team and my mother had three boys. Although you had to walk over a mile to practice, that was of little consequence because we would be away from home for a few hours. That was important! Bernard and I tried to arrange a few games with teams in Woodbury but there was no one to transport our team. Eventually, our team dissolved because we tired of playing among ourselves. Mr. Bixby was well-intentioned but, like everything else in Mizpah, many things failed for lack of resources to follow up. Impromptu baseball games were easier to arrange and sometimes Bernard and I would steal an hour and join some of the other kids up the road from us who had the same urge. Mother was often away and during those times, we were not allowed to leave the house. We had a large backyard so the four of us literally carved a baseball diamond in the field behind our house. My sister and I would team up against my two brothers. We made our own fun.

Life for us was structured so free time was cherished, particularly if you had to be creative to find it. The four of us never lacked for imagination and much of the stuff we did, Mother would not have approved. We made a pact never to tell her until we were adults living away from home. Homework, household chores, and church on Sunday were my existence. During the summer, whole families, including ours, became paid labor picking blueberries at six cents a pint for eight to 10 hours a day. We also picked strawberries, raspberries, and tomatoes. Time passed but not quickly enough for me. The more I read, the more a larger universe beckoned me.

My birthday held no particular significance for me until the year I turned ten: June 25, 1950. What I recall is seeing a photograph in a magazine of an American soldier looking out over a valley from a mountaintop somewhere in South Korea. This must have been one of the earlier photographs taken in the early days of the war. I know I never forgot it. On that day, a struggle between two ideologies broke out in a faraway place called Korea. I was the child who, for the lack of reading materials beyond my textbooks, an occasional magazine, or two, sought intellectual refuge in that set of old encyclopedias. Where was Korea and why was it significant? I wondered as I thumbed through the pages looking for anything I could find about this place called Korea. Little did I know the influence this country and its people would have on the trajectory of my life and decisions I would make affecting my family. By the time we left Mizpah, there were several Korean War veterans in the community, one of whom became a cherished family friend. He came into our lives after my father abandoned us. His was a steady, firm, but friendly presence and Mother relaxed when he would visit. He certainly did care about us more so than my father apparently did.

I suppose the salient fact of my life in Mizpah, even after the first five years, was that I never felt connected to the place. Hardships were standard fare; there was never enough money in our house, the world I knew was stifling, and I felt trapped. Put another way, no one I knew had a hunger to leave Mizpah; there was no passion for life, no thirst to know, to see, and to do. This was a tough period for me, but, as the obedient child my Mother always said I was, I adjusted. I had no other choice.

When I entered the eighth grade in the fall of 1953, I had a small circle of friends, all of whom looked forward to experiencing high school together. One member of this circle was a young girl I had a crush on since the third grade. Contemplating the future, I could already envision her as my date for the senior prom four years hence. Events beyond my control would conspire against the realization of this simple dream.

CHAPTER 2

CAMDEN

When my father said goodbye to all of us at 7:50 pm the night of January 8, 1951, we were all standing around the oil stove near the front door as we customarily did whenever he would make an extended road trip. He would say to us, "You kids mind your mother and be good!" His parting words to her were "Emma, I will see you in two weeks." And with that, he was out the door. Daddy always parked his truck across the road at the entrance to the summer camp because it was too large for our driveway. There was also the fact that it made too much noise so close to the house. Engine technology was not so advanced then as it is today.

We had no idea we would not see him again for over ten years. My father was an interstate trucker who spent considerable time on the open road. Often, according to mother, he was required to "make a run to Florida." She, and we, fully expected him to return in two weeks. Why not? He never failed to return home from previous trips. Two weeks passed and when he did not return, mother was naturally worried. We had neither telephone nor electricity and news, even bad news, traveled slowly. Mother wondered if perhaps he had been hurt, or worse, killed. A Black man was still an endangered species on the highways in the southern states in the late 1940s and early 1950s. Days of no news became weeks turned into months, and still not one word. Even my father's road buddies there in Mizpah professed not to know his whereabouts. Mother always suspected they knew more than they let on but there was no way to prove it.

My father's absence had an immediate impact on us financially. Ours was a "cash and carry" existence. Otherwise, it was Postal Money Orders. Rent, although only $25.00 monthly, may as well have been $200.00, an unheard of sum in those days. We did not have money and this was winter on the eastern seaboard: cold, blustery winds and snow up to our knees some days. By the way, my brother and I still cut wood even when the snow complicated our ability to do so. Mother's early recourse was to turn to family and friends for help. Then, it was the New Jersey State Welfare Board. She did what she had to do to keep her family safe.

Just a personal note on this. To this day, I fail to understand the mentality that seeks to become a ward of the welfare system. Our case worker was a young white woman; younger than mother, but who treated her as someone unworthy of respect, compassion, or understanding. She would inspect our home for profligate purchases of food, clothing, or household items she deemed excessive. Of course, she never found anything. She reserved unto herself the right to determine what constituted a family necessity. I promised myself to avoid any life's circumstance that reduced my options to dependency on the state welfare system. Again, mother did what she had to but it did hurt. My father's actions reduced us to that level of contempt and I never forgot it.

Beginning 1952, we began each new year wondering about my father; would this be the year he returned? Two years passed and we persevered. It was now early 1954, three years later and it was clear, at least to my siblings and me, that daddy had permanently separated from us. That he did so without so much as a letter really mystified us. The State Welfare Board considered a telephone a luxury and that made it even more difficult to try and locate him. Daddy was seldom at home due to his extended road trips, but for the first two years after his departure, mother always held out hope he would return. Gradually, she, too, became less hopeful and more accepting of this new reality. The change in mother brought about by our diminished circumstances was evolutionary. Although she was her customary strong-willed self throughout daddy's absence, she was a lot more intense; there were fewer light moments and she did not laugh as often as she once did. Since I was the child that never slept, I could hear her crying and praying every night. We had to hide our homework every night because to mother, it was just another piece of paper to compute the family budget. There was just never enough money.

Frugality was the new mantra in our household. It was "don't waste this," and "you can fix that and make it last longer." Life for us had become more desperate and the toll on mother was real. There were no part time jobs in Mizpah, only summer employment, so my siblings and I were unable to contribute financially. Our contribution was limited to remaining in school and not giving mother cause to worry. Everything was about to change again!

One day in February 1954, mother told the four of us to begin packing our few household possessions because we were moving! I thought we were about to be evicted and I asked, "mom, are we being evicted? To which she promptly said "No!" "Just start packing!" This meant the end of school, books, and the world I had painfully come to know and enjoy. Shortly thereafter, mother announced that we were moving to Camden. "Camden, I thought! Why Camden?" And then it occurred to me: Camden made sense because many of mother's friends lived there. That considered, I was still schizophrenic about this big change. The reality of moving was very difficult for me. In retrospect, I was more affected by the move away from Mizpah than the move to Mizpah because even in this tiny, sparsely populated, isolated community, my intellectual universe had grown over the past six years, thanks to my teachers at Mays Landing School. Moreover, I was a teenager now; I had real friends and relationships I looked forward to developing during our high school years, which for me, was just a few short months away. At the heart of those relationships was a girl I had a crush on since third grade. High school would mean four more years to hopefully strengthen that relationship. Her name was Marian and I was convinced she was the cutest girl I had ever seen: beautiful brown skin, a twinkle in her brown eyes and an infectious smile. But, who remembers details? I was transfixed and had been for five years. In the third grade, I sat next to her and often she would taunt me mercilessly because I stammered. In spite of my embarrassment, I was still smitten. We were now in the eighth grade; both of us were approaching 14 and I was determined to gain my sea legs with her. She did not know it but I had a plan for our future together.

High school for me meant not only sustaining some important relationships, but also opportunities to excel academically; maybe even earn a college scholarship. This may have been a distant dream but it was the only one I had. A scholarship was my only hope because we certainly could not afford the expense of a college education - as much as mother wanted me to have it. I still had two siblings at home and mother struggled just to keep food on the table and a roof over our heads. Assistance from the State Welfare Board did not cover necessities, not with four growing children.

I had also worked very hard to fit into the community of Mizpah. I was doing well at Mays Landing School and had established a solid reputation as a serious student among my teachers and classmates. To my credit, I had even earned some level of tacit respect from the local bullies, whose gauntlet I had to run after school from the post office to Mr. Ausby's store and then home. The only thing I would not miss by moving to Camden was the burdensome chore of cutting firewood before and after school and all day Saturday. I have not taken an axe to any tree since we left Mizpah in early 1954.

Reluctantly, my siblings and I obeyed mother's wishes and began to pack our meager belongings in preparation for the move to Camden. It was March and we made the move quickly; mother wanted to avoid a lengthy interruption in our schooling. Goodbyes were hurried and that saddened me. I would miss graduating with my eighth grade class. Before leaving, however, I did arrange with my teachers to return to Mays Landing School for the class trip to the United Nations and to visit the Gary Moore show in New York City later that spring. I also arranged to meet my former class for their trip to the Philadelphia Zoo. For six years, I labored and earned friendships I was not ready to sever in such an abrupt fashion. I saw Marian but only briefly. I had a head and a heart full of thoughts but the words just did not come. I really did want her to know how I felt about her. Camden was 46 miles from Mizpah, less than two hours drive in the rickety, open-top truck my mother had hired from a family friend. We arrived early afternoon on a grey day in March 1954. Fortunately for us, it had not snowed recently and the streets in Camden were dry. The trip to Camden had been uneventful. My siblings and I did not engage in our usual chatter; we were still trying to digest the change to the unknown once again.

When the truck stopped in front of 312 Summit Street, an old and graying, limestone row house 50 feet from Penn Street, Camden's major artery, my older brother Bernard whispered to me, "This is the slums!" I had not seen anything quite like this neighborhood before, even during an occasional visit to Philadelphia with mother. Two of my grandmother's brothers lived in Philadelphia as did my paternal grandparents and my father's younger brother, Uncle Thomas Kennedy. Picture if you can, a typical inner city block of the 1950s devoid of houses except for two old grey row houses on our side of the street, one of which was our new home, and two directly across from us. The other houses all had been demolished with some of the rubble still visible. Residents on neighboring streets used the vacant lots on Summit Street as available parking spaces and to burn trash. At first glance, this was worse than Mizpah had been been. Mizpah was rural; it lacked infrastructure. Here, it was expected; we were living amid urban blight. At the end of the half city block that was Summit Street sat Powell Elementary School. My younger brother Michael would spend the eternity of the sixth grade there before entering Clara S. Burrough Junior High. The upside of the move to Camden was that we were now only ten miles from the familiar surroundings of Woodbury and our grandparents. Public transportation was now just a few minutes from the house and the fare to Woodbury was just twenty-five cents. Many times though, that fare was difficult to come by. The family's financial condition had not improved materially by this move; mother was closer to job opportunities and Bernard and I could find part time jobs. Being close to my maternal grandparents again was important to me. Their house in Woodbury, was in some respects, an anchor, a cornerstone of my life. My grandparent's house was built on contested ground and I always thought it significant that I was the only one of their ten grandchildren to be born in their house. This made me special; at least I think my grandfather thought so.

This man, George W. Elam, was not only my grandfather but also the principal male figure in my life while growing up in the 1940s and early 1950s. He was the keeper of the values that became cornerstones in my life. Born of modest circumstances on June 26, 1893 in South Carolina, like many African-Americans of his generation, he migrated north following his service overseas in WWl seeking employment and to escape the indignities imposed by the rigid segregation he experienced daily both in the U.S. Army and back at home in South Carolina. Eventually, he and my grandmother settled in Woodbury.

Our house on Summit Street was turn of the century (20th Century) construction or before, therefore old and quite small: three rooms (two bedrooms on the second floor and a living room on the first floor) and a kitchen – all on two floors. Toilet facilities and limited storage space were in the basement. The backyard was your typical urban postage stamp: ten-by-twelve feet surrounded on three sides by an old and decrepit wooden fence. An alley behind the house led to the next street. The walls in all of the rooms were covered with old and faded wallpaper that had seen its best days. The house needed a good coat of paint and caulking around the windows. Window shades were missing and the kitchen stove would have to be replaced immediately. I could already see what lay ahead. Mother was thinking she had the manpower to make the place livable, and she did. There was no central heating and the house was dreadfully cold. I did wonder how we were going to survive that first winter.

Potatoes were cheap and we ate potato soup several days a week. Mother was never a great cook, but potato soup! Well, it kept us alive. I dislike potato soup to this day. During the balance of that first winter, the kitchen served a variety of living purposes: eating, bathing, and doing homework because it was the warmest room in the house. We achieved that by turning on all of the burners on the gas range and lighting the oven. This practice was less dangerous in 1954 than it is today, but for many households, that was their only option. Poverty does limit your choices, including how to keep warm. Most of the row homes directly behind us had outhouses. That was a startling discovery. At least we were spared that indignity. Still, I was not happy about this change but it was not my place to question mother's decision to relocate the family. Financially, we were desperate even with limited assistance from the State Welfare Board. Even on that first day, mother sensed our collective apprehension but she held us together. Mother's commitment to family was rock solid and I am indebted to her eternally for that.

Camden in the early 1950s was a universe away from the simplicity of life in Mizpah. This was a real city; the fifth largest in New Jersey at that time. Most neighborhoods were segregated along racial or ethnic lines, but each had its share of families struggling to survive. In 1950, public housing in Camden was segregated. There was no obvious social ferment, just unwritten rules about who was hired for certain jobs. The Mayor of Camden was alternately Italian and Irish. Public sector positions were denied to Blacks in the 1950s. Black women were limited to jobs as "domestics" in Jewish and Italian neighborhoods, and similar positions in hospitals. A vivid, iconic image in many urban centers then was the Black women with their ever-present shopping bags waiting for the bus to go to "work." My mother was one of them.

Here in the city, there were sights, sounds, challenges, opportunities, and social phenomena that literally unnerved the impressionable 14-year old teenager I had become. Most of the older guys in the neighborhood whiled away their little free time at the pool hall on the corner from Summit Street, or at the social club across the street from the pool hall. Younger teens spent their free time at Jack Bass's luncheonette a block away on the corner of 11th and Cooper Street. Jack Bass had a bank of public telephones, a major convenience for those families without telephone service at home. In an era before Motown, "Do Wop" was in vogue and North Camden also had its share of vocal groups who harmonized outside Bass's luncheonette most spring and summer nights. At 9 pm, the police would ride by and say, "I want that corner!" That meant it was time for everyone to be at home off the streets. There was never a problem, never an argument, never an altercation with the police. Many of the older guys proudly pointed out that many of the police who patrolled North Camden never drew their weapons except on the firing range. Contrast that with today! As young Black men, we were not an endangered species; we did not fear the police as we were no threat to anyone.

George Evans, a classmate and neighbor, helped me to navigate the terrain between home and my new school, about a mile away. George offered friendship and I gratefully accepted it. Very quickly, I learned that life on the surface was raw. As the proverbial new kid on the block, I was an outsider, soon to learn that relationships were more difficult to build than had been the case in Mizpah. People acted on their feelings about you. For the first time, I had to test the solidity of the "social ground" I walked on daily. Life was about the quality of your relationships. My well-being and, on occasion, physical safety, depended upon relationships, who I knew. If I was to survive, much less prosper, on some of Camden's mean streets, I had to learn who the "Alpha" males were, not only in my North Camden community, but also in East Camden where I went to high school, and in South Camden where some of my teachers lived, as well as most of my mother's friends to whom she would often send me on errands.

Again, I owe a debt of gratitude to George Evans. George was a Camden product, well liked, outgoing, and the most natural basketball player I have ever observed in life. Michael Jordan, with all his vaunted ability, had nothing on George Evans. George could take off from the key, do a 360-degree turn and dunk the ball in 1954. That was unheard of in junior high school basketball at that time; at least it was news in Camden. Perhaps Wilt Chamberlain had accomplished a similar feat at his high school in Philadelphia, but if he had, the press never wrote about it.

Traversing some of the streets in South Camden was harrowing because if you did not know the right kid on a particular block or in a particular neighborhood, which I often did not during the early years, it was all too easy to become involved in a serious altercation with kids from that neighborhood. Van Hook Street, and the First and Third Wards in South Camden were neighborhoods I tried to avoid. You could not convince me that even the weather in South Camden was not different than elsewhere. The sky appeared darker and threats seemed to lurk everywhere. While running errands for mother in those sections of the city, my brother Bernard instructed me on how to comport myself to avoid undue attention from ever watchful eyes. I learned, for example, that how I carried a bag in my hand could indicate that I was an outsider. Therefore, strangers were easy to spot.

Guns and drugs were not as ubiquitous as they are today, but I was 14 and unaccustomed to the downside of inner city life. Knives were the preferred weapon then and I did not relish the idea of being in a fight with a skilled knife fighter. The only knife I had handled was a kitchen knife and mother's trusty butcher knife. The perpetual admonition from my mother was, "by all means, protect yourself and your clothes," because if one of us came home bloodied and with torn clothes, we had a worse fury to contend with – Mother. Little did mother know - or seemingly understand – how I dreaded being her emissary delivering messages to her friends, particularly in South Camden. It was the menacing looks from kids I did not know, and wondering if I was in imminent danger; the questions about who I was and why I was in their neighborhood. What I feared was being told to stay out of their neighborhood. I would just have to cross that bridge if I had to. There were those few occasions when friends visiting girl friends across town were asked where they were from. If your tormenter just happened to have had a bad experience with someone in your neighborhood, your day suddenly took a turn for the worse. How could I tell mother I would have preferred to stay at home and read or study? In response to this frequent circumstance, I developed an almost encyclopedic knowledge of the city by learning the back streets and alleys; the alternate, more circuitous routes from our house (point A) to the intended recipient of mother's message (point B). For me, this was survival 101. Meanwhile, I learned how to posture myself not only among African-Americans, but also among the Irish, the Poles, the Puerto Ricans, the Jews, and the Italian Americans.

Life at Clara S. Burrough Junior High School on Camden's Haddon Avenue reminded me of scenes from that 1950s classic film with Sidney Poitier, "Blackboard Jungle." No one ethnic group feared any other group, so there was not the option of positioning myself with a predominant group for safety and security. Who you knew and what you had in common mattered. Most of the kids in North Camden grew up together – childhood friends. I could not compete with the bonds they shared but I knew I had to fit in.

In fairness, I think my mother knew Camden was a tough environment for a Black teenager, but she had three boys and she knew we were going to be out there. She understood from the other mothers with boys that a Black kid's success on the streets depended on having your head and your ass wired together at all times because temptations came in various forms: sex, gang life, petty crime, menial jobs, and early parenthood. Parents struggled to feed, clothe, and house growing and inquisitive teenagers. Money in every household was in short supply, so having a few quarters in your pocket for discretionary spending was a luxury. Money unlocked the door to the streets and all of its temptations. The fact that I did not have any just may have been my salvation.

Although George Evans and I were classmates and newfound friends, he did not "have my back" as the expression goes. My real guide and role model during those early years in Camden was my older brother Bernard. Bernard, according to his teachers and friends, was brilliant and wise beyond his years. One of his favorite pastimes, I discovered, was reciting poetry by Kahil Gibran. I used to wonder "who the hell is Kahil Gibran?" Bernard was also "street smart." He thrived in our new inner-city environment. The energy and the pace of life in Camden nourished him. While I struggled to gain my footing, he sprouted wings and began to fly. He would often say to me, "life is not lived in those books; you'd better get out in the street and meet people where they live." Like my brother, I was in the streets everyday, but Bernard's admonition implied that I was not learning real survival skills; I was just passing through. Initially, I defended my reluctance to "get out there" as he put it, but I always tagged along with him as often as I could because I knew he would not mislead me. He and I both understood that my survival depended upon how quickly I learned; he would not always be there for me. As I think back, he and I did a lot together. In just under two years, we did just about anything to earn extra money: ice cream vendors, handymen, service station attendants, pinsetters at our local bowling alley, and busing dishes in a restaurant. We even capitalized on natural disasters such as hurricanes by pushing stranded cars from flooded areas of the highway before the city crews showed up with their tow trucks.

A bizarre incident revealed in stark terms the truth of my brother's admonition about understanding people where they lived. That same incident also laid the foundation for a friendship that would endure between one of my antagonists and me during my early years in Camden and for the next four decades. One day in 1955, while walking home from school, I heard someone behind me call my name. "Alfred, stop, I want to talk to you!" It was Vincent Cream, the youngest son of Jersey Joe Walcott, the former heavyweight champion of the boxing world in the early 1950s. Vincent called me by my middle name because at home, and among those who were part of my early childhood, they knew me as Alfred.

"Alfred," Vincent said, "I dreamt you stole my girl and I am going to kick your butt!" I was dumbfounded and fearful at the same time. I knew by reputation that Vincent was a highly skilled boxer. Inwardly, I remained calm, thinking "this is Mizpah all over again." As Vincent called out my name, I never stopped walking, but tried to defuse the situation by talking, talking, and more talking. "Are you crazy?" I asked him. "I have never heard of such nonsense; starting a fight over something you dreamt?" The more I talked, the less agitated he became and the closer we drew to his house. At the corner of his street, he turned to go home, but before he did, he said "Alfred, you're crazy, but you're alright." He laughed and walked away. I had gotten through the day, but then there was tomorrow. The next day, I had an identical experience, only this time with another kid by the name of George Boyer. This George imitated whatever Vincent did, so if Vincent had a dream that I stole his girl, Boyer had to have the same dream – only a day later. Boyer, however, appeared to be more humorous than threatening.

Although I felt emotionally wounded by both attacks, I, again, understood how necessary it was to develop effective survival skills for Camden's streets. Sometimes the skills would involve an ability to engage someone verbally with the demeanor of someone with greater self-confidence than I possessed. Those streets also included the corridors of Burrough Junior High School. The teachers there were accustomed to dealing with rough and highly vocal inner city kids and I was neither. If you happened to be in the wrong corridor, especially in some of the unused classrooms, you just might witness acts of intimacy more appropriate for the privacy of one's home. To me, the larger concern was how to convey this dilemma, the need to develop survival skills, to my mother who knew the latest slang, but did not appreciate that the use of it was necessary to survive on the streets. I decided not to tell her, just look for opportunities to be on the street, legitimately, as Bernard had suggested. I said earlier, perhaps mother did understand this, but there were times when I thought she did not. As part of adapting to my environment, I knew my reputation as an outstanding student, but one who stammered, would have to be tempered. I did not have any idea how to do this; it just occurred to me that it might become necessary. For example, I again dreaded those moments when I was singled out, this time, by Ms. Mansfield, my homeroom teacher, or Ms. Fittipaldi, Social Studies, for exceptional performance on a test. I could not have been more vulnerable than to have a bulls-eye pinned on my back and chest. To mitigate the harassment that always accompanied being singled out like this, I decided to become an athlete as well. All of the important guys were, especially from North Camden. Those that were not athletes had other attributes: the "gift of gab." Between the athletes and the "smooth talkers," they had all the girls. I was not blessed with the gift of gab so academics and, secondarily, athletics were the only options available to me.

Vincent Cream was one of the premier athletes in school and its star quarter-miler. Naïve as I was, I thought that becoming an athlete might be an approach to developing a relationship with him. One day, before the track season began, I said, "Vince, I am thinking about running the quarter mile. What if I practice with you?" I had never run a measured quarter-mile before but I did love to run. No one else knew that. Vincent looked at me, laughed in my face and said, "Alfred, you're no athlete; you had better stick to your books." Again, he laughed. By the end of the day, it seemed that every kid in the school knew that I thought I could run the quarter-mile. It only got worse. The next day during physical exercise period in a field behind the school, Vincent challenged me to run with him. The school did not have a stadium or athletic field. We would run the perimeter of an unused parking lot of a utility company. That is where Vincent trained and he was familiar with it. The object, of course, was to humiliate me in front of his friends. Smarting from my humiliation the day before, I had to accept. Vincent won, but not by much. "Alfred," he said, "you can run? Why don't you try out for the track team?" I was in! I had been accepted, or so I thought. I had not known it, but Vincent, too, had been looking for a friend. He just had to accept me on his own terms. I was learning the rules. Finally, I did begin to "fit in" in my new surroundings.

As life began to settle down, I was able to focus on re-establishing myself as a serious student (mother required that) and now as an athlete. Eventually, I was able to broaden my circle of friends and developed several relationships that lasted for many years after high school. As an added bonus, mail came directly to our house.

In 1955, I graduated from Burrough Junior High and I looked forward with great anticipation to following my older brother to Woodrow Wilson High School in East Camden. Wherever he was, I wanted to be. He was also my biggest and most vociferous supporter at track meets and football games. When I became a high school sophomore in 1955, Bernard should have been a senior. His devotion to mother and his siblings meant he chose part time jobs over school much of the time. His grades suffered and he had to repeat his junior year. Another consequence was he and I sat next to each other in typing class and that was too much for him. In his mind, he was still my senior. He was an outstanding typist, by the way. I could never match his speed and accuracy. Moreover, I never knew how the class setback affected him until years later when mother told me. My father's decision to abandon us combined with our continuing financial condition at home weighed heavily on my older brother. School was the last thing on his mind. Bernard was conflicted and hurt by the absence of our father. He had become the head of the house and we respected his self-ascribed role – as did mother. Bernard was now 17 and he viewed military service as a means to gain real experience and contribute financially to help at home. His next step was to join the Marine Corps. I don't recall that he shared this decision with me because I would have been opposed to it. Bernard was selfless; he saved the family and in the process, altered the direction of his life.

Another momentous development that year was our move off Summit Street to 1191 ½ Penn Street, two blocks away. What a boost to our morale. Our new landlord, Harry Edelstein, owned the small corner grocery store almost equal distance between the old address on Summit Street and the new house on Penn Street. We lived at the Penn Street address for over ten years without incident. Harry Edelstein became a true family friend. Although the house was small, it was larger, newer, and more comfortable. It was also directly across the street from our church. Life was good again.

High school represented the culmination of several key quests in my life. I was a 15-year old who had made a successful transition to Camden. Secure in my identity and place in our close-knit North Camden community, I was a respected student and athlete and had earned a level of recognition by many of my coaches and teachers. Moreover, I was now the president of a prominent young men's social club and had begun to build a reputation among some of the older African-American men in North Camden as a serious young man with a future. It was as a tenth-grader at Wilson High School that I would encounter someone who would have a profound influence on my life; someone who regularly encouraged me to pursue my dreams. Moreover, he could coach me on how to chart a course to the future we both felt was my destiny. Additionally, he offered real adult male friendship. I think I needed that more than anything, especially since my older brother was no longer within easy reach. This larger than life figure was one of my tenth-grade teachers, Mr. Frederick L. Adams.

Apart from school and athletics, there was always a need to earn pocket money for bus tickets, lunch, and those movies on Sunday with Aretha. Oh, I forgot to mention that I was able to survive the separation from Marian in Mizpah. Indeed, I almost forgot her name. Aretha Johnson was a very pretty girl who lived a few doors from us when we lived on Summit Street. Although I noticed her in Junior High School, we did not begin to date until our junior year at Wilson three years later.

Mr. Adams was a new teacher at Wilson High School in 1955: flamboyant, gregarious, and likable. He was also a big hit among the students, myself included. One day after class, Mr. Adams asked if I was interested in a part-time job. Earlier that day, he had asked if any of us in his business practices class was looking for a part-time job. Seeing this as an opportunity to finance those necessary extras that I knew my mother could not afford, I said, "yes" immediately. Mr. Adams had recently moved into a new apartment in South Camden with his bride and it required painting. Later, I would paint the house they occupied after moving from the apartment pending the birth of their first child. On that day after class, Mr. Adams asked if I knew how to paint. I was overjoyed and relieved. Having helped my grandfather paint his house almost every summer, I confidently replied, "yes, I can paint!"

At first, I was excited just to earn some extra money. Gradually, however, Fred and Marlene Adams became real friends. Clearly, I could not reveal this friendship to other students. One evening at dinner with Fred and Marlene, after spending several hours painting, they asked, "Ken, have you considered going to college?" (They called me "Ken.") "Yes" I replied, but "unless I receive an athletic scholarship, it would be financially impossible...the family cannot afford the expense." Both Fred and I knew that although several African-American students were standout athletes at Wilson High, an informal group of city fathers pressured the coaches not to seek scholarships for African-American athletes. The coaches' efforts, in their view, should concentrate on white athletes no matter how mediocre their talents may have been. I was the only African-American student/athlete in my graduating class to earn academic recognition and the coveted varsity jacket for accomplishments in both varsity football and varsity track and field. I had earned the requisite four varsity letters. Vincent and all of my antagonists from those early days in 1954 were there to congratulate me. Winning their approval was an unparalleled accomplishment at that time. Finally, I knew I was one of them.

I also knew that I was an unlikely candidate for an academic scholarship for similar reasons: insensitive school guidance counselors. Our counselors were not predisposed to advance the academic careers of African-American students. I attributed my modest academic recognition at my high school graduation ceremony to the fact that my girlfriend, Aretha, was a student aide to the teacher responsible for compiling grade averages for students in the field of Business Education. I happened to have one of the highest academic averages in the business curriculum and Aretha pointed that out to the teacher. Had she not been there that day, my academic performance most likely would have gone unnoticed.

Fred and Marlene resolved to help me find the means to go to college. Their hope was that I would attend Fred's alma mater,

Trenton State Teachers' College in Trenton, not too far from Camden. By my senior year in 1957, I had been accepted as part of the Adams' family. I grieved with them over the loss of their first child and was a reliable babysitter for their second child, Robin. Meanwhile, a group of Wilson alumni resident in North Camden were all too familiar with how African-American athletes were denied scholarship opportunities. Several members of that group introduced me to the head football coach at Shaw University during one of his summer recruiting trips to Camden's African-American neighborhoods. In the 1950s, coaches from the predominantly African-American colleges of the Central Intercollegiate Athletic Association (CIAA) recruited many of their athletes from high schools in New York, Pennsylvania, and New Jersey. Shaw University in Raleigh, North Carolina, was one of the favored schools for kids from Camden. CIAA coaches were able to harvest the rich talent the northern high schools developed because as coaches, themselves often products of northern schools, they were aware of the dearth of scholarships available through white coaches. If an African-American athlete was offered an athletic scholarship, sight unseen by a southern university, engineered by a high school coach, he was turned away the day he arrived on campus. Such athletes also wound up at CIAA schools. This was the experience of a high school classmate and fellow traveler on our high school gridiron. He, too, came to Shaw University the fall of 1958 but he did not stay too long. Some of the coaches at northern high schools were capable of this level of cruelty. Were it not for the CIAA schools, much of the African-American talent available to professional sports in the 1950s and 1960s would not have been developed.

Although I had been invited to trials for Shaw's football team in late summer 1958, I did not have the means to travel to North Carolina. The means were made available to me on a Sunday morning in May 1958. That day, Fred Adams, now president of his men's club, attended the morning service at my church. He knew I would be there but did not tell me he would visit or why. When visitors were announced, Fred stood, introduced himself and his organization and asked if he could make an announcement. He announced to the entire congregation "This year, Alfred Kennedy is the recipient of our scholarship award; that he was chosen because he was an outstanding student as well as an accomplished athlete. We feel Alfred Kennedy has a future and we wanted to invest in his future and who we think he has the ability to become." While I knew he wanted to help, I did not know of this decision by their club. I was surprised and grateful beyond speech. That was a good day for me. Mother could not have been more proud.

Later that week over dinner at his house, he said, "Ken, you have a great future ahead of you; be true to yourself, your ideals, and never give up on your dreams. You do that, and wherever you are destined to land, you'll get there."

CHAPTER 3

FROM RALEIGH TO VICENZA

The scholarship from Fred Adams and his men's club meant that I could seriously plan to attend Shaw University in Raleigh, North Carolina the fall of 1958. For the first time, the next phase of my future was taking shape. The journey I felt I was destined to make had its first destination. That summer, I became a full-time employee at the Best Supermarket luncheonette a few blocks from the house across from Sears & Roebuck on Camden's famed Admiral Wilson Boulevard. Previously, I had been a part-time employee and Rose, the Italian-American manager, was glad to see me. Rose was another supporter who shared my dreams and was a source of inspiration.

"Welcome back, George," she said when I appeared for work the day after my high school graduation. For some odd reason, Rose preferred to call me George, unlike everyone else in my universe of family and friends.

"Thank you," I replied; "I am pleased to be back." Rose, who knew about the scholarship said, "You are going to need all of the extra money you can earn." During her brief absences, she also trusted me to manage the lunch counter, including our busy kitchen, by myself. I also prepared meals for customers but she did the cooking.

One day as she prepared to go home, she turned to me and said, "George, I am going to let you run the place more often...you may work as many hours as you can." This was great news to me. All I could say was "Thank you, I won't let you down," or something to that effect. I wanted her to know that I appreciated her confidence in me. "I know," Rose replied. The job at the luncheonette was a good job. I mean that it wasn't backbreaking work, but it was exhausting. You were on your feet all the time and, at times, the pace was frenetic. I took Rose up on her offer and worked the maximum number of hours permissible. Most of the waitresses were pleasant, efficient, and were a great help to me, especially when I was alone. Only one of them ever became testy with me when she felt I was not responsive enough to one of her requests. The luncheonette had a steady lunch clientele from Sears, their automotive service center, the local car wash, several car dealers in the area, and the N.J. Motor Vehicle Inspection Station less than a hundred yards away. We had to be fast. It was not unusual for customers to form lines behind the stools at the counter.

Rose was one of those rare gems that pass through the lives of the fortunate, in this case - me. I could always count on her to do whatever she could to boost me up. Late one afternoon in August while returning from the dry cleaners, I saw Vincent on the street and it was then I learned he, too, had been invited to try out for the football team at Shaw. So, in early September, ten days before student registration, Vincent and I arrived in Raleigh and proceeded directly to the Shaw campus. Coach Anderson had already advised us to go directly to Tupper Hall, the freshman men's dormitory, once we arrived on campus.

Shaw's campus in September 1958 was small with a student population of slightly over 600 students; reminiscent of a southern plantation, with large trees that provided a canopy between two old red brick buildings, themselves covered in ivy that extended to the fifth floors. These two buildings were the women's dormitories. Concrete walkways punctuated the well manicured commons with a central driveway through an ornate wrought iron front gate. Off to the right partially obscured by trees was the residence of the university president. An interstate highway through the heart of the campus to the left of Tupper Hall separated the administration building, the school library, and the School of Divinity from the main campus – the locus of student activity. To the rear of the main campus was the dining hall with the auditorium on the second level, the Campus Inn and Bookstore, the Science Building, classrooms, the gymnasium and the upperclass men's dormitory.

The Shaw Campus, and its sister institutions throughout the South and the Southwest, offered an idyllic setting to nurture young African-American men and women who were later to confront the challenges of the early Civil Rights Movement and the Vietnam War. It was from these campuses that we created a generation of leaders and followers for the lunch counter sit-ins near Raleigh's St. Augustine College in 1959 and 1960. I was pleased at the beauty and pleasantness of the campus because I had steeled myself for the worst, and I was prepared to tough it out no matter how much I may have disliked being back in the South.

This was my only opportunity for a college education and I had to set aside old memories. The problem was, my memories of the summer of 1948 in South Carolina ten years earlier with uncle Clarence and aunt Mattie were still all too vivid.

Early the next morning, Vincent and I, as the first of the new arrivals, headed to the dining hall for breakfast. We were so early, the steam table had not opened yet. As we entered, Vincent saw a piano and, as he was wont to do whenever that happened, sat down to play while awaiting the student servers to staff the breakfast line. Vincent had barely begun to play when a voice thundered, "Who authorized you to play that piano?"

"Who do you think you are coming in here establishing your own rules?" "Get up!"

Vincent and I, momentarily jarred by such a shrill and direct order, turned to face the university's infamous dietician, Ms. Francine McKeenan. I almost lost control of myself. Within seconds, we were nose to nose with this short, stocky Black woman and it was not pretty. From the moment we heard her voice until she descended upon us, no more than a few seconds passed and she had crossed what seemed to be 30 yards of tables and chairs. She literally put the fear of God into us for what we perceived as a fairly benign act. To Ms. McKeenan, Vincent's simple act represented a major intrusion into her domain; one she did not countenance. She made it abundantly clear that, as she put it, "No one touches that piano without my authorization." Imagine this scene: both Vincent and I were six feet in height and this short, stocky Black female at least six-to-eight inches shorter than either of us, hands on hips, head shaking and in our faces. In retrospect, I am surprised she permitted us to eat breakfast. She was really upset! Vincent and I decided after that brief but unpleasant encounter to forego lunch and wait until dinner. Perhaps, by that time she would have calmed down. Fortunately for us, other players arrived during the day and dinner offered us the safety and comfort of numbers. The student servers, all sophomores, and apparently amused by Vincent's misfortune, spread the word among the returning upper classmen about that morning's incident. Todd McNair, a sophomore from Camden, advised Vincent to avoid any direct contact with Ms. McKeenan for a while.

Most of the athletes participating in team trials the fall of 1958 were from New York, New Jersey, and Pennsylvania. Of course, there was the sizable contingent from North Carolina and West Virginia. Several of the returnees were from Camden High School, a cross-town rival at home. Because some of the players from Camden had seen the coach that summer, they had heard my name. I had crossed paths with several of them on the gridiron at home and this worked to my advantage during freshman initiation. It is true I was hazed during freshmen orientation, but the hazing involving nothing more benign than being told to blow out a light bulb in the football team captain's room and making up his bed on several occasions during the first week of trials. I was never paddled or roughed up in any way.

Vincent, on the other hand, coming from a prominent family, was himself a high-strung teenager and accustomed to preferential treatment from everyone, including coaches, throughout his secondary school career. He was also challenged frequently during his early public school years and that usually meant having to fight his way out of situations. He caught several kinds of hell from several upper classmen at Shaw, themselves former products of Camden's school system. His most persistent antagonist was the team Center from North Jersey. His goal was to goad Vincent into a fight. He was rugged, as a team center had to be, and talked trash constantly. This was Vincent's trial by fire and I wish he had been able to tough it out. I do believe Vincent handled the rough treatment as well as he could under the circumstances. The malevolent intentions of several of our teammates turned what should have been a traditional college rite-of-passage into something more ominous. Vincent emerged unscathed physically, but psychologically, he had had enough. Several days later, he left campus and managed to transfer to Howard University in Washington, D.C. I was unable to persuade him to stay and for the first time in four years, we were separated.

Fall trials were physically demanding but I was in good physical condition and enjoyed testing myself against older and more experienced athletes. Shortly before the first game, coach Anderson made his selections for the team and I made the cut. The next step was a scheduled meeting with the university's athletic director, Mr. Lytle, to discuss financial aid. I harbored the illusion that if I made the team, I would be receiving a full scholarship and my financial problems would be resolved. Never one to be late for an appointment, any appointment, I arrived at Mr. Lytle's office a few minutes early and sat down. Mr. Lytle was direct and to the point. He asked, "George, how much can you contribute to your expenses for tuition, room and board?" Stunned by the question, I remained calm, my heart pounding and, in response, I said, "I cannot contribute anything, Mr. Lytle. The small scholarship I received from home and some money I was able to earn this summer was enough to buy some clothes, a trunk to ship them in, and the cost of my ticket to school." I did wonder at that moment if

I had misunderstood coach Anderson when he told me in Camden that I would be on scholarship if I made the team? Well, I had made the team! Was my brief college career about to end before it began? I knew my mother could not help me financially because I still had a brother and sister at home, both in high school.

We can offer you a partial scholarship," Mr. Lytle said, "and a part-time job as statistician for the baseball team in the spring. The balance will be your responsibility." On that jarring note, the meeting was over. I was in a quandary dreading the call I knew I would have to make to my mother. That night, I called home with the news. Mother took it well, but I knew she was as surprised as I was about this development. "Don't worry," mother said. "You stay there, play well and make me proud. We'll find the extra money."

I settled into room 209 at Tupper Hall, the primary residence for freshmen males. My new roommate, Bruce Johnson, was an older student, ex-military veteran, and laid-back. I enjoyed this relationship because Bruce was an easy-going, friendly conversationalist willing to talk about his experiences in the Army, growing up in New Rochelle, New York; women, and just about everything else. Above all, he accommodated my inquisitive nature. Hell, I was still a teenager! Although Bruce tried out for the football team, as an older student in his mid-twenties, he lacked the passion to risk injury to make the team. I was in exactly the same position eight years later. "My life is about more than football now," he told me as I was trying to encourage him to put out more on the practice field. Bruce was financially independent. He worked out with the team for the exercise and the camaraderie. I, on the other hand, was 18 and still passionate not only about the sport, but also about competing. Bruce was beyond that phase of life. His military experience had tempered him in ways I had yet to appreciate. Little did I realize how soon I would come to appreciate how life can temper you.

I will share an interesting short story with you about life with Bruce in 209 Tupper Hall. Early in the semester, I was heading out to class one morning while Bruce was in bed lying on his left side facing the wall. His back was to me and I could not see if he was asleep or awake. I knew that he had a class and I did not want him to sleep through it. I approached Bruce shaking him lightly: "Bruce, Bruce, wake up, you have a class...I'm leaving now!" Before I could retract my hand and complete my sentence, Bruce rolled out the bed in a defensive crouch and, in a split second, had me pinned against the wall with both hands gripping my shirt. Bruce was about 6' 3" or 6' 4", well over 200

lbs and in good physical shape. The expression on his face was, well...
frightening.

"Bruce," I yelled, "Bruce, it's me, George, your roommate."
Over several interminable seconds, Bruce relaxed his grip on my
shirt. His demeanor changed and he apologized. "I forgot to tell you
something," he began. "When I was in the Army, I was part of an elite
unit and our training included conditioning yourself to not only sleep
lightly but with your eyes open." He went on to say, "To wake me, if
you think I am asleep, just take the broom and touch me lightly on the
shoulder." He talked about how rigorous their training had been and
that sudden jolts still conditioned his reflexes as though he were being
attacked. His brother also had been pinned against a wall at home in
a similar fashion and, thereafter, refused ever to awaken him again. In
that frightening instant, his brother could have spoken for the two of us.

Later that night, I said, "Bruce, we have to talk. You scared the
hell out of me this morning!" He, again, spoke in some detail about his
training and the residual effect of some aspects of that training, even
then. "In time," he said, "I will be less affected by it." Oh, by the
way, he went on to say, "I see everything going on in the room, even
though I may appear to be asleep." I wondered why my uncle (my
mother's brother) never spoke of such training and he spent more than a
decade with the 82nd Airborne Division at Fort Bragg, North Carolina.
Eventually, I became less fearful of waking Bruce, but I was certainly
intrigued by that last revelation about seeing everything in the room
when he appeared to be asleep.

The social life for a young African-American male at Shaw
University was unlimited, provided of course that you apportion your
time among meeting individual class requirements, a part-time job on
campus, football practice or traveling with our university choir, doing
personal laundry, and attending mandatory Vespers service at the
Campus Chapel on Sunday afternoon. The young women on campus
were the equivalent of eye candy. I had never seen so many beautiful
young African-American women of every hue, size, and shape. The
challenge for hormone-crazed young men was to stay focussed. The
melodic cadence of southern women when they spoke reminded me
of my uncle's Tennessee-born wife, Marian: the lilt was seductive.
There was that one embarrassing incident with my first student advisor
when she called my name and I did not recognize her pronunciation of
my surname. Phonetically, I heard "Canady", not the more northern
pronunciation of "Kennedy" and assumed she was speaking to someone
else, not me! I happened to turn in her direction and once I understood

she was talking to me, I was mortified, apologized profusely, tried to explain my lack of response. I don't think she ever forgave me for that perceived slight.

Academically, the Shaw campus was a hospitable environment. The student body numbered about 632 students and everyone knew everyone else before the end of your first semester on campus. The faculty was demanding, meticulous, and professional. As our mentors and sherpas, they were entrusted with developing and nurturing undeveloped young men and women to confront and overcome the challenges that were beginning to emerge regarding change in the South. Each member of Shaw's faculty took this responsibility seriously and they required a total commitment from each student. The other students and I were reminded daily that the academic preparation we would receive there would qualify us to compete with anyone, anywhere similarly educated.

A prime example of this commitment to excellence was Ms. Madeline Watson, my English professor. She put this commitment on her part in stark context for her students our first day of class in freshmen English. I never forgot her words and the unique way she introduced her English course requirements and how she would grade us. See if this sends a small shiver up your spine. She said, "In my class, there will be no 'A' grades. A grade of 'A' means you are qualified to teach me, which none of you are." She continued with her trademark broad smile, "A few of you will earn Bs, most Cs, some Ds and a few Fs." I could hear hearts beat, including my own. I was accustomed to doing well in English. It was always one of my favorite classes, even in primary school. She concluded on this note: "Some of you may wish to transfer to another class" and she paused to see if there were any takers. "If there are no questions" she said, "let's begin." I elected to remain in her class and, in retrospect, that was one of my better decisions that semester. Regularly, even today, I refer to the textbook we used that year: "A Complete Course in Freshman English." Children of friends and colleagues, my son, and my nieces and nephews have used that book. It accompanied me throughout my career and today, occupies hallowed space on my office bookshelf.

The class that semester was rigorous and conducted under the exacting standards that defined Ms. Watson's reputation. On many a night studying and on many an examination, I thanked my eighth grade English teacher, Mr. Davies, for insisting on perfection. I had decided to concentrate my effort on doing well on class exams and, to a lesser extent, on well-timed interventions in class. In other words, even though 50 percent of our final grade would be based on oral presentations, I was prepared to sacrifice part of that, given my speech defect and a fear that I would embarrass myself in front of my classmates. Remember, I was still 18 and did not feel confident enough to acquit myself well under the circumstances of her classroom. I admit that Ms. Watson intimidated me.

I thrived on my new freedom, the responsibility to manage my life, my schedule, and the relationships that were now important to my well-being as a student athlete. My other classes were less demanding with the exception of mathematics and physics. My major adjustment was to the clamor in our dormitory at night. Most evenings, I studied at the library, returning to my room when the library closed at ll pm. Occasionally, I would join a study group at the home of one of the other freshmen students from Raleigh.

There were other dimensions to life on campus; the fun stuff that college freshmen look forward to to build memories. Every freshmen class at Shaw becomes quickly aware of the exploits of previous classes and seeks to create its own legacy. You only get one shot at it. Our class was no different. Panty raids, for example, ranked high on the list, but at Shaw, the residence hall matrons were notoriously hyper-vigilant and, from what we were told, thwarted all previous efforts to raid the women's dorms. A small group of us formed a committee, met in the recreation room of Tupper Hall and planned our assault - all good naturedly, of course. We laid out a plan which we executed with military-style precision. We did the unexpected; we accessed the upperclass women's dorm from a location no one would expect: Under a street light using a human ladder to enter from the second floor. In fairness, we also had one of the women acting as a lookout and opened the door once our guy was in place. Our man actually roamed several floors, visited quite a few rooms and returned with a treasure trove of lace delectables. Ours was a coup which earned us bragging rights in the Campus Inn for several weeks.

We also accepted a challenge from the campus nymph, but I will not go into details except to say our "champion," unfortunately did not register on the "satisfaction scale." He was demoralized for a brief period but he recovered quickly. We joined an illustrious list that had grown quite lengthy. Our freshmen class was considered to be more active than most at that time, but we were careful to limit our activities to the safety of the campus. Raleigh could be hostile to the off-campus pranks of college kids, especially if they were Black. There were kids from Raleigh's all-Black Ligon High in our group and they were less inclined to support anything that meant going off campus.

During the fall that year, a very popular film was showing at several theaters in Raleigh and a number of us wanted to see it. Just the simple act of going to the movies became a project. We were freshmen and were advised in unambiguous terms it would be preferable to have several upperclassmen with us and that we should go in a group. We did not argue; we just wanted to see the film. The theater was naturally segregated with the "Colored" entrance on a side street. The ticket booth was small, cramped and dirty. You immediately ascended the dimly lit wooded stairs to the second floor reserved for "Colored" people. Their refreshment stand was an aluminum bucket filled with ice and several bottles of Coca Cola. You ordered popcorn from a glass container; the popcorn was brought up from the concession stand on the first floor and dumped into the glass container. Yes, the popcorn was cold. The seats were wooden, many broken, and some were unserviceable. As you stepped into the aisles, there was so much dust on the floor, it felt like a carpet. We saw the film, promptly left the theater and walked back to campus. I never saw another film for the balance of the year.

I settled into a routine made easier by self discipline: my classes, doing personal laundry, a work-study job, and football practice. When football season ended, I joined the track team. That first semester was a blur. Our football team performed poorly that fall season. As for me, I sat on the bench because of my class schedule. The team lacked something that year but it did not diminish my desire to play. The season was mercifully over and it was time for finals. I felt fairly confident about my grades the first semester, but the big unknown was Ms. Watson. Finals were over and she scheduled individual conferences before passing out grades. Her's was my last conference and it was right before lunch. Until that last conference, I had achieved all "As" and "Bs" and was hoping for a "C" from her. I reasoned that I had performed well on the periodic tests and the final exam; surely that merited a "C." My hope was that the balance of my performance would compensate for my reluctance to speak often in class. Each of my class presentations had been thoughtful, brief, and accurate. Ms. Watson did not countenance "showboating" in the hope she would be impressed. Although we had been warned, there were those students who were counting on achieving the larger part of their grade through oral presentations. We would call them "jumping jacks" because they were constantly on their feet. Ms. Watson's style was to let you dig a hole deep enough to embarrass yourself. When you thought you had acquitted yourself well, she would tell you to remain standing while she offered her critique. Ms. Watson was fair, but when you taxed her patience, her critique was withering, never delivered with malice, and always with a smile. Generally, she would say, "Thank you for your response; you earned a 'D' or 'F'....now you may sit down." No one dared breathe. Her message, again,was simple: do not waste valuable class time trying to impress anyone, least of all her. As I said, some students, mainly from the School of Divinity, never learned, most did. I was certainly one of the latter.

It was just before lunch; I knocked and entered Ms. Watson's office. I was prepared to eat whatever was on the lunch menu to get over the "C" I expected. "Good morning, Ms. Watson" as I approached. "Good morning, Mr.Kennedy...please sit down." She continued, "Mr. Kennedy, you did well this semester" never looking up from her desk and the grade slip she had prepared. She did raise her head, smiled, and handed me the grade slip. When I saw that smile, my heart sank because I had seen that smile before just before she handed one of my classmates his head. I looked at the slip and saw a 'B.' Reflexively, I said, "Ms. Watson, you gave me a 'B.' is this a mistake?" "No, Mr. Kennedy," she replied, "but I can change it if you want me to." "No ma'am," I said, "thank you, thank you," I gushed. As I got up to leave, she said, "You earned it." I recall eating lunch that day, but I do not recall if my feet touched the ground between her office and the dining hall.

Academically and socially, my freshman year was a success. Although the football team did not do well, I was told I would have made the starting team had I been willing to cut my fifth period religion class to arrive at practice an hour earlier. My larger concern was not about increasing my playing time, but assigning greater priority to my education. I had already begun to doubt that I could return for my sophomore year and I did not want a failing grade on my transcript. I would take my chances with the football team, but not with my education. My freshman year might be my only college experience for quite some time, I reasoned. My roommate, Bruce, thought my assessment a bit too grim. "Look," he said, "you had a successful first year...While you did not make the starting team, your prospects for next year are good, provided of course, you can return in September." I also knew that a return in the fall would mean having to adjust my class schedule without compromising the integrity of my academic schedule. That first year, the coach understood the choices I made to focus on my education while trying to remain competitive as an athlete.

That year also had a softer dimension to it. Cassie Palmerson, one of the young women that served us breakfast my first day on campus was from Raleigh on a summer work program. She and I had become good friends since that fateful encounter with her supervisor, the school dietitian. She later became my guardian angel by sending me food. We would study together, attend church together, and I would visit her at her dormitory on Sundays during visiting hours. For the longest time, I felt obligated to her because she was there for me. The social norm on small African-American campuses then was, if two people spent a fair amount of time together, everyone assumed they were a couple, they were "going together." Other women would not spend time with you to avoid offending someone else. I suppose I fell into a pattern, while not prepared to state intentions that were unclear at the time. Aretha and I wrote each other several times weekly. She and I had history I did not want to ignore. This was the classic dilemma of the average college freshman. I was 18 and enjoying the freedom of new friends, new interests, and looking forward to new relationships. According to Fred Adams, this was part of the whole college experience. Had I returned to Shaw the fall of 1959, I would have spent much less time with Cassie. Again, I felt more a sense of obligation to her because she really did rescue me from starvation.

Financially, my freshman had been troubling for me. The money my mother did manage to send did not arrive before the 15th of the month thus leaving me with an open account and an outstanding balance. An open account with the university's finance office meant that I could not receive a pass to the dining room until the 15th of every month. So, for the first 15 days of each month, I could not, and did not, eat in the campus dining room on a regular basis. I basically survived on food Cassie would often send through my roommate, Bruce. Although I never asked her to send food, she would say to Bruce, "take this to George." I could not have survived without the risks she took for me. Had she been caught by Ms. McKeenan, she would have been expelled from the university. Because of this arrangement, I did not have to survive totally on Ritz crackers and peanut butter.

Several students, unfortunately, had no other choice. The university's financial resources were meager and many students lived on the edge of hunger, or dropping out altogether. Students employed every known device to remain in school. I recall the plight of David Watson, a sophomore from Camden High. His basketball scholarship did not suffice to cover the expense of a meal ticket. When not in class, he was in bed. He never walked quickly or exerted himself unnecessarily. His constant refrain was "it is mind over matter...I have to conserve my energy." At night, other students would buy sodas from the gas station just off campus and bring him the empty bottles. Each bottle was worth two cents when returned. Most of the available floor space in David's room was filled with empty pop bottles. Each evening, David would redeem enough to buy a small carton of milk or some peanut butter and a box of Ritz crackers. Care packages for other students often contained something for David. We were a "family" and, within our meager resources, we tried to help him survive as best we could. It bears mentioning that in the 1950s, many of my classmates, myself included, represented the first generation in their family to set foot on a college campus as a student.

Raleigh, North Carolina was a racially segregated city, so looking for a part time job off campus was futile. Haircuts were possible because at the edge of our campus was a barber college for African-American students. Raleigh, in 1958 and 1959, like so many southern cities was also hostile to a young African-American male who did not understand "how to comport himself" in southern white society. Having grown up to have and display personal pride, I and many of my classmates from New York, New Jersey, and Pennsylvania did have adjustment problems. My mother always said, "Once you bend your back to grovel, you can never stand up straight again."

Raleigh was the State capitol. On several occasions, there were physical altercations between small groups of whites and individual African-Americans. The favorite tactic of whites was to walk five and six abreast on city sidewalks whenever they saw an African-American approaching. To avoid conflict, the African-American would step off into the street and wait while they passed. When our students were involved in incidents like this, the student was invariably from one of the northern states, unaccustomed to these more overt forms of racism. New students, especially from out of state, were encouraged by the university administration to remain on campus and, when going to the movies, to travel in groups, never alone. Options to earn extra money were available only on campus or, in the local Black community if you did not live on campus. To university officials, this fact alone minimized our need to be off campus for extended periods of time. On Sunday afternoons, carloads of white students from the University of North Carolina at Chapel Hill would drive past the campus and shout racial epithets at those of us sitting out on campus after lunch. We ignored them or someone would "flip" them off. I would hope for any one of them to experience mechanical problems during their drive-by.

I know the campus has expanded since my day, but at that time, I loved the intimacy of Shaw's campus and the deep friendships made possible by a small student body. Both the faculty and the students shared a recognition of the burden they carried to be prepared for life after Shaw. If the faculty did not demand the best from us, who would? If the faculty did not nurture and care for Shaw's students, who would?

Classmates rallied to the support of those who required extra tutoring. Failure truly was not an easy option; it was hard to fail. Help was everywhere!

Sororities and fraternities were an extension of the academic experience. Everyone wanted to belong for the friendship, the support, and the unique traditions of Greek organizations on African-American campuses in the 1950s. I pledged Alpha Phi Alpha because most of the upperclassmen from Camden and from New Jersey, and many on the football team, were Alpha men.

In May 1959, I successfully completed my freshman year and returned to Camden. Life was about to take a 180-degree turn. I took a weekend for myself and the following week, my thoughts were on my future. What was my next step going to be? Shaw had been a defining experience, one that I had every desire to complete at some point. However, I could not escape the deeper, foreboding thought that I would not be returning to campus in September. I had made some important friendships there, ones I would miss dearly, including my guardian angel, Cassie. We did promise to keep in touch. Aretha, meanwhile, was in a serious relationship and was, in fact, pregnant, I was to learn later. We'll get to that.

I think my first telephone conversation early that first week was to Fred and Marlene to let them know I was home. What I really hoped for was an opportunity to earn some money. I was broke! Perhaps they could still use me in some capacity. I also called my grandfather in Woodbury thinking he could use my help with some of his accounts. Earlier in my youth, I had accompanied him on his rounds to maintain the homes and grounds of affluent whites in Woodbury. I told him I was coming down to visit later that week. I was older now and maybe he would allow me to manage some of his accounts. I needed money because living at home was not free.

Marlene and Fred invited me over for dinner so we could talk. They were still important friends and I was eager to share with them impressions of my freshman year. Fred had spoken often of his experiences while a student at Trenton State Teachers College and now I could add my own; no longer in my former position of quiet envy. I knew Fred well enough to know he would enjoy listening and comparing notes. The serious part of our dinner conversation was all about the linkage between the graduation date they foresaw three years hence and the future they envisioned for me. I could be honest with them so I told them how difficult it had been for me financially and how my mother had struggled to help me and, that now, I needed to be able to earn enough money to return to Shaw in the fall.

Fred was silent for a moment and then he said, "Ken, I will need you to help us with a house we're planning to buy…it needs a lot of work." That was a start. "Thanks," I said, "I was really hoping you had something for me to do." Later that week, I met Fred to visit the house they planned to purchase and he was right: there was a lot to do. For me, the more work to do, the better. The following week, I plunged in. Two dollars an hour in 1959 was good money for a 19-year old teenager in Camden.

I also took the time to review the classified ads in the local daily, The Camden Courier, to see what job opportunities might be available. I needed something full-time and then work for Fred in the evenings and on weekends. He would understand. While I did not delude myself into thinking I stood a reasonable chance of being selected for jobs all teenagers sought during the summer months, I also saw no harm in pursuing any reasonable leads. I noticed several office jobs as clerk-typists and the only posted job prerequisite was a high school diploma. I was not only an excellent typist, I was also a business administration major with a successful year of college. I knew to appear bright and early the following morning to be the first applicant to appear in person. That afternoon, I called the contact number and was told by a Mrs. Anderson that the job had not been filled. I called Fred to tell him of my plans and that I would be late the next day because of the job interview. He understood and wished me well.

The next morning, I dressed appropriately and went early to the department store that had posted the ad. As luck would have it, I was the first applicant to appear. In an envelope, I had a copy of my high school diploma, a list of the business courses I had taken, and my college transcript. I could type an average of 60 wpm and felt confident I could pass any typing test. A Mrs. Anderson approached and before she could say more than "good morning," I asked, "are you Mrs. Anderson?" "My name is George Kennedy…we spoke yesterday afternoon about the clerk typist position advertised in The Camden Courier." I then showed her the ad. "Oh! You're George Kennedy," she said. "Well, I have to tell you, the position has been filled; I am sorry." I should note that I was never asked to accompany her into her office for even a pro-forma interview. Instinctively, I knew she was lying. The position had not been filled, unless it was after office hours the night before. There was nothing I could do but leave. Several days later, the ad was still listed. This was the beginning of a series of professional disappointments that served to impede what was, at this point in my life, a burning desire to continue my education and lay a foundation for my life. Giving up in the face of these not-so-subtle forms of racism was absolutely out of the question. For me, the question became, what strategies could I employ to overcome obstacles like Mrs. Anderson and maintain some forward momentum.

While recounting the events of the day with Marlene and Fred, Marlene told me she was not surprised at the outcome of my experience earlier in the day. As she explained it, I needed to experience the kind of discrimination most commonly employed outside the South; more subtle. She had had similar experiences. So, for me, it was back to painting their new house.

In early June, I was in Woodbury visiting with my grandparents and my grandmother began to tell me about a new program she had heard was being offered by the U.S. Army whereby an enlistee could select the school of his choice. Not many females fell into the category of regular Army enlistees at that time. My grandmother knew I wanted to complete my college education and she saw this new program as an opportunity to do so. She did not have all of the details, but told me to speak with the Army recruiter there in Woodbury - and so I did.

I never viewed military service as a career option but, out of respect, listened to my grandmother's advice to look into whatever possibilities such a program might offer. Later that afternoon, I went to see the U.S. Army recruiter who explained the Army's newest recruiting "tool." As he explained it, the Army's approach was straight forward: "Enlist for the school of your choice." "Does that mean college or university?" I asked. "It means you can select the professional training which determines the military occupational specialty you are ultimately assigned," the recruiter said. More importantly he went on to say, "You would also be eligible for the G.I. Bill of Rights to help defray the expense of a college education when your service enlistment is completed."

Suddenly, I began to see something I had not realized before. I knew that as an unemployed, young African-American male, I was a natural target for the Selective Service Board in Camden. The zealotry of the Selective Service Board on Cooper Street in Camden in targeting African-American males was legendary. This explained why most of the African-American males in Camden were Air Force veterans: they preferred to enlist for four years and have some choices than to be drafted for two years with no choice and be assigned to some infantry unit in Germany or Korea. Moreover, most of the Air Force vets had served in Japan, an exciting possibility if I chose the Air Force. Here is how I was reasoning after my meeting with the Army recruiter. I thought that by enlisting, or volunteering for the draft, I could continue my emphasis on business administration and education, avoid being drafted at some untimely point in the future, send an allotment of money home to help mother with two siblings still dependent upon her, and, most importantly, have an opportunity to travel. I looked at the package of benefits and saw in it an opportunity too good to dismiss outright.

When I got back to my grandparents' house, I shared with my grandmother my understanding of the program she had alerted me to. I also wanted to use her as a sounding board for a tentative decision I thought I might make. It was tentative because I had not yet presented it to mother who I knew would be opposed to it. An enlistment in the U.S. military was not what she ever had in mind for this particular son. To Mrs. Kennedy, my calling should be education. She had wanted that for me since birth. She always envisioned my name in front of my desk: G. Alfred Kennedy. My grandmother whose husband and only son had served in the military, was not as unalterably opposed to the military as a valuable experience for a young man as her daughter was. With my grandmother's encouragement, I went home to talk to mother. The bus ride from Woodbury to Camden and the walk home from the bus stop gave me more time to marshal my arguments in favor of seeking even more information on this new program. That would involve visiting Whitehall, the main recruiting office in Newark, 78 miles upstate.

"Absolutely not!" my mother said following what I thought was a convincing presentation. "We'll make it, you will be able to return to school in September...don't waste your life!" She was almost frantic, imploring me not to consider the military alternative. I saw my best option at that moment as to continue to talk…"at least allow me to spend a free weekend with other guys like myself at Whitehall in Newark. I'll go up, take the tests, spend the weekend at the Army's expense and come back" I said. I really pressed the point that it would not cost us a dime. I was relentless. Finally, mother said, "Fine, but you be back here in three days!" I met a number of other young guys like myself at Whitehall. They, too, were curious about the new Army recruitment program and pleased to be away from home for a weekend. In spite of the job shortage, what we each had in common was no clear intention to join the Army. The hotel was clean and comfortable. This may sound odd, but this was the first time I had ever been a guest in a hotel. By the third day, the presentations and initial testing were over and the group of us, about twenty, were assembled for a final session with the Officer-in-Charge (OIC). I was already thinking ahead to the departure time for the return bus ride to Camden. I was distracted and not paying full attention to what was being said. Had I been more attentive, I would have been better prepared for what was coming next.

"On your feet!" said a tall, immaculately groomed sergeant. His uniform was obviously tailored and his shoes glistened - spit shined. He identified himself as the senior NCO (Non-Commissioned Officer) at Whitehall. In a loud and clear voice, he said, "If there is anyone here who does not wish to be sworn in, please step forward." At this command, everyone seemed to be focused. There were anxious glances, each of us waiting for someone else to take that first step forward so he could join them. There were no females among us. No one stepped forward, and I did not want to be the first or only one to do so. I did not think I could handle the embarrassed stares I felt would be directed at me. I later learned that military recruiters at the time depended on this unspoken peer pressure to bring in new recruits. It worked!

The Officer-in-Charge stepped in front of us and said, "Raise your right hand and repeat after me!" Right hands went up in unison and each of us swore an oath of allegiance to the Constitution of the United States and to the U.S. Army. I recall Thomas "Greek" Dent, one of the guys from North Jersey asking, "what does this mean?" "You're in the U.S. Army now" barked the senior NCO again. We had crossed the Rubicon. "You have two hours to call home and get ready to ship out to Fort Dix. Every one of us newly sworn-in recruits was now confronted with the stark realization that we would not be returning home as each of us, myself, included, had promised; we had joined the Army!

"Damn," I said. "How am I going to explain this?" "What have I done?" My carefully constructed rationale for possibly joining the Army seemed less convincing when confronted with the reality of having made the decision. I was in the damn Army! My hand trembled as I dialed the phone to talk to my mother. We still did not have a telephone at home. I called the Micklins who owned the small, family-owned grocery store across the street. Marty, their son, went to get my mother - as he always did whenever mother would receive a call from someone. The Micklins were always gracious about this inconvenience. "Mom, I began…guess what? I'm in the Army." I paused for her reaction. "You'd better be on the bus tonight" she laughed; apparently thinking I was springing a bad joke on her. "Mom, I'm serious, I joined the Army!" There was a pause and, when she spoke again, her voice had a different, more ominous, quality to it. "You did what?" she said. "I joined the Army today, but mom, don't worry, it's a good thing." Trying to keep from stammering too badly, I carefully explained my rationale, including new information I had acquired, hoping this would assuage the pain I realized I had caused. I wanted her to accept a decision I could not reverse. Still talking, I felt a pat on the back. "George, I need the phone." "Greek" was next in line and I was taking too much time. "We only have two hours" he said. As I was about to hang up, I said, "mom, I'll call you from Fort Dix." At that, I hung up.

An hour later, my latest group of friends and I were on a bus headed for Fort Dix. I could not help but reflect on my brief conversation with my mother. Well, I thought, I am not going AWOL (Absent Without Leave), so it's done! Upon arrival at Fort Dix that evening, our group was ushered off the bus angled into a barracks. It was all very orderly; no screaming and trying to put the fear of God into us. After some brief processing, we were assigned bunks and it was off to the dining hall. That night, lying in my bunk, I marveled at the sudden, unexpected change in the direction of my life. It had been only a month since my return from Shaw and, now, here I was, in the Army. This was indeed a dramatic turn of events. The next several days were a blur of more processing, aptitude tests, haircuts, and the issuance of an Army duffel bag with my basic wardrobe. Naturally, there were more calls home. Life was different but I was largely unfazed by the drastic change. The daily routine was as my uncle, himself a paratrooper in the Army's 82nd Airborne Division, had described it often to my siblings and me. My brother Bernard had been a Marine at Parris Island, South Carolina and a seaman recruit at the U.S. Navy's Recruit Training Command in Bainbridge, Maryland. Other first cousins had served in the U.S. Navy, the Army Reserves, and the Air Force. The large, unanswered question was, would I be assigned to Fort Dix, less than an hour from home? That would have been the best of all possible worlds. The answer came the following day when assignments for basic recruit training were posted.

There is a twist to this part of the story. The Army had recently instituted a policy of sending recruits from the northern states to military bases in the South for their basic training. Conversely, recruits from the South were assigned to training commands in the North. Fort Dix, the ideal assignment, suddenly became the reality of Fort Benning, Georgia, prompting another call home. This time, I kept it short. There was no need to say much more than where I was being assigned and that I would write when I could. I had traveled to the deep south only once earlier in my life when my older brother and I spent the summer of 1948 in South Carolina. Now, I was returning to the South again. I had never been to Georgia before, but I felt, or hoped, the Army would provide some insulation from the racism I knew existed there. They did, but not much.

The departure for Fort Benning became a nightmare for those of us assigned there. Earlier, each of us had believed we would be traveling by train, not air. The location of McGuire Air Force Base, contiguous to Fort Dix, simplified the logistics for the Army. When we assembled at the air terminal and were ordered to board the aircraft, at first, not one of us moved. The fact is, none of us had flown before, and the aircraft, a World War 11-vintage DC-3, was old and had the appearance of having seen its best days. As a first-time experience, the sight of that aircraft did not engender confidence, at least not for my group.

"Get on the plane!" an NCO shouted, "Now!" Again, no one moved. "Get on the plane or each of you will be court-martialed for failure to obey a lawful, direct order!" The other recruits and I looked at each other and, reluctantly, we boarded the plane. As the aged DC-3 taxied to the runway for takeoff, I gripped both armrests so tightly, my knuckles turned white. About an hour into the flight, perhaps less, the pilot announced that he was experiencing engine trouble and would have to return to McGuire. The aircraft only had two engines and one of them was malfunctioning. I think each of us was thinking, "if this thing makes in back to the base safely and I can get off, I will never board an airplane again." After that announcement, you could hear a pin drop - as my mother used to say. No one uttered a sound until the plane landed and taxied to a halt at the terminal. Within seconds, the plane had been emptied. No one panicked, but no one hesitated about getting off that plane.

The scene surrounding the re-boarding several hours later was straight out of central casting at a major Hollywood studio. Military Police (MPs) had surrounded all of us. We were, again, under threat of courts martial and ordered to re-board the same aircraft. There was no alternative. A court martial had a life-altering, ominous ring to it as the words burned into my brain. I headed toward the aircraft behind my buddy "Greek." Although a light meal was served route to Georgia, most of us did not eat. The silence on the plane was punctuated quite a few times by the sound of someone using their "comfort bag."

Life turned deadly serious when 32 new recruits and I became part of the famed 2nd Infantry Division. The recruit training area was Fort Benning's Kelly Hill. Charley "C" Company, First Battle Group, Eighty-Seventh Infantry, our new home, was under the direct command of 1st Lt. Willie L. Johnson. To my surprise, Lt. Johnson was African-American. My platoon sergeant was Sergeant First Class Pollack, a Korean War veteran. He was Third Platoon's guiding light for the next eight weeks.

One comedic event on the first day left an indelible impression on us as the recruits who bore witness. Sergeant Pollack had begun in earnest to instill the fear of God into us when I heard someone laugh and make an unintelligible remark. It was the "Greek." I knew it was him because I was standing to his immediate right. "Who laughed?" Sergeant Pollack demanded to know. He seemed to know it was the "Greek" because, as if radar-guided, Sergeant Pollack bore in on him. The "Greek" was suddenly nose-to-nose with Sergeant Pollack who not only questioned his genealogy, but also ordered him to stand nose-to-nose with a telephone pole nearby and shout out loud, "I will not laugh in ranks" until instructed to rejoin the group. From that day forward, Sergeant Pollack had everyone's undivided attention, even when he was not present during evenings and weekends.

I was selected as a trainee squad leader. I was accustomed to leadership roles so I just flowed with my duties as Sergeant Pollack laid them out for me and the other three squad leaders. Midway through the training cycle, I was moved up to trainee platoon leader because the previous platoon leader had really screwed up badly managing to embarrass Sergeant Pollack in the process. His dismissal was loud, ugly, and public. Leading a squad was one thing but, now, I had 32 people, some of whom were real screw-ups. I knew from previous conversations with my uncle that there were no longer individual transgressions. He had been a platoon sergeant. Whenever anyone failed to perform, I, as platoon leader, would be held responsible. My first challenge was to get 32 guys to work as a team under my leadership. They would now fail or succeed as a team, not individually. Several in the platoon delighted in marching against the tide, but, eventually, incessant work details, drills, and sleepless weekends persuaded them that teamwork was the better course. I, of course, got tired of being chewed out because of their misdeeds.

I mainly enjoyed the daily physical regimen, courses on basic infantry tactics, and formation drills. I had been an athlete since the eighth grade and physical training was something I was accustomed to. The heat and humidity of Georgia was no worse than the blueberry fields in New Jersey or the cotton fields of South Carolina. Moreover, I was an insomniac and sleep deprivation training had no effect on me; I didn't sleep anyway. Self-discipline was not an issue. Shortly after assuming my new role, Sergeant Pollack told me that the Third Platoon had to win the company commander's trophy for being the most "squared away" - in recognition of its outstanding military bearing and adherence to Army practices. The key was to be the top platoon during the daily inspection conducted by the company Executive Officer, Sergeant Pollack and the other platoon sergeants.

Preparing for the daily inspection was a study in the mastery of seemingly inconsequential minutiae. For example, everything, and I mean everything, had to pass a white glove inspection including the underside of your wall locker, your bed (called the rack), the window frames and sills, the latrine, even the inside of the large trash cans in the platoon bays (the large, open space in which we lived, slept, and trained on occasion). We cleaned and mopped the floor constantly while in our stocking feet to avoid leaving scuff marks from our boots. We were up at 4 am and cleaned until breakfast. After breakfast, it was back to the company platoon area to check last minute details before going outside for the first of many formations that day.

At the end of the seventh week of training, the result of the daily inspections were announced: Third Platoon had won. Our motto was "WETSU." "We Eat This Shit Up!" Seven weeks of hard work, 100-degree heat and humidity, sleepless weekends, endless drills and inspections, no time off, and the seeming omnipresence of Sergeant Pollack had reaped great dividends for me and Third Platoon. Sergeant Pollack called me aside and said, "George, great job!" "Let your men relax during the last week." "I don't care what they do as long as they don't forget that they are still in the Army." The guys had responded well to my leadership and took that last week to relax. The Third Platoon had the most deficiencies of the four platoons every day that last week. It didn't matter; Sergeant Pollack had earned bragging rights among the other platoon sergeants. Assignments rolled around and it was time to say goodbye again.

"Kennedy - Army Administration School, Fort Knox, Kentucky," said Sergeant Pollack as individual assignments were being read. As graduating recruits, we were entitled to a week's leave before reporting for advanced training at our next duty station. After the next phase, it would be a permanent assignment. This time however, it was possible to choose our modes of transportation home. I elected to travel by Greyhound bus. I had had my fill of air travel for a while. Following the traditional pledges to stay in touch with each other - which no one ever did - several of us from New Jersey and New York boarded the bus destined for the main Greyhound Bus Terminal in Philadelphia, Pennsylvania. The ride was uneventful until we reached a scheduled stop at a restaurant somewhere in South Carolina. It was early in the morning following all night travel from Columbus, Georgia.

"Greek," five others from our group, and I filed off the bus and into the restaurant. As we made our selections, I was second in line moving toward the cashier. "Greek" paid the cashier and began looking for an empty table. I handed the cashier my money and looked for "Greek" while awaiting my change. As I turned toward the cashier expecting my change, she seemed perplexed, as my money lay on the counter. "Here is my money" I said. The cashier seemed anxious but did not pick up the money. "George, what's the holdup?" someone asked. It still had not dawned on me. "I don't know, she is not taking my money!" As I looked around, I noticed that everyone in the restaurant had stopped eating and was looking in my direction. Directly over the cashier's left shoulder, I noticed a separate room that said "Colored Dining Room." Several of the African-Americans there were casting anxious glances in my direction, as if their eyes were saying, "come this way." Finally, it occurred to me why the cashier was refusing to take my money.

"No way!" I told her. "I am hungry, I am in uniform, and I am an American citizen. You had better call the manager!" Well, by this time, "Greek" had returned to the cashier and had become extremely vocal. The guys traveling with us, all in uniform, had crowded around the cashier, berating her and calling for the manager. "Guys, cool it," I said. "Lets wait for the manager." When he appeared and asked, "what's the problem? I responded, "I am in uniform, I am hungry, I only want to eat and leave. I do not intend to eat in some back room. Your cashier refuses to take my money." "Greek" and the others had by now become agitated and reiterated what I had said. "We are in uniform; either we eat as a group or none of us eat!" The manager, to defuse what had become a very tense situation, consented. He may have lost his job, who knows! This was blatant racism, and I was prepared to confront it. This was apparently the first time the others had experienced anything like this before. They literally could not stop talking about it.

I admit to a certain apprehension about going home in uniform. Mother had been unhappy about my decision to enter the Army. My fears were quelled when I walked through the front door. She smiled, hugged me, and wanted to know how I was. Her reaction was important to me. The older guys in the neighborhood all understood. They, too, had made similar decisions during and after the Korean War. Grandmom and grandpop were especially proud. I told grandmom I did not regret the decision and that I would make the best of it. Following a week at home, I was back on the bus headed to Fort Knox, Kentucky. Fort Knox was a key phase of my military experience because it was there I would learn the basics of Army administrative policies, processes, and procedures. This was, after all, one of my prime motivators for joining the Army. Sergeant Dudley, the new platoon sergeant, also an African-American, selected me as one of his squad leaders. As a squad leader, or Acting NCO, I could join the other NCOs in the NCO dining room, a nice perk I did not enjoy at Fort Benning. Life in advanced training was considerably less stressful; drills were conducted less frequently, and evenings were free. On several occasions during our eight weeks there, a group of us took the bus to Louisville to break the monotony of life on base. Louisville was another of those traditional southern cities in 1959. Segregation was policy and practice; no, it was the law! There were a few nightclubs, bars, and small hotels that catered to the resident African-American community and the African-American GI's from the Army base. Louisville had limited appeal to me. I did not drink and could not rationalize spending any portion of my $78.00 monthly salary on Louisville's limited "delights."

During Advanced Training,I became familiar with many Army regulations (ARs), particularly those that would govern my life as a new private in the Army. The Army, like civilian life, had its rules. I wanted to understand these because I intended to take full advantage of the opportunities they made available.

The timing of my arrival at Fort Knox was coincident with football season. Over dinner, someone brought up the fact that we had a football team; in fact he knew the coach. If we had a team, I intended to try out for it. I went to see the coach and was invited to practice the following day. He chose to test me in my military fatigues and boots. All I could imagine was slipping on the grass. After all, I was a power running back and smooth soles with my speed was a disaster waiting to happen. He asked me to take a handoff, run a pattern and stop in front of him. I managed to retain my footing during a couple of handoffs and that must have been enough for him. I was selected to be the third member of the starting backfield.

My daily routine had the feel of normalcy now: classes during the day; drills several times a week - which I would conduct as a squad leader, and daily football practice. When I found a gym some distance from our barracks, I would go over and work out. Our team did well that year and made the division playoffs. My permanent assignment came through and the timing of my departure from Fort Knox meant that I would miss the playoffs.

In November 1959, I graduated from Army Administration School, to learn that I was being assigned permanently to the 124th Signal Company in Vicenza, Italy, home of the Southern European Task Force (SETAF). To those stationed there, it was known as "Something Even The Army Forgot." I was the only one in my class to be assigned to Italy. None of the other NCOs had ever served there, as distinct from Germany, Korea, or Japan, so I had no early intelligence regarding what to expect. Following another week of leave at home, I was on my first transatlantic flight to Germany. A new phase of my journey had begun.

CHAPTER 4

ITALY – ALONE IN THE WORLD

My mother had always encouraged her children to make the best of every opportunity we encountered in life. She was encouraging us to "be all that you can be" decades before the U.S. Army adopted it as a recruiting slogan. Italy, as distant as it was, represented a very unique opportunity to get away from her watchful eye, to mature away from home as other male relatives had done, to test some assumptions regarding my undeveloped world views, and to live in a larger universe. Until that point, my views on human interaction, personal behavior and life in general were largely shaped through the prism that was my mother, the eternity of that summer in South Carolina at the age of eight, and a year at Shaw University. From an early age, especially my mid-teens, I do admit to misgivings about some of mother's ideas. I saw Italy as a unique chapter in my life to be my own man. In a very real sense, I felt that I was extricating myself from the "backyard" that Camden had become. I never knew how, or when, I would be making my break; I just knew it would happen. Now it was finally happening and I was determined to enjoy the journey - and my journey was taking me to Europe.

The first hurdle was to learn to relax on a flight that took me from New York's former Idylwild Airport to Gander, New Foundland. The memory of that initial flight to Fort Benning was still fresh. From New Foundland, it was across the North Atlantic to refuel in Shannon, Ireland. Several hours later, I landed in Frankfurt, Germany. To my pleasant surprise the flight across the Atlantic was smooth and comfortable albeit sleepless. I had two seats to myself; not bad compensation for the constant drone of the four-engine propeller aircraft we were on.

Most U.S. Army personnel assigned to the European Theater of Operations in the late 50s were administratively processed through the 7th Army's large personnel center in Frankfurt. We arrived in early

December to grey, overcast skies, no snow, but fairly typical for a late fall day in Germany I was told. Everything appeared grey, dull, lifeless: the buildings, the automobiles, the clothes people wore, even the Germans themselves. I spent my first three days there and then it was back on the plane to Milan, Italy. I was hoping for better weather further south. In Milan, I was met by an Army transportation officer who informed me that I would be traveling by train to Vicenza, five hours to the north. The Pullman coaches used by the American military in Italy for personnel traveling overnight were comfortable and, as I subsequently learned, preferable to many of the regular trains in the Italian rail system. At eight pm, the train arrived in Vicenza and I, along with several other men newly assigned there, were met and transported by bus to Caserma Ederle, the principal military installation in Vicenza and my new duty station. The driver called my name and said, "Kennedy, 124th Signal, this is your stop." I got off the bus in front of a modern, two story building, already a pleasant change from the larger, multi-story, grey buildings in Frankfurt. I entered and saw the overhead sign "Orderly Room." Upon entering, I dropped my duffel bag, snapped to attention and said ""Private Kennedy reporting for duty, sir! I signed in and, after being assigned a room on the second floor, and trying to digest a late dinner, I laid in my bunk wondering who my seven roommates were. Would I have difficulty fitting in? Well, I would know soon enough. I heard Taps at 11 pm and drifted off to sleep sometime after that. The next morning, it was just the normal processing in, familiar routine by now.

A note about the 124th Signal Company. This outfit was a "Line Outfit." That meant its mission was vital to the success of any American combat activity in southern Europe. Signal company personnel manned "Yankee Relay," a strategic communication's relay station in the Dolomite Mountains between Headquarters, U.S. Army Europe in Heidelberg, Germany and the Southern European Task Force's four principal commands in Italy. Since the equipment we maintained was vital to communication in the event of hostilities, training and field exercises were common for officers and men of the 124th. The company commander, Captain Casper King, I learned, was not a particularly strong or effective leader. He drank heavily and regularly; had a troubled home life, and was not well respected by his peers, or his men. The troops in his unit called him "Shakey" from drinking so much. His hands trembled and his official signature reflected this condition.

Captain King was obsessed with being promoted to major and thought he could earn his promotion by driving his men relentlessly. Promotions above the rank of captain for officers stationed on our base were rare, more difficult to earn than in Germany. The troops of the U.S. 7th Army stationed in Germany were considered the bulwark of America's forward defense against the Russians. They were the first line of defense against any massed land attack through the Fulda Gap against western Europe; the finger in the dike. Captain King simply was not up to the caliber of leadership expected of officers assigned to those forward-deployed units. Many of us doubted his promotability were he assigned to a comparable-sized unit in Germany. The joke among his men, including several of his NCOs, was that when the captain looked in the mirror, he saw General Patton. Everyone else saw a closet alcoholic.

A product of the Army's old "spit and polish" school, Captain King loved inspections - of everything - and would insist, for example, that all of the 97 vehicles under his command, most of which were two-and-a-half-ton with a communication's van, be washed and waxed regularly. When parked, they were to be brought on line using a lengthy piece of field wire. When you saw one vehicle, you saw the bumpers of all 97. It was of less importance that many of these vehicles could not operate at peak efficiency, a reasonable expectation of combat vehicles. To our captain, appearances were everything. A full-field display by the 124th Signal Company was the most impressive sight on the base. Everything glistened, including us. We were without peer among the other units on base. In a combat situation, we would be visible for miles because of the sun's reflection on our equipment, not a desirable state of affairs on a sunny day. We would have to hope for rain or heavy cloud cover. Two of his four platoons were scheduled for field maneuvers eight-to-ten days monthly. It was that penchant for appearances that resulted in an unusual admonition from our newly arrived base commander, Colonel Coffin, during his initial visit to the 124th. This was to be a command appearance, a chance to impress the "old man," perhaps improve the captain's chances to be promoted. Colonel Coffin arrived in our company motor pool, took one step out of his staff car, left foot still in the car with the right foot on the ground, took one look at our impressive display of vehicles and their OVM equipment glistening on the ground in front of each vehicle, and instructed Captain King to "dull everything down; make them combat-ready...your outfit would be too big a target." He got back in his car and left. Captain King was crestfallen. Appearances were out; combat readiness was in and we, the troops, could not have been more pleased. We had spent countless days and nights in the company motor pool listening to the derisory comments of friends from other outfits while we polished equipment already painted olive drab. Ironically, requests for transfer among Captain King's troops were low because he was known for rapidly promoting them. This policy brought troop loyalty, but not their respect.

I was a company clerk, assigned to Captain King, his executive office, Captain Angus Trasker, and the First Sergeant, Vernel Prophet. In my capacity as administrative support staff, I traveled to the field only when the captain had to establish a temporary field command. Otherwise, my daily life consisted of hot meals and clean sheets, in my own bunk every night; not a field uniform in a sleeping bag, on the side of a snow-covered mountain eating C-rations. I should explain something here. The front office in an Army unit was known as the Orderly Room. Our senior company clerk was Paul Mancin, a Swiss-American. Paul and I got on very well, initially. Soon, it was all too apparent that my growth potential under his tutelage was limited. Paul saw to that! He was "the man" in that shop and I was just an extra pair of hands for the less glamorous tasks that frequently rose: type this, go get that, take this to.... Tensions arising during the day spilled over into our off-duty hours because we were also bunkmates. Eventually, the tension between us escalated to the point that I was transferred to the Supply and Maintenance Platoon (S & M) within the company. Paul arranged this. I was now a supply and maintenance clerk counting and sorting spare parts for 1940s and 50s communications equipment. My new office was a 6' x 6' van on a two-and-a-half-ton truck in the company motor pool. I shared this office with a Private First Class Smith who thought this was exciting duty. In the platoon, he was known as "Smitty" and he thrived on performing such mundane tasks as sorting the types of fuses we kept on hand for our radios.

Once I had an established daily routine in the S & M Platoon, I was able to continue classes in the on-base University of Maryland's Overseas Extension Program. My monthly payroll allotment had not been processed yet and I still had enough to pay that semester's tuition. I had not lost sight of my educational objectives to either complete my undergraduate degree or earn credits toward a degree. In a strange environment, civilian or military, friends are a key ingredient for survival. The situation I confronted on a new continent with a new culture, and a new language, increased the probability that early missteps on my part could have serious consequences very quickly. I understood this. During my first week in the 124th Signal, I met someone from the Communication's Platoon whose friendship, advice and guidance would prove invaluable to me over the next 31 months of service in Italy. Private First Class Stanley Tilman, an African-American in his early twenties from Washington, DC, had been in country for two years and was an ardent student of Italian history, culture, and language. Moreover, he was also a brilliant radio engineer. To my great fortune, he quite literally took me under his wing. Early on in our relationship, Tilman made a key point, one that I never forgot. He said "Italians, like African-Americans, are a sensitive people. They are proud, warm, and generous...first impressions are important." He went on to say that, "generally, you did not want to use a second meeting to correct an egregious mistake made during that all-important first encounter, no matter what the circumstances of that initial encounter were." In other words, "never apologize; never explain," (just don't repeat the same mistake.) Stanley Tilman showed me how to avoid easy, but natural mistakes and to sidestep the cultural minefields that tripped up many a young, naïve, and often arrogant American newcomer to Italy.

Most evenings, when I was not in my international relations class, Tilman and I would sit either in the barracks, or at Luigi's bar directly across from the main gate. While Tilman drank chilled red wine, he talked about his experiences as one of the first African-American soldiers to be assigned to Vicenza in 1957, after U.S. Forces established a more permanent presence there. Tilman contrasted that earlier period with the Italy I would encounter in 1959 and beyond. He would be rotating back to the states in another year. Tilman pointed out a salient fact: in the mid-1950s, many Italians in northern Italy had never seen African-Americans before, not even during World War 11. Some Italians had impressions derived from tales they had been told by the first contingent of white American soldiers that transferred from Vienna, Austria to Italy in 1955, many of whom came from southern states. Of course, their impressions were all negative. An objective among the white soldiers was to persuade Italian men and mothers to minimize contact between the few African-American soldiers among them and Italian women. This was common in Europe in the 1950s when racial strife and altercations between white and Black soldiers were a frequent occurrence. Southern white soldiers, and some from elsewhere in the U.S., tried to replicate conditions in their home towns while in Italy or Germany. Some Europeans resisted this, but many German proprietors saw economic advantage by accommodating one group or the other by refusing to serve the "out" group in their bar or restaurant.

Tilman's sage advice covered an array of topics, all of which were important to me. For example, he said, "don't be offended if a curious Italian rubs your skin to see if your color comes off on his hand, or, if they look behind you to see if you have a tail...these are things they have been told by white troops." Some mothers may fear contact between you and their daughter out of fear you may have syphilitic blood. Babies may be shielded from you as mothers approach you on the street out of fear you will eat them. "Don't react badly; show them that none of these tales is true." "Make an honest effort to communicate with Italians in their own language." "Your humanity will become obvious and they will reciprocate." "Italy," he continued, "has a rich and lengthy history...learn something about it." Vicenza was the perfect place to start. Stanley Tilman came to represent an early, but influential, intellectual force in the life I would ultimately embrace as a Foreign Service officer some 13 years later. As I travelled, my early Italian experience taught me to view each new assignment, its people and culture through the prism of a civilization, not a government at a distinct juncture in history.

All of Tilman's advice made imminent good sense. He knew that my means were limited but he suggested that "within your limits, see as much of the country as you can...avoid life in the bars." That last tip was easy advice. I did not drink. When Tilman talked, that was my time to be the easy listener I was. Here was wisdom and I resolved to absorb as much of it as I could. Tilman also introduced me to two other people, one of whom became a life long friend: James Nance, also from Washington, D.C. The other, Leon Cheatham, was someone else with whom I maintained contact beyond our service together in Italy. With Tilman, Nance, and Cheatham, I developed friendships that gave life texture, laughter, meaning, and equally as important, good memories that I savor today.

My larger group of friends was part of the Headquarters and Headquarters Company (730001) on base. Here is what attracted me to them. Their jobs were less mechanical, but more diverse than most of the job specialties in the 124th. They were legal clerks, graphic artists, and educational specialists; specialists in food service, chaplain's assistant, weapons maintenance, supply and logistics, finance, personnel, transportation, and communications. One of the guys I met in the dining hall one day had actually been part of the design team for Disneyland. I also gravitated to the guys at Headquarters and Headquarters Company because they were also more diverse in their life experiences, had higher levels of education, careers they aspired to and broader insights into the military. Few of them entertained the idea of reenlisting because most of them had been drafted. I do not want to be misunderstood on this point. They were not pacifists or conscientious objectors. They were good soldiers, valued their experiences in uniform, but saw military careers as less desirable than other alternatives.

These new friends had other advantages. In large measure, they were not required to do field duty. Their daily routines confined them to the base because they staffed all of the headquarters' command functions.

I spent so much off-duty time at Headquarters and Headquarters Company, I became aware of a vacancy in the office of Captain Geddes, the Command Transportation Officer. Both the senior NCO there and one of his deputies were African-American. The more junior of the two NCOs was a 1950s graduate of Camden High School, the cross-town rival of my alma mater, Woodrow Wilson High School. I learned more about the position and requested a meeting with the ranking NCO in the office. We hit it off and he told me if I could be released from the 124th, he would speak to the transportation officer on my behalf. I did request a transfer and, to my surprise, it was granted. Maybe I had been a misfit at the 124th. I did, however, welcome the transfer.

I will frame my request for transfer from the 124th in larger context. I worked hard to fit in at the 124th because it was my duty assignment; I had responsibilities and my goal was to fulfill them. There were variables, however, beyond my control. My limited finances put me on a collision course with one of Captain King's projects to enhance his prospects for promotion. Just prior to my arrival, the command announced a U.S. Savings Bond drive. Captain King was vying to become the first unit commander to achieve 100 percent participation. My allotment was going to reduce my monthly net pay to $13 monthly. I simply could not afford to contribute $5.00 monthly towards a Savings Bond. Captain King, as the company's paymaster, was aware of my allotment because he signed the forms. Yet, he encouraged the First Sergeant to pressure me to ensure full participation. I had to refuse and this did not sit well. Hallway scuttlebutt had it that King was disappointed, even upset with me. This was strike one.

Unit basketball trials were over before I arrived and the 124th had fielded a decent team; not championship caliber, but a good team. While I was comfortable playing pickup ball in the gym on Saturdays at Shaw University, basketball was not my game. Football and track and field, yes! But not basketball. Again, the First Sergeant was on me constantly about joining the company team. I knew I could not acquit myself well in regular competition and, again, I declined. Within my first month, I had two strikes against me. I came to learn very quickly that the 124th Signal Company was more than a military unit; it was a culture shaped largely by its commanding officer. Your success there was contingent upon your willingness not only to fit, but also be willing to lose even that measure of independent thinking the military allowed. There was a cultural fault-line and I was on the other side of it. Paul Mancin, my immediate supervisor reflected the captain's unhappiness with me by creating an unpleasant work environment in the Orderly Room. I knew life was going to be untenable at the 124th when Paul and

I had a major altercation in our room one night. The cumulative effect was to transfer me to another platoon within the company. I wanted to fit, to perform well but I was the square peg trying to fit into the round hole. The timing of the opening in the Post Transportation Office was perfect. Captain King must have taken delight in approving my transfer.

My new job title became Transportation Movement Specialist. The transition was painless because the new position was largely administrative. The change in position did not, however, exempt me from Guard Duty as was the case with other functions in Headquarters and Headquarters Company. During my initial briefing with the Transportation Officer, I was told that other aspects of the job could be learned through an apprenticeship with one of the NCOs responsible for liaison with the Italian customs community. A major benefit of the transfer was more frequent personal contact not only with the Italians occupying professional positions on base, but also with Italians in the Veneto Region of northern Italy; those Italians who provided essential support services for the Army and its counterpart organizations in the Italian Army. Transportation Services at the command level included not only the physical movement of troops, but also the processing and movement of the personal and household effects of all American military and civilian personnel from our command entering and departing the country. Moreover, the command was responsible for the movement and distribution of petroleum, oil, and lubricants (POL) to support air and ground operations during field maneuvers, maintaining relations with Italian customs officials and railroad stationmasters throughout northern Italy. There was also the added responsibility of the evacuation of non-essential personnel (the dependents of military and civilian officials assigned to the command) in the event of hostilities. My job involved all of these areas thus my administrative training at Fort Knox became invaluable.

I understood at the outset that at least a working knowledge of Italian would significantly enhance my operational effectiveness, given the complexity of the responsibilities I could ultimately assume. Daily conversations with my Italian colleagues in the office allowed me to practice vocabulary, grammar, and sentence structure learned during my off-duty Italian class. Now I had a real job, one that stimulated me intellectually because of the volume of Army Regulations (ARs) governing our operation. I now had responsibilities that placed me in direct contact with Italians and a broader understanding of Italian life and society. It was also obvious that I would experience new challenges and become aware of new opportunities for advancement. Working with Sergeant Essex, who handled all outside operations, I learned the less mechanical aspects of the job: how to be an effective customs agent. He was expecting to be transferred to the U.S. soon and it was important for office continuity that I get up to speed quickly. Sergeant Essex was away most of the time and the beauty of his job was that he did not have a direct field supervisor, only the senior NCO back at the office. Captain Geddes, the Transportation Officer, trusted his judgment. If trust, maturity, and good judgment were the hallmarks of Sergeant Essex's performance, then that was my new standard. During command maneuvers, he was the only member of the Transportation Office required to be in the field. The difference was that he functioned independently, had a dedicated vehicle and additional personnel support if he deemed it necessary. This was the way to pull field duty. As someone not favorably disposed to field duty, it did not get any better than this for one Private First Class Kennedy.

When I received my overseas assignment at Fort Knox, it was with the understanding that my overseas tour was not to exceed 22 months and that I could expect a normal rotation date back to the U.S. during October 1961. Prior to 1961, a rotation date was the closest thing to a fixed contract with the Army: you could take it to the bank! So, now that I was in country, I was interested in maximizing my possibilities. Although my net monthly pay was meager to say the least, I decided to travel within my means. I needed a plan because most of my monthly pay was allotted to my mother. That just did not leave much to satisfy the normal desires of a 19-year old overseas for the first, and perhaps only, time in his life, so I planned carefully.

One day in the office, while looking at a large, detailed map of the Veneto Region, I got an idea. I plotted most of the cities in the region with stickpins on the map, almost as if I were planning a strategic operation with the designated cities as mission objectives. My thought was, why not plan a series of day-trips and overnight, or weekend trips to many of the small cities in the Veneto Region? I could not afford a car, not even a used one, as many of the other guys could; those whose monthly pay was not encumbered. The more I planned, the less alone I felt. Train travel was cheap. I would even travel third class if that is what it would take to see and experience more of my Italian "backyard." If necessary, I could sleep on the train. Travel in this manner offered endless opportunities to project a different image of African-Americans to Italians from all walks of life, and to improve my command of the language. If I could not afford a hotel at my chosen destination, the solution was simple: order a plate of spaghetti at a local restaurant, have dinner and return to Vicenza late in the evening. A roundtrip ticket was as good as a security blanket. That ticket guaranteed that I would always have a place to sleep, if necessary, and that I would arrive back on base before reveille on Monday morning.   I was on the road frequently; therefore, I knew the proximity of the local train stations to the cities in most locations in the Veneto Region. Most of the train stations in the Veneto Region had been constructed with Marshall Plan funds after World War 11 since most of them had been destroyed during the war.

The stations were situated perpendicular to the main street in these small towns. This meant I could leave the train station on foot, walk directly down the main street and eventually, arrive at the largest hotel in the city.   This basic knowledge gave me a psychological advantage and boosted my confidence. I could appear knowledgeable, while familiarizing myself with the city. These day and weekend trips were small voyages of miraculous discovery and took me beyond the range of the experience of many guys on base. Those who had cars did not travel by train, and they were more interested in the larger, more populated destinations of Verona, Florence, Milan, Pisa, and Bologna. Those with the financial wherewithal, but lacked the mobility of a private automobile, traveled by air to the same destinations to include Rome and Naples.

I ate, drank, and slept in the homes of ordinary Italians, farmers, even local officials I met at the railheads. Many of those I met in these towns and villages had been an active part of Italy's recent pre- and-post World War 11 history. I listened while they recounted details of their experiences and observations of the German occupation during the war. Some had been among the resistance – Partigiani – and actively fought against the Germans, often at great personal sacrifice. I saw dozens, even hundreds, of photographs of friends and family members killed during raids against their German occupiers. Mostly, I was intrigued by their perceptions of America and Americans because it was precisely when we began to talk about the States that I could influence what they thought.

One memorable winter night in Beluno while on maneuvers, I was briefly kidnapped by an Italian paratrooper (Bersaglieri) and several of his friends, all of whom were being discharged from Italian military service the next day. Separating from the Italian Army was a real cause to celebrate. They thought we lived like royalty when compared with their facilities. These three paratroopers had seen me in a local hotel earlier that evening and thought I was "molto sympatico," meaning that I seemed to be nice, approachable, and appreciated Italian language. They followed me into the street, surrounded me and encouraged me, in a good-natured way, to join them at a local bar they apparently knew well. The owner of the bar and his family were warm, gracious, and very generous. I never saw money exchange hands but I am sure my Italian military host must have compensated them before the evening was over. For the first time in my life, I drank wine and sang Italian songs; I laughed at jokes I partially understood, but I really felt comfortable with them. That evening with those Italians in that bar became one of my memorable experiences while on duty in Italy. Framed mementos from that evening, along with a photograph of one of the Italian paratroopers, occupy a prominent place on a wall in my office at home today.

My travels throughout northern Italy in my official capacity as a field customs agent, were not without adventure, moments of extreme levity, and the occasional challenge. My experiences while in uniform varied considerably from those as a young GI in civilian attire walking down the main street of a small Italian town. In those small towns where a Black face was a rarity, reactions varied from curiosity to initial avoidance. By the next day, if I were there overnight, the reluctance to engage me had changed to one of warm acceptance. I was frequently invited to their homes and to return to their town – and on many occasions, I did. To navigate the Veneto, I spent considerable time traversing the Dolomite mountains. I became so familiar with the railheads at various locations in the region that I could almost drive the mountains at night with my eyes closed. I never tried to do so, but I do recall driving on a few occasions when I should have been asleep, not driving.

I was often in Beluno, a town high in the Dolomites, because it had one of the newest railheads in that part of Italy. On this particular trip, I was required to divide my time – a total of ten days – between directing the railhead at Beluno and another one in Conegliano, further down the valley. Extended field operations require that shower units be set up in the field by the third or fourth day. Even in winter, a hot shower becomes a necessity, about on par with hot meals instead of cold C-rations; no Meals-Ready-To-Eat (MREs) for us. I lived in my comfortable panel truck, not with four other guys in a tent with a heater that may, or may not, have been functioning. On day three, the word was circulated among the units that the shower unit would be operational by day four. On day four, the word was that the water pumps were faulty and would be repaired by that evening. On day five, there were still no showers. By now, I was sleeping with open windows in my truck. Sergeant Huskey, an NCO from the Quartermaster Company, and whose unit was responsible for the shower units, was also on duty at the railhead. He and I decided to approach the local police chief whose station was contiguous to the train station. I knew the police had installed showers as part of a recent modernization project.

"Capitano," I began in Italian, "possiamo utilizzare I vostri docce? La nostra non sono operativi e si e' passati cinque giorni da quando abbiamo fatto il bagno." ("may we use your showers? Ours are not operational and it has been five days since we bathed.") "Certainly," he said. "Go through the barracks and the showers are at the rear of the building to the right." To show my appreciation, I later gave him a carton of cigarettes. Cigarettes and chocolate were still coin of the realm at that time. Now that we could take a shower, I returned to my truck, picked up my shaving kit, a towel, and some clean underwear and proceeded to the police station. Before I undressed, I turned on both faucets, and found an empty locker. The room had began to fill up with steam and as I contemplated my good fortune, I wondered if I should tell the other guys. There were too many of them and I did not want to ruin my relationship with the police chief; I would need him in the future. As I approached the shower, the steam felt cold but that could be remedied by adding more hot water. As I reached for the handle to add more hot water, I noticed it was wide open. Quickly turning off the cold water, I discovered there was no hot water. The water was freezing to the touch and I stepped back. I hated the idea of a cold shower and had never taken one in my life. I waited and waited and waited. Meanwhile, the water seemed to get colder. I was dirty and not prepared to remain in that condition even for another day. To prepare myself for the ordeal, I began to scream at the top of my lungs and stepped into the cold water. It felt like a thousand knives boring into my flesh. The water was so cold, it took my breath away. For a moment, I felt paralyzed; I could not move I was so cold. I tried to use my soap but it would not lather. The water was just that cold. That became the quickest shower, certainly the coldest, I had ever taken – or would ever take – in my life. A few minutes later when I returned to my truck, I put on every piece of winter clothing I had with me, including my overcoat. It took a week before I began to feel warm again. The shower unit never did function during that entire ten-day period.

When petroleum, oil, and lubricants were shipped to a railhead in either 55-gallon drums or in five-thousand-gallon tank cars, the tank cars had to be inspected from the top. During the same ten-day field exercise, I had occasion to inspect several tank cars that had arrived overnight from Livorno, the SETAF logistics command headquarters. I shouldered my M-1 rifle, butt down, and climbed up on a tank car to inspect its contents. The tank cars were parked at a rail siding to facilitate access by personnel from the 110th Aviation Unit requiring fuel for their helicopters and light observation aircraft. As required even for an inspection, I was also wearing my steel helmet. As I reached the top of the tank car and opened the hatch, my helmet struck something metallic. This startled me and reflexively, I lowered my head and looked up rather than reaching up with my other hand to identify what struck me on the head. As I looked up, I saw overhead electric power lines. In that instant, my blood ran cold; I began to shake. I had hit a power line. Had that tank car been parked anywhere other than at that siding where the power lines had been turned off, I would have been incinerated in a fireball of five thousand gallons of highly flammable aviation fuel. I slowly climbed down while struggling mightily to calm my nerves. I had been lucky, but decided not to tell anyone about this particular incident. Next time, I would be sure to check the height of the power lines above a tank car before I climbed up. Also, I would leave my steel helmet and weapon on the ground, regulations be damned! There were other incidents of greater consequence during field maneuvers, events that brought me into direct contact with the Italian Judicial System.

It was now spring and the units at Caserma Ederle were again in the field, this time in Conegliano, a fair-sized city several hours north of Vicenza. I had traveled up to Conegliano to receive several flatcars loaded with dozens of 55-gallon drums of gasoline. Gasoline prices in Italy were perennially high and black marketeers were constantly targeting Army supplies, especially during military maneuvers when many personnel were less vigilant about controls. In fact, several American Army personnel at a major Italian seaport had been prosecuted for black market activities. Shortly after my arrival at the railhead that particular day, several Italians approached me asking if I would be willing to "lose" two drums of fuel for a price. "It would never be missed, particularly during a field exercise," one of them pointed out. Although he was right, I was not interested and told them so. I was adamant and when it became clear that their little venture would not succeed, they left. There were no harsh words exchanged; they just left and I assumed that was the end of it.

At noon, I left the railhead for lunch, as I was authorized to do. No one had ever tried to steal a 55-gallon drum of fuel before, so security was not a concern. None of the barrels were lying on the ground; they were still secured to the flatbed car. An hour later, I returned. I noticed tracks on the sandy ground by the flatcar, the kind of evenly spaced tracks made by the ridges of a 55-gallon drum when it is rolled across a soft surface. Apparently, someone had climbed up on the flatcar, untied the ropes securing the drums and pushed two of the barrels onto the ground. In addition, there were two sets of footprints between the telltale tracks as the barrels were rolled across the ground. The tracks led through a small clump of wild grass and down an earthen incline. Someone must have been waiting with a vehicle because the tracks ended abruptly. I promptly notified the stationmaster, who then called the local police chief. I then reported the theft to the Transportation Office back at base. That afternoon, the new Transportation Officer, Captain George Crespino, arrived to conduct a joint investigation with the town's police chief. "These guys are pretty stupid," I commented to the police chief. "They were not smart enough to cover their tracks." The police chief noted that "someone had to see them because it's daylight, and the railhead is in a heavily populated part of the city."

Two small children were playing in the area and the Transportation Officer, himself an Italian- American and bi-lingual, approached them. In a brief conversation with the two kids, they told him they saw the two men drive up in a small truck, climb aboard the flatcar and remove the barrels of fuel. Under gentle questioning by the police chief, the boys provided enough of a description for him to draw a reasonable conclusion as to their identities. He arrested the two men that evening. The captain returned to Vicenza and I remained behind at the railhead. The next day, I was advised by the police chief that the captain and I would be required to return at a later date for the trial. Several weeks later at the trial, I saw that the culprits were the same two men who had approached me earlier about "losing" two barrels of fuel. They professed not to have met me at all. The trial proceedings, while serious, revealed a judge with a delightful sense of humor. The judge wondered aloud about the nature of the crime. In addressing the two defendants, he put it to them in the following manner: "You stole from the U.S. Army in broad daylight with witnesses....." "You did not have the presence of mind to cover your tracks. Moreover, the two barrels of fuel with US Army stamped on them were found in your possession. Furthermore, while the Americans are not pressing charges," he continued, "I have no choice but to incarcerate the two of you for rank stupidity!" The circumstances surrounding this incident pre-ordained the outcome. With serious criminals, malevolently intentioned, the outcome could have been different. Someone could have been seriously hurt, me perhaps; most certainly the two small children. The incident did not reflect badly on me because I had meticulously followed Army procedures. Railheads were not secure locations and I was not authorized to use deadly force in the event of an attempted theft. In fact, Sergeant Essex had briefed me earlier of the possibility that something like this could happen because Army fuel was a high value item. He said I was to protect my cargo but not at the expense of physical harm or the threat of loss of life; that if there was the threat of violence to effect a theft, not to resist and report the incident to the local authorities and the Transportation Office – as I did. Fortunately that was the only incident of its type during my tour of duty in Italy.

There also were those times when military life, even in Italy, could be a little monotonous. When Tilman, Nance, and I were practically broke but needed a respite, we caught one of the day trains to Venice and spent the day people-watching in St. Mark's Square while nursing a bottle of Coca-Cola. It takes a GI to nurse a coke. We could make a single bottle of Coca Cola last practically a half day. St. Mark's remains one of the perfect places in the world to people-watch. You never knew what the most prominent language would be on any given day because the tourists were visiting from many points around the globe. There was always something interesting to see and interesting people to talk to. We met many young female tourists in this fashion. Three African -Americans sitting at an outdoor cafe in St. Mark's Square in Venice was not a common occurrence in the late 1950s. I must have made that trip several dozen times.

Stanley Tilman's intellectual range even at the age of 22 set him apart from most of the guys on base. On these frequent trips to Venice, we spent hours debating Italian politics, base policies and procedures, and discussing the fine points of Italian grammar. A favorite topic for everyone was the military as a career option versus life after the military. When you were with Tilman, there was always an issue, a discussion that made the universe smaller because he broadened your understanding of something new and different. Tilman read extensively, especially during those isolated tours manning the Yankee Relay station up in the Dolomites. For me, these experiences were impossible to replicate back home in Camden. I was living the advice offered by my brother Bernard when he said "get in the street and meet people where they live." I was just taking it to a level beyond the mean streets of Camden. In fact, I had chosen a well-worn path within family traditions. My maternal grandfather had served in France during World War 1. My father's brother served in Europe during World War 11. My uncle George spent many memorable years in the Philippines in the late 1940s. My older brother had served aboard a destroyer in the North Atlantic and many of my first cousins practically lived in Japan, courtesy of the U.S. Air Force. To round out the family commitment to its military traditions, my younger brother Michael entered the U.S. Marine Corps in August 1961, after graduation from high school. He would subsequently spend ten years in Japan and perfect his command of the Japanese language.

In the late summer of 1960, Jim Nance and I decided to go to

Rome. After all, Rome was obligatory for a first time visitor to Italy, even low-paid GIs. Also, 1960 was the year of the Rome Summer Olympics. Why not go? Jim and I had been able to reserve a room through the United Services Organization (USO) at a family-run hotel on a quaint side street not far from center city. Rome was "all the way live" during the Olympics. We walked practically everywhere to save cab fares, which had trebled due to the influx of tourists. We saw Wilma Rudolph achieve her stunning victories, wandered through Rome's famous Piazze, threw coins in the Fontana di Trevi, climbed the Coliseum, visited as many Olympic venues as we could and, by night, entertained ourselves on the fewest dollars we could spend. Most of our money was spent on food in Rome's restaurants.

The trip to Rome was practically the mid-point of my 22-month overseas tour. In October 1960, I would have only 12 months remaining. At Christmas that year, I was taking advantage of special flights for those GIs in Europe wishing to spend Christmas at home. It took a year to pay for the $325 airline ticket, but I felt it would be worth it. The flight home was frightful, so turbulent that the pilot authorized the stewardesses to allow a generous consumption of alcohol samples. The headwinds were apparently fierce. As the plane landed in New York, everyone noticed that the wheels were sliding, not rolling. That meant an icy runway. The plane took forever before it turned to taxi to the terminal. When we exited the aircraft, several of us got down and kissed the ground. A few hours later, I walked in on my mother. She gasped because she did not expect me. Her reaction said everything.

My Christmas vacation of 1960 was unremarkable, pretty much what I expected. It was just good to be home. The first night, I sat up listening to my mother bringing me up to date on all family matters, eating good food and just enjoying being home again. I think by this time she had forgiven me for having enlisted in the first place. After several hours sleep, the next day I visited with former classmates to catch up with them. My grandparents were next on my list. I had to have some of grandmom's cooking. My mother could cook, but she was not in the same league with grandmom. Grandmothers are in a class by themselves. As an aside, my grandmother told me my mother did not speak to her for several months after I enlisted attributing my decision to do so to her informing me about the Army program. Again, I told grandmom that I had no regrets and thanked her for sharing the information with me. Moreover, I told grandmom that the decision to enlist was the best decision I could have made at the time since my employment prospects were so limited. And then there was that little matter of family tradition. Grandmom understood.

I returned to Vicenza in mid-January 1961 and promptly checked off 20 days on my "short-timers" calendar. Every GI had a short-timers calendar taped inside of his wardrobe – or wall locker. 1097 days was a full three-year tour. This was 1961, a memorable year for me. With ten months remaining on my overseas tour, I wanted to see as much of Europe as I could. Who knew if I would ever have such an opportunity again? Several months later, another friend, Lionell Washington from Indiana, and I took advantage of a long weekend and boarded a train to Zurich, Switzerland. Zurich's nightclubs were rumored to have great jazz and few American soldiers walked its streets. On our second day, while sitting at an outdoor cafe on the canal in Old Zurich, Washington was drinking a heavy Swiss beer. "Check that label, George," he said. "This is a special Easter brew," he noted while pointing to the label. I was not a beer drinker and that particular bit of trivia did not register with me. As the afternoon wore on, Washington had been trying to goad me to "just take a swallow, this is good beer...one swallow will not hurt you." Then he said, "I'll make you an offer: you finish the little that's left in the bottle and I'll buy dinner." What harm could that small amount of beer do? I thought. "Okay," I said. I had not really noticed that Washington had been sipping the beer, not gulping it. I took the bottle and in two gulps, drained the contents. We kept talking and, about 30-minutes later, he said while getting up, "let's go." I got up, or so I thought. My body seemed to move, but my head did not. Someone (the beer) had hit me on the head with a hammer. The lofty altitude of six-feet off the ground was two-feet above what my head could manage at that moment. Washington was naturally amused. He knew! The beer's high alcoholic content would have an immediate effect on me because I was unaccustomed to it. Even I had to laugh because I was high, worse than I had been that night up in Beluno drinking wine with the Carabinieri. Later, while returning to our hotel, I had a sudden, irrational urge to run part of the way. "You'd better stop running, fool!" Washington yelled at me. Still feeling the effect of the beer, I had decided to hurdle a wall several yards away, why I do not know. I had been a hurdler in high school and the wall did not appear to be more than three feet high. As I approached the wall, I decided at the last moment to stop. As I did, my forward momentum almost propelled me over the wall and into a small canal below. I didn't swim and I could have drowned. Imagine Washington having to explain how it happened. I laughed lightly to myself, but knew I had better sober up quickly. At night, we walked the streets and tried to slip into as many clubs as we could talk our way into, a favorite GI pastime. The ruse was we were students trying to find some friends we were supposed to meet. During the day, we hung out at a center city park by a lake with other young people. What I found unusual was that the beach was not sandy, it was all grass.

That summer, three recent arrivals in the Transportation Office told me of a trip they were planning to the Italian, French, and Spanish Riviera and they needed a fourth man to share the costs and the driving. Individually, the cost of the trip was prohibitive, but divided by four, it became "Hell yes!" The drive would take two-to-three days. From Vicenza, we drove to Torino, crossed the Italian border into France and proceeded along the French coast to Cannes and Nice. The drive was memorable for another reason. Being a World War 11 history buff, I always insisted we stop for a few minutes whenever we spotted German fortifications in southern Italy and France left from the war. They were an endless source of fascination for me. Those fortifications, I learned later, were strategically placed to offer a commanding view of approaches to key German strong points. The weather for the trip was perfect. The women we encountered on the beaches were beautiful, and we had time to be distracted. After a full day spent trying to mingle with the crowds in France for the earlier Cannes Film Festival and vacation, we were back on the road through the French countryside to the Spanish border. We changed drivers at the border and at some point, and while driving, I nodded for a split second. Everyone heard a sharp noise and I pulled over. At the moment I nodded, I was passing a large truck on the opposite side and I must have drifted to my left striking the truck's rear mud flap. I knew what happened, but did not want to alarm my sleeping colleagues. They thought I had hit a pothole and I left it at that.

Barcelona's beaches and nightlife were simply overwhelming. Elements of the U.S. Sixth Fleet had recently departed, thus eliminating the competition. Those guys, numbering in the thousands during each shore leave, had too much money to spend. Barcelona for the four of us was paradise discovered. The operative rule there was, "In Rome, do as the Romans do." We spent six days wandering the city looking very much like tourists with cameras flapping around our necks. At night, we prowled the city's famous clubs and took full advantage of its delights. Daily, we hit the beach around noon to chat up the locals. Cheap restaurants and hotels were the order of the day. Before we knew it, it was over. What we did have were the photographs and the memories.

Fall was rapidly approaching and I had fewer than 90-days remaining on the overseas portion of my three-year enlistment. Once I returned to the States, I would spend the last eight months closer to home and preparing for my transition to civilian life again. This earned me the title that all soldiers covet: "short-timer" and the bragging rights that came with the status. I could say things like, "I am so short, I don't have time for a long conversation, and, "I'll have dinner, but I'll have to take dessert to go." Being a short-timer is one tremendous boost to someone's morale; it means it is almost over. Early one morning, around 4 am, the silence was shattered by the shrill sound of a whistle. The duty NCO came through the sleeping quarters shouting "Alert! Alert! Alert!" Well, this was highly unusual because under normal circumstances, we in Headquarters and Headquarters Company were forewarned about all military alerts. After all, our mission was to manage the base itself. How could we not know? This had to be something else.

We scrambled out of bed, donned combat gear, and began to report to our duty stations. Those of us with ENEP (Evacuation of Non-Essential Personnel) responsibility for notifying Army personnel and their dependents living in the Italian community, ran to the Motor Pool to pick up our vehicles. Within minutes, I was racing through the Italian night with a list of those personnel I had to notify about the alert. They were not notified by telephone because the exercise was designed to simulate wartime conditions. In the event of hostilities, all telephone communications could be down. By now it was not quite 4:30 am and I am thinking, "this is highly irregular!" Alerts in this command are exercises, never consequential; this is not Germany or Korea!

Two hours later, I was back at company headquarters and, as expected, there was bedlam. Normally, as I said, these are orderly affairs; everyone knows what to expect and goes through the motions. The First Sergeant then ordered us into two-and-half-ton trucks assembled behind the barracks. An hour later, we were still sitting in those trucks. No one seemed to know anything. This was classic Army, "hurry up and wait." Later, toward mid-morning, while still in Alert status, we learned that the Russians had begun to physically divide Berlin. The infamous Berlin Wall was being built. Life changed that day for all American military personnel stationed in Europe, even for those of us in Europe's (inconsequential) Southern Command – SETAF. By the second day, normalcy reappeared, but with a twist: the NCOs and officers were more tense than normal. The soldier's bible, the Stars and Stripes newspaper, had graphic photos of the face-off between American and Russian tanks in Berlin. Numerous articles described barbed-wire barriers being erected and a concrete wall under construction. The question at the street level where I lived was, "Are we going to war?" The 124th Signal Company and the 80th and 82nd Missile Battalions were already in the field. The rest of our command was in standby status. Even those NCOs that were veterans of World War 11 and the Korean Conflict, normally unfazed by an Alert of any kind, were a little more tense than usual.

Several weeks later, when I began to inquire about my orders reassigning me back to the States, I was informed by our company clerk that all Permanent Change of Station (PCS) orders had been cancelled. At first, I could not believe it. I was then told that I would be extended in Italy until November as a direct result of events in Berlin. That's not so bad, I thought; I would still be home for Christmas. Since my mother was expecting me stateside soon, I wrote to tell her of the change. The Army would have to assign me to Fort Dix this time, I reasoned. In November, the extension was moved back to December. Well, now the game had a new set of rules. The contract the Army had with me had been broken. A guy I knew in the 124th Signal Company had to be physically restrained after being told he would have to be extended beyond the date of his separation (ETS) from the Army. The reason cited for his extension was that he occupied a critical Military Occupational Specialty (MOS). My MOS was not critical as far as I knew. My replacements were already in the command. This soldier was just another ordinary grunt doing his time. Why was he critical now, he wanted to know. "Can they do that?" he yelled. "I've been a good soldier, never got into trouble and now you tell me I can't go home! This is crazy!" All of this unsettling information about a critical MOS was being reported second-hand, but under the circumstances, it was credible. I admit that for a time, I did think the worse. Perhaps we were going to war. Events in Berlin, according to reports in military channels, were tense, but there had been no exchange of fire; just a very tense face-off.

The new year rolled around in January 1962 and the First Sergeant called to tell me that I had been extended indefinitely. "What does that mean?" I asked. He had been under siege for several months now by others in my new state of psychological disequilibria. All he could say was "I'll let you know!" I was now in the 25th month of a 22-month assignment. My mother had become frantic, but beyond advising her of my new status, there was nothing more I could do. I even stopped writing to her because there was nothing else to tell her. She reported to the Red Cross that she had not heard from her son, that she was worried, and could they find out what had happened. Naturally, that came down through channels and infuriated the First Sergeant. I talked him down and wrote home telling my mother she was not helping my situation.

I was now a Corporal, which meant I lived farther from the edge of poverty. As a corporal with over two years of service, my base pay of $150 monthly gave me a little more money in my pocket even after deducting my monthly allotment home. I had to get away. I was entitled to 30-days of annual leave, did not know when I was going home, had already trained my replacement, so vacation was the next best thing. I simply had to clear my head. Leave requests for guys in my status were routinely approved forthwith as a gesture of compassion. With a train ticket in hand, I was en-route to Copenhagen. I had read a bit about Scandinavia so why not see it while I can. Twenty-four hours on a train can be an adventure in itself. There was time to strike up conversations, read, and allow your mind to wander while seeing but not seeing some of the best European scenery imaginable. The rhythmic clicking of the wheels was relaxing and I managed to get some sleep.

Thirty-days in Copenhagen was the prescription I needed; the best vacation by far – including the Riviera trip and the sensuous isolation of Barcelona. I met quite a few guys like myself from some of the famed Army units in Germany including the artillery, mechanized infantry, guys who lived on maneuvers for months during the year. They, too, had been extended but the difference was these guys played real war compared to the benign Alert drills in Italy. Italy was Something Even The Army Forgot – remember? The Stars and Stripes was always filled with graphic photographs of Army maneuvers at Grafenwoehr, one of Germany's more infamous war-game sites. I recall "Winter Shield 1" and "Winter Shield 2" splashed across the front pages. For many of the guys I met there, Copenhagen was home away from Germany. Whenever they could escape life in the field, they were in Copenhagen. It did not take me long to understand why. Danes were socially more progressive than many countries in Europe and they harbored no prejudice toward African-Americans.

I buddied-up with another young African-American airman from an obscure American Air Force installation in Bari at the heel of the Italian boot. We explored the city's nightclubs with our Danish female guides, played tourist by day and slept when we could. In Copenhagen at that time, if you spent time with an unmarried woman, she checked into your hotel with you. This was allowed by the police for better control. They would check the hotel rosters at night. For that 30-days, the events in Berlin were secondary to anything else on my mind. I returned 28-days later with fabulous memories and the address of a beautiful Danish nurse I intended to stay in touch with. For 26 of my 28 days there, she was a constant companion when not on duty at her hospital. The four of us took long walks, visited the famous museum commemorating the Danish Resistance Movement during World War 11, saw Danish movies, bought hot dogs to go, and the two of us decided we wanted to remain in touch.

The spring of 1962 came. My enlistment was due to terminate on June 30, 1962. It was now early May and I had no orders. The thought did occur to me that I, too, might be extended beyond my enlistment date even though my job was not critical. By now, I had served almost 30-months in an overseas assignment. That was a record for a first-term enlistment in my company. When I did receive orders directing me to return via surface travel to the Continental United States (CONUS) for discharge on June 14, I would actually be discharged two-weeks early. That was not much consolation for being extended an additional eight months, but I would take it. In early June, I bade farewell to my closest friends and settled down for the long train ride to Bremerhaven, Germany. I joined 6,000 other guys returning home by the troopship USNS Gordon. I was now going to spend ten days on the Atlantic, another new experience. Although I was going home, I really did not look forward to spending ten days at sea with guys sleeping five deep in stacked bunks, seasickness, night sounds, and being confined for the most part to the troop area below deck. The food was bad, and for several days, we did not have fresh water to take showers. Try to make soap lather with salt water.

The Army and my military service in Italy had been a life-defining experience for this 21 -year old young man who first set foot on Italian soil almost three years earlier. I had listened and learned from all those Italians and Americans who became an integral part of my experiences. Moreover, I discovered that I was comfortable in a larger universe of diverse cultures, languages, political and educational systems, and contrarian views. It had been my experience that regardless of who you are, each of us has the ability to be a force for good, for friendship, and for understanding. In my case, it was also across cultural and linguistic lines. For the first time, I had been accepted on the basis of who I was as a human being, not for what I was – a man with a different hue. The color of my skin, for the first time was irrelevant, nothing more than a curiosity. What a marvelous feeling! I now understood how white Americans felt at home. It was obvious that my Italian odyssey had shaped the trajectory of my life yet to come. I just had to give it content, purpose, and direction.

There is a special footnote to this chapter. My experience in Italy, especially the military component, could have shaped my thinking about my life and a career differently than it did. Perhaps it is true that everything happens for a reason. At the time I volunteered for the draft, I was an average African-American male teenager of the 1950s with one possible exception: I felt since the age of ten that I was destined to live in a large universe of ideas and challenges, beyond anything I could conceive at the time. Second, I knew I had to shape, to design any role I was destined to play in the world I would ultimately inhabit.

The average young soldier of that era, whether a draftee or regular Army, entertained, if only briefly, the idea of the Army as a viable career choice. They may not have admitted it to their buddies, but the idea did cross their minds. We were the equivalent of a Tabula Rasa, just waiting to be written on. I was no different. For most of us, the experiences, the opportunities that shape career choices were yet to be. The military has always been a choice; it may not have been the most desirable choice, but it was a choice. My thoughts about the Army were not shaped by my experiences at Fort Benning or at Fort Knox. To the contrary! It was the 124th Signal Company and the 1st Missile Command in Northern Italy: Caserma Ederle, my duty station. Had I been assigned elsewhere, perhaps my outlook would have been different. I have to allow for that possibility.

The officer corps at our command were, for the most part, southern – social products of their era. Blacks, to them, were not their professional or social equal. They accepted them as officer colleagues because it was Army policy. Of the approximately 3,000 officers and enlisted personnel on post, at least 90-percent were white – many southern. There were dozens of officers but only six African-Americans and that included an African-American investigator of dubious status with the Office of Criminal Investigations. He may have been an NCO authorized to wear civilian clothing. Racial strife was a fact of life and the idea of fairness of outcomes in numerous altercations between Blacks and whites was an unreasonable expectation. Blacks were routinely passed over for promotion and routinely subject to Article 15 non-judicial punishment resulting in loss of rank and pay.

One of our base commanders was from Athens, Georgia and he was reviled by contacts between African-Americans and Italian women. Setting aside individual preferences as in "boy-meets-girl," consider the "supply-and-demand" approach: there were no African-American female enlisted personnel. There were only white female nurses. Social contacts between enlisted personnel and officers were against Army regulations. Moreover, I doubt that any white nurse would have been willing to endure risking her career by dating a single African-American officer – which there were none. They dated Italians and the few single white male officers available.

The officers assigned to us exhibited few of the leadership skills or qualities that inspired their men or impressionable young men like myself to emulate their career example. It was the conduct of our officers that gave rise to the alternate designation of our command "Something Even The Army Forgot." The reputation of our command at USAREUR (United States Army Europe), according to contacts many of my colleagues in Headquarters and Headquarters Company maintained with counterparts in Heidelberg, was that good officers did not wish to be assigned there. They preferred Germany or Korea.

Perhaps this was unique to our command, but it was common knowledge that many officers did not always sleep at their own residences. I was struck by how easily they fell into bed with women who were the wives of other officers. This, I witnessed. Two critical sentry posts confirm this: the Officers' Club and the officer housing area. This behavior was not restricted to the officer ranks. I knew early on that had I chosen to become a military officer, I would never marry. I did entertain this choice as a career option until my trip home the Christmas of 1960.

In 1962, it was base policy, at least in my company, that departing first-term enlisted personnel meet with the re-enlistment NCO for a total of six counseling sessions before they could administratively depart the command. I reached an agreement with the sergeant to have one meeting during which he would make the case for the military as a career option and I would make my case to leave the military. If he felt I had made a reasonable case, he would sign my case card indicating five previous meetings. We talked for over an hour. At the conclusion of our meeting, he said in all earnestness, "Kennedy, you do not need the Army...you're an independent thinker and you do ask questions. Furthermore, I honestly doubt that you will achieve the level of satisfaction you seek." He did say though that the Army needs more young men like myself. We parted amicably and I had my six signatures. The foundation of my argument was poor leadership, unfairness and racial bias in adjudicating disputes, residual racism, questionable moral behavior. I was not a Puritan, but I was young with reasonable expectations of those selected to lead. I was not prepared to re-enlist for six years (your only option at that time if you re-enlisted) and risk my future with the Army. My future lay elsewhere; I just did not know where.

CHAPTER 5

CHOICES – THE ROAD AHEAD

On June 14, 1962, 11 days before my twenty-second birthday, we arrived at Fort Hamilton, New York aboard the USNS Gordon. When we docked, I was below deck. I saw no need to rush topside with the guys crowding up the stairs. During our pre-arrival briefing, we had been told that upon docking at the port, it would be another several hours before we could disembark. I recall lying in my bunk feeling relieved that the voyage was over; it had not been that pleasant. Also on my mind were thoughts about tomorrow and the days after. At that moment on that day, only a formal discharge ceremony separated me from the continuation of a journey I was going to make. In a few hours, that portion of the journey, my military career, would be over.

Someone shouted for an "Alfred Kennedy." "Is there an Alfred Kennedy down here?" he asked. "Yeah, I'm over here," I responded. "Kennedy, your mom is dockside, she's asking for you!" Well, that was a surprising bit of news. She knew I was coming home and I had forgotten just how much detail I had given her about when we would dock. I should not have been surprised because mom did things that way. I scrambled up the steps; guys were lined three and four deep at the railing shouting to family members. It's a wonder anyone heard anything! I made my way through the crush of hundreds of bodies jockeying for position along and the rail and I could see her before I arrived within ear shot. I waved to let her know I had seen her. Mom was still beautiful; tall, that broad and beautiful smile. She had aged a little. She also had a grey streak on the right side and I remember thinking it was quite striking; I liked it. I tried to tell her it would be at least a couple of hours before I could disembark; that she should go over to the family section and wait for me there. I would find her. She must have understood because she turned to leave.

I went back downstairs and laid on the bunk. For some odd

reason, now that I had seen mother, my thoughts seemed more urgent. I guess it was the reality I knew to be her. Again, the question, What was I going to do? The one thing I did know was that I was profoundly and permanently affected by my European experience. Trying to bring some order to my thought process, I saw the immediate challenge to be reintegrating the Camden I knew might offer even less than before. I say this because I left Camden as a teenager with the worldview and expectations of a teenager. I was now almost 22, a veteran with different needs and expectations. My greatest need now was access to jobs and opportunity. The idea of Camden and opportunity was just a little scary. I knew that I was not prepared to join the ranks of those ex-veterans of the Korean War and the 1950s in my neighborhood (my neighbor being among them) who returned home with similar expectations but had to settle for less satisfying jobs and a deflated sense of self. That prospect did not sit well with me. But, I also knew I would do whatever it took to avoid that outcome. I was motivated and I was driven. Now, I had to be about channeling my energy in a positive direction. For many of the older ex-vets in North Camden, the best days of their lives were behind them. While lying there, this scene played like a movie because it was so familiar, and I imagined it had not changed. Every Saturday at the community barber shop on the southwest corner of Eleventh and Cooper Streets, I heard them arguing passionately about boxing, baseball teams and scores, individual players, and politics. They also retold with great fondness, their adventures as a young soldier or airman in Korea or Japan of the early 1950s. They lived on memories. The difference for me was that I wanted the success of achieving my dreams. If I sound impatient before arriving home, it was because I was impatient. Italy was a launching pad. I had a sense of self worth and it was important that I find something of value to validate myself.

A couple of hours later, the order came to disembark. We filed into a cavernous hall filled with chairs. In a few minutes, we were told, an Army officer would arrive, formally declare our group of returnees discharged from active military service and I would be on my way. As you can imagine, the dynamic within the hall was interesting. Here is what happened. At first, not one of us sat down. We were all hyped, closer to home, and anxious to get going. Minutes passed and no officer appeared. I remembered sitting down, but also recall sitting on something. I lifted myself slightly and saw that I had sat on a large manila envelope. The upper left corner was stamped "U.S. Department of Defense." In the envelope was a variety of information sheets and pamphlets describing opportunities for Veterans. I did not look at it carefully. I put it all back in the envelope, and in the spirit of the moment, stood briefly and sat down again. This time, I held the envelope in my hand, feet tapping the floor nervously. "Where in the hell is that officer?" I wondered aloud. Again, I stood up while reflexively placing that manila envelope on the chair under me. I didn't want it anyway. Again, no officer! By now, everyone was growing increasingly impatient and very vocal. I sat down again, but this time, when I picked up the envelope on my chair, I opened it and examined its contents more closely, not much, just a little more than a few minutes earlier. As returning veterans, we qualified for federal employment, according to one of the information sheets. There were notices of position openings at a number of federal agencies in Washington, D.C. That may as well have been a world away. I put the envelope in my small travel bag and forgot about it. Eventually, the officer arrived, discharged us and I was out the door to find mother. Many of those leaving the hall, at least those I could see, left their envelopes on their chairs, or discarded it in one of the large bins by each exit. The Army was already well into a recycling program. My decision to put that manila envelope into my travel bag turned out to be life altering, however, the gravity of my decision was not apparent to me at the time. Once outside, I found mother, we embraced, tears on both sides. She looked good and I let her do the talking. We headed toward the buses that were there to facilitate everyone's travel needs. We bought tickets and settled in for the long ride back to the Trailways Bus Terminal in Camden.

Several days later, while finally unpacking my bag and my Army duffel bag, I noticed the manila envelope, the one I had inadvertently put in my bag. This time, I sat on the side of the bed and carefully examined everything. I came across an announcement from the U.S. Department of State describing various opportunities for veterans and others with a background in communications, foreign experience, or a familiarity with foreign languages. Thus far, I was batting a thousand percent. The positions at the State Department were consistent with my background. The pay was $4,110 per annum with benefits. The clincher for me was the availability of positions in Europe. That did it! A few minutes passed as I began to think seriously about what I was reading.

I tried to remember something. I knew there had been an American Consulate in Venice, and Jim Nance and I did walk past the American Embassy in Rome on that city's famed Via Veneto. It also occurred to me that it was unlikely the Department of State would seriously consider me. African-American kids of that era, especially males, were not encouraged to extend their horizons beyond a military experience let alone the remote idea of a possible career in international diplomacy. On the other hand, I thought, "nothing ventured, nothing gained." I did not have a job; I had the time, so why not follow up. What I honestly envisioned was a day in the distant future when I would receive a letter thanking me for my interest, but advising me that "nothing is available at this time." This thought process was my reality check; you had to have that! I could no longer think the way I did in Italy. Thoughts about equal opportunity and equal treatment were dangerous and could lead to much frustration and disappointment. This was Camden of the early 1960s and I had better readjust; the sooner the better.

Mother was at work on the day I examined the contents of that manila envelope, particularly the flyer from the Department of State. There was a copy of the old lengthy Standard Form 171 (Application for Federal Employment). It took a couple of days on my old Remington typewriter (from high school), but I managed to get some carbon paper and complete the application in multiple copies. I signed it, mailed it and promptly forgot about it! Again, "what now?" That question had settled on my brain and it was going to plague me until I had an answer. One of my high school classmates, James Webb, was discharged from the Air Force around that same time. He, like so many others from our class, had joined right after graduation in 1958. I spent a year at Shaw University and three years in the Army while Jim completed a four-year stint in the Air Force. Part of that tour of duty was spent in Japan. We had seen each other on that first Sunday home in church. Our family church was quite literally across the street from my house on Penn Street.

Later that Sunday afternoon, I walked around to his house on Carpenter Street. Jim opened the door. "What's up?" I asked. "Not much, man...I know I've got to find a job." "You know how it is in my house," Jim said. "Too many mouths to feed." Jim came from a very large, multi-generational family many of whom still lived in their three-story house. I had been there on many occasions when we were in high school and I well understood the situation he was referring to.

In discussing our situation, he said, "I think we qualify for unemployment benefits." "So, we should go to the employment office down on Broadway and register." As it turned out, I was entitled to $37.00 weekly; Jim's benefits amounted to $29.00. That was enough to keep the "Wolf" away from the door – as that popular colloquial expression goes. I was an avid saver and thus managed to save $10.00 weekly after paying rent for my mother and helping her with a few bills. Daily, Jim and I would buy the local paper, The Camden Courier, scour the classified ads and list the jobs we felt qualified for. It was important that we make an honest effort to secure employment to avoid losing our benefits.

The process and the outcome developed a familiar pattern quickly: call about the job, identify yourself. Confirm the vacancy late in the afternoon. Obtain the name of the contact person. Arrange an interview for the next day and be told early the next morning the position had been filled. All of this after you were the first applicant to appear on each occasion. Each rejection only strengthened my resolve to succeed, not to be psychologically bludgeoned into my place, whatever that was. I now knew what it was to be accepted as a human being and that was my new standard, consequences be damned!

Civil society in Camden of the early 1960s was polite. African-Americans and white-collar jobs were still a contradiction in terms, especially in city government, the banking and hotel industry, and much of retail. We were welcome however as consumers. I was prepared to push the envelope for access, up to the point that jail was the next step in the process. At that point, I would back off, but only momentarily. Of course, in the back of my mind was the "return-to-military-service" option which several of the older ex-vets counseled while lamenting the fact they regretted not having done so. As each of them so aptly put it, "there is nothing here in Camden but factory jobs – if you can get a good one."

The Army allowed a veteran to reenlist at prior rank within 90-days from separation. Even before separating from the Army, and while still in Italy, I had conditioned myself to believe that I would not find a job before the 91st day after discharge. I had already ruled out reenlisting; it was not an option. My only point in bringing this up is that in my circumstances, it did cross my mind. I had to stay focussed. Enjoying Europe was one thing; reenlisting was quite another. Three years was quite sufficient in my case. There just had to be another way forward. For the balance of the summer that year, Jim would borrow a car from one of his older brothers and we would hang out in Atlantic City or some of the suburban communities around Camden. There was always a small house party and new people to meet. At long as we could put a few dollars worth of gas in the car and afford a meal, we were good to go.

My old friend Vincent still lived in North Camden and I had not seen him in quite some time. A quick trip to his parents' home produced a home address and telephone number. While tossing around a football one day down at Pyne Point Park, I caught up with events in his life. He was a proud, young father now and working full time in Philadelphia. Although I had wanted more for him, he seemed content with the choices he had made after leaving Howard University several years earlier. I asked him about my former girlfriend Aretha and learned that she and her family were living in Parkside near Camden High School. I decided against contacting her; she had moved on. I would see her soon enough. Vincent and I attended the same church and both of us sang in the church choir. Maintaining contact was easier with him. He had also told me that good jobs were difficult to come by and in short supply. "Alfred," he said, "Camden is not for you, it never was. Get away from here – you can do better!" I loved that about him. Other than my older brother, Vince was a one-man booster club for me. Fred and Marlene were mentors – thus in a slightly different category. Vincent, on the other hand, was heart and soul - the basis for our connection.

On the 94th day after separating from the Army, Jim and I found employment as custodians with GEX (Government Employees Exchange), a major discount chain. The store was a few miles from home near the old Camden City Airport. The starting salary was $44.00 weekly. It was now September and Jim and I had only a few months remaining on unemployment benefits that would expire around Christmas. That would have been disastrous. Better a job, even as janitors. So it was good to have a job. A full-time job also meant that we could no longer hang out in Atlantic City and party as much as we did. Not having a job also had its benefits: an active social life.

Something else happened later that fall that brought more light to the Kennedy household: My younger brother Michael was home on Christmas furlough. I had not seen him since before my enlistment three years earlier. Mike looked great in his Marine uniform. He talked about boot camp at Parris Island and subsequent duty at Cherry Point in North Carolina. Everything he encountered in boot camp was as Bernard had recounted it seven years earlier when he was there. Mike was full of tales about "life with the locals" in North Carolina and had me in stitches laughing. Some of what he experienced, I could relate to from my year in Raleigh. Bernard was still in Camden and my sister Earlene was living with her family on Haddon Avenue. This was a rare event for my mother: having all four of her children close at the same time. It became increasingly rare.

Meanwhile, I had been involved in an exchange of correspondence with the Department of State in Washington, D.C. Whatever information they requested, I would provide. I was still waiting for their "thank you, but no thank you!" response. By late October and November, I had completed the application at some personal expense, traveled to their regional office in Philadelphia for certain aspects of the application process, provided background check information, typed a paper and had my fingerprints taken. The only people I could share the details of the application process with were Fred and Marlene. My mother was less than enthusiastic about the possibility that I might leave home again so soon. When she would ask about it, I would always tell her the odds were against me thinking that would ameliorate the situation a little.

One day in November, a neighbor knocked on the door to ask if I was in any trouble. The question seemed out of the ordinary, but in response, I said "not to my knowledge ...why do you ask?" "Well," he said, "the FBI has been talking to people in the neighborhood about you, asking questions about your character." I thought for a moment and then laughed. "Don't worry, that is probably in conjunction with a job I am applying for. A background investigation is part of the process," I said. I thanked him for bringing this to my attention. I promptly forgot it. That November, just after Thanksgiving, I also received a $6.00 per week increase in my salary. Fifty dollars a week meant I finally could afford to buy a car. Having my own car would mean I could decrease my dependence on Jim and others for transportation – even to work. I had to walk the five miles home at 4 am every morning when Jim and our other colleague arrived at the store to relieve me. That was a long five miles when it was the bitter cold of November and December.

Jim and I found a 1956 Chevrolet Bel Air, 4-door sedan with a '57 Chevy V-8 engine and a standard transmission; asking price - $695.00. I put $200.00 down, agreed on the financing and it was a done deal. I was now on "wheels," my first car. Almost overnight, my social prospects changed. Suddenly, I had female admirers that did not exist previously. My motto became "if you didn't see me when I was walking, you don't see me now." I'm still the same person. In some respects, being mobile deadened the psychological impact of being a janitor. I could get away from the house on my own when the weight of my thoughts was more than I could manage – which was often. Unconsciously, I was still comparing the expanse of life as I lived it in Europe with the uncertainty and the confines of my existence at home.

In mid-December, Fred and Marlene invited me to a Christmas party at their home. Fred said they would be inviting someone they wanted me to meet. I looked forward to that because I usually enjoyed the friends they introduced me to. Truth be told, their friends were the only interesting people I had the opportunity to me. "I'll be there, thanks," I replied. The Christmas party was a typical Fred and Marlene affair: good food and great music; not just your standard holiday fare.

Moreover, there were many people I had not previously met, which usually meant good conversation. While engaged in a conversation with a former high school teacher, Fred tapped me on the shoulder saying, "Ken, I'd like you to meet Donald Watson." I turned briefly to shake Donald's hand. Fred continued, "I've told Donald about you and your application with the State Department. The two of you should talk!" Donald and I excused ourselves and went looking for a quiet place to talk." I mentioned to Donald he was held in high regard by both Fred and Marlene. I also said, "Fred told me you were previously in the Foreign Service, and that you would be willing to share something of your experience with me." "Were you in the Foreign Service?" I asked. "Yes! Back in the 1950s...there were only a few African-Americans then." He spoke briefly about a trip he made to the Far East." "Where are you in the application process?" "Well, the FBI has been talking to people on my street and elsewhere." Before I could continue, Donald interrupted and said, "You've been accepted. They just have not told you yet." How do you know that?" I wanted to know. He would only say "that is the way the process works. If there was something in your background of major concern to them, they would not have interviewed your friends and neighbors, and teachers...Trust me!"

Although I was heartened by Donald's response, an inner restraint kept the skeptic in me alive. "What you say is very encouraging, but, I'll believe it when I receive something in writing." "When you receive the letter, not if, let me know" he replied. Later Fred asked me what I thought about Donald and his sense of my prospects. I expressed concern about building myself up for the letdown I felt would come at some future date. Fred understood but told me he was still optimistic.

By the end of January 1963, Jim and I knew that there was no possibility for advancement at GEX. The assistant manager, Mr. Harrison, was very unpleasant and obviously not inclined to consider us as prospects for other vacancies in the store. We had met other store employees who had started as custodians in other stores, but were offered opportunities in the stock room, shipping, sales, and security. Mr. Harrison's attitude left the unmistakable impression that Jim and I were doing what he had hired us to do and that there would be nothing else available to us. I wanted out, but to where?

One day, Jim said, "George, let's play some politics. That's what they do." "What politics?" "What are you talking about?" I asked. "Let's go see our Ward Leader Collie Hairston," Jim replied. "I know he gets people jobs...I just didn't think of this before." I asked, "who is Collie Hairston and what does he do?" Jim said, "he lives two blocks from you on Cooper Street and he is supposed to represent our community's interests at City Hall." "Fine" I replied, "anything beats working at GEX." When we met with Mr. Hairston, his first and only question was, "Are you guys registered to vote?" "No!" we both responded. "Come with me; we're going to City Hall. We have to get you guys registered to vote. You're Democrats, by the way." Speaking for both of us, I said "we will be whatever improved our prospects for a better job. Once we had registered, Collie said, "you guys come see me tomorrow night, I may have something for you."

The next evening, Collie shared with us some of the history surrounding his attempts to get jobs for African-Americans at City Hall – other than in the Sanitation Department. There was one office in particular he wanted to crack and that was the Office of Water and Sewer Taxes. "There are administrative positions there that you are qualified for," he told me, but "the office administrator is difficult." "Are you up to a good challenge?" he asked. "If so, bring me a copy of your high school transcript, your transcript from Shaw, and your DD-214" (Official separation from the U.S. Army.) Collie continued, "you are a resident of Camden with a good record and you are a veteran...None of the other guys in that office at the level I have in mind have ever served in the military...I'll be in touch!"

I worked the graveyard shift at GEX, therefore, I slept from the time I returned home at 4 am until about 8 am. As I lay in bed early one morning, someone knocked at the front door. My mother had already left for work. When I opened the door, it was Collie Hairston. "Good news, George" as he came into the living room. "I got you into the Water and Sewer Office...get dressed, we're going to City Hall." An hour later, I was being introduced to Steven Sparelli, the office manager. Steven was Italian-American, probably first-generation because he still spoke fluent Italian. Steven had to be in his mid-forties. The only other African-American in the office was an older minister from Philadelphia who had actual civil service status. They couldn't touch him. The other three audit clerks were "patronage" hires. Collie Hairston had persuaded Steven to let me in, otherwise, he would publicly challenge office hiring practices.

I promptly quit my job at GEX and reported to City Hall where I became the fourth member of a small, congenial group of audit and account clerks that audited water and sewer tax receipts. With one exception, they were all recent graduates of Camden High School. That one exception was an Irish guy named Russell, a '48 graduate of Wilson High School. Another member of that group, a second-generation Italian

American, Nelson Paccione, and I frequently played basketball together at a court in Nelson's neighborhood – an Italian-American enclave in South Camden. There was never an incident. After working up a good sweat for an hour or so, he would drive me back to North Camden. Since we were all patronage hires, politically, we were vulnerable, but I'm getting ahead of the story.

The beauty of this job for me was that it was within walking distance of home. I could walk to work! The $3,000 per annum salary for a 30-hour workweek was "manna from heaven." I did wonder how long this could, or would, last. As long as it did last, I had plans. That level of income for a 30-hour week revealed the disparities in income among the races at that time. Many African-Americans earned that much with a minimum of a 40-hour work week that included the expense of a commute. Another dimension of my political education had begun. I wanted to capitalize quickly with a plan to finance the balance of the college education I had interrupted four years earlier. It should be obvious that this goal had become a quiet obsession with me. While I did not plan to return to Shaw, there were other colleges in New Jersey and Pennsylvania within reach. The reason I chose not to return to Shaw is easily explained. At Shaw, you were a member of a class. You entered with and graduated with a class. All of my former classmates had graduated, with one exception I knew of, and I did not want to start over with people I did not know. It would not be the same. I already had history.

As the newest member of the group in the tax office, I assumed it would be good politics if I volunteered to take late lunch. My three colleagues liked to lunch together when they could and I was trying to signal that I wanted to fit in. My gesture would now permit the office to function during the noon hour without interruption. On one memorable day, several weeks into my tenure there, an elderly Italian couple came into the office and approached the counter. When the husband tried to speak in broken English, I asked him in Italian, if he was Italian ("Scusate ma, Lei e' Italiano?") "Si, sono Italiano": (yes, I am Italian). "Ma, Lei parla bene Italiano!" (you speak very good Italian) he replied. "Ma, come' mai? Lei non e' Italiano." (why is that? You are not Italian!) "No, I'm not Italian" I explained, again in Italian. "I speak Italian because I lived in Italy and I am familiar with the language." Both of them stood there in stunned silence for a moment. I, again, asked, "May I help you?" (Come' posso aiutarVi?) They were unfamiliar with Camden's 18-story City Hall and were seeking directions to an office for an appointment elsewhere in the building. They told me the name of the office they were looking for and I directed them to the floor directly above us. They thanked me, smiled gently and left. I thought no more about it, but I was pleased to have been able to help them.

There is more to the story. A week later, my colleagues and I were cloistered around the account registers when we heard Steven Sparelli's telephone ring. It was around 10:30 a.m. The telephone rang in his office everyday around that same time. On that day, Steven picked up the receiver and, while responding to the caller in Italian, stood in his doorway – as he customarily did. During Steven 's conversation, I laughed almost inaudibly to myself. Why I reacted that day, I'll never know, but I did. "What are you laughing at George?" Nelson asked. "Oh, just something Steven said to his wife." "You understand what he's saying?" "Yes, why are you asking?" I responded. "Steven gets that call almost everyday and we never know what he's talking about... he always speaks in Italian." I explained, innocently, that it was just a call from his wife; that they were talking about the children and what she is preparing for dinner. I was familiar with that routine because it was a ritual among many Italian men I had met in Vicenza.

The next day, I noticed something odd. Steven had closed his door, something he rarely did. In the office, Steven was a creature of habit; he liked his door open. Although I thought it a bit odd, it was just one of those bits of minutiae I noticed, thought about for an instant and promptly forgot about. The job was going well. I had begun to increase my savings, but somehow there was always something my mother needed. Preliminary research revealed that there were affordable colleges in New Jersey and the Philadelphia area. I was going to have to narrow my selections, look at some catalogues, and explore the idea of going to school at night and on weekends for the coming fall term. The dream of returning to college never faded, even though the balance in my savings account often fluctuated.

The events of Christmas past had just about receded from memory. This was definitely the case regarding Donald Watson's confident pronouncement that I had been hired by the State Department. It was now spring and in early April, I received a letter from the State Department, among others in the mail that day. "Well, here it is," I thought, "the thank you, but no thank you." I opened the letter and just as I had suspected, it began: "Dear Mr. Kennedy, we regret that we are unable to offer you employment at this time. We will retain your application on file as we assess future needs. Again, we appreciate your interest." It took them a year to tell me that! In a way, I was relieved rather than surprised. A submerged part of me, the idealistic George I rarely revealed, hoped that Donald Watson had been prophetic, that he was right, that I would be hired. This was supposed to be the letter informing me that I had been hired. The pragmatic George, the George that was grappling with the reality of being young, African-American, without a college education and living in Camden, said, "I knew it!" Well, nothing ventured, nothing gained, I reasoned. At least I had the satisfaction of knowing that I had pursued an opportunity ostensibly available to ex-veterans like myself. As circumspect as I tried to be about the rejection, I did feel hurt. Why could they not see that I was right for the job; that I would be great in that job? Is this rejection indicative of the struggle I am going to face as an African-American whenever I apply for jobs of this caliber? An added level of disappointment stemmed from the fact that I still harbored an abiding desire to return to Europe. This would have been my ticket back.

The address I vowed not to lose when I returned from Copenhagen 18-months ago was now very much in play. I had been corresponding with the young nurse I had met while on vacation there and, through her, Europe was still very much alive in me. We wrote of shared memories, familiar places, common interests, and even the future. Why not? For me, dreams were a form of insulation against the reality of Camden, especially now that the Department of State had slammed the door on me. I shared the news with Marlene and Fred. Somehow, they remained optimistic that an offer would materialize at some future point. I decided to close the door on this chapter and move on.

That weekend, Jimmy Webb and I went to Atlantic City. The city's famed Club Harlem and Club 500 on Arctic Avenue were just the balm I needed to assuage the pain I felt about being rejected. A month later, almost to the day, another letter arrived from the State Department. Now, I was intrigued; what did they want? How many times do they need to reject me? This time, the letter began: "Dear Mr. Kennedy, we are pleased to offer you an appointment as a Pouch Clerk at our embassy in Bonn, Germany." I was so excited I almost had to scrape myself off the ceiling. I was in orbit once again when I saw that my starting salary would be $4,110 per annum, a thousand dollars more than my-then current princely salary of $3,000. Of course, I would be working a 40-hour week, but who cared! The reporting date was June 1963, provided I accepted the appointment. "Provided I accept the appointment" I screamed to myself. "Hell yes! I accept." I had to tell my mother immediately even though she was away at work. I ran to Jack Bass's corner drugstore to use the telephone. We still did not have a telephone at home. Fingers trembling, this time for joy, I dialed mom's number. "Mom! Mom! I shouted. Guess what? The Foreign Service has offered me an appointment. I'm going to Germany." The news caught her totally off guard. "You just returned from overseas, I won't let you go." Without thinking, I responded, "But mom, you can't stop me!" Both of us paused at that moment. My mother knew she couldn't stop me and I had wanted to avoid disappointing her, while remaining true to my career aspirations and to myself. In an instant, the competing desires collided. I knew what I had to do to be true to myself. My mother also knew. The dream of a ten-year old that hot Sunday at that old country church in Mizpah was now beginning to take shape. I could almost see the way forward. My next call was to Fred and Marlene. That night, we had dinner and it was all that they could do to contain my enthusiasm.

The next day, I met with Bill, the older African-American minister in the Tax Office to tell him of my good fortune. Bill was pleased and said, "This is a good thing. This office is no place for you in the long run." Did Bill know something that I didn't? I decided to take Bill's comments to mean that the Foreign Service was a better opportunity than remaining in the Tax Office. Bill then shared with me how upset Steven Sparelli became when he learned of my facility with his language. Either he was acquainted with the elderly Italian couple that visited the office that day, or he picked up something through his community grapevine. In either case, he was unhappy and I had to go. Well, I was now going to save him the trouble. I then contacted the State Department's Regional Office in Philadelphia to formally accept the appointment. Shortly before my 23rd birthday, I arrived in Washington, D.C. for two weeks of orientation.

CHAPTER 6

BACK IN EUROPE – FINDING VALUE IN WHAT I DID

Leaving home this time was different than it had been four years earlier when I joined the Army. I would not have the emotional insulation of the telephone. This time, I had to do it face to face and, emotionally, it was more difficult. Mother always wanted the best for me and in her heart, I think she felt the Foreign Service was a phenomenal opportunity for me to launch a career and find real value in something I did. If she understood this, it was not evident in her face or her words. She could not, however, disguise her bitter disappointment that I was leaving her again, and so soon. It had been a year since I returned from Italy. I thought that surely she would understand. She, above everyone else, knew of my plans to return to school and find something of value with career potential. We got through the goodbyes and I was in my car on the way to Washington, D.C. Mother could not know the complete exhilaration I felt about leaving Camden, perhaps permanently.

The closer I drew to Washington, the more excited I became. As any young novice, I had visions of my new job and, more importantly, where it might lead. I also knew it was not going to be easy and I would have to deal with some of the same retrograde attitudes encountered while in uniform and at home in Camden. So, what else was new? Brimming with self-confidence, I had convinced myself I could cope with any new challenge. Ah, what youthful exuberance!

I settled temporarily in Washington and re-connected with my old Army buddy, Jim Nance, then working as a Permit Officer with the Office of Permit Control, a division within the DC Government's Department of Motor Vehicles. I had arranged temporary residence with an aunt of my former college girlfriend who was spending the summer in Washington. They were living at 4th & L Streets in the North West section of the city. For the first time since leaving Shaw in May 1959, Cassie and I would spend time together. Corresponding for three years and a single visit since my return a year ago just could not compare with the time we now had to catch up with each other. The problem for me was simple: it took six months to save enough to purchase a car and, later, between job demands and not much money in my pocket, it was difficult to spend a weekend in Washington. The distance of 142 miles may as well have been a thousand. Unfortunately, this was not the best of times for us because I was leaving again and she was unhappy to say the least. We could do no more than agree to stay in touch since marriage was the furthest thing from my mind. Cassie had graduated from Shaw in 1961 and was teaching in the North Carolina Public School System. She was established in a career; I was not. I tried to explain to her that the Foreign Service offered me the chance to accomplish both of my objectives. I could not wait for opportunity to come to me; I had to be flexible enough and mobile enough to respond to opportunities where they presented themselves. If that meant returning to Europe, I was prepared to do that. I could only hope that she understood what my priorities had to be at that time.

The orientation I received at the Department of State was more about navigating my way from office to office along some of official Washington longest corridors, than a structured series of briefings about current events: Kennedy Administration foreign policy, the Foreign Service, key State Department personnel and their roles, and the functions of an American embassy. I admit I was a novice in international diplomacy in 1963, but the Kennedy administration was defining its role in Vietnam and we had concluded a nuclear test ban treaty with the (former) Soviet Union. Vietnam may have been a "bridge-too-far" for the average American at that time but the Cold War, however, had conditioned the reflexes of my generation and our European counterparts. I was headed to Germany, the buffer between two superpowers and my orientation did not include even a conversation with the German desk officer. In fact, my orientation was so unstructured, I was temporarily assigned to an office within the Office of Personnel to help with some filing – busy work. Within four hours, I had completed a task someone thought would occupy me for two days. I was amused when the file supervisor asked her boss, "He's finished already; what do I do with him now?" I went to lunch.

In the Passport Office, I was issued my first passport, an Official Passport, one level above that of a regular tourist passport and one below the highly prized diplomatic passport. In the Travel Office, I was advised that I had a choice between air and surface as a mode of transport to Germany. The travel clerk there suggested I consider surface travel for a variety of reasons: I could travel first-class on a luxurious ocean liner, the S.S. America, one of two luxury liners operated by the U.S. Second, I would have a private, single cabin on the Main Deck. Moreover, my car would accompany me aboard ship. That meant I could disembark in Hamburg and drive to Bonn. Surface travel was not a difficult sale with me. I did recall hearing how comfortable the accommodations were for officers and their families during our Atlantic crossing from Bremerhaven last summer. Shortly after applying for official travel to Germany, I received my travel orders, first-class tickets, a roadmap of Northern and Central Germany and a date by which I had to deliver my car to the transportation officer at the pier in Brooklyn, New York.

Fred, Marlene, and my mother accompanied me to the pier for my departure. While boarding that magnificent ocean liner, I literally had to pinch myself. Was all of this real? The scene was surreal and more reminiscent of some old Hollywood films I had seen with Spencer Tracy and Kathryn Hepburn. As we boarded, we were given streamers and confetti to throw overboard. The ship's foghorn was blaring; well-wishers and relatives were shouting farewell and those of us aboard were in a festive mood. Think about it! This was heady stuff for a young African-American male in the summer of 1963.

The nine-day trans-Atlantic crossing was the perfect balm for the hurts and slights of the past year and it fulfilled any expectations I might have entertained. I teamed up with the son of an American Air Force general also assigned to Europe. Our dynamic duo explored practically every inch of the ship, even in areas off-limits to first-class passengers. At dinner the first night at sea, I met Brendan A. Dietz, an Army lieutenant colonel and the new Assistant Army Attache, also en-route to Embassy Bonn. He knew who I was and commented, "So you're the guy who bumped me from bringing my car with me on the ship...you had precedence over me." I, of course, was unaware of this development and, in my own defense, said "I was just advised that I could have my car accompany me if I chose to. Naturally, I took the option as opposed to a delivery date some time later in the summer. I am sorry if I inconvenienced you." Col. Dietz had not intended to be confrontational, and said, "I would have done the same thing had our roles been reversed." The two of us did become social friends while serving together in Bonn. There was yet a third person aboard the ship also assigned to Embassy Bonn. Both he and I had been assigned to the embassy's Communications Section. More on him later.

Surface travel at this level of accommodation was a world away from the troopship, USNS Gordon. Here I was - assigned to Cabin 41 on the Main Deck of the S.S. America. Life was really quite pleasant: single accommodations, my own waiter in the dining room, 'round the clock room service, and no one mistaking me for a waiter. The crossing was smooth and nine glorious days later, early on a Sunday morning, we docked in Hamburg. I watched my car being off-loaded. As a former transportation clerk, I held my breath until it was on the ground because I knew of cars being dropped accidentally from considerable heights during off-loading. After clearing passport control and German customs, I was sitting behind the wheel of my car looking at the map. The drive would not be difficult nor would it take more than seven-to-nine hours to reach Bonn. German autobahns were a post-World War 11 marvel and a driver's dream: long and generally straight, almost boring but traffic flowed at speeds in excess of 100 miles per hour. My 1956 Chevy could not technically rise to that level of sustained performance, but I did enjoy driving in such fast company. I watched the passing tail lights of many a flashing Mercedes, BMW, and Porsche. In fact, the German highway patrol sported green and while Porsches with a telescoping blue light. The prudent thing for me to do was stay in the right lane, which I did. By late Sunday afternoon, I arrived in Bonn. I spoke no German, therefore I chose not to seek more precise directions from anyone on the street, at least not yet. This might seem a typical male reaction, but that was my plan. Really, had I chosen to seek directions, how would I have managed?

"What was embassy in Germany?" I wondered. I decided to keep driving, at least a while longer. A few minutes later, I saw a sign "Amerikanische Botschaft." Instinctively, I felt that this must be it. The sign directed me away from center city Bonn. Soon I was out of town looking for a second sign that read "Amerikanische Botschaft." Off to my right, I saw the sign pointing left toward the Rhine River. It was a winding road that descended gradually toward the river. Several hundreds meters later, I was facing a gray, weathered office complex that almost rivaled the immensity of the main State Department building in Washington: seven-stories tall with four four-story wings, eight two-story wings, a separate annex for the ambassador, his deputy, their immediate support staff and the political counselor; and a castle. "This must be it" I said aloud. Directly above the front entrance was the official seal of the Department of State. For a moments, I sat in the car reflecting on the reality of what I was about to embrace.

Taking a deep breath, I entered the embassy, introduced myself to the Marine Guard on duty and signed in. It was late Sunday afternoon and the embassy was officially closed. I had been instructed to notify the embassy's counselor for administration, Brinton Casemeyer, upon arrival. His number was listed and I called him. Mr. Casemeyer welcomed me and gave me instructions to Plittersdorf, the embassy's residential community for American personnel. According to his instructions, I had passed it while searching for the embassy. He also informed me that a room at the embassy guesthouse had been reserved in my name. I made my way back to the embassy housing area, found the guesthouse and signed in. I was back in Germany, but this time in a totally different capacity. I owed this change in circumstances to that officer at Fort Hamilton who failed to appear on time. Had he been on time, I, like so many other returning veterans, would have pitched that manila envelope while exiting the hall that day.

Later that evening after a few hour's rest, I asked the concierge on duty for directions to a local restaurant. He directed me to the Embassy Club, fewer than a hundred yards away. Following a light dinner, I walked around the community. It was immense, over four hundred apartments, its own entertainment/sports complex, two schools, a theater, shopping center, gift shops, multi-denominational church, service station, and a guesthouse – where I was now a guest. I don't think I slept more than three hours that night. This was a lot of change to digest. I returned to the embassy the next morning and was directed to the Personnel Office where Ms. Ramona Petersen, the American secretary, welcomed me with one of the warmest smiles I had seen anywhere. After some initial processing, she escorted me to the Pouch Room to meet my supervisor, Danny Giannelli. Ours' was an instant connection because he was a first-generation Italian American. He spoke Italian, and called his wife every morning to talk about the kids and the dinner menu. I could relate to all of this. Frequently, we conversed in Italian.

As a new member of the embassy's Pouch Room, I made the internal embassy mail run (pickup and delivery) five times a day. Many of the corridors were 100 yards long. I often wished I had a pedometer. Within the first few weeks, I knew every American in the embassy and most of the German national staff. My very first day, I was assigned a comfortable apartment at 13/12 Kolumbusring at the rear of the housing complex known as "bachelors' row." Almost immediately, I became a topic of conversation. The question going around was "How did I, as a newcomer, manage to move directly into a single apartment? " It was then I became familiar with the politics of embassy housing. Here is the story. Upon learning of my assignment to Embassy Bonn, the housing officer planned to assign me and another single male member of the communication's staff to a larger family unit, as he customarily did pending the availability of a single unit. When he learned that I was African-American and that he had teamed me with a white male from Atlanta, Georgia, he became a victim of his worst instincts: his own myopic view of the world. He thought that pairing the two of us would be a prescription for disaster. He took what he assumed to be the prudent course of action and assigned me to the next available single apartment, the one I occupied the day after my arrival. The ironic twist to this tale is that the white male in question, Demond W. Talmadge, and I not only became neighbors, but also the best of friends. Our friendship endured a full decade beyond his single Foreign Service assignment. Friends in the embassy Personnel Office later told me they wished they had just followed normal housing assignment's policy. They over-reacted.

My arrival in Bonn was coincident with the timing of a European Chiefs of Mission Conference chaired by Dean Rusk, the American Secretary of State. Every American ambassador in the European Bureau, including Canada, was required to attend. At that time, Canada was part of the European Bureau. For purposes of policy, planning, and resource allocation, geographic divisions are essential. The other bureaus then were Latin America and the Caribbean, the Middle East and North Africa, Sub-Saharan Africa, The Soviet Union and Eastern Europe, the Near East and South Asia, and East Asia and the Pacific. Secretary Rusk and his team descended upon us for the better part of a week. Danny briefed me regarding revised procedures for routine mail delivery during that week. Our mission in the Pouch Room was to ensure that each member of the Washington delegation received select telegrams and other documents for their information, review, and appropriate action in a timely fashion. That was simple enough.

On the first day of the conference, I had just returned from my second run of the morning when Danny literally met me at the door to the mailroom in a high state of agitation. "George, they want you! They want you! What did you do?" Slightly taken aback, I asked "What are you talking about? Who wants me?" Danny told me "A Deputy Assistant Secretary Cheston Clifton called here asking for you." Again, the question was "what did you do?" "I didn't do anything...I delivered mail to everyone on the delegation list you gave me. I picked up mail from their secretaries...here it is!" Perhaps I had picked up the wrong mail or delivered something to the wrong addressee" I suggested. Danny replied "he didn't know what the problem is...that Deputy Assistant Secretary Clifton wants to see you, that's all I know."

I checked my list but Mr. Clifton was not scheduled for either a delivery or a pickup. "Well," Danny said, "here is his office number, go and see him – now!" Danny was easily excited but his demeanor now was on the verge of panic. I mentally retraced my steps, did not see any missteps, and headed off to see Mr. Clifton. When I entered, I introduced myself as George Kennedy, "you sent for me, sir!" "Please sit down, George, relax" as he gestured toward a chair near his desk." "Relax!" I am thinking he must be kidding. He was the only African-American I had seen in the delegation. " Thank you," I said nervously. Mr. Clifton sensed my discomfort and spent several minutes trying to put me at ease. I was a sight to behold, sitting ramrod straight, in true military fashion, on the first six inches of my chair. Both hands resting on my knees. He queried me gently about my job, working at the embassy, and how well I had been received as a member of the embassy family. He was interested in my impressions of Germany. He had a keen interest in the social-psychological environment for a young, single African-American male in this setting. I kept my responses short and factual: I liked my job, had been well received, and enjoyed being back in Europe. Near the end of the meeting, Mr. Clifton asked me what my plans were toward the end of the week, then just two days away. I told him I had planned to attend Happy Hour at the Marine House on Friday. He then asked if he could visit me at home around 6 pm Friday evening. "Fine," I said, thinking I would have to cancel my plans to play host to a high-level visitor. I remembered from my orientation briefing that on rare occasions, junior staff may be called upon to make themselves available to assist the ambassador. This appeared to be one of those occasions. I knew Secretary Rusk and his team would be gone in a few days so this would be a minor inconvenience. I could check out Happy Hour next week.

At 6 pm that Friday, the doorbell sounded: it was Mr. Clifton. My German housekeeper had been there that day and the apartment was spotless. On the way home, I stopped at the embassy commissary to pick up a few steaks in the event it became a full evening. Meanwhile, I am still apprehensive and very much on guard. I needed the opportunity this assignment offered and, since I was still relatively new and did not know Mr. Clifton, I was determined not to let my guard down. I would continue to parse my words carefully and volunteer nothing. He came in, shed his suit jacket, put his feet up on the coffee table, loosened his tie and asked, "Do you have any scotch?" In that instant, something clicked. I knew this was a friend, a "good brother." "Ballantyne Scotch, if that suits you," I offered. "Perfect, where is it?" For the next two hours, Cheston Clifton and I shared details of our respective backgrounds, how he became part of the Kennedy Administration, and what life was like at the top as the Deputy Assistant Secretary for Congressional Relations and, concurrently, Deputy Chief of the Office of Protocol at the State Department. Describing his own background, he told me how the psychological impact of the battle for the Pusan Perimeter during the Korean War provided the motivation he needed to write his master's thesis while on duty there, a feat he was unable to accomplish while in college before the war. He had been a combatant and Korea became the defining experience of his life. He returned to California after the war, earned a law degree, became a juvenile court judge and, through friends, got involved with the Kennedy campaign.

Cheston Clifton offered sage career advice and recommended a particular book he would send later. Above all, he offered friendship and a willingness to serve as sounding board for ideas I may develop about my future plans. He then went to the bottom line, the real purpose of his travels with Secretary Rusk: to learn where the African-Americans are at our missions overseas; to know more about what they are doing and how they are being treated. "Secretary Rusk genuinely wanted to know and no one in the Office of Personnel in Washington could, for example, tell him how many African-Americans there were in the Foreign Service, where they were assigned, and the kinds of responsibilities they held." "Secretary Rusk asked me to find out as unobtrusively as possible." He went on to say, "when I saw you in the hallway, I wanted to know who you were; that is why I sent for you." He made another salient point that did not surprise me. "The Foreign Service is still hostile territory for us!" "The officers and your colleagues here speak highly of you... keep up the good work." Regarding the Secretary's interest in the status of African-Americans in the Foreign Service; his daughter married an African-American and Dean Rusk was a southerner. That union may have conditioned his reflexes just a little.

At one point in our conversation, Mr. Clifton asked about the party at the Marine House; he had not forgotten. In fact, we could hear the music from the Marine House which was less than 50 yards away. He said he preferred that I keep my original plans for the evening and that he would like to accompany me to the Marine House. Oh! He said, "don't tell them who I am, I want to relax." By this time, I am thinking this guy is definitely a "good brother" because within minutes after our arrival, several young women approached us. Given the smile on his face, he was obviously enjoying a respite from his responsibilities that week. The conference ended that weekend, but I now had something infinitely more valuable: a new friend and mentor, someone who acted in both capacities until his sudden death of a heart attack in 1985.

Bonn was the capitol city of the Federal Republic of Germany in 1963. For a federal city, it was also quaint, very quiet, and largely a residential community on the Rhine River. The city had one small night club that closed before 10 pm on Friday and Saturday. Restaurants were also few. Whenever I sought a change from the embassy club, the alternative was the local hotel in Bonn because the view of the park from the hotel dining room was spectacular. Social life within the embassy community was designed for families, less so for single staff members and young, childless couples. The place to hear the best European renditions of good old-fashioned American "Rock n' Roll" was in Koln, 15 miles away. On many weekends, you would find me there. On one particular weekend in August 1963, I met Tayo Oremule, a young Nigerian medical student at a university in Koln. We actually met on the dance floor at the TABU club. Tayo and I were a good fit: both 23, single, loved to dance, enjoyed meeting Germans and having a good laugh. The more we got to know each other, I learned we shared something else: a determination to optimize our opportunities while there. For the duration of my tour in Germany, we were brothers at heart. He, as a full-time student, could speak, read, and write fluent German and was of considerable help to me in my efforts to learn the language and German customs. I would laugh uncontrollably when he recounted for me some of his experiences with his German landlady. There was this one occasion when I laughed so hard, I cried. "George," he began, "she actually thought I did not know what a light switch was. She would flip the switch on and off and smile at me as if to say, now you see light, now you don't." He continued: "It was the same approach with the toilet in the Water Closet (WC) and the refrigerator and stove in the kitchen." At first, I did not believe him, but it takes Tayo to tell the story with his accent. When I realized he was serious, I really lost it; I was practically on the floor. Tayo was also a serious student of West African history and politics, a real eye-opener for me. He was familiar with the U.S. role in destabilizing the Congo with the assassination of former Prime Minister Patrice Lumumba and, like many young Africans, was bitter about the American CIA's involvement on the African Continent. Tayo reminded me of my friend Stanley Tilman: serious, broad-gauged, and incredibly knowledgeable. Tayo and I were teachers and friends to each other for two years and our relationship was one of the highlights of my tour in Germany.

It was now the fall of 1963 and thus far, my transition into embassy life had been painless. I had a new circle of friends, both American and German, and life for me was good. Life, however, was about to change. Following a dispute with a colleague, Reginald Johnson, about an agreement with me he chose not to honor, my branch supervisor, Pauline Vishon, became involved and decided fault lay with me. It mattered not to her that Reginald not only reneged on an agreement affecting both his job and mine, he admitted as much to me by telling me "this agreement just does not work for me any more; I am sorry." When I protested, Pauline became concerned and decided I was to be made an example. Her over-reaction to this trivial incident did surprise me. It was a stark reminder that I was still under the microscope I thought had escaped. With Reginald Johnson, there were "human elements" to be considered. With me, I rightly sensed something deeper (this was later confirmed by several colleagues in Frankfurt who had heard about the incident), a mindset reflecting an entrenched set of attitudes about me and what I represented. There is important context in most situations including this one.

During the decade of the 1960s, I often heard the State Department and its venerable Foreign Service referred to as the "Last Bastion," in contrast to the Department of Agriculture's reputation as the "Last Plantation." The embassy in Bonn was among the largest this country maintained overseas and there were only two African-Americans, both of us clerks in the communication's section. The other African-American was eventually sent back to Washington before the completion of his tour. On a subliminal level, I believe Pauline was reminding me that foreign affairs, even at the clerical level, was still the unwise choice for me. I felt she wondered why I had not chosen a more domestic profession or something related to the struggle for civil rights; that my talents and energy were best utilized there.

My encounter with Pauline and Reginald did have a favorable outcome for me, but I later learned, at an egregious cost to my direct supervisor, Danny Giannelli. Danny refused to go along with Pauline's scheme to transfer me from Bonn. His reason was simple: Reginald had been in the wrong and he found no fault in my performance. Pauline, in an act of gratuitous cruelty, proceeded to derail Danny's career. Danny never told me about it; I learned from his colleagues in the Pouch Room at the State Department. That experience was a timely reminder that I could not afford the delusion of total acceptance because Pauline and others of a similar mindset were not an anomaly. I transferred from the embassy Pouch Room to the Communications File Room under the direct supervision of Denise Robertson. All of my prior administrative training, education, and experience combined to make my new job one of the most interesting ever. I would gain knowledge that would serve me well into the future.

It was now late fall and on the evening of November 22, 1963, I drove to Koln for the evening. Tayo was studying so I chose to have dinner alone and maybe even try a German language film. While I would not have had total comprehension, my experience in Italy taught me the importance of developing a sense of the natural flow of a language. Films were great for that purpose; I could try to pair dialogue with gestures and actions. At any rate, I was sitting in a restaurant across the street from the TABU, having just given my order to the waiter. I noticed people in the street were running, others were crying, shouting "Kennedy Todt." A German gentleman came into the restaurant and was speaking in excited tones to one of the waiters and several others sitting at the counter. I heard him make reference to President Kennedy having been shot, and that he was looking for a newspaper. Before my order arrived, I raced into the street looking for a newspaper. When I found one at a kiosk not far away, the headline read "Kennedy Geschossen" (Kennedy Shot!). Another column read "Kennedy Ermordert" (Kennedy murdered). The news sickened me in the pit of my stomach and I was not quite sure what I should do. I remember eating quickly and driving immediately back to the embassy. A long line of Germans had already formed at the front entrance to sign the first of many, many, many condolence books.

Germans took Kennedy's death to heart because, just prior to my arrival in Bonn, President Kennedy had uttered his "Ich bin ein Berliner" line in Berlin. He and Jacqueline Kennedy had electrified Germany. In a word, they came, saw, and conquered the hearts of all Germans. That this young and energetic president had been struck down by an assassin's bullet was inconceivable to them. We in the official embassy family went into mourning. President Kennedy had also touched our hearts, we who represented a generation of the Foreign Service who believed in the promise of the better world that this young president described. We believed in a world that required a prominent role for the United States, a world that looked to American leadership for vision and purpose. The spirit of President Kennedy's "New Frontier" moved young Americans of my generation at Embassy Bonn. Each of us believed in public service and each of us, myself included, were proud to represent our country abroad. To us, to me, there was no higher calling. Our service was a noble mission. President Kennedy had just told my colleagues of our shared mission during his visit to the embassy. We were not accustomed to seeing American presidents up close and, now, he was dead. The shock and grief was palpable, but in time, it passed but was never forgotten. November 22, 1963 became a benchmark date in history. Everyone I knew, or encountered, old enough to remember that day, could tell me where they were on that fateful day and exactly what they were doing.

Recovering from the shock of November 22 that year paled in significance to the news I was to receive in a letter from mother in early December: my maternal grandfather, George W. Elam, had died on December 4th from Cancer. My world was now shattered. Grandpop as everyone called him, was the patriarch of a large, multi-generational and multi-state, extended family of Kennedys and Elams. His death hurt because I had planned to bring him to Europe to close the loop on an earlier experience of his in World War 1 while serving in France.

My grandfather, like many of his neighbors, was a World War 1 veteran willing to fight and, if necessary, die for the land of his birth. He was relegated to a segregated service unit. For him, it was as a corporal with the 814th Company in the Transportation Corps of the American Army. Oddly enough, I, too, would serve in the U.S. Army Transportation Corps four decades later. My grandfather would return from service overseas with a limp that plagued him throughout his life. I was my father's son but my apple did not fall far from my grandfather's tree. Although life was a daily contest with all of its indignities, even in uniform, my grandfather was proud of his service and it was my dream to bring him back to Europe once again to visit the France of his youth. There is an unspoken need among veterans to return to the place of their military service, especially if it involved a period of conflict outside the U.S. It brings a form of closure that only those who served can understand. It stamps paid on a life-defining chapter for many of us – myself included even though I did not serve in combat. When my mother wrote to tell me of his death, I cried; I looked into space and asked no one in particular, where was the retirement he had earned? What about the quiet walks and talks he and I would have from time to time? He never revealed his inner turmoil, the pain he felt, but I knew it was there. He, too, had his desperate hours. He was a veteran of the war to end all wars, yet he returned home to a hostile country and he once again became invisible. He had served his country for the birthright to be a second class citizen. Now that he was dead, I vowed that the cycle of desperation would end with him. Social mores restrained him in a fashion I knew I had to overcome. I was going to fulfill his dream and my own by bringing value to my life and to my career and, in the process, validate the life and the dreams he could never fulfill.

Life in Bonn offered a panoply of opportunities to develop relationships in both the German and the American diplomatic communities. I was well known, approachable and, according to some at the embassy that had spent time with me, considered an interesting conversationalist. I brought a world-view unfamiliar to many Americans in the official community and to Germans. There was a reason for this, at least for the Germans. Bonn did not host an American military installation and there were none of the frequent daily contacts between Germans and American soldiers common in cities such as Wiesbaden, Frankfurt, Munich, Kaiserslautern, and Berlin, for example. Contacts between Germans and young African males were generally limited to a few African students pursuing medical degrees at the University of Bonn. Perhaps it was the zeitgeist, but I thrived in my new surroundings. I also confounded some of my colleagues.

Many of them considered the most unlikely relationship that which existed between Demond W. Talmadge and myself. I was African-American, urban, a veteran and socialized in the north. Demond, on the other hand, was an aloof, white, middle class southern male product of privilege and a 1962 graduate of the University of Georgia. His educational and social background set him apart from many of his white colleagues in the Communication's Office. Contrary to all, and I mean all, expectations, Demond and I forged an easy relationship. It took time, but we did it. We borrowed money from each other, drove each other's automobiles, explored Bonn's environs together and, on occasion, double-dated. We were constantly amused by the reactions of others. Hanging in my living room was a framed, signed watercolor I received from Demond as a gift. He was also quite the artist. I always credit Demond for introducing me to James Bond – or sort of!

One particular weekend, I planned to attend a film showing at the British Embassy community in Koln but my car was being repaired. Demond agreed to lend me his sporty, red Alpine, two-door convertible since he was on duty that weekend and would not be using it. The film that night was the first of the James Bond series. I had not heard of James Bond or the British actor, Sean Connery. I knew it was going to be different but nothing more precise than that. At the conclusion of the film, we were all invited for light refreshments. I recall someone asking what I (as an American) thought of the James Bond character. "Bond's exploits rival those of John Wayne, Henry Fonda, James Stewart, and Kirk Douglas combined," I commented. "007 is every man's fantasy, including my own." At lunch the next day in the embassy's eighth-floor cafeteria, I was telling some of my male colleagues about the film since I was the only American in attendance the previous evening. It seemed the more I talked about the film, the less interested they became. Somehow, their lack of interest was unimportant. I was a film buff and thoroughly enjoyed the film as well as the chance to meet some of the British staff. Many of my colleagues were content not to venture outside the American community of Plittersdorf. This fact was noted by several observant German journalists who wrote scathing articles about the "Amerkanische Seidlungen am Rhein." I was broadening my circle of contacts which now included the British. My name was on their mailing list for future programs, films, and social events. Today, I have all of the Bond films, some in three formats. Thanks, Demond!

While engaged in a game of pickup basketball at the gymnasium in the American sports center one evening, a German visitor beckoned in my direction. I noticed but did not pay particular attention. "I think he means you, George," one of the guys said. I did not recognize him but approached him nonetheless. He introduced himself in good English as Herman Kaufman. Apparently, he had seen me on several occasions and wanted to introduce himself. Curiously enough, he asked if I was a sprinter – 100 meters. "Yes, I am," I responded, "why do you ask?" He told me about his membership in a local sports' club and their interest in building a sprint relay team. Herman then asked if I would consider visiting the club's facilities with him and meeting some of its members. I saw no harm and said I would, but at the moment, I wanted to finish my game. When we finished, some thirty minutes later, Herman was still there. While walking out, I agreed to meet him that Friday. He lived less than a mile from me and was a frequent visitor to the embassy club. He told me he liked the great view of the Rhine River. The American Club extended membership to all foreign diplomats accredited to the Federal Republic of Germany resident in Bonn and some residents of the local German community – Herman among them.

On Friday, Herman picked me up at my apartment and we headed over to his house. There, I met his wife Brigitte, their daughter Brigitte Kaufman and her young son. Edith's son was biracial and, for a moment, I sensed an ulterior motive. Herman and I did become friends, in fact in short order, I felt a member of the family. To Herman, I became the son he never had. Often, he would introduce me as his son. I thought he did it for the "shock" value so I would play along. I enjoyed working out with the sprint relay team at his athletic club because it was a great way to keep in shape. One evening after practice, the coach and Herman approached me about becoming the fourth member of the team. Given my work schedule and other extracurricular activities, I explained how honored I was to be considered, but a commitment to a rigorous training schedule along with occasional travel was just not possible. Both understood and that made it easier for me to continue to work out with them and to maintain a very good relationship with the Kaufmanns. I was not dating anyone at that time and Brigitte Kaufman and I did become close. She remained among my closest friends for 25 years.

One spring evening in March 1964, I was jogging through the community just to get some exercise and an African diplomat stopped me seeking directions to an address he was having difficulty finding. This tall, distinguished gentleman was Paul Bamela Engo, Deputy Chief of the Embassy of the Cameroons in Bonn. His English was impeccable. After giving him directions, he asked if I was a recent arrival. "I arrived about nine months ago," I said. We talked briefly and I learned that he had a history of American friendships in his other "postings" abroad. We would say assignments. As he turned to leave, he handed me one of his business cards and said, "perhaps we can get together soon." I was just a clerk and thus was not required to have business cards. I did see, however, how it would be useful to have a card that would identify who I was and my association with the American Embassy. Several days later, I called Paul honestly thinking he would not remember me. On any given day, his level of official and social contacts were considerably above my lowly status. To my surprise he instantly remembered and we agreed to meet that weekend. It did not go unnoticed that Saturday morning when Paul arrived at my apartment to pick me up in a beautiful midnight blue Mercedes. Paul loved to drive and thus was not chauffeur-driven.

Through Paul, I was introduced to most of the African diplomatic community in Bonn and socialized with levels of diplomatic representation one would expect of more senior officers at the American Embassy. Several evenings a week, I was a guest at Paul's home on the outskirts of Bonn. Paul seemed to be the focal point for social activities within the African community. Although he was not the most senior officer in his mission, he was extremely popular. His role was that of counselor and advisor to many of the younger members of the African community and he relished it. Paul's wife was an American from New York City. It was in his home that I developed a lifelong appreciation for West African food and learned to dance the Highlife, a very popular dance among West Africans. Africa was experiencing liberation from European control and through Paul's tutelage, I gained valuable insights into the Cameroonian and Nigerian perspective on a variety of economic and political issues – all new to me. I became familiar with contemporary political figures in West African politics and, for the first time, began to entertain becoming a Foreign Service officer. When I shared that with Paul, my formal tutelage became more structured to include mock interviews. Paul was a legal scholar and the first African judge in the Cameroons after independence. In that context, Paul had a national reputation at home. Occasionally, he would invite me to accompany him on official trips to Holland and the Low Countries (the Netherlands and Luxembourg). He would give me sufficient notice so that I could apply for vacation days. It was on trips of this nature that I became familiar with Cameroonian agricultural policy, the purpose of his travel. Agricultural trade played an important role in the development of the economy of the Cameroons during the early years of independence.

Another side benefit of traveling with Paul was having time to appreciate the Mercedes as the world class automobile it was. Here was a level of automotive engineering and technology far superior to anything I had driven in my life. My love affair with this automobile had begun. Italian Fiats and Alfa Romeos from my Italian experience did not compare. I promised myself that one day, I would own one – and I did. Again, this was a relationship I could not share with my embassy colleagues for two reasons: my American officer colleagues would have resented it, and, more importantly, the Africans preferred it that way. Foreign ambassadors and their senior staff at that time did not, as a matter of custom and practice, socialize with junior staff, even from other major embassies. In this instance, according to Paul, there was mutual satisfaction derived from the relationships he facilitated among his colleagues and I was not about to deprive myself of the value these friendships represented in my life. Again, I was a clerk, but on another level, my African friends validated my ideas and were willing to contribute to my political, social, and cultural growth. I believe that everything happens for a reason. It was through my African friends that I was able to develop and nurture a relationship that would have a profound impact on my life.

I was attending a social event hosted by one of the West African embassies and had the good fortune to meet a couple from the Caribbean. Craig and Jean Williamson were both employed by Deutsche Welle, a German broadcast company with an office in Koln. We talked a great deal that evening; they were interesting, travelled, and multi-lingual, but I never thought much about them after that evening. Through Paul and his friends, I was introduced to a broad spectrum of non-German society and I was constantly sorting people and places and how they related to my evolving international interests. Well, here is what happened. About a month later, Craig and Jean were in Bonn one evening for an interview and decided to visit with me. Apparently, I had given them my address. Knowing they were taking a chance that I might not be at home, they rang my doorbell. My neighbor had seen me go out and she went to tell them I was not at home. To be helpful, she offered to take a message for me. Craig and Jean told her they would take a walk and return later. My neighbor invited them to wait in her apartment. An hour or so later, they heard me return. I was surprised to see the Williamsons and, even more so, to see them emerge from my neighbor's apartment.

Craig told me that I had a truly gracious, friendly, and interesting neighbor. I saw my neighbor, Elsie Kent, daily, but contact between us was strictly perfunctory. Craig went on to say, "she thinks highly of you, George, so much so that I recommend you reach out to her." "She certainly seems pleasant enough" I responded. "You already know her better than I do and she is my neighbor...I should be embarrassed." A perfect opportunity to meet her had been created. After work the next day, I knocked on Elsie's door and she invited me in. I thanked her for being so kind to my guests and we began to talk. From that day forward, Elsie and I were to develop a friendship that would allow me to fulfill my most cherished goal in life at that time.

Elsie was one of the most unusual people I had ever met. As a first generation Norwegian American, hers was an intriguing mix of two cultures: one very American and the other with strong family roots and traditions in Northern Europe. Deeply spiritual, Elsie spoke with a simple eloquence that captivated me. She was fluent in both languages and, at first, I was uncertain which perspective would condition a response to one of my many questions. A product of pre-World War 11 Europe, she immigrated to America before the outbreak of hostilities. She was not just spiritual, Elsie was a devout Christian and would quote from the Bible, or refer me to a specific passage if it would help to make her point. I was the first African-American she had met, thus the stage was set for conversations that sometimes began on Friday and concluded Sunday evening. One of the two of us would prepare dinner with contributions from both households and the conversations would continue. Elsie was a senior secretary in the Office of the Military Assistance Advisory Group (MAAG) of the Department of Defense under the command of Air Force Major General Haugen. Unlike the State Department, Elsie was on an extended assignment. The military did not set limits on the overseas tours of its support staff and so extended assignments were the norm. Elsie knew Germany well and on several weekends, she guided me through the scenic Rhine Valley. I thought I had seen most of it with the Kaufmanns, but Elsie took me places that were entirely new. On one memorable weekend, we attended a Formula One race at the old, but famous, Nurburgring in Germany. I was like a kid in a candy shop. The sounds and smells of Formula One cars and their finely-tuned engines was addictive to the auto enthusiast I was. First, it was the Mercedes Benz; now it was Formula One. I developed an interest in Formula One that endures to this day.

All of these relationships (the Kaufmanns, Paul Engo, the Williamsons, Elsic Kent, to name a few because there were others) shapcd the still highly impressionable 23-year old that I was. No one seemed to have ulterior motives and this allowed me to lower my guard; to not fear revealing private thoughts in a fashion I never considered before beyond Fred and Marlene. Others brought me into their confidence and I felt comfortable reciprocating. I felt a complete sense of belonging, a degree of inclusion that allowed me to entertain new ideas regarding the direction of my personal growth and educational and career development. I could dream out loud and find a voice and encouragement for what to others might have seemed unlikely.

Another denizen of bachelors' row, and friend, Marian Mesropian, helped to give life to my thoughts of becoming an architect. Marian was secretary to the Labor Attache and she knew of his contacts with the American Institute of Architects (AIA). She said she would ask her boss to meet with me. When I shared with her a childhood dream of becoming an architect, I would temper it because I felt access was just unlikely. Marian was the idealist and disagreed with me, hence her willingness to approach her boss on my behalf. There is an interesting side story to Marian. Marian was a "hand model," which means whenever advertisers were looking for the perfect hand to pitch their product, Marian's hands were often used. She told me the hand silhouette used on the original CARE products was none other than hers. The Labor Attache did agree to meet with me and over time, we felt comfortable enough with each other for him to help me where he could. "You need information, George. What I can do is reach out to my contacts at the AIA and request materials that can help you formulate ideas and provide useful background on certain undergraduate programs, opportunities, and scholarships available to young, qualified people." Here, again, was someone offering good advice and friendship. It gets better.

Standing in line at the community theater one evening, I struck up a conversation with the wife of our Agricultural Attache, Nelson Berman. When she learned that I was relatively new, in the spirit of friendship, she invited me to dinner. They lived just one street over from me. Nelson was one engaging conversationalist which made for a special evening. Nelson, as he preferred to be called, was Jewish and he exhibited a genuine ability to empathize with the frustrations, the anxiety, and loneliness members of America's minority community, especially African-Americans, often feel. Our friendship evolved so it took me a while to arrive at this conclusion. We would spend evenings in intense conversation that opened my mind to a completely different world view. Nelson made good sense when he said that these "feelings of frustration could inhibit an ability to remain rational, or impartial, when trying to establish credibility...that becoming a captive of your emotions often makes you your own worst enemy." "Never allow someone to shift your attention to extraneous issues while they marshal their forces against a more valid position you are trying to establish." "Focus" he said, "establish your priorities...remain centered." He offered one piece of advice I never forgot. He said, "There are more battles and enemies than you can fight...pick one or two issues that are the most important to you and concentrate your energy there...become an advocate for those issues." I promised myself that I would make that simple advice a hallmark of my life. I had to, otherwise, I would spread myself too thin and become marginal, if not totally ineffective.

By the spring of 1964, while thriving in my position in the file room of the Communication's Section, I decided to enroll in a correspondence course offered by the State Department's Foreign Service Institute in Washington. The course, "Immigration Law and Visa Operations," was a 12-month course and it required an extensive familiarity with, and practical experience in, State Department Consular Operations. I had neither, but I was prepared to learn. No other courses were available through the embassy and I was looking for professional growth and intellectual stimulation. Should I decide to make the Foreign Service a career, I knew it would not be in communications. I was also looking ahead to the possibility of an ongoing assignment and I did not want to be tracked as a communication's professional, as was the case with many of the more seasoned staff in our unit. I had to do what I could to influence those who would decide my fate.

All of the embassy's junior officers were required to serve in the embassy's Consular Office. They were all challenged by many of the legal issues that office had to address when it came to the issuance of passports and visas, immigration questions, and the special consular services Americans abroad required, including members of the resident American business community. I knew that several of these officers would offer to help me sort out some of the complexities beyond my ability to research or reason my way through. The Chief of the Consular Affairs Section, Henry Wechsler, told me he would make the resources of his office available to me should I require additional support. Henry commended me for taking such initiative. "I rarely see that among junior staff" he told me. With the friends and supporters like Henry Wechsler and Denise Robertson, Elsie Kent, Marian Mesropian, and Ramona Peterson, plus the Bermans, how could I not flourish in this environment? In the Personnel Office, I was told I have established a precedent. The senior German assistant said, "never in our collective memory has a junior staff employee ever requested enrichment through a correspondence course. That is why we do not maintain much information on course offerings in this office. No one ever requests anything." Herr Steiner said, "we were pleasantly surprised when you insisted that we contact the Foreign Service Institute on your behalf."

My transfer from the Pouch Room to the Central File Room was a strategic move. Denise Robertson was considered by the American staff to be a class act. She was deeply admired and respected and I needed the change. Although she, too, was subordinate to Pauline, she outranked Pauline, and Pauline was less inclined to antagonize Denise. She needed Denise and everyone knew it – including Denise. The File Room was a vault within a vault, the super-secret realm of the most classified materials available at the embassy – including materials requiring a "Q Clearance" for access. My colleague, Gene Swankowski controlled access to all classified materials. Because of the sensitive nature of documents delivered by armed, escorted military courier, there was yet a third internal vault. Across my desk flowed all non-telegraphic classified and unclassified communications (Airgrams, official correspondence, Aides-Memoir, Diplomatic Notes) addressed to the embassy from Washington, the German Government, and other diplomatic missions in Bonn, and from other American missions around the globe. My specific responsibility was to assign a file designation to each piece of correspondence for future reference. Therefore, I had to know the classification manual. What I did not know or could not find, Denise did. I became familiar with the complex and the arcane of American foreign policy in general and American-German relations in particular. My desk became my tutorial. Insights I gained at my desk allowed me to follow topical issues in the local press with greater precision and understanding. Between meeting the demands of my correspondence course and my new responsibilities, this was intellectual stimulation at its practical best.

The file room occupied a significant amount of space on the first floor toward the rear of the main embassy building. In the back of the room was a large wire-enclosed space containing dozens of cartons no one ever sought access to. I was curious and asked Denise, "What's in those cartons?" She said, "Those cartons contain copies of the transcripts from the Nuremberg War Crimes Trials." "Some of it is really interesting reading." Naturally I was intrigued and spent my lunch hour one day going through the cartons within easy reach. I don't know what the process was that created white print on a black background, but it was not too difficult to read. I picked up several files and began to read. The more I read, the more angry I became. The materials I selected contained transcripts of interviews and discussions involving German civilian treatment of captured American and Allied pilots. Pilots were often captured and tortured to death. Others were treated for their wounds and then tortured and killed. American and Allied losses during bombing raids over German numbered in the tens of thousands. It is easy to assume that most were killed and those that were captured were either imprisoned or shot. Torture just did not enter into my consciousness. I mean, why would anyone nurse someone back to health and then torture and kill them with a pitchfork or an axe? The bestial behavior of some Germans exhibited toward these captured pilots rivaled the treatment of African-Americans in the hands of southern whites up to the period after World War 11 – even when in uniform. After an hour, I had had enough. This was an aspect of the trials I was unfamiliar with and chose to leave it that way. I never returned to that section of the File Room nor did I share with Denise or anyone else the contents of the few files I managed to read. My curiosity had been satisfied.

I led a full and balanced life, but I continued to correspond with Cassie. For some reason, I could not move beyond my connection with her in any other relationship. Although we had been separated for five of the last six years (1959 – 1964), our letters sustained our relationship. And now, we were discussing marriage. The odd thing is I could not help but feel uneasy about taking this next step. I felt as though I loved her on some level, but something did not feel right. I wish I could offer a better explanation. Perhaps because of what I felt for her and partly because I had not really gotten to know her outside our limited and constrained relationship at Shaw, I felt I should not judge her too harshly without giving her and the development of our relationship an even chance. My inner conflict never dissipated and yet, I found myself on a plane headed to New York in early June 1964. We had decided to have a June wedding at home in Camden at the new church across from my house. This would be the first wedding in the new church and that added a dimension to the wedding plans that created considerable discomfort for both Cassie and me. Our wedding became the social event neither of us wanted. At the time we decided to marry, I was still in Germany and Cassie was teaching in Washington, D.C. My mother offered to assist in the planning. Nature abhors a void and the wedding became mother's project. Cassie and I took the path of least resistance because we knew we would be leaving Camden right after the wedding. Why create bruised feelings unnecessarily? At least that's how we reasoned.

I had shopping to do as did Cassie. There were several rehearsals, logistics, a photographer and, oddly enough, an oil painting had been requested. Costs began to mount and that became a concern when it should not have been. On June 27, 1964, Cassie Palmerson and I were married at the Mount Calvary Baptist Church at 12th and Penn Street in Camden, New Jersey. Several of Cassie's classmates from Shaw were bridesmaids and my older brother Bernard was my best man. Cassie's parents were deceased but her older brother William was there to walk her down the aisle. The ceremony was marred only by the discomfort of the heat and humidity because the air-conditioning unit in the new church had not been installed.

On an emotional level, I was in turmoil. I had expected that the exchanging of vows, the pageantry, and the emotion of the occasion to evoke some level of joy and reassurance in my decision to marry. Instead, this was my wedding day and I felt a deep sense of foreboding. I knew instinctively I had just made the biggest mistake of my life. I suppressed my feelings as best I could and vowed to myself, and to my mother who sensed something was wrong, that I would do everything in my power to make the marriage work. If there was one thing about me that was true, it was that I had a deep-seated sense of responsibility and a strong feeling of obligation to fulfill promises I made. Perhaps there should have been an exception under these circumstances but this was the quality of my thinking at that time. Grandpop's words rang in my ear: "A man is only as good as his word." By exchanging wedding vows, I had given my word; now I was going to keep it – cheerfully.

Following a brief honeymoon in New York City and a visit to the 1964 World's Fair, Cassie and I returned to Camden to pack. From there, I had scheduled a week of consultations at the State Department before returning to Germany. Cassie had not applied for her passport as I asked her to do nor had she completed the obligatory physical examination required of all prospective Foreign Service employees and immediate family members prior to an overseas assignment. We began to experience difficulty right after our marriage and before we departed for Washington. Upon arriving back in Camden, I told Cassie, "pack your clothes; I am going to make our travel arrangements to Washington... I have to make several calls and I will be back in 30 to 45 minutes." We still did not have a telephone at home so I went to the Gulf service station behind the house. Cassie was alone in the house.

I was back in approximately 30-minutes and found my new wife practically passed out across her suitcase. My first thought was she must be sick. I got down on my knees and held her around her shoulders to steady her and asked, "Cassie, what happened?" It was then I smelled the wine. She was drunk! I was floored but went immediately into "damage-control" mode. I am thinking, "This is new, this is bad, I can handle it!" She could not stand so I laid her on the bed while I went to make some coffee. Fortunately, my mother was not at home. Perhaps it would have been better had she been there. For the next several hours, I tried to sober up my new bride in time to make a later bus connection to D.C. I do not drink and I do admit a low tolerance for anyone that drinks to the excess. This was just the first of many surprises to come.

Notwithstanding her assurances (by letter) to me of her good health, Cassie had several medical challenges that required treatment and she had neglected to have some dental work done. Both were unacceptable by Department of State standards for overseas assignment. Ultimately, she was cleared because of the availability of first-class facilities in Germany. With her passport in hand and a conditional medical and dental clearance, we boarded the plane for Germany. I no longer felt like a newlywed.

Once back in Germany, Cassie wanted to resume her teaching career. My earlier plan was to give her the balance of the summer to settle into the marriage and living abroad for the first time. Not only was she away from North Carolina, she was also in a new universe of change. Several weeks later, on a Saturday, if I recall, the telephone rang and I picked it up. The caller was from a Ford dealership in North Carolina wanting to know if he could speak to "Cassie...her car payments were overdue and he wanted to know when he could expect payment." For those unaccustomed to social relations between African-Americans and whites in the south, white southerners did not accord African-Americans the respect of Mr. or Mrs. It was always your first name, age and status notwithstanding. I had dealt with people like this previously and informed him that he was mistaken, that "Mrs. Kennedy's" debts had been discharged and, that I did not appreciate his tone. Cassie knew I was upset and as I turned to her, said, "Cassie, tell this guy your car is paid for and that he should check his records!" Cassie hesitated as I held out the phone to her. She said, "I still owe money, I just did not tell you about it." It only got worse. She knew how I felt about debt. She also knew I was saving to return to school. She also knew I had believed her when she assured me her only debt was the car and that it would be paid for before we got married.

I quickly came to realize that my wife had misrepresented herself to the extent I had to ask her, "What else have you not told me?" Cassie must have felt secure now that we were married because she looked me in the eye, smiled and said, "George, if I had let you know what I was really like, you would not have married me. My friends told me it was not necessary to do many of the things you asked me to do before we went to Germany...that they could be done afterwards." I sat down and just looked at her. "What is it that your friends knew about living abroad and the Foreign Service that I did not?" I asked. "What made their advice so much more valuable than mine?" For the next several hours, we talked through what I foresaw as the financial consequences for us. To begin, I did not have dental insurance and the costs of her dental work would be considerable. She seemed to know that. There were the added costs from the wedding and, now, the outstanding debt on her car – which was almost two thousand dollars. Remember, this is 1964. I was in debt before anything else. She was not working and had no savings. I was also young, passionate, and could not accept that my wife was capable of this kind of deception. I knew that marriage was a risk, but I think I was prepared for anything but dishonesty. We had spent months talking about everything: getting rid of the debt, that we did not want to start married life with bills; her health, getting to the dentist, etc. And then there was the drinking. How serious was this? I wondered. The most immediate problem was financial. I could not handle everything on my own; my salary did not reach that far. The only solution was a job; Cassie was going to have to work. Without debt, we could have enjoyed life as young newlyweds without upsetting my plans to return to school. I am grateful that she wanted to resume her teaching career. All of my plans were taking flight and I was not reacting well. For months thereafter, we argued constantly.

I had met the director of the International School in Bonn and felt comfortable approaching him on my wife's behalf. Conveniently located in our community, the school was a stone's throw from where we lived on Kolumbusring. We were blessed with good fortune because following an interview, Cassie was offered one of the coveted few teaching positions there. The International School accepted students from Bonn's diplomatic community and the competition for available spaces was intense. That the school was located in the heart of the American community only heightened the prestige factor. This job offer was not only fortuitous for Cassie's career, it was necessary to help defray some of the residual debt she left behind in North Carolina.

Europe was a new experience for Cassie and following a period of adjustment, she slowly began to feel comfortable in her new role as a wife in a foreign culture. This was the first time she had to adjust to life outside North Carolina or the nation's capitol since birth. It bears reminding that she was a product of a segregated South and the transition had to be slow. For a while, there had been only two African-Americans at what was then the largest embassy this country maintained abroad. When my colleague was sent back to Washington, I was alone again. With the arrival of an African-American female teacher and an African-American secretary with the Defense Attache's Office, Cassie's comfort level rose; the three of them could get together and hang out.

I got a little ahead of the story, not by much, about a month or two. In August of 1964, I requested additional vacation time just prior to the launch of a new school year and took Cassie on a driving tour of Southern Europe. Munich was our first stop enroute to the Italian Alps. Then it was down through the Dolomites and on to Vicenza. I wanted Cassie to see where I had recently spent three momentous years of my life. While walking around the base, I saw one of my former Army buddies. He told me he was the only one remaining from my time in Headquarters and Headquarters Company. In fact, he had reenlisted to remain in Vicenza. From Vicenza, Cassie and I headed south to Florence, with Rome as our ultimate destination. My intent was to bring something pleasant into our otherwise turbulent lives. My grandmother told me just before we married that "the success of getting old is having good memories." I hoped this trip would be one for our book of memories.

Cassie was the consummate professional and thrived in her new job. At the end of the first semester, the director of the International School rated her as his most effective teacher that semester. The one thing Cassie did do was work hard to be successful. All of her students loved her and several parents were maneuvering to have their child transferred to her class. I was aware of this because I knew some of the parents and they were consistent in their praise of Cassie's ability to inspire children to learn. Although several of Cassie's more senior colleagues resented such an evaluation of a new teacher, she was able to assuage any bruised egos. Cassie and I also downplayed any potential racial animus that some of her colleagues harbored. To us, that was not going to be an issue. Cassie handled herself well in that situation, something the school's director greatly admired and appreciated. He, too, understood how explosive the issue of race was. I only wish my wife had handled the situation at home with a comparable level of understanding and maturity that she brought to her role as a teacher. I willingly accept my share of the responsibility for the difficulties we experienced. My problem was I did not know what else I could do to "fix things." I felt hopeless most of the time until one day when I was at my wits end, Cassie said, "George, there is nothing you can do to fix us...this is just the way things are. The problem is me!"

The Christmas holidays were approaching and the plan was to relax in Bonn; no travel, just spend time with friends. That December, I experienced a first, something I could not have anticipated: recognition by the Ambassador of the Cameroons in Bonn. January 1st is the Independence Day of the Republic of the Cameroons and invitations to their Independence Day activities were generally non-existent. Cassie and I were the only foreigners invited to a special dinner and dance hosted by their ambassador at his residence. Had my embassy colleagues known of this, they could have made life unpleasant for me, particularly with the supervisor who sought to make an example of me over the Johnson affair. This event had the distinction of being the simultaneous highlight and low point of my life. Here's why. I knew from Paul that foreigners were rarely invited to this special dinner hosted by his ambassador. Therefore, ranking among the most junior members at American Embassy, Bonn, I felt honored to be a guest. I explained this to Cassie and said that she should relax and enjoy herself; that she would be among friends.

The protocol for the event was that the ambassador would begin the evening's events by a brief dance with Cassie, as the spouse of his guest, followed by a dance with his wife. This was carefully explained beforehand. We arrive, everyone is in a festive mood and, professionally, I was relishing the honor of being an invited guest. The ambassador approached Cassie and extended his hand. To my absolute horror, Cassie refused to acknowledge him. Paul and his wife were mortified. Going into full damage control mode, Paul's wife sprang into action, firmly took Cassie's arm while explaining to the ambassador that Cassie was slightly ill and pulled her into the ladies' room. I can only imagine the conversation that ensued between the two of then. If I knew Betty, it was more a monologue with Cassie doing most of the listening. When Cassie and Betty Engo emerged, Cassie seemed to have a better grasp of the situation. Eventually, she did dance with the ambassador, but by that time, I was already imagining a casual conversation between this ambassador and mine. My ambassador was George C. McGhee, an oil-millionaire, expert geologist and personal friend of President Johnson. He had a short temper and, I learned later, would fire anyone, including German nationals at the embassy, if they displeased him. Having Steven Sparelli, his Counselor for Administration, send me back to Washington for a breach of protocol would have been the end of my career before it was really launched. Again, all I could see was my career out the window. Paul managed to defuse the situation with his ambassador because it was at his suggestion that we were invited as guests. I may have been overwrought, but that incident sealed my fate with Cassie. I knew that if I was going to pursue the Foreign Service as a career, we could not do it as a team. The gulf between us was vast and growing.

I had now completed 18-months of my two-year assignment and I had a decision to make: resign from the Foreign Service and seek access to one of the colleges I hoped might accept me or, take another assignment, save more money and await an actual college acceptance letter. If I accepted another assignment pending acceptance at the University of Wisconsin (my first choice), I could defer my starting date and resign from the Foreign Service after completing the first year of my second assignment and still travel at government expense. I was, therefore, reluctant to resign without the guarantee of acceptance at school. Timing compelled me to accept an assignment to our embassy in Manila. My scheduled arrival date was October 1965.

The assignment was attractive for several reasons. I had received favorable evaluations for the quality of my written assignments in the correspondence course I had taken. On my final test, the proctor commended me for having done so well, considering my lack of consular experience. On the strength of my success in that course and the availability of a position, I was assigned as the Consular Records Supervisor in the American Consulate General at the embassy in Manila. A second advantage was an increased level of responsibility in a new area of Foreign Service operations. I would have a staff of eight and, third, I had been told informally that a promotion was practically assured. This was a good career move for me and I felt grateful for the advice and counsel of friends.

In early June 1965, following my commitment to the assignment in Manila, the hoped-for acceptance letter arrived from the University Of Wisconsin at Madison. I had been accepted for that fall term. To preserve a future place for myself, I asked for a year's deferment. I wrote a detailed letter, with the assistance of my friend the Labor Attache, explaining my circumstances. Next, I shared the news of my acceptance with all of the many friends and supporters who had encouraged me the past two years. Elsie had already invested in me by giving me an unsolicited, interest-free loan to ensure my financial survival during that critical first year. I had been away from an on-campus environment since May 1959 and Elsie did not minimize the psychological difficulty of reintegration. When I asked her why she was prepared to make such an investment without any guarantees, her response was classic Elsie: direct and uncomplicated. "George, I believe in you. I know you will succeed and, one day, I will be able to have the personal satisfaction of knowing that I helped your success to become a reality." I did not cry easily but I came close. There was nothing I could say except "thank you" with a warm embrace. With friends like Elsie, Ramona Petersen, Paul Engo, Cheston Clifton, the Labor and Agricultural Attaches, and Fred and Marlene Adams, I knew I had to succeed. I could not bear the burden of disappointing so many people.

Cassie also had a highly successful year. Many of her students cried upon learning that she would not be returning for the Fall term. I had one more surprise that left me practically speechless. While making travel arrangements for our return home and my onward travel to the Philippines, the German travel assistant at the embassy, a good friend of mine, told me she could arrange first class accommodations for the two of us on the Queen Elizabeth, the original QE-1. We would sail from the Port of LeHavre in France. In addition, there was space aboard another American ship sailing from San Francisco to Manila with a brief stop in Hawaii. The shock, surprise, and gratitude at such a gesture was visible. Oddly enough, all of this was legal. The travel assistant, even though a good friend, did not have to reveal the availability of this option to me. To her, my reaction spoke volumes. She smiled and said "You are welcome! I will call you when the tickets are ready." It never would have occurred to me to ask for a return by a surface mode of travel. Remember, I had travelled to Europe aboard the S.S. America. Among my prized possessions are several framed photographs of Cassie and myself on the QE-1 en-route to New York in July 1965.

On the train from Bonn to LeHavre, I commented to Cassie "good friends are the substance of good memories." That simple declarative statement summarized my feelings about my assignment to Bonn. I left with a renewed sense of hope about my future, however that future might evolve. I also had sufficient resources to defray much of the cost of my first year at school. Moreover, I had been accepted at a major mid-western university with a recognized School of Allied Arts and Architecture. Also in my chest of blessings were indelible memories of innumerable acts of genuine friendship, kindness, understanding, tolerance, accommodation, and generosity. How rich I felt at that moment.

Since the night at the Embassy of the Cameroons six months earlier, Cassie and I became increasingly distant for a variety of reasons. We were the match made in Hell. We grew apart because even though we had known each other for six years, we had spent most of that time apart. We struggled through appearances but the degree of disharmony between us compounded daily. The years we spent apart we grew apart. Letters did not suffice for lives lived apart. We differed in outlook, expectations of each other and what marriage meant. Then there was the Foreign Service as a possible career rather than the comfortable, middle-class existence of an African-American teacher at home. The stress of being part of a volatile relationship at night while struggling through daily appearances had aged me and I felt it. I do not want to minimize the stress Cassie was feeling. As we prepared to depart Bonn for the trip home, we both knew we were not destined to survive as a viable partnership.

Now, I looked forward to the leisurely pace of the return cruise. For the five-day Atlantic crossing, we would have time to assess next steps, hopefully in calm, measured conversation. It seemed the more we talked, the more intractable our positions became and the outcome of each conversation was the same: division. We were just too different. After the first day, we resolved to keep contentious issues off the table and try to relax. The voyage then became the quiet, comfortable interlude we both needed.

Fred and Marlene were at the pier the day the Queen Elizabeth docked. This was to be a celebration of our homecoming. Fred had made reservations at the Playboy Club for dinner and a show. When the ship's porters unloaded the cabin baggage onto the pier, they managed to separate most of our luggage. I had to spend four hours searching through thousands of pieces of luggage on the pier for the missing pieces. It was difficult to approach other passengers' luggage without incurring a disapproving stare or a loud "Hey! What are you looking for?" When we were able to join Marlene and Fred, they, too, were exhausted from standing at the pier literally the entire day. I was hot, sweaty, and frustrated. Cassie was also tired. The planned celebration was cancelled in favor of a quiet dinner to relax and catch up. Once again, Cassie and I struggled to maintain appearances. It was more difficult this time because we were both practically at our worst. Fred, however, sensed that something was wrong and I knew to expect a question or two later.

Marlene slept during the ride from Brooklyn to Camden. I interrupted the silence and told Fred "I will be going to Manila alone." The ladies were asleep so I continued to talk, almost in a whisper. "It has been tough, Fred. I need the time and distance....I couldn't go to school now if I wanted to." I continued, "emotionally, I am a wreck and I have to regain a sense of myself and perspective on my marriage to Cassie." Fred smiled and said, "there's time; we will talk later."

Soon it was late summer and I had to find a modest tropical wardrobe for Manila's oppressive heat and humidity. I had been looking for summer clothes since my return to Camden, but fall fashions were already on display. Several trips to Philadelphia's garment district on South Street produced three pairs of summer trousers, one summer suit, two sport coats, and a hat. Everything except the hat was washable. Whatever else I needed, I could have made in Manila. At least I had enough to get started.

Cassie and I decided to officially separate following a particularly nasty exchange early one morning. I offered to take her to Washington or

North Carolina, but she wanted to remain in New Jersey, at my mother's home. She had immediate family in both locations and she, too, wanted time and distance from inquiring minds. Even though we both knew in our hearts that separation was the best thing for us, I was emotionally devastated. I had a deep sense of personal failure. I had not kept my word. I questioned whether I had taken the path of least resistance. I began to question who I thought I was as a man. Everyone in both families would be disappointed in me. Was I not man enough to handle this situation and make a go of it...for better or worse? Not until several years after our divorce in 1966, several years of nagging self-doubt, did I realize that I really had little choice. The reality of our situation was that we were ill-suited for each other to survive and prosper in a marriage. I believe that had we continued under the circumstances we had created, it would have lead to mental, and possibly, physical self-destruction.

I notified the State Department that I would be unaccompanied on this next assignment. During the last days of summer that year and before my departure for Manila, Cassie applied for and received, a temporary teaching position in the Camden School System. By late August, my focus shifted to Manila now that I knew Cassie was going to be fine. Also around that time, a letter arrived from the State Department notifying me of a change in my travel plans. My predecessor had departed post early and I was needed in Manila earlier than had been the case when my travel arrangements were first made that spring. The surface travel I looked forward to was cancelled. The ticket for my flight to Manila was enclosed. I was however able to negotiate several days in Hawaii to visit with my younger brother Michael and his wife Betty.

CHAPTER 7

WHO IS THAT CHILD'S MOTHER?

My brief stopover in Hawaii served several important purposes. First, I could begin to acclimate myself to the oppressive heat and humidity I would experience in Manila. Then, there would be time to spend with my brother Michael, who was stationed at the Western Pacific Marine Headquarters Command there. I think it was called FMFPAC (Fleet Marine Force Pacific). Mike and his wife Brenda (who was pregnant at the time) had been there for approximately a year. Mike had requested several days leave so we could hang out together for the first time since Christmas 1962. My stay was all too brief, but it was relaxing and fun. I did not realize how much I missed Mike's laugh and it was good to hear it again. I really enjoyed just catching up with him on developments in our respective lives. Mike had a great staff job, liked Hawaii, and was thriving in the Corps. Moreover, he had decided to reenlist.

Once we got through the family stuff, Mike told me he was keeping an eye on developments in Vietnam; that he might become part of a deployment there at some point. That raised a question I had been grappling with since the summer of 1964. I told him when I came home to get married last June, I saw a former classmate back in uniform that I knew had been discharged with me in '62. Roger Williams had not reenlisted but had been recalled. I was naturally concerned because I thought I might also be vulnerable. Mike said, "Al, keep your head down because our involvement in Vietnam is going to grow; this war is going to get a lot worse before it gets better." Materials he was seeing and conversations he overheard suggested to him Vietnam for us was only beginning. On the third day, Mike took me to the airport.

The flight to Manila was long and claustrophobic; I just wanted off that plane. Every seat was occupied and there was no getting comfortable. When I stepped off the plane at Manila's International

Airport, the glare and intensity of the sun and humidity hit me like a one-two punch and I could feel the heat welling up my trousers and sleeves. The humidity was stifling and I momentarily gasped for air while crossing that hot tarmac. Years earlier, my uncle George had spoken frequently of his days as a young soldier in Manila in the late 1940s. His accounts of his escapades were lucid, full of drama, and that element of risk he seemed to like. We called him "Brother." I never thought that one day, I, too, would find myself in the Philippines. Now it was my turn. This climate was going to take some adjustment, more so than tours in Europe had required.

Vernell Savage, a colleague from the consulate was there to welcome me, shepherd me through customs and immigration, and escort me to the Philippinas Hotel on Roxas Boulevard directly across from the embassy. This particular hotel was a local landmark and had survived the ravages of World War 11 and the Japanese occupation. Although vestiges of former luxury were evident, the place still needed a major facelift. I was more exhausted than I realized because I slept through a dinner my new colleagues had arranged for me that evening. They graciously allowed me to sleep and I was grateful at not being disturbed. The effects of jet lag were the worst in my experience to date. The following morning, Vernell came by to escort me to the embassy for the usual processing. Everything was routine except housing. I was junior staff, therefore I qualified for housing at the embassy's housing and community support compound (Seafront) several miles down Roxas Boulevard in Pasay City. There was a vacant apartment on the local economy directly behind the Seafront Compound and furniture would be supplied by the embassy. The owner of that building was reputable and known to the embassy Housing Office. The advantage of temporarily occupying that apartment, I was told, is that you are within walking distance of the rear gate of the American Compound. An embassy shuttle bus commutes from the compound to the embassy several times daily.

I was then taken to meet Lawson Glasgow, the American Consul General in Manila, my boss. At first, Mr. Glasgow apologized for interrupting my earlier travel schedule, but I quickly set that aside as he began to talk about the scope of consular operations in the country. His overview included a broad overview of the political and psychological climate that affected the conduct of American policy initiatives at that time. This was the fall of 1965 and the purely domestic aspects of US-Philippine relations were enough to consume one's attentions. And then, there was that other growing distraction called Vietnam. Lawson Glasgow's words still ring in my head decades later: "George," he said, my best advice to you is to "grow into your job. Grow into the context of the Philippines and its relations with its neighbors...This will be one of the most fascinating assignments you will ever have." In retrospect, he was right.

The other members of the consulate team were collegial enough, but Mr. Glasgow was cut from different cloth. He impressed me as one of those people whose insights shape history, but history would somehow overlook. I later learned from his deputy Ray Bastiani that Mr. Glasgow was somewhat of a maverick within the ranks of the Department's Asia hands. He marched to a different tune, but his insights, knowledge of the country, and his contacts among influential Filipinos were difficult to challenge – even for his political betters back in Washington.

The administrative requirements for the new job were less onerous than I had anticipated. My staff managed themselves and kept me apprised of whatever was important enough for my attention. I focussed on individual case files and became more familiar with specific sections of the Immigration and Nationality Act. It was important to me that I understand the nuances of individual cases because Manila had the third highest number of visa fraud cases of any embassy worldwide. I kept voluminous notes and when the Consul General was not available for consultation, I would buttonhole Tracy Philips, one of the vice consuls who manned the visa window every day. Often, Philips would come into my office to vent after an hour or so of interviews. His cases consumed more of my time than any of our other colleagues. Regularly, I would be invited to observe while he and the other vice consuls interviewed prospective visitors. It soon became obvious why Manila confronted the challenges it did on visa issuance. Filipinos were desperate to escape the grinding, abject poverty that was their lot in life. The extent to which applicants misrepresented even basic facts was enough to make a cynic out of an altar boy. Unscrupulous travel agents controlled the highly profitable industry of intermediaries for those seeking non-immigrant (travel) visas to the United States. For a fee, they would coach the applicant on how to respond to questions. Every applicant offered the identical response to each question regardless of how you phrased the question. For example, in response to the question, "where will you be traveling in the States?" The response invariably was "San Francisco, Chicago, New York, and Washington, D.C." Each applicant would produce a new bank book with the requisite amount of $500 on deposit from one of the major local banks. This amount showed financial wherewithal to purchase a ticket and handle their expenses while in the States. We knew that the money had been deposited the day before (for a fee) and that the bank book was to be surrendered to the travel agent if a visa was issued. When a non-immigrant visiting the States, for whatever reason, decided to remain there, they were required to file for an Adjustment of Status (to that of immigrant). That form had to be filed in the States and forwarded by U.S. Immigration to the embassy that issued the original travel visa. I understood very quickly why Tracy Philips instructed me to complete the Adjustment of Status form whenever we issued a non-immigrant visa: he knew they would not be returning. This was the era of typewriters and he just wanted to save time by having the partially completed form on file.

In reality, the average Filipino did not qualify for a travel visa at that time. Had our refusal rate reflected our best judgments, it would have generated a backlash from the Philippine Government at a politically delicate time when we were pressuring the government of President Ferdinand Marcos to contribute to our growing military involvement in Vietnam. In short order, I felt less like an observer at the Consul General's early morning staff meetings and more the participant.

The other primary purpose in my life was to sort myself out emotionally. There was no prescription for this; only the passage of time and making an effort every day to be positive. By late fall that year, I had moved from my apartment just behind the American Compound into the compound itself, just one block away. My short residency in that apartment did have its bizarre and comedic moments. You will find aspects of this story amusing. Between my apartment and the embassy compound was a large vacant lot I would pass daily. Often there were squatters who would move onto the lot the previous night. Since the lot was vacant, it was difficult to dislodge them. Well, I had a daily companion during my early morning commute. The first time my companion visited with me, I was taken aback, but then I became amused by his antics. The second or third day after settling into my apartment, I was walking to the compound to catch the embassy shuttle when I heard a small child, no more than five or six years of age, shouting and running in my direction. At first, I did not understand what he was shouting because he was in full tilt. As he approached, he was shouting "Nigger! Nigger! Nigger!" I was momentarily dumbfounded. Imagine this child, dirty from head to toe, unbathed, clad in a filthy T-shirt, no pants and no shoes, standing there, chest heaving and out of breath calling me a "Nigger!" I took stock of the situation: I bathed that morning, fully clothed, housed, well-fed and enjoying my lot in life. I could only conclude that someone was responsible for this child; most likely squatters living in a hovel, themselves as ignorant as they were raising their son to become. He greeted me every morning with a smile. One morning, he did not come. I waited for a few minutes;

he was part of my day. I missed him. This was the comedic. Now for the bizarre.

If I am not mistaken, my uncle spent a great deal of time in Pasay City while visiting Manila. Well, I also learned from my capable staff that Pasay City was a favorite target for terrorist attacks by the country's more well known domestic terrorist group, the "Huks" (Huk Bala Hap). The Huks were a reality, one I experienced from a short distance. Again, on my way to work one morning, I noticed a large group of people crowding the sidewalk about 30 to 40 yards from me as I passed. I decided not to let my curiosity get the best of me so I kept moving. Several hours later in the office, one of my local staff came to tell me that eight people in Pasay City near the American Compound had been murdered the night before and their bodies laid out on the sidewalk as a message. The crowd of people I witnessed several hours earlier, according to local press reports later in the day, were the family and neighbors of those slain. I promptly told Mr. Glasgow what my staff had told me. He picked up his telephone as I left his office. The "Huks" unnerved me. I was pleased to move into the compound. Living there offered a different perspective on life in Pasay City. The compound was literally yards from Manila Bay and the sunsets we enjoyed across the Bay were purported to be the most magnificent in the world. Although the compound was considerably smaller than the housing community in Bonn, it did represent an island of tranquility in the uncertain sea that was Pasay City in 1965. The disparity of income and life circumstance between the Americans who lived within the confines of the compound and the Filipinos in the community did encourage some of them to breach our security perimeter. Their target on one occasion was the Marine Gunnery Sergeant in charge of our Marine Security Guard Detachment. Apparently, their Filipino maid had drugged the family the night before and, since their apartment was close to the perimeter wall, they were a natural target. That prompted an intense scrutiny of each of the Filipino housekeepers employed within the compound – including the one I had recently hired. There was the time I was kidnapped by a taxi driver who was in the employ of Manila's infamous "Binny Boys." I was lucky and managed to get away. Although I did have in my possession an embassy list of approved cab companies, this cab was a new air-conditioned Toyota. It was not on the list, but I made the false assumption that since it was new, unlike most cabs that plied their trade on our section of Roxas Boulevard, it had not been added to the embassy's list. Was I ever mistaken!

Manila in 1965 did occasionally present images from American frontier folklore. For example, it was not an uncommon occurrence to see two Filipinos settling their differences with firearms, sometimes in full view of the public. Some of them, in their desperate attempts to gain a financial foothold would even engage in the "sport" of Russian roulette. Life was cheap. Per capita income in the mid-60s, if I recall correctly, was below $50 per annum; firearms were ubiquitous, unemployment was high, poverty was rampant, and the well-off were convenient targets for robbery or kidnapping. There were two worlds: the poor, the unemployed and hungry, and then there were those who lived behind walled compounds. An ambitious politician or businessman could easily eliminate the competition by offering one of the city's dispossessed a meal to do his dirty work for him. Nothing, not even basic security, could be taken for granted in this place.

Seafront, as the American housing compound was known, provided comfortable, air-conditioned apartments for junior staff and the embassy's complement of Marine guards. The club amenities included a pool, dining room, entertainment, tennis and basketball courts, and space for other outdoor activities. Here, everyone felt reasonably secure – even with the occasional perimeter breach. Evenings and weekends for me early on were confined to Seafront. It was there that I could heal in comfortable anonymity. My other purpose in choosing to remain at home was simple: Manila in the mid-1960s could be a dangerous place. You could never forget that life was cheap – even my own. I was a new guy in town, so why tempt fate and become too adventurous too soon? This was not Europe.

It was a Saturday, shortly after returning from a swimming lesson that I noticed a Filipina nanny trying to keep up with the most beautiful child imaginable. The child so captivated my attention, I did the unthinkable. I ran after the nanny, apologized to avoid scaring her and asked, "whose child is that?" "Miss Marilee" she responded. "Miss Marilee" was Marilee Rousseau, executive assistant to the American Labor Attache. She was also my downstairs neighbor. Marilee was an African-American who rode the embassy shuttle with me every morning. Initially, I was reluctant to approach her about her child for fear I would be misunderstood. I mustered up the courage to tell her about my encounter with Tessie, her daughter's nanny and Marilee's daughter Solange. Before she could interrupt me, I told her if she ever needed a babysitter, I would be willing to do so. Having broken the ice, the two of us would talk on the way to the embassy. To add to her comfort about a man offering to be a babysitter, I offered to take her to dinner at the club. Whatever reservations she may have had we could deal with over dinner. After all, I was talking about her daughter. Marilee worked in the main chancery building and I spent my days in the consulate building 50 yards away, so there was not much opportunity for the two of us to talk during the day.

Several weeks after I made my offer to baby sit, I was sitting at home one evening when I heard a knock at the front door. It was Marilee and she needed a babysitter. "Is your offer to baby sit still good, George?" she asked. "Yes, it is," I replied happily. Marilee had a date and her regular babysitter, Tessie, was not available. Solange was a bright, precocious child who was accustomed to commanding the world that was her domain. That evening, the seeds of a relationship were sown that endures to this day. Solange became the daughter, the child I never had, and I credit her with restoring my sense of self-worth. Solange became my world away from the embassy. I would often remark, "the world of a two-year old is below the knees of an adult... they see what adults do not...they look down, we look up." I never knew that getting down on all fours, crawling through grass with a small child could reveal the existence of a world I did not even remember from my own childhood. As my relationship with Marilee grew, she became a lifesaver for me. She was the pleasant distraction I needed at a very low point in my life.

Marilee Smith was erudite, self-confident and quite comfortable in her own skin as a single African-American female and mother in this predominantly white male institution called the Department of State. She was also a strikingly attractive redhead who became the bridge that connected what I did not know and what I felt a need to know at my level of responsibility. In myriad conversations with her, I developed insights into the politics of the embassy. I learned who the ambassador's closest advisors were and what made them valuable to him. Marilee's thumbnail sketch of the political terrain brought many of the basics into sharp relief. Manila in 1965 was a hotbed of political intrigue. The country had a popular new president and first lady who embodied the hopes and dreams of the country's downtrodden millions. Ferdinand and Imelda Marcos were their equivalent of President Kennedy and his vivacious wife Jackie.

The Philippines was a major American ally and the embassy had to keep them in our camp since the war in Vietnam was beginning to heat up. The first major American military operation in Vietnam's Ia Drang Valley signaled to the world and the Pacific Rim countries a deeper American commitment to that war; a commitment President Lyndon Johnson and Defense Secretary Robert McNamara wanted our Pacific allies to share. That included the Philippines. Marilee pointed me in the direction of connecting all the dots on the tapestry that was

America's connection to South East Asia.

I had noticed the increasing number of merchant ships in Manila Bay, but had not connected that development with Vietnam. It was during one of our early morning staff meetings that I learned Manila Bay was a strategic staging area for American supplies and munitions destined for the war effort in Vietnam. Port facilities in that country in 1965 were limited and the overflow was staged in Manila Bay until the ships could be offloaded in Vietnam. A consequence was the growth of a large, dangerous, and thriving black market in downtown Manila involving equipment and arms destined for Vietnam. The mission of our ambassador, Justin C. Tracewell, was to persuade President Marcos to equip and train 10,000 Filipino soldiers to augment the American military presence in Vietnam. The group would be called "The Philippine Civil Action Group (PHILCAG). We, of course, would finance it. This request sent political shock waves through Manila's political elite. As they saw it, such a request would mean a serious drain on the country's meager resources. They certainly were not prepared to send their sons to support "President Johnson's War."

The consulate, a mere 50 yards from the chancery, seemed to be insulated from the global issues that consumed the embassy staff. The one principal exception would have been Mr. Glasgow. Marilee was part of this world and the hours I spent with her shaped the larger perspective the Consul General spoke of on my first day in country. The big picture he sketched for me now had shape, color and contours. Marilee's boss was one of the ambassador's trusted advisors, thus the path to his door was well worn. Marilee knew everyone. I began to meet all of the junior officers and many of their mid-career colleagues tasked with drafting the hundreds of telegrams that are the life's blood of an American diplomatic mission. I knew from my days in Bonn how consumed the embassy was with every aspect of Filipino life. In the few months Marilee and I served together in Manila, she extended my horizons to the point I was having difficulty absorbing the myriad topics with which she was conversant. This woman had worked at the Kennedy White House, served on the support staff of the Secretary of State, and had been an assistant to the American Ambassador in Belgium in her first overseas assignment. She had also sat for the Foreign Service oral exam and would often subject me to mock interviews. Moreover, Marilee not only encouraged me to return to college, but also helped me prepare for the challenges I would again confront as a student.

My small library at home had begun to grow in preparation for future coursework. Marilee had been there. Her consistent encouragement was important because I knew what it took to become a Foreign Service officer. In addition, Marilee was accustomed to working in the presence of senior government officials and knew her "nitty gritty." This was how I learned that Mr. Glasgow had the most extensive and reliable network of contacts of any officer in the embassy. He was known and trusted by many in Manila's political establishment, a fact that was the source of some envy among his embassy colleagues. Ambassador Tracewell was well aware of Lawson Glasgow's extensive ties to the community and made strategic use of his Consul General. Glasgow was an old Asia hand who had spent a career understanding what conditioned the reflexes of Asians in their relations with westerners, especially Americans. And so it was that textbooks did not adequately prepare the unseasoned officer for the Manila of the 1960s.

The future direction of a likely professional career was taking shape. The Foreign Service offered the diversity in lifestyle, professional growth, and exposure to the world's cultures to which I was gravitating. While in Bonn, I had taken the Foreign Service Examination just for the experience. That was the first hurdle; the oral examination was the second. Although I had not passed the written examination, I was not discouraged. The experience of an eight-hour examination was what I had sought. Equally important, I was gaining valuable life's experience: three years in Italy, two years in Germany and, now, the Philippines. The way I reasoned at that time, the key to any future success I would enjoy was my college education. The key then would be to marry that with my growing body of diverse experiences.

The Christmas holidays were rapidly approaching and I became increasingly amused by the traditional sounds of Christmas juxtaposed against the backdrop of the heat and humidity of the tropics. "Dashing through the snow," I would muse, with everyone crowding around the swimming pool, or seeking relief inside from temperatures in excess of 100 degrees Fahrenheit. Having picked cotton in South Carolina and tomatoes, blueberries, strawberries, and raspberries during the summer heat of southern New Jersey, I thought I knew what heat was. The most oppressive summer temperatures on the east coast of the United States within my memory did not compare to the stifling heat and humidity of Manila. From noon until mid-afternoon, one did not venture out of doors unless it was necessary. "In tropical climes" goes one of Noel Coward's famous lyrics, "there are certain times of day when all the citizens retire to tear their clothes off and perspire." Hear! Hear! Mr. Coward. Christmas day with Solange and Marilee provided some semblance of a more familiar Christmas. To Solange, it was a fun, happy day, and for me, that mattered more than anything else.

I did not know that my uncle George, now in the U.S. Navy, was on active duty at the giant American Naval Base in Subic Bay north of Manila. I became aware of this in a surprise phone call in early January 1966. When my phone rang and I picked it up, I heard this all-too-familiar voice say, "Alfred, how are you? I have been telling my buddies up here that my favorite nephew is assigned to the American Embassy in Manila." His was the last voice I expected to hear. "I'm fine," I said; "good to hear from you...I can't believe we're in the same country at the same time. When are you coming to Manila?" I asked. "Soon" he replied, "do you have room for me?" "Yeah" I replied. "I have a two-bedroom apartment...let me know when you're coming." This was an incredible struck of luck. Finally, a revered uncle and a favored nephew would have a shared experience. I got real excited and called Marilee. Maybe she would offer to have Tessie prepare one of her local dishes I had come to favor. "Brother" told me several weeks later over dinner at Marilee's apartment that he was a crew chief on American Navy flights into and out of Vietnam. He supplied other fascinating details about the importance of the Naval base at Subic to our involvement in Vietnam. In response to my question regarding the vulnerability of flights like his, I noticed he tried to minimize the risks. On a subliminal level however, I sensed that the danger was greater than he was willing to admit. I had heard reports from some of the American airmen at the embassy that it was common for hostile fire to be directed at American military aircraft over the South China Sea, but the reports could not be confirmed. I am sure my uncle knew more about this than he was willing to discuss with me. I also knew I would never rest easy on this until he had returned to the States or was reassigned.

Other important events were about to affect me. Spring was on the horizon and Marilee's scheduled departure for her new assignment in Bogota, Columbia was fast approaching. I had already begun to steel myself emotionally for what I knew would be the effect of their departure. Emotionally, I had healed from the devastating effects of my failed marriage. Solange was important to my healing and, now, she would be gone. Marilee was excited about her new assignment, an excitement I gamely tried to share. In the end, however, I chose not to see them off at the airport because I did not want Solange to see me break down emotionally. She would have looked at me with puzzled, innocent eyes and asked why I was unhappy. Nothing I could have said would have made me feel any better than I did. In my heart, I readily acknowledge that Solange was the presence, the glorious distraction, that pure childish spirit that gave me the impetus to heal. Marilee gave strength to my dreams through countless, selfless acts: verbal assurance during moments of doubt; emotional and psychological support, and timely and important introductions to official embassy visitors whose support was instrumental to future plans to return to school. Through a daily association with these two, I emerged from behind the psychological prison I had meticulously constructed to protect a fragile psyche. Teaching Solange to read, to be unafraid of the dark, to be less selfish, and those small acts that contribute to a child's development, helped to restore my feelings of self-worth. Solange was a wonderful spirit who loved me unconditionally. The sweetest sound I heard daily was "Hi, uncle George." Time, distance, and inspiration from my new "family" accelerated the healing process and, ultimately, I felt emotionally strong enough to move on with my life.

In the days and weeks following their departure, I poured all of my energy into my job, trying to untangle the web of issues in US-Philippine relations and the connection to the war in Vietnam. The Consul General touched on the issue regularly in our morning staff meetings. I also began to wonder if my own life would be affected by a deepening American commitment to that conflict. My brother and I had touched on just this very issue. Moreover, I had memories of friends whose lives and plans – including my own - were temporarily shattered by the events of August 1961: the erection of the Berlin Wall and the crisis that ensued. Also fresh in my head was a brief conversation I had had recently with Jackson Passmore, the embassy's political counselor. On that day, as he normally did, Jackson was standing in front of the embassy around noon but, this time, in Navy whites. I was curious and I asked, "Jackson, why are you in uniform?" His response sent a chill up my spine: "I have been recalled to active duty" he said. Jackson was the first Foreign Service officer at the embassy during my brief tenure there to be so directly affected by the growing conflict in Vietnam. I could not help but wonder if there would be others similarly affected. Perhaps I, too, would be recalled. I was just 26, unattached, and a veteran. Somehow, I seemed a prime candidate. The thought of being recalled was very unnerving. Powerless to exclude such a possibility, I shifted my attention once again to understanding the issues that consumed everyone's day, my consul general among them. Focusing on things more tangible and closer to home made more sense than anything else I could do.

It was during this time that I was admitted to the military hospital at the sprawling Clark Air Base 90 miles north of Manila for some previously scheduled minor surgery. My recovery period at that hospital brought home the horror of war in all of its most graphic manifestations. I took the train to Clark and checked into the hospital for what I had been advised would be a stay of four-to-five-days. This was not my first stay in a hospital and I was unconcerned. The surgery was minor and with a competent staff in my office, I felt comfortable being away for a few days. In early afternoon the day of my arrival, I was assigned a room and, as I entered, I noticed a doctor attending a young African-American patient. What struck me immediately was the unusual angle of the doctor's right hand while treating the patient. The doctor's right elbow was elevated at an unusually high angle and I could not imagine what form of treatment could be involved.

I settled in bed and began reading some material I brought with me. A few minutes later, the doctor left the room. I looked over at this young guy who was in obvious pain. "I'm George Kennedy. What happened to you?" I asked. He responded, "my name is Paul Johnson and I got shot while on patrol in the bush." I put my reading material aside and sat up on the left side of my bed facing him. I guessed he was no more than 18 or 19 years of age, but his expression and a distant look in his eyes revealed someone already aged by a harsh, even traumatic experience. I learned later that what I saw in his eyes was commonly referred to by combat vets as "the thousand yard stare." "How did it happen?" I asked curiously. Paul began, "I was on patrol carrying an M-60 machine gun when this enemy soldier popped up in front of me. I had never seen the enemy before" he said. "Both of us were equally startled and we both froze for an instant. He pulled the trigger before I did and the impact of his bullet sent me backwards." He went on to say, "as I began to fall, I squeezed the trigger and I remember seeing his body disintegrate and the brush around him catch fire before I lost consciousness. My guys told me later that I had emptied a full clip into his body. The tracers literally ignited the brush in front of him." Paul said he vaguely remembered being air-lifted but nothing really in detail until his arrival at Clark Hospital.

I sat on the side of my bed mesmerized by Paul's account of how he was wounded. He spoke without emotion in simple, but eloquent, detail. This was no war story. This kid was in pain, responding to a question he had been asked at least once and had no reason impress me. Watching this kid, I thought, "this is war, this is Vietnam...God, am I fortunate, he could be me!" I felt a tremendous surge of emotion, a mixture of fear and simultaneous relief. For the next several hours, the two of us talked about things familiar: home, girl friends, family, the past, and tomorrow's dreams. He was just one of many thousands of kids like himself: drafted into a war he wanted no part of but just doing his job. Early the next morning, I was wheeled into surgery and, several hours later, I was back in my room, somewhat groggy from the anesthesia and mildly discomforted by the stitches. Paul showed me his wound: a gaping hole the size of a baseball just below his left collarbone. I had not seen such a wound before and I almost lost it. Now, I understood what the doctor had been doing the day before when he had to raise his right arm to an unusually high level to insert his hand into the wound to adjust the dressing and to ensure that it was draining properly. Later that afternoon, I was moved from my semi-private room to a ward. I said goodbye to Paul not knowing if the two of us would meet again. In fact, I never saw him again. I often wondered if he survived the war. I wanted to believe that he had a million-dollar wound, the kind that gets you shipped home instead of back into a theater of war. My ward was filled with guys being treated for wounds most of us only experience vicariously in some Hollywood production: "Saving Private Ryan" or "We Were Soldiers" or "Black Hawk Down."

As I lay there absorbing the totality of this new setting, I felt overwhelmed by the enormity of it all. All around me were young men like myself who were caught up in the maelstrom of combat, living and dying for each other, trying to heal shattered bodies and wounded psyches, wondering, sometimes aloud, about what tomorrow would bring. For the balance of my stay at Clark Hospital, I made it my mission to meet and talk to as many of these soldiers as I could. Sometimes I missed meals because I would wander from ward to ward introducing myself to as many soldiers and sailors as possible. I wanted to hear their stories, the stories that would not make the press, stories that the world would not hear. It was also striking that most of those around me were African-Americans from America's inner cities: Newark, New Jersey; Chicago, Illinois, Brooklyn, New York; Los Angeles, San Francisco, and Oakland, California; Philadelphia, Pennsylvania, and Detroit, Michigan. The guys I talked to lying in those beds were the walking wounded and they were taking it in stride. To them, being alive, broken, and having missing limbs was preferable to being dead. They knew many former buddies who were going home in body bags. For some of them, they did have the "million-dollar" wound. They had a one-way ticket home. The most unnerving aspect of my experience at the hospital was saying goodnight to one guy before going to sleep and saying good morning to someone different occupying the same bed the next morning. Sometimes, the occupant in the beds on both sides would change twice while I slept. I never quite got over that. The war was now real in a way it had never been.

Several days later, I was preparing to return to Manila. My only thoughts at that point were the stories I had heard about combat, misguided leadership, questions about why America was involved in this war; accounts of moments in battle when American-made weapons malfunctioned and people were killed. I was having difficulty reconciling a lot of what I had been hearing from people on the business end of the war. They did not have a political agenda; they were not seeking glory. They were trying to survive and keep their buddies safe from harm. Back in Manila, I tried to reach my uncle, only to be told by a duty officer that he was away and would be returning in several days. "He's flying another mission into Vietnam" I thought. I just said a silent prayer and hoped that he would call me when he got back. By the time I left Manila in September, I had the uneasy feeling that this war was not going to turn out well for us.

It was time to think ahead. There was school and transition back to the States. Although I had been accepted at both the University of Wisconsin at Madison and at the University of Oregon at Eugene, I ultimately chose the latter school. The reason was simple. In Madison, temperatures were known to drop to -50 degrees Fahrenheit during the winter months. I was coming directly from a tropical climate and that was just too radical a change for me. Oregon in the fall was already going to be a shock on my system.

Although I was on the cusp of realizing a dream I had pursued for seven years, giving up a career was not easy. A promotion had recently come through and that opened up the possibility for consideration as a Vice Consul right here in Manila. The Consul General supported my candidacy for the vacant slot and the request was forwarded to the Department for approval. The response was direct and simple: No! The background to this is interesting. Audrey Simpson, a Foreign Service secretary in Tokyo had been assigned to the position in Manila, a position she did not want. I was to train her for a position I practically occupied. Audrey Simpson arrived in late summer 1966. Meanwhile, I had received notice that orientation and classes at the University of Oregon would begin the first week of September. I could not travel at government expense until the first week of October, the one-year anniversary of my arrival in Manila. At that time, I would have been at post for a full year and thus eligible for official travel.

I approached the embassy's Personnel Officer and asked if "Washington would grant me an exception to travel a month early?" She said "I don't know, George, but it is worth a try. We support you because it is for educational purposes." My boss, the Consul General and the embassy's Personnel Officer endorsed the request, only to be denied with the simple explanation "not in the best interest of the (Foreign) service." I was disappointed. My choice was clear: leave Manila at my own expense and be on time for classes, or wait until

October and miss that critical first month of classes. I had been away from a structured, total immersion academic setting for seven years and I was anxious about falling behind.

I went in to see the Consul General and asked, "what would you do, sir?" What I always appreciated about Mr. Glasgow was his sincerity, his honesty, and his thoughtfulness. He said, "this is your future" George...you have done a great job for me and I appreciate that. Go ahead and bear the expense and be on time. We will miss you, but you will never regret your decision." Mr. Glasgow was right. The expense of moving back to the states and being on time that first day of classes was worth the investment many times over. I located him just before his death but was unable to meet with him. I wanted to thank him for his support. I also wanted him to know that I, too, had ended my career as a consul general. He was my role model for what I felt a senior Foreign Service officer should represent.

Within a week, I had sold most of my possessions, packed those I wanted to keep, and purchased an airline ticket for my return trip. My trusted friend, Elsie Kent was now living in San Francisco. I knew I could forward my few possessions to her for safekeeping, which I promptly did. In my briefcase, however, was a photograph of Consul General Glasgow, my old colleagues and myself at the American Consulate in Manila. That photograph hangs on my wall today. Mr. Glasgow died last year and my one regret is I never got the opportunity to thank him for his support. I think he knows how grateful I am.

As the Northwest Airlines flight headed toward San Francisco, I reflected on what had been one of the most memorable years of my life. My abbreviated 11-month tour in the Philippines had been memorable. It had been a period of healing. I arrived an emotionally scarred man, depressed, and with a newly developed "bunker mentality" of emotional isolation. The last thing I imagined was being able to attach myself emotionally to anyone and, yet, I did just that and no one could have prescribed better medicine for me. I emerged an emotionally healthy person with a clear sense of direction and the courage to make the decisions that would get me back on the road to my future. Thanks to Marilee and Solange, what had appeared to be the end of the road was no more than a temporary bend in the road. The next important thing I had to do was to call my brother Michael during our brief stop in Hawaii. The next phase of my odyssey was already unfolding.

CHAPTER 8

THE PACIFIC NORTHWEST – KEEPING A PROMISE

We landed in Honolulu and I had just enough time before re-boarding to call my brother. I was transiting and there would be no time for a visit. I found a telephone and called Mike. It was late and I wasn't sure he would be awake. On the third ring, Mike answered. "Mike, it's me, Al; how are you? Listen, I don't have much time...I am between flights and just wanted to let you know that I left Manila and am heading back to Oregon to attend the University of Oregon this fall." Mike was one for details: "What are you talking about? When did this happen?" Before I could respond, he went on to say, "there have been changes in my life, also. Brenda and I are not doing well!" Well, that was a development from a year ago. I thought I heard my flight being announced over the public address system so I had to finish up. "Mike, listen, when I get settled at school, I'll write...we can catch up then. Take care, I'll be in touch." I do wish there had been time for a visit because years later, Mike told me he was having the same kind of problems with Brenda that I had experienced with Cassie. The complicating factor in their marriage was children.

Elsie met me at the San Francisco International Airport and, as always, I was delighted to see her. She was one of my more staunch supporters. Without her financial support, I knew the next chapter in my life would have been written differently. Going back to school was another major change in my life and the decade was only six years old. By the age of 26, I had spent a year in college, three years in the Army – most of which were spent in Italy; a year at home, two years with the Foreign Service in Germany and another year in the Philippines and, now, I was headed to Eugene, Oregon for more of the unknown. Elsie was wearing a trench coat, something I had not seen anyone do in over a year. I felt the slight chill in the evening air; a sign of what awaited me in Oregon. My blood was thin, a reminder of the abrupt change in climate between Manila and San Francisco, and I was already shivering.

Now it was time to catch up with developments in Elsie's life. I wanted to know how she liked living there? When did she leave Bonn and why? "Tell me everything" I said. Elsie laughed because she knew that was the way I am. "Life is so very different than it was in Bonn," she said, "but, I really enjoy it...the city offers the diversity in people, entertainment, and the cultural activities I was looking for." She told me that I would appreciate that when I had time to return for a visit. Little did I know it would be for an entirely different reason.

The view from Elsie's apartment on Broderick Street captured the beauty of San Francisco by night. Broderick Street was on a hill and the view was spectacular. Pointing off in the distance, she said "the Japanese are constructing a new cultural center here in San Francisco." "Because of your letters, George, I am now interested in the Pacific region." "When the center is completed, I plan to learn more about the programs and activities they offer." This was the Elsie I remembered: exuberant, alive, and intrigued by the differences in people and cultures. Elsie's enthusiasm was infectious and, were our roles reversed, I would have responded to her in a similar fashion. Although I wanted to spend more time in conversation, I was exhausted; jet lag had overtaken me and I just wanted to crash on anything comfortable. The next day, I had to make the last leg of my trip to Eugene and I wanted to feel more rested than I was. A few minutes after lying down, I was out like a light. My transpacific flight had been a bear. There were no vacant seats available on a flight that had been overbooked. The pilot announced that the aircraft was so heavy that we would be landing in Guam to take on additional fuel.

I slept soundly because I do not recall being awake half the night as is usually the case with me. Oddly enough, I did awake early enough to have breakfast with Elsie before heading to the airport. It was really good seeing her again and I shared with her how much I missed our all-night conversations, being neighbors, and that I was delighted we were still friends. Elsie had become an anchor in my life, something I needed. She had a special smile that spoke volumes for me. "Manila was good for me both emotionally and psychologically," I said. "It was the interregnum I needed before resuming life as a student again. I could not have done this a year ago." "How do you feel about such an abrupt change in your lifestyle?" she asked. "Truthfully, I said, I am a little anxious about it, but I am looking forward to getting back in school. This is something I have to do!" "Somehow, I feel that this is what my life has been all about." The pursuit of an education is what took me into the Army and two tours in the Foreign Service. Ever the optimist, Elsie said, "you will do well; of that, I have no doubt." Elsie's faith in me was still strong and I needed that now more than ever. I may have appeared confident, but that belied the trepidation I felt about becoming a student again. It was time to go. En-route to the airport, I recall we laughed a lot about nothing in particular. We used to do that often, especially on weekends. She dropped me off, we embraced and I watched her pull away until she was out of sight. Elsie was a true friend and I felt blessed to count her among the few real friends I had.

The campus of the University of Oregon was considerably more vast, but less intimate, than that at Shaw University, although the city of Eugene was smaller in population than Raleigh, North Carolina. What a universe of difference between a student population of slightly more than 600 and a small community of 18,000 students. Eugene had the feel of the Pacific Northwest: vast, open but not intimidating. The air smelled clean, crisp with enough bite to remind me that I was not prepared for it. This new campus environment would have had a different effect on me as an 18-year old freshman. Today, as a 26-year old freshman, it did not matter. It was just more terrain to navigate. I was now a full-time student, not a student-athlete with the distractions, interruptions and responsibilities that status entailed. I was an entering, non-resident freshman thus required to live in the freshman dormitory. Having lived through the chaos of life in a freshman dormitory at Shaw, I again sought refuge in the university library. Again, I would spend most of my study hours away from my room with the exception of a two-hour block of time right after lunch when the dorm was relatively quiet.

The paroxysm of activity I had expected on a major university campus was in full force when I arrived. Orientation was serious business for me this time. I took full advantage of most of the sessions offered that week. By the second day, I had identified several older students like myself and we talked about the kind and location of resources we would need to survive here. This was, after all, an institution of 18,000 +, overwhelmingly white, and predominantly in-state residents. There were fewer than 100 African-American students in all categories and no African-American faculty members. My decision to leave Manila "on my own nickel" to avoid a late arrival had been the prudent thing to do. Remaining academically competitive with a universe of students much younger than I was would be daunting enough. But trying to play catch-up with a mid-October arrival could have been fatal academically. It felt good to be back on a university campus but my anxiety level was rising.

At the age of 26, I was older than the student body at large, including the graduate students, and many of the teaching assistants. The university operated on an academic quarter basis rather than two academic semesters and, for me, that was a major change. Compared to my earlier experience at Shaw, this system was the equivalent of compressing a year-and-a-half of instruction into one academic year. Therefore, I needed to know the course load I could comfortably carry after an absence of seven years. My faculty advisor, Professor Altman, advised me to proceed gradually, perhaps with 12 credits rather than the 17 I selected, to establish a comfort level. At that pace, he said, "you can probably graduate in slightly more than four years." "Four years!" I said, "what about my transfer credits from Shaw?" He told me to "discuss that with the Registrar's Office." "My role," he continued, "is to advise you on course selection, your academic major, and questions you may have germane to your academic life as a student." My next stop was the Admissions' Office. They did accept some of my transfer credits giving me advanced freshman standing. To graduate, however, I would need a total of 180 credit hours. That was the university requirement. There were also requirements for my specific major and requirements for my academic group. Some of my transfer credits could be applied to meet some of these requirements. Otherwise, I would receive recognition for having successfully completed course work, but those courses would not be applicable to meet requirements at Oregon. I quickly reasoned that I was looking at a minimum of four years of course work to earn my undergraduate degree.

I took the plunge and enrolled for 17 credits the fall quarter that year thinking I would know by December if the seven-year absence was a handicap. That first quarter was a whirlwind. Over that three-month period, I discovered I could function effectively on as little as four hours sleep a night while studying seven days a week. I managed to earn a "B" average for my first time at bat. Now here is the rest of the story. That "B" average did not come easy and I owe my success to several graduate students who not only befriended me, but also tutored me every unencumbered hour I had . They admired me, they said, because I had given up a promising and interesting career to pursue an education they felt was of dubious value. I was unaccustomed to this level of cynicism among people this young, but they were bright and willing to help me.

The idea of becoming an architect still enthralled me and that was my first choice for an academic major. While reviewing the degree requirements, it was obvious I needed a stronger foundation in mathematics. I had not had a math course since 1958 and I would have to begin with intermediate algebra. An undergraduate degree in architecture is a five-year commitment and it presumes success every quarter – no mean feat for the best students. I was still an unproven quantity. I had to be honest with myself – it would have taken considerably longer for me at my current level of academic preparation. However, not one to quit, I had to know if I could meet the math requirement. During the fall quarter that year, I took intermediate algebra and I worked hard. The class was held in an amphitheater; the pace was fast and it presumed skills these students possessed, but I no longer had. For them, this was a refresher course; for me, it was practically a vertical climb. For all of my effort, I received a "D." My overall grade point average that quarter was 3.0, but it came at a tremendous cost: time spent in the student health center with infected sinuses, weight loss, stress, and anxiety. My overnight transition from the tropical climate of Manila had been too rapid. My blood was thin, too thin for the colder fall season in Eugene. Much of that first fall term I spent at the university health center fighting head colds and a serious allergy condition. I was determined, however, to succeed. I had to because I was also terrified at the thought of failure. Becoming an architect would have to remain a dream. Otherwise, I felt confident that I could do well if I learned to relax and reduce the self-induced pressure. If not, I knew I would burn out.

A "B" average bolstered my confidence given it was my first time at bat. The fall quarter was a blur but I was able to establish a rhythm that gave me the confidence to readjust to the demands of being a full-time student. I only spent a few hours a day in my dorm room, and that included meals. I would meet with my tutors in their rooms, or some other quiet location on campus. Sure my health was an issue, but the risks seemed worth it at the time. Although I was still a young man, a social life did not rank high on my list of priorities at this stage of the game. Sure, I went to a movie once with a graduate student from Houston, but nothing beyond that. I think we saw Dr. Zhivago. There would be time, I kept telling myself. The distractions were everywhere and remaining focussed was not always an easy thing to do. I was still a young man. For the moment, life was on hold. Between classes I had met a few of the older graduate students and teaching assistants at the student center. Most of them were from out-of-state. Time passed quickly and I then had to think about final exams.

The Christmas holidays loomed on the horizon and mother had asked me to come home if I could. Cassie was living with my mother and she and I agreed to resolve our differences once and for all. I had asked for a divorce. I went home with the understanding that she would agree to the divorce; she did. Our differences were as evident as always, but we both agreed we wanted to preserve the relationship. There was nothing to be gained from a lifetime of enmity. Marriage just did not work for us. We did remain friends until her death several decades later. The holidays were the perfect interlude for what I had in mind for the second quarter. On the strength of my performance that first quarter, I decided to sidestep the recommended approach to course selection: 100-level courses for freshmen, 200-level for sophomores, 300-level for juniors, and 400-level for seniors and graduate students. The university preferred this more orderly, sequential approach to course selection to estimate the number of students enrolling in a course, to manage instructor-student ratios, and because it was theoretically an indicator of a student's preparation to enroll in higher-level courses. While my confidence was high, I moved immediately to 200-level and 300-level courses during the second and third quarters of my first academic year. I could only do this with the concurrence of my faculty advisor.

At the end of the first quarter, I had the obligatory meeting to review my progress and to make course selections for the winter quarter. Professor Altman's signature on my course selections was a prerequisite to register. When I showed him my selections, he said "George, you did very well this quarter considering you carried 17 credits after a seven-year absence"...it would appear you will make my job easier than many of my other students." "I like the fact that you want to stretch yourself... You will be carrying 16 credits this next quarter, and that seems about right judging by your performance so far." "Professor Altman," I began.."I have a reason to be here and my focus is on graduating as quickly as I can. I will be 30 in four years...I do have plans for my life. What is important is that I continue to test myself." Continuing, I said "This next quarter will tell me if the first quarter was just a fluke. I need to know the level of course work I can manage as early as I can. If I have difficulty, I will be the first to let you know. I did not come here to fail. If I need to adjust my plans, I will." "George," he responded, "I think you really don't need my advice...just tell me what you plan to do and I'll work with you." I needed his vote of confidence to set my plan in motion.

The second quarter went by even more quickly than the first and I had reached two conclusions: the first was to change my major to political science. The University of Oregon was by reputation host to one of the country's leading behaviorist Political Science departments. Understanding politics from a behavioral perspective rather than from the more classical study of political institutions allowed me to draw on my life's experience shaped largely by multi-lingual and multi-cultural experiences in three countries and exposure to many others. I had a reputation as an engaging conversationalist by former colleagues. It just seemed to me that behaviorism offered a more natural approach to articulating, advocating, and understanding both the domestic and foreign policy issues that roiled college campuses and American society in the mid-1960s. For me, it was not enough to discuss the role of institutions in society. I identified with the school of thought that said institution are people. People make decisions based on perspectives gained from education, their life's experience, and socio-economic status in society. My life's experience persuaded me it was necessary to understand the forces that conditioned the reflexes of decision-makers and to understand their motivation and worldview. A clash of the two prevailing schools of thought was inevitable. There were those born between 1946 and 1950 demanding a more humanist approach to policy formulation and addressing social ills. Then, there were those of the older, pre-World War 11 generation, survivors of the Great Depression, World War 11 and the Korean Conflict who were uncomfortable with having rapid change foisted upon them. To many in this older generation, the unrest, the chaos, the public demands for change, was nothing more than anarchy. The mid-1960s was largely about this clash of world views and I was caught up in it along with others like myself. It was also an exciting time to be alive and involved with a generation demanding change.

The second conclusion I reached was to try and reduce the length of time it would take to earn my undergraduate degree. Four years was too long; perhaps I could accomplish the same goal in three.

As winter 1967 became spring, by now confident in my transition to student life, I was also more sensitive to and integrated in other campus activities. And, I was spending less time with my tutors. The Vietnam War had split the student body into noisy, activist factions whose members contained a few ex-veterans. I sought them out because I was a veteran and because some of them had served in Vietnam. I wanted to contrast their on-the-ground experiences with what I learned in Manila, and with the news reports that gave us Vietnam raw during the dinner hour. While I knew I had no desire to participate in marches, demonstrations, or attempts to occupy university administration buildings, I did see avenues to engage in dialogue with students about the Vietnam War, foreign policy issues, America's social policies, the "Black Power" movement, urban unrest in the country's principal cities, and the rise of the Black Panther Party for Self Defense. As an older student, I thought I could tone down the temperature that characterized most individual and group encounters and get some people talking to each other and not at each other. There were those moments when I did succeed. I thought it was worth the time and effort because some of these young and impressionable white students could one day be in a position to make decisions that would affect the lives of many, including African-Americans, perhaps even my own. The more they understood why African-Americans and migrant workers, for example, were demanding change, the better informed their decisions could be and the more tolerant they might be of others who were different from themselves. Because many of these white students were willing to listen, unlike many of their parents' generation, the educational experience many of them had as students took on a different coloration. A goodly number of them became allies with several of the campus groups working with the university administrators to bring about change in admissions' policies, hiring minorities at the staff and faculty level, and making the university more aware of its role as a "change agent" within the City of Eugene. The students who were our allies earned my respect because most of them had been "disowned" by their parents: not allowed to come home between quarters and cut off without financial support. They were literally on their own for the first time in their lives. I had never heard the term "disowned" before. I actually believed there was a legal process involved. The white parents of these student "activists" - as they were labeled – could not understand, nor accept, changing their academic majors, their commitment to contemporary social issues, or their concerns for people of color. I was in the right place at the right time because some of those kids were emotionally bereft. They were dealing with a side of their parents never before witnessed. I told them they would not have as long as the choices they made were consistent with the future they wanted for their children. We presume to know our parents, what they would understand and countenance, as long as we do not test them

The success I achieved academically by the end of the spring quarter of 1967 had me firmly established as a solid B+ student As the summer quarter approached, Carlos Jimenez, a Poly Sci. major from Hawaii, and I rented a house within walking distance from campus. In many respects, despite a six-year age difference, I being the older, Carlos and I were fellow travelers. He had been an early volunteer in the old VISTA Program (Volunteers in Service to America). While working in the American south and with poor migrant workers in Texas, Carlos, who was Filipino-Chinese, gained a perspective starkly different from many of his generation. He, too, found himself philosophically at odds with many of the white students on campus, and from the insulation and social isolation that was Eugene, Oregon in 1967. Carlos came from comfortable middle-class circumstances, but the experience that shaped the man he had become was similar to that of a sharecropper in the south, or a poor Mexican migrant worker in New Mexico, Texas, Arizona, and California. Carlos and I were enrolled in many of the same political science courses and Carlos felt comfortable approaching me about renting a house off-campus. The friendship we began during that time endured for years. Carlos liked to cook and I did not mind the less onerous chore of washing the dishes. We shared general housekeeping duties and paying the bills.

The summer quarter at Oregon also offered a Summer Teachers' Institute: teacher-training seminars for public school teachers around the country. Several of the returning teachers were alumni of the university. The larger student body was smaller during the summer with a larger percentage of older students with whom I could interact. The summer session was attractive to many of the participating teachers because of the fame of Professor Arthur Pearl, author of the highly acclaimed book "New Careers for the Poor." Pearl was an advocate of non-traditional approaches to addressing many of the problems public school teachers confronted in educating inner-city youth. I had become attracted to the program because of my association with the Warfield brothers. They were administrators in the Michigan public school system, consultants to public school systems in Oregon, and some of the most dynamic graduate students on campus. John and Charles "Chuck" Warfield both suggested I take a look at what they were doing in the field of education with Dr. Pearl. I liked Dr. Pearl's teaching philosophy and the opportunities he created for his students to gain practicum experience in Oregon's public schools. His students became resources to public school administrators on a volunteer basis while pursuing graduate degrees in education. During that first summer quarter, I carried 15 credit hours, a full-load for a summer period, including graduate-level courses in political science and sociology. I was feeling on top of my game and decided to accept "Chuck" Warfield's invitation to accompany him on several field trips to public schools in Eugene and cities farther west in the state. Evenings were generally devoted to discussion groups Carlos and I hosted at our off-campus house with many of the teachers enrolled in the summer institute. Most of them were years away from their college experience and they were trying to understand the mood among today's students, the unrest over the War, events quite distant from the lives they were leading.

Oregon in the 1960s was right-of-center on the political spectrum. Some observers characterized it as the second most conservative state after Barry Goldwater's Arizona. Many of Eugene's residents resented the student activities on campus. More to the point, they publicly lamented the intrusion of "outsiders" with their insistent demands for more diversity in the university's faculty and its student body. Why was it necessary, local editorials asked, to broaden the course offerings with courses on "The African Diaspora," "Slavery – America's Sorrow?" These were but two examples of courses recommended by a group commissioned by the University President Arthur Fleming to review course offerings and report back on options the faculty could consider. There were many other suggestions from other groups as well. I was part of the group that made recommendations on changes in the student dining menus. Fleming had previously served as the Secretary of Health, Education, and Welfare under President Eisenhower. I remember one editorial that raised the question we felt most qualified to respond to: "Who are these outsiders who presume to know better than Oregon's public school officials and parents what their students should learn?" What the local editorial board refused to acknowledge was the success Dr. Pearl's graduate students were achieving in working with the public school system in the state. Teachers and administrators were receptive to new approaches; they wanted to succeed.

Logging and heavy equipment operations were major local industries and there were reports of altercations between several of the African students on campus and blue-collar workers from a local lumber mill. My first roommate, an older male student from Ghana, Maurice Doku, was attacked and beaten not far from the main campus. Maurice had been walking with a white female friend when, according to the police report, they were set upon by two young white males in a blue pickup truck. In spite of the fact that Maurice and his friend were able to describe their two assailants, the color and make of the truck, and provide a license number, the local police were never able to locate the two attackers. No one wondered why. African-American students were advised to remain on campus after dark. Carlos and I had profiles that made us natural targets. When Carlos and his girlfriend were attacked one evening after class while returning home, we decided that walking at night was dangerous. I went to San Francisco to talk to Elsie about buying a car. Carlos purchased one in Eugene. We had to be mobile and flexible now that our lives were at stake.

I was now dating a student from Medford, Oregon, someone I cared for and she had been threatened by receiving a razor blade in the mail. My concern for her safety was greater than for my own because she was more vulnerable. We also thought it prudent not to share this development with family, particularly hers, because they were opposed to our relationship. We spent a full evening in dialogue with her parents at their home about our relationship. Sarah had a stubborn side and, while I admired that, it did heighten my concern that she might take risks because she refused to allow anyone to restrict freedoms she took for granted. Her greatest sin was being associated with me, caring for me, and being willing to lend her voice on causes and issues she felt strongly about. I suppose this made her a natural target. Along with the razor blade was a note with vile and racist language. Our home telephone number was listed and most evenings, Carlos and I received at least two death threats each. Beyond taking prudent steps to protect ourselves and those we cared for, Carlos and I chose not to panic. The situation deteriorated materially following our appearance on a local radio talk show during which we tried to broaden the public debate over the riots in Newark and Detroit and their links to student activities on the Eugene campus and elsewhere in the country. The vitriol from some in the city kept the threats alive and our telephone ringing off the hook. Eventually, we were forced to contact the FBI in Portland and they agreed to monitor our telephone. We were not alone. The pressure was on to shut us down.

Most African-American students, especially the out-of-state doctoral candidates, lived off campus in the city. Because of their work in the State's public school system, they traveled frequently. Their families were isolated and vulnerable, and several were harassed at night. Naturally, we turned to city authorities for help. The meetings we were able to arrange with the City Manager were fruitless. In one noteworthy meeting, the City Manager told us, "the only problem this city has are you niggers on campus." To reassure anxious family members, we established a network of "safe houses" among the African-American students closer to the main campus, in the event families in more distant locations came under attack at night. Some of the African-American students on campus had volunteered to share their dormitory rooms in the event of an emergency. Our door at home was always open. The plan we African-American students formulated was a military-style operation modeled after the system I knew best from my Army days in Italy when we would practice evacuation of non-essential personnel. Everyone had a car, a telephone, and a directory of safe locations for families who were threatened. Again, this was Oregon in 1967. Activism had its rewards and its risks. The more experienced graduate students were in Oregon because Professor Pearl's program made the sacrifice worthwhile for those African-American educators who interrupted their careers to pursue doctorates under him. Dr. Charles Warfield, his brother Dr. John Warfield, and their cousin James Warfield, all from Detroit, ranked among the program's graduates. Dr. Francine Brown, a prominent African-American educator, was another.

Academically, I had a successful Summer quarter in 1967 with an A- average. My accelerated graduation program was bearing fruit. I had amassed enough credits to be classified a junior. The old equation danced in my head again. I told Carlos, "I think I can graduate in two years, not three or four." Although he had placed himself on a similar track, he did not feel the same time pressures that I did. At his current rate of progress, Carlos would complete his course work in three years and graduate in 1969, not 1968, as I was planning to do. Carlos did graduate in 1969. My faculty advisor, by this time, would just endorse the course selections I brought to him. Professor Altman remarked "I have never had a more disciplined, a more focussed student. I do believe that you will achieve the goals you have set." He also added that my progress at the university had been impressive.

In mid-summer 1967, I received the news that I had been selected as a Residence Hall Counselor for the Fall term. The responsibilities of a residence hall counselor took on special significance during the evening hours, therefore, I would have to give up my off-campus house with Carlos. I needed the distance, the quietude, and the personal space the off-campus house offered and I told Carlos that I would continue to pay my share of the rent with the money I saved from free room and board. Although I was required to spend nights in the dorm, I would be at the house on weekends. Of course, Carlos was relieved because he did not want to begin a search for a new roommate. In early September, I moved back into the dormitory to help prepare for the entering class of 1967. As a member of the university staff, I was entitled to parking privileges, a highly prized perk.

Working with discussion groups at the house kept me attuned to current events but it was now approaching the fall term and I had to shift my focus to another objective – career planning. The Foreign Service examination was being offered in December that year and I planned to sit for it. Looking past the exam was the waiting game, the serious side of the process. Many a candidate became dispirited while waiting and moved on to other options. The Foreign Service was also a long shot via the examination route and I knew it. Plan B required a more practical, more parochial approach. I was impressed with the success professor Pearl was achieving through his doctoral program in the State's public school system. Scholarship funds were available and I was seriously considering pursuing a doctoral degree in education. Why not? I had the grades. Dr. Pearl had selected me as one of his summer group leaders, and I would again be working with him the coming fall quarter. It was a plan, it made sense, there were scholarship funds, and I had Dr. Pearl's support. More immediate though was preparing myself for the challenge of becoming a residence hall counselor.

New Student Week had one amusing highlight. Several of the

parents were surprised to learn that their son's counselor was African-American. In private meetings with the university's housing director, some parents asked, "does this mean that my son will be living in a Black dormitory?" The housing director immediately scheduled a meeting with me to voice these parents' concerns. I listened as he struggled to put a humane, rational face on racism. The more he talked, the less I was inclined to rescue him from an obviously uncomfortable position. With the exception of my military service time, I wore a beard all of my adult life – even in high school. The visage of the proud, articulate, African-American male of that period was made even more menacing to white Americans if his hair was more than an eighth of an inch in length and he wore a beard. I was the embodiment of their greatest fear, and now their child was under my direction. Horror of horrors! What was America coming to?

I really enjoyed what came next. The director cleared his throat and asked, "George, would you consider shaving your beard." I smiled and said, "I would if you are prepared to ask Professor James C. Davies (an international authority on the theory of revolution and a tenured professor at the university) if he would shave his." "Better yet," I went on to say, "how do you think he would respond were you to ask him to shave his beard to satisfy the concerns of parents?" To his credit, the matter was dropped. I offered to meet with any parents who were willing to meet with me. He knew this was absurd but I could only conclude that he thought the request was worth a shot. Common sense must have prevailed because parents' fears were quickly allayed and the routine of life in our dormitory settled in. I assumed the parents' fears were quelled because no parent ever asked to meet with me. And the housing director never scheduled another meeting on this subject.

Life was fairly comfortable for me now. Bob, my co-counselor, was a second-year law student who was quite laid-back and mature. He was also nimble and fleet of foot. We had to be to keep up with the few more immature students who saw the dorm more as a playpen rather than a place for more studious pursuits. Bob and I were perfectly matched in temperament, a major factor in maintaining the stable environment parents expected, students needed, and the university required. As the Fall quarter drew to a close, I decided not to go home for Christmas. I checked out of my dorm room and temporarily moved back in with Carlos. In 1968, several of my closest friends on campus graduated. For the first time, I felt a sense of loss. They had been supporters and mentors as I was finding my footing as a student again. I also knew that this would be the year I would amass enough credits to graduate. My target date was the end of the '68 Summer quarter.

College campuses in 1968 were fertile territory for student activists and our campus in Eugene was not to be spared its share of headaches. The assassinations of Bobby Kennedy and Martin Luther King, Jr. had a cataclysmic effect on the students at our campus in Eugene. Many of them openly despaired about the future; some thought the country was on the verge of civil war. The shroud over all of this was the success of the North Vietnamese Tet Offensive earlier in January. Many students now knew personally, or had knowledge of, friends killed in Vietnam. It was not the best of times and I, too, began to wonder about the direction of this country. Everyone I knew, with the exception of a group of student members of the Young Americans for Freedom (YAF), were terrified over the prospect of a Nixon presidency.

Early that spring, I received the news I had not passed the Foreign Service examination, but I did receive an invitation to sit for an oral interview in San Francisco. A week before the interview, I called Elsie to tell her I would be in San Francisco to interview with the State Department's Board of Examiners; that they would be interviewing potential officer candidates from the west coast. At first she was delighted, but then asked "if this was not what I wanted?" "Yes, I responded, but let's get through the oral first. You never know what these examining boards are looking for." I also asked her if she could pick me up at the airport.

During the flight to San Francisco, I put myself through another of a series of mock interviews. I calculated that there would be at least two or three questions on contemporary social issues, perhaps a question on the Vietnam War, and a hypothetical situation to test reasoning ability. Feeling reasonably confident, I was able to relax the rest of the flight. The interview went well and I was told I would be receiving a follow-up letter from the Department's Board of Examiners (BEX) when final assessments were completed. I knew from my prior Foreign Service experience that considerable time could lapse before I received that letter. Moreover, there were no guarantees. My best course of action was to resume the current direction of my life as if the Foreign Service career option did not exist. I had seen and heard of many other officer candidates that became captives of the "waiting game." I did not intend to sit by the telephone.

The Summer quarter of 1968 marked the end of a quest begun ten years earlier. I would be graduating. This moment of personal triumph was the culmination of a dream both my mother and I harbored, and I needed to share it with her. Fred and Marlene had moved to Maryland in connection with a new position he had been offered, otherwise, I am sure they would have made an effort to be there. The rest of my supporters were still abroad. My girlfriend had taken a summer job in San Francisco and she could not be there. The plan, our plan, the one we discussed before she left, called for a celebration when she returned for the Fall quarter. I would be the first of several generations of Kennedy's to earn a university degree. To mark such a historical family milestone, my mother and sister were flying out to be part of my great moment. I felt great because key pieces of my life were falling into place even though there was nothing definitive from the Foreign Service. Reflecting on that summer quarter, it had been one of the most challenging thus far.

While reviewing all of my reading assignments for that nine weeks, I calculated to have read the equivalent of almost 33 books. It would not have been possible without the benefit of a speed reading course I had taken two years earlier. The reading requirements at Oregon were legendary. I was told shortly after my decision to major in Poly Sci that if I did not wear glasses beforehand, I would probably need them eventually. I was also advised that if my reading skills were average, around 250- 300 words per minute, I would not make it. My reading skills were average and, fortunately for me, one of the freshmen in my dormitory had taken the Evelyn Woods Dynamic Reading Course. His roommate told a group of us that he had been one of the more successful students to take the course. His speed and comprehension were the stuff of local legend. Several of us decided to put him to the test, with the assistance of his roommate. We wanted to select materials he had not read. What we witnessed just blew our minds and we asked him if he would consent to offering an unofficial course for a small group of us in the dorm. He was reluctant initially, but we prevailed. Contrary to policy, he met with us several nights a week in our dining room for very intensive instruction in techniques. It was all about technique and how to focus without distraction. Learning the basics of speed reading was one of my better decisions.

All of my courses that last Summer quarter were graduate level and I earned a 4.0 grade point average. Taking graduate level courses as an undergraduate reduced the number of graduate level courses I would have to take later. Since I had decided to enroll in Dr. Pearl's doctoral program beginning the Fall term, I was effectively ahead of the game. I graduated with an overall grade point average of 3.7 in my major and a 3.5 as a full time student.

Some time during that last week, I received two telephone calls.

The first was from my faculty advisor, Dr. Altman. "George, can you stop by my office this afternoon?" he asked. "Absolutely!" I responded. I told him I could be there around 3 pm. When I knocked and entered, he was sitting at his desk. As I sat down, he said, "George, I can't tell you how proud I am of the work you've done here. In two years, you have accomplished what it takes the average student four years to do... some take a fifth year." At that, he reached into his desk drawer and pulled out two glasses and a chilled bottle of apple cider. Neither he nor I drank alcohol. "No need to tell the other students, but this is cause for celebration...yours is a remarkable achievement." I expected a sincere "well done," but I was completely taken aback by the generosity of his comments. I did thank him for believing in me and supporting my plan. We sat there for almost two hours talking about some of the changes under discussion within the university administration, current events, and my plans for the Fall quarter. He knew I was actively considering Dr. Pearl's doctoral program. "Art Pearl is doing some exciting things in primary school curriculum development and you will fit in well there. You will still be on campus, so stay in touch."

The second call was from Dr. Pearl. He, too, wanted to see me. Art Pearl was more difficult to schedule because he maintained such a frenetic pace. I did track him down for a noon meeting two or three days later. He got right to the point. "George, I know you plan to enroll in my program this Fall, but there is something I'd like you to consider...it would be exciting...just your cup of tea." "Moreover," he said, "you could make a real contribution and it would give you more of a foundation in the field of education." With that introduction, he described an effort underway in Washington, DC to establish the first urban land grant college in America. It was the new Federal City College. I had not heard of it. Pearl went on to say that Senator Wayne Morse, of Oregon, sponsored the legislation establishing the college, and he was in the process of selecting a small team of educators, several from the department of political science, to serve as the nucleus of a transition and development team. Several members of the team had been in Washington for several months and they were recruiting faculty and staff. He said, "George, think about taking a year or two to help establish the school; put it on a solid footing and then return to resume your program here." "One of my students, Jay Jones, will be the Director of Student Affairs there...talk to him...he will be going back to Washington soon." "Furthermore, he knows you and he has some ideas about positions that might interest you."

Dr. Pearl's suggestion made good sense to me because it was well known that all of his most successful students were educators. A stint at a new college, particularly one with a totally urban constituency, would be a departure from the history of Land Grant colleges in America. When the Morrill Act of 1862 established land grant colleges, the country was largely agricultural and rural. Degree programs had a heavy emphasis on animal husbandry, farming techniques, and liberal arts. It had been decades since the last land grant college had been established in the United States. The District of Columbia was urban, not rural, and it did not have the equivalent of a "State" institution of higher learning. All of the colleges and universities in the District were private and beyond the financial reach of most of its citizens, particularly that segment of the population that depends most heavily upon State institutions of higher learning. The Morrill Act contained the tool to establish a public institution whose purpose was to provide affordable, high quality education for an urban constituency. I called Jay, this was important! He asked me if I would be available to have dinner with him that evening. I said I could.

Later that evening, Jay briefed me about the school, the team in Washington, and the positions the school needed to fill to open in September. As for how and where I might fit in, he said, "George, I highly recommend the Admissions' Office...I know the director, Jack Whittaker and he needs someone like you." "Would you be interested?" he asked. I asked a few more questions and the more Jay talked, the more interested I became. Since Art felt this would be a good move, I said, "yes, I am, but what can you tell me about transportation expenses, salary, housing, etc?" By the end of the evening, I knew I was going to have to make a quick decision. I was excited about the opportunity and I did want to be part of it. Dr. Pearl had assured me I could return to his program as did his other students in similarly situated. As we talked, I said, "Jay, help me reason through this. I will be graduating soon which means I can be in Washington by early September. To do that, I will need official authorization from the school to incur the expense of shipping my effects and driving across country." "Can you arrange that for me?" Jay returned to Washington later in the week and, to my surprise, by the middle of the following week, the authorization I requested arrived in the mail. I was already impressed by how quickly things were beginning to fall in place. Another new, but unanticipated, chapter was about to begin.

Before that, there was graduation. More importantly, I had to call my girlfriend in San Francisco. This development was not something we had anticipated. To the contrary, we were headed in the direction of planning a future. Well, the big day came; my mother and sister were there. It was beautiful that day and the number of African-American families present was just beautiful to behold. Their sons and daughters embodied generations of hopes and dreams, tears, expense, and now everything would culminate in this one awesome moment. I know what my mother was thinking. For us, this, too, was a family affair, an effort of shared sacrifice years in the making. Mother and my sister positioned themselves to get that photograph for posterity; the moment when I walked across the stage, held up the piece of paper, lingered for a moment and flashed the smile we would all remember for the years to come. Well, that was the plan. What came next was truly bizarre and cast a pall over the crowd.

The Chancellor stepped to the microphone and asked all candidates for Masters and Baccalaureate degrees to stand. We promptly stood, some students faced slightly to the right expecting the usual procession to the stage. At that moment, the Chancellor said, "I now confer upon each of you the degree which you have earned...please be seated." Students and parents were stunned into momentary silence. You could hear the gasps from the crowd. I was thinking this could not be – but it was. I looked over and saw mother; she was in tears. Several of the students close by talked about getting up and leaving. Later, many of them said the only reason they participated in the ceremony was because of its importance to family and friends, many of whom traveled considerable distances to be there. Many of us would have been content to have the actual degree mailed to us. We earned it, we knew it; it was now prologue. Only the doctoral candidates were accorded individual recognition that hot August day in 1968.

At dinner that evening, it was time for family. Family also included Carlos, my collaborator, friend, and roommate. "Mom Kennedy," as he affectionately called her, made sure he was seated next to her. Carlos missed his family and my mother sensed his loss. She would pinch hit for the week she was visiting with us. Mother hugged him frequently and he hugged her right back. It was also a time for reflection, prayer, and gratitude. Mother and I were standing out on the front porch one evening and I remember saying to her, "I thought it would be over when I achieved this. It took ten years, but it's not over. My journey has only begun!" I was reminded of a line from one of the Beatles songs that summed up my feelings: all I've done is purchase "a ticket to ride." Mother smiled and said, "that's right Al, but now you're on your way...the dues you paid to get here were well worth it." She continued, "look at the life you've had thus far and you're only 28.

A few days after their return home, mother called with news that rocked the foundations of my life for years to come, a call I never forgot.

"Al, … yeah, mom, what's up?" "It's Bernard" (my older brother). The tone of her voice signaled the worst and I knew the news was not good. I thought I heard her voice crack and at that point, I remember holding my breath. I can be excitable on occasion but, oddly enough, this was not one of those times.

"Is he dead?" I asked. "Yes!" Mom replied. I could tell she was fighting tears and the urge to scream. Mom and Bernard had a strong relationship; he was her first born and they often spoke in a shorthand that spared them the need for details.

"How did he die?" "Where was he when it happened?" I asked. By this time, I'm asking questions in such rapid succession I forgot to breathe – and I do stutter badly. "Sit down, Mom," I said. "I need to understand what happened." This was the one thing the family dreaded because Bernard, even as a child, always said he would never live to be 30. Old folks used to say, "you could mark yourself for death."

Mother explained that Bernard had been involved in a dispute with his landlord where he had been living temporarily in South Carolina. She had heard from the local police and the landlord's wife that the proprietor of the rooming house did not like my brother and, that he was trying to provoke him into an altercation. According to the police report, Bernard was settling his bill at the desk and the proprietor confronted him. Bernard said he did not have time to argue with him; that he had a bus to catch. Bernard put his receipt in his pocket, picked up his bag and turned to leave. The proprietor then produced a weapon and shot him in the back. He was dead before his body hit the floor. So, why was he in South Carolina? My brother had heard my father might be living there and he went to investigate; something he always said he would do. He, among all of my siblings, missed daddy the most. Even as a kid, he always said, "one day, I am going to find my daddy." Well, he had and that pursuit cost him his life. Just before mother hung up, I said "he almost made it." Within the family, the feeling was, if Bernard saw his 30th birthday, he would live forever – a long and normal life.

Two days later, I was back in Camden for the funeral. Bernard had been the Rock of Gibraltar for us. He was there for each of my siblings and for me, especially mother. Often, Bernard and mother would sit up at night; mother would cook and they would talk until dawn. Bernard was her first born and they were soul mates. That day in church, mother was almost hysterical with grief. It would take years for us to fully recover from his untimely death. December 3, Bernard's birthday, was always special in our home. That was the one day we left mother alone and we did not mention Bernard's name. She would just retreat into herself. The change for me was more psychological. I was now the head of the family, a position I never wanted. I liked being son number two. Up until my mother died in 2008, I would sign letters and cards to mother as "Son #2, Al." Bernard's place as the first son is reserved for him in perpetuity. Mike, my younger brother always signed letters and cards as "Son #3, Mike."

I flew back to Oregon to prepare for the drive across country. Following the obligatory round of farewells with friends and certain faculty members, I packed my car and headed south to San Francisco. Carlos and I agreed this was not farewell, just a temporary parting. As I backed my car out of the driveway, Carlos was sitting on the front porch strumming his guitar. I also knew that both of us were masking a lot of feelings. We had a lifetime of experiences in the time we walked the Eugene campus together.

I drove to San Francisco to pick up several of my belongings in temporary storage with Elsie. I also had to say goodbye to my girlfriend and, that, I did not look forward to. Both of them were important and now I was leaving them behind. Elsie and I had a different relationship, but my girlfriend, that was different. I guess I could have said no to this opportunity in Washington. I could have chosen a different path, what, I don't know. I was driven, I knew that. There was something over the horizon I was destined to accomplish and just settling in Oregon with someone I loved somehow did not suffice. Not then! I had to go.

On a bright Monday morning in early September, I headed east. I had never driven across country before; another new experience. That memorable trip was a study in itself. I discovered ours is a majestic country with some of the most magnificent vistas, landscapes, and geologic wonders on the face of the earth. I drove 10 hours a day, and as each day passed, I promised myself to make the trip again, but at a more leisurely pace. Six days after leaving San Francisco, I was in Washington.

CHAPTER 9

1968 – ANNUS HORRIBILIS:
RACE, POLITICS, AND EDUCATION

To paraphrase Britain's monarch, Queen Elizabeth, 1968 was *"annus horribilis."* The caveat is that it was America's madness. Public debate over the war in Vietnam reached a feverish pitch that pitted one generation against another; parents against children, and the American military establishment against a society upon which it depended to sustain their war effort in a tiny corner of southeast Asia. In January of that year, the North Vietnamese launched the Tet Offensive and further weakened our resolve at home. Robert McNamara, the Secretary of Defense, and a major architect of our war strategy, had recently left the Pentagon. Martin Luther King, Jr. and presidential candidate, Robert F. Kennedy, were brutally gunned down, and publicly. The fragile sinews holding America together were weakened even further. The last straw was popular news anchor Walter Cronkite's assessment of our war effort which lead to President's Johnson's announcement that he would not be a candidate for re-election that fall.

The "police riot" in Chicago at the Democratic National Convention temporarily became the world's indictment of the world's greatest democracy. The epicenter of the debate over America's purpose in Vietnam was shifting to the nation's capitol. This was a presidential election year and Republican presidential candidate, Richard Nixon, was artfully exploiting the schism in the country with his appeals to the "silent majority."

In September 1968, I became a new addition to our nation's capitol, a city in rapid transition from a sleepy, southern town on the Potomac River in the death grip of its southern colonialist masters in the Congress, to a twentieth century, urban metropolis with an aroused polity seeking to throw off the shackles of 20th century-style political, social, and economic enslavement. For example, many Americans, myself included, were unaware that the District's residents collectively remitted more of their income in the form of federal income taxes to the national treasury than the combined populations of several states in the American union. People in the District of Columbia wanted Statehood and the right to choose their own political representation. I thought this was a reasonable request. Alas, as the "last plantation," the politics of the historic Boston Tea Party were not applicable to these American defenders of the Republic.

The riot that year on Washington's famed Georgia Avenue had tattered the framework of an old social order. The Chairman of the House District Committee (recognized as the de facto mayor of Washington) from South Carolina was apoplectic. Order on his reservation had been breached. Maryland suburbanites, many of whose daily commute into the District carried them down Georgia Avenue, were fearful of driving into the city. The gentry of Washington's "Gold Coast," the illustrious alumni of Howard University, and the descendants of the city's Freedmen, all discovered in the immutable words of Washington Post columnist William raspberry, that "Fear is Mutual, Tolerance Isn't." These African-Americans were now lumped together with the rioters in the streets. Shattered almost overnight was the thin veneer of respectability Gold Coasters thought separated them from the "others." White people were frightened and all African-Americans looked alike. The African-American judge driving down 16th Street in his imported automobile became "just another nigger" when he was stopped by a frightened, young white member of the National Guard who pointed his weapon at the judge and told him to stop. There was a curfew! Why was this Black man on the street? I can imagine the inner horror of that judge at having been reduced to sub-human status. The ubiquitous African-American taxi driver, the equally ubiquitous African-American elevator operator at the Department of Agriculture, and that outraged judge, all had one thing in common: their color. These events and countless others were immutable fact, the proverbial bottom line. The social landscape in 1968 Washington also included life at this level. Add to this the social and psychological impact of the nation's newest Land Grant institution.

425 2nd Street, N.W. had become a well-known address in Washington by the time I arrived. It was the address of the main campus of The Federal City College (FCC). The Federal City College was unique in the annals of Land Grant College history because it represented the first attempt in decades to translate the guiding principles of a traditional land grant college with a rural, agricultural-based population to those that would serve a modern, urban population. The school's administrators,

faculty, and staff were grappling with myriad challenges, but among the most complex issues they had to confront was determining the urban equivalent of a course in animal husbandry; or, the urban equivalent of a course on techniques to improve crop production. This was an experiment of historical dimension and it had its supporters and a growing legion of detractors, many of whom were right there in the nation's capitol.

The main campus building was a three-story, nondescript, grey building that had been vacated to serve its current purpose. I found a parking spot and went inside looking for Jay Jones. In short order, a student directed me to Jay's office. Jay spotted me. "George, good to see you!" he said. "When did you arrive?" "Last night," I repied. "I checked into a motel and managed to get a decent night's rest." "We'll talk later," he said, "but first, let me take you to meet the Dean of Students, our boss, Robert Hassler. His office is down the hall." Looking about as we walked, Jay said, "as you can see, we are managing chaos here...everyone is excited because this is history in the making. You'll catch the fever." Robert Hassler was entering his office as we approached. Jay caught his attention. "Bob, this is George Kennedy, the new addition to the admissions' office you and I discussed." Dean Hassler had come over from the Peace Corps, where he had built a reputation as an efficient, but thoughtful, administrator. He saw real value in my Foreign Service experience – and said so. He also understood the uniqueness of the Foreign Service as an attractive career and he asked me if it was my intention to resume that career at some point. I did tell him that it was on a short list of attractive options I was prepared to pursue. In the interest of full disclosure, I pointed out that my commitment to the college was for a minimum of two years and that I intended to honor that commitment.

Hassler then spoke at length about the activities of concern to his office and even more about the demographic that was the school's natural constituency. The more I learned about the school and the importance of the admissions' office, the more excited I became. An hour into the meeting, Bob said, "we will have ample opportunity to talk, but, now, you need to meet your boss, Jack Whittaker, the Director of Admissions." By this time, Jay had returned to his office and Bob escorted me to the admissions' office, one floor below. Whittaker was on the telephone when we walked in. He terminated the call and got up to greet us. "You must be George Kennedy." Whittaker had the grip of a former boxer, but experience in Germany had taught me to prepare for handshakes with strangers, especially strangers the size of Whittaker. "Man, it's good to see you. Sit down!" I had a good feeling about

Whittaker as he, too, began to talk about his program.

Jack Whittaker was a retired Army Lieutenant Colonel who had seen real combat during the Korean Conflict. In conversations with him, it was obvious the colonel, or "Jack" as he liked to be called, was a "closer" - someone who recognized the importance of closing that all-important last six-inch gap in communications. In Whittaker's case, he was passionate about selling the virtues of the brand of education The Federal City College was developing. Whittaker had a quick wit and enjoyed a good laugh. He also well understood the seriousness of the responsibility he had accepted in his role as the director of admissions. I also met my secretary, Yvonne Turner, a vivacious, young African-American woman who had already begun to organize my office. Whittaker told me to go and get settled, so I took the balance of the day to complete the ritual processing.

Later that afternoon, as I was roaming the hallways familiarizing myself with my new surroundings, I saw a face I instantly recognized, but was astounded to see it in this place. "Malea, Malea Kiblan," I shouted. "Is that you?" Malea was also a '68 graduate of the University of Oregon's Department of Political Science. She, Carlos Jimenez, and I were previously members of a political science study group that worked, conducted research, and studied our way through school. I had not known she was part of the team in Washington. Jay would not have known her at Oregon because he was in the school of education. "What are you doing here?" I asked as we embraced in the middle of the hallway. Again, I commented, "I had no idea you were here!" "I'm a teaching assistant in the political science department, as is my former roommate, Nicki Thomas. We arrived about two weeks ago right after graduation."

Malea went on to describe a meeting she had had with Professor James Klonoski, someone I knew from Oregon's political science department. He had been tapped as Assistant Provost at FCC. It just so happened that Klonoski was Malea's faculty advisor and, through him, she learned of the college and his appointment. He asked Malea and her roommate to consider coming as teaching assistants. They saw this as a unique opportunity and took him up on his offer. Malea then told me something that gave me pause. "The other reason I came, George, was because of you, the many arguments and discussions we used to have about commitment, getting involved, putting all of one's eggs in one basket." "When Professor Klonoski described what The Federal City was about, I saw it as my time to get involved. That's why I am here." "So, where are you staying? she asked. I replied that I would be temporarily bunking in with with Jay Jones and his family; that it would be a tight fit because he has three kids." "Nicki and I have this delightful old townhouse on Capitol Hill...it has three bedrooms, so come with us. Plus, it's walking distance to the school. I'll tell Nicki, you can move in tomorrow." Well, this was a stroke of good fortune because housing was at the top of my "to do" list. Malea was a good friend, someone I knew well and could trust. Ours was as she put it, a friendship forged over countless cups of coffee, shouting matches (some public), and a mutual desire to understand and support each other. We had succeeded and now we would share in a venture that would test both of us in ways we could not even imagine at this point.

Processing-in took little time and I wanted to complete my tour of the facility. As I walked outside and and looked at the area around the building, it was clear that this was designed to be a real urban educational experience. In front of our building, a block away, was the headquarters of the Metropolitan Police Department for the District. To the rear of the college were Union Station, Capitol Hill, three banks, and the headquarters for the Teamsters' Union. Under construction directly in front of the main building was an extension of Interstate-295 North (I-295). Parking was on the street; much of it diminished by construction and the construction crews that arrived earlier than anyone else. I was last in Washington back in 1962 right after separating from the Army. My purpose then was to visit with Jimmy Nance and Cassie, and check out a few job openings with the federal government. This time, I was back for the duration.

I followed Jay to his home later in the afternoon. Jay had found a large, affordable, three bedroom apartment out in Prince George's County, Maryland. During the drive home, I contemplated my future and my good fortune. FCC was history in the making and I would be part of it. I would live the dream of many young African-Americans of my generation: to create something that would uplift Blacks in this country and those who shared our goals for a better America. If this college was the outgrowth of an idea long overdue, then perhaps it could provide solutions to some of the ills that plagued America. My position in the admissions' office paid $10, 270 a year, almost twice my salary when I left the Foreign Service just two years earlier. Whittaker had told me how multifaceted the role of admissions' counselor was to be. Each of his counselors would be required to handle the multiple challenges of recruiting, advising and mentoring, and serving as a resource to community groups. Each of us would wear at least three hats. I would recruit in Washington's top three academic high schools and all of the high schools in predominantly white Montgomery County, a prosperous political jurisdiction north of the District in Maryland. FCC would also have a significant number of foreign students, primarily from Africa and the Caribbean. Given my Foreign Service background and experience as a discussion group leader at Oregon, Whittaker asked me to take on the added responsibility of Foreign Student Advisor.

I saw a natural connection between the birth of the Federal City College and its importance to the City of Washington and the Civil Rights Movement. By extension, my role was not only to recruit a new generation of African-American youth, but also a new generation of white Americans that saw the promise of America reflected in this new institution. Mine was to be an uphill battle because the obstacles between this new generation and me, were the parents – of all ethnicities – who with their intense philosophical convictions, opposed the very concept of this new college. The dream of white parents in particular was to see their sons and daughters graduate from one of the city's prestigious, established, private universities; not an untested, upstart college with a predominantly African-American, lower income, urban student body. Upper middle-class Blacks shared this aspiration. At a minimum, Howard University was an acceptable substitute. This generation of oppositionists apparently never knew, or had forgotten, that the Morrill Act of 1862 was passed to bring higher educational opportunity to that class of American the elite, eastern Ivy League schools did not accept during the early years of the American Republic.

I was ready to delve right into the new fall term, but after almost two weeks of living with Malea and Nicki, and the comfortable commute from Capitol Hill to the college, I had to find a place to live. A colleague, Jim Cardwell, offered to take me out to southeast Washington's Southern Avenue to look at the apartment complex where he lived. Just across the boundary line from there was Prince George's County. Prince George's County in 1968 was the less affluent political cousin to the more northern Montgomery County. I had seen an ad in the real estate section of the Washington Post about a possible vacancy at the Carriage Hill Apartments in Hillcrest Heights, a stone's throw from Southern Avenue just across the line in Prince George's County. Jim said it was a relatively new apartment complex and was worth checking out. It was only a few minutes drive from Jim's place.

The resident manager, a white female, demonstrated an amusing degree of curiosity about me, my background, educational level, how long I had been in the Metropolitan Area, and how long I intended to stay in Washington. She had not been hostile, but more aloof, more curious than interested in me as a prospective resident. As I completed the application and prepared to leave, the manager advised me to call the next day. I said I would. On the way out, Jim said, "George, you got an apartment!" "What makes you think so?" I asked. "She was impressed with your demeanor, your background...I can tell...trust me. In fact, George, don't call her. We will come out to see her tomorrow." The next afternoon, Jim and I drove out to Carriage Hill for my second meeting with the resident manager. I did like the complex and was hopeful that something would be available. The manager obviously saw us pull up because she approached us as we walked into her office. "Good afternoon! Mr. Kennedy. You should have called. It wasn't necessary to drive out here from downtown." "Welcome!" she said. "I hope you will enjoy it here with us. In fact, Mr. Kennedy, you are the second Negro to be accepted here at Carriage Hill." Her tone, body language, and an approving smile seemed somewhat self-congratulatory. I decided that it was not necessary to comment beyond expressing my appreciation at her having accepted my application.

I was thoroughly amused because the previous day, this same person said she thought "something might become available." Today, I was even offered my choice of two apartments, including an apartment in their pricier high-rise. I took possession of an affordable terrace apartment and moved in that night. Malea and Nikki gave me blankets and I slept on the floor. I was pleased to be settled with an address. I decided to look for furniture over the weekend.

The team at Federal City was strengthening daily, including our team in the admissions' office. There was a buzz, a pulse to the main campus, it was seductive, even exhilarating. And all of us were willing captives. We were building a new world of hope and promise; a world designed to develop, enrich, stimulate, and deepen African-American and white intellect, to extend student horizons into new and uncharted territory. When I was not in meetings that first week, I was preparing the presentation I would make to the guidance counselors and principals of the schools I would be visiting. Skeptics would be lined up to greet me and I knew it. I took a strategic approach by developing and mastering two, five, and fifteen-minute presentations. Prior experience with Dr. Pearl's program at the University of Oregon convinced me that if I could capture a counselor's attention in two-minutes, I could further their interest in five-minutes, and possibly convince them to schedule a meeting with junior and senior-level students.

Before taking my show on the road, I did a few dry runs with Whittaker. Whittaker knew the local school systems and the intellectual rigidity each of his three counselors would confront. He put me in the "lion's den," as he labelled it, because Jay Jones told him I was the man for the job. I had finished one of my fifteen-minute presentations when Whittaker said he liked my approach and suggested that "I was going to have some fun out there." His mischievous smile and that twinkle in his eye reassured me. A critical piece of my life was now under control. I felt I had a grip on what Whittaker expected of me as one of his recruiters. He had validated my approach, and now it was time to "battle test" it. My new role was going to consume all of my time, at least for the first month, and there was one thing I had to do beforehand: reestablish contact with friends of long-standing and let them know I was now in Washington. Elsie, of course, would always know, and she did. My time was going to be severely constrained; even good friends would not see very much of me. Jim Nance was only a block away from where I was at 425 2nd Street, so I walked over to see him. There had been that hurried phone call shortly after my arrival; now we would have more time to talk, and I could fill in the blanks for him. Chet and Claudia Carter were still in New York City in connection with his responsibilities as Vice President for Overseas Sales at Seagram's Corporation. I called Chet only to learn that they were negotiating a new business venture that would shortly bring them back to Washington. I shared with him some of the changes in my own life and that I would supply more detail in a letter. Chet and Jim were important to me and now those bases were covered.

The fall semester of 1968 opened later that September than projected, but that did not diminish the enthusiasm of the entering students. There actually were more students showing up for classes than there were places for them. Classes were overcrowded, but no one raised a voice in protest. That, alone, set them apart from most entering freshmen classes I was aware of. The students at Federal City College did not fit the typical profile of an 18-year old high school graduate seeking an education to obtain employment, or to build a career. The average freshman at FCC that year was 28 to 30 years of age, married with a family, an ex-veteran if a male, and with at least 10-years of work experience. Their educational objective was not to qualify for a job, but to earn a degree to strengthen their promotion potential. That distinguished our students from the average entering class of freshmen at any college or university in the country. Our students that year had jobs. Most of them were federal or city employees who were being denied promotions ostensibly because they did not have college degrees. Their supervisors were generally white, southern, and living in Virginia.

This was the 1960s and many federal agencies were modeled after 19th Century plantations in the south. Blacks were concentrated in the lower grades: GS-1 through GS-10. Whites occupied the majority of the positions from GS-11 through GS-18. All of the professional studies conducted to determine the demand for higher education among Washington's lower-to-middle income residents revealed one startling fact: demand was off the charts, beyond national norms. Prospective students from the Greater Washington Metropolitan Area inclined to seek student status at a Land Grant College in the District of Columbia would pursue a degree to improve their prospects for career advancement. They wanted to break through the glass ceilings that confined them to the lower ranks of the career Civil Service system. Their motivation was the stability, the flexibility, the life choices higher income and greater professional status would confer. This was a different set of goals from that of your typical entering college freshman. As an entering class, they were more mature, secure in their identities, focused and, above all, hungry for knowledge. As one student told me, "I am here for a reason, not for the season."

Again, I was the third member of a team of three recruiters. Barbara and Phyllis, the other two members of our team, were native to the area; products of the local school system, and I drew heavily on tips, guidance, and other insights they could offer. I was the new kid and I did not want to make any more mistakes than I had to. I read voraciously, studied maps of the city and of Montgomery County. I worked the phones to the guidance counselors at each of my schools. Early that fall, I arranged initial visits to Wilson, Western, and Roosevelt High Schools in Washington. I followed up those visits with a visit to all of the high schools in Montgomery County, Maryland. My approach was honest and straightforward. In all of my discussions with interested and prospective students and guidance counselors, and with those parents I would meet with in the evenings, I consistently advanced several themes. Those themes were: first, that The Federal City College, although the newest Land Grant institution in the nation, accepted its unique mission, and as a public institution, it was committed to offering its students an educational experience designed to meet the needs of a modern, urban society. Second, that The Federal City College would ultimately offer the rich and comprehensive curriculum at the undergraduate and graduate-level typical of any institution of its type. And, third, those students from the Greater Washington Metropolitan Area would benefit from the diversity of experience and outlook FCC's students and faculty offered.

By November, I noticed a slight shift in some students' attitudes regarding the quality of education being offered at FCC. Early in the semester, as expected, parents, guidance counselors, teachers, and students reacted almost as if speaking from a script..."The Federal City College does not meet the academic standard of the schools in the city's consortium of universities." Where did that come from? In small groups, often in the hallway of the school I was visiting that day, without school administrators present, students approached me and told me they were excited about the concept of The Federal City College. They said they would welcome a chance to meet with some of the faculty and students, to visit the campus, but their parents would never permit it. Several students revealed that their parents were adamantly opposed to a Land Grant college with a predominantly African-American student body, but that they could accept Howard University and its sister institutions because they were in a different category. One student, I recall, said, "Mr. Kennedy, my parents, and many of the parents here, are racist...that if FCC were largely white, they would be supportive of it, primarily because it is new and innovative." Other students standing within earshot of this conversation nodded in agreement. When I shared my observation about this shift in attitude with my colleagues in the admissions office, they told me they, too, had noticed the same thing. We concluded, and rightly so, that we were reaching the students, those who were ideologically and philosophically less rigid than their parents and friends.

Undaunted by the active resistance the students told me I would encounter, my colleagues and I strove to maximize the impact of each visit to an area high school. Ours' was a mission to lay the foundation for a new concept in higher education and success, therefore, could not be defined or measured in quantifiable terms e.g., the number of graduating seniors from my target high schools matriculating to his new college. This was going to take time. On an intellectual level, I thrived on the exchange of ideas I came to expect. What I looked for was gradual reduction in resistance at the "knee-jerk" level, to the point that an honest exchange of views was possible. The initial goal of recruiting prospective students became one of altering mindsets. The Federal City College was going to be a permanent feature on Washington's landscape, so why not try to build tomorrow's base of support? At the end of each day, I was fueled by my commitment to the philosophy of FCC, a deep desire to affirm the good we sought to do, and confidence in my ability to present the best case for our college, its faculty, the students, and the academic program. The Provost, Dr. Klonoski, lived in Montgomery County and would, on occasion, sit in on my presentations. Through him, Jack Whittaker became more aware of the reputation I had developed as a representative of the college. The other two recruiters were more successful in their recruiting efforts because predominantly African-Americans populated their schools. Some of their parents had fewer options, unless their child received a scholarship from an out-of-state institution

The role of Foreign Student Advisor was less challenging, but important nonetheless. Most of the early foreign students were from Nigeria and less affluent than their countrymen attending Howard University and other schools in Washington. For the foreign student attracted to The Federal City College, the school meant the prospect of full time student status rather than driving a taxicab to support the costs of part-time status at one of the District's more expensive, private universities. The African students, as a group, were easy to work with. In this role, I drew heavily on my experiences with the African diplomatic community in Bonn five years earlier. Several of the Nigerian students had heard of Paul Bamela Engo and were impressed that I, an American, knew him as a friend. That revelation led to many interesting conversations about Nigerian politics and the contrast between early African independence movements and the demands for social change in our country at that time.

Each member of the professional staff at FCC was expected to contribute time to local community groups that were affiliated with the college through the Community Education Division and its extension programs. Most days were 15 to 18 hours at a stretch, but that was the level of commitment expected of us. That was the norm. Moreover, I had to find time for a young men's club that sought me out as its advisor. Life for me was full, rich, and all-too-often, exhausting. The downside was little time for a personal life, and no time to nurture the girlfriend back in Oregon. We remained in touch throughout the fall of 1968, but I could tell from the tone of her letters and our weekly conversations that the physical separation and the constant pressure from her parents to sever our relationship, was weakening her resolve. She told me she was just tired and wanted a more normal life. I could no more terminate my current responsibilities than she could leave Oregon and come to Washington. That was the reality neither of us could ignore. In our last conversation in early December, I knew it was over. The night, I was standing in my kitchen with this hollow feeling in the pit of my stomach. The last time I felt that kind of anguish was when Solange left the Philippines.

To fill the void, I drove home to Camden, New Jersey to spend time with family and friends. Christmas at home was the perfect balm for what I was feeling. The smells, sights, and sounds were reminiscent of many Christmases past when the promise of going to grandmom's for the holidays would inspire my siblings and me to angelic-levels of behavior for weeks on end. Several of my high school classmates were still in the area and we caught up on developments since graduating ten years earlier. Christmas that year was not noteworthy in any respect; I was just grateful for life, the richness of it, new opportunities, new friends, old friends, and family. I returned to Washington right after the New Year.

In mid-January, I invited a friend to the movies. She was a young lady I had met through one of my colleagues: brown-skinned, very attractive, and pleasant to be with. My intentions were so honorable, I told her of my girlfriend (before the breakup) in Oregon. We would talk casually, but we did not spend much time together. I did not have much time. On that particular evening, she was surprised I asked her if she wanted to go out with me. En-route to the movies, she and I were sitting at a red light at Constitution Avenue, N.W. behind a Volkswagen, having just emerged from the 12th Street Tunnel. In an instant, everything changed. Apparently, a drunk driver in a borrowed vehicle, had passed out at the wheel while traveling in excess of 90 miles per hour coming through the tunnel. He hit us and two other cars from the rear. The forward impact propelled my car into the car in front of me. I recall a violent crash and a thunderous noise. The front seat of my car lifted up from its tracks and jerked backward before it crashed to the floor. We were both quite shaken, but able to exit the car. Five vehicles had sustained major damage, including my own. The two impact vehicles had fused together. I looked at my beautiful 1964 Chevrolet Impala, 4-door sedan. That car was my pride and joy. We had survived Oregon together, and it carried me across the United States. The front end was crumpled, as was the trunk.

Slightly dazed, I told my friend to sit in the backseat while I went to survey the accident and to assist anyone that I could. The police arrived in short order, as did several emergency medical vehicles. My friend and I were transported via police cruiser to a hospital on Capitol Hill, even though Georgetown Medical Center was more convenient. The interesting thing about the ride was the police driver kept trying to persuade the two of us to contact a lawyer and an orthopedist he knew. He even produced business cards for them. Although we were in some pain, I do recall wondering if this particular officer stretched some ethical boundaries. He was actually "shilling" for business. At the hospital, we were treated as outpatients and subsequently taken to a police sub-station to file a report. I also had to retrieve my car that had been towed there by the police. To my surprise, I was able to drive it home. Fortunately, neither of us had sustained major injury. I did, however, sustain back injuries that were sufficient to confine me at home for the next three months. My routine consisted of daily visits to an orthopedist referred by my colleague, Jim Cardwell; prescription painkillers, bed rest, and moderate exercise. Mother came down to nurse me back to health. Initially, Whittaker was supportive and told me to go home because I did go to work the next day, injuries notwithstanding. My date that memorable evening recovered more quickly than I did. In one of our subsequent conversations following the accident, she said, "what a memorable date, George. Maybe the next time, we should stay at home." We both laughed, but I did feel terrible about what had happened. There never was a second date, nor did we get to see that movie.

One of the benefits we enjoyed as professional staff at the college was unlimited sick leave. Therefore, I was unconcerned about being confined temporarily at home. As weeks spent convalescing became months, Whittaker's attitude changed. When I was able to return to the office that spring on a part-time basis, my colleagues told me Whittaker had been trying to have me replaced. This news came as a surprise because Whittaker and I spoke at least weekly and never during any of our conversations did he intimate that my absence had become untenable for him. I put in even longer hours to compensate for my forced absence and to rebuild my relationship with Whittaker. Although we continued to work together, the easy rapport and friendship we once enjoyed was never the same again. If Whittaker wanted a change, then it was incumbent upon me to explore my options.

My work with community groups brought me into frequent contact with Dr. James Williams and Professor Alan Trawick, respectively, the Dean and Associate Dean of the school's Community Education Division. Dr. Trawick was in heavy demand as a speaker and I would accompany him to many of his engagements. Alan had been a student activist in the early 60s and I knew I could learn from him. Working with Alan Trawick during the '68 – '69 academic year broadened my knowledge of Washington from the ground up. Moreover, I was able to extend my range of contacts with local educators, community activists, and an emerging generation of African-American politicians, including those destined to become first generation African-American mayors and members of Congress. I kept Whittaker informed of my activities, but as my community and political involvements became more extensive, the rhythm of our relationship, already strained, changed even more. The easy camaraderie was gone. Our meetings were more structured, and Jim Cardwell, now his deputy, became the third party. They were not overtly hostile, but I sensed an estrangement. Something other than my recent extended absence was going on and I was groping to understand what it was. My two colleagues in the admissions office provided the context I needed. Between the access I had to key members of the school's administration, who were fellow Oregonians, and my outreach activities through Dr. Trawick, I was managing a volume of information and important relationships greater than Jack Whittaker. Whittaker, the old Army officer, was accustomed to a more hierarchical flow of information from the top down. Emotionally, he was still tethered to the structured universe of the military culture that had shaped him. To Whittaker, we were his troops and our growth and access he felt should evolve through him. I respected Whittaker, but this behavior was a stark reminder of why I separated from the Army. Whittaker did not see that his instincts to control us was in contradistinction to his earlier advice to provide community service and to become a part of the larger community we served. I was motivated to grow into an expanding universe of relationships, opportunities and knowledge. That simple approach had been drummed into my head since childhood. Shoehorning myself into the "tent" that was Whittaker's comfort zone ran contrary to my instincts. I was now sitting on the horns of a dilemma. Artificially limiting my personal and professional growth to accommodate Whittaker's ego was a non-choice. Therefore, if I wished to remain with the college, it would have to be in another capacity. I shared my concerns privately with Dr. Klonoski, the new Provost; Dr. Cortada, the new Assistant Provost, and Alan Trawick.

In September 1969, Dr. Trawick invited me to lunch. He said, "George, I can use someone like you in my outreach program...maybe you and Whittaker have reached an accommodation, but would you consider leaving the admissions' office? Whittaker may not want to lose you, but here is what I need." Dr. Trawick was known for his straightforward manner and here it was. He continued, "The U.S. Department of Education is prepared to fund several projects I am bidding on, but I do not have anyone to develop the proposals I need. One project is worth $55,000, the other $500,000. I need one proposal within two weeks, the other within six months. The position I have pays $15,000 annually." I think my salary at the beginning of the second year was $11,800 and now I was being offered $15,000. While I enjoyed the freedom I had in the admissions' office to set my daily agenda, Alan Trawick was offering a major bump in salary and a window of opportunity that would serve me and the college well. Moreover, he was offering an opportunity to gain a level of experience more germane to the requirements of the doctoral degree I still planned to pursue back at the University of Oregon. My relationship with Whittaker had deteriorated to the extent he was prepared to divide my responsibilities between my two colleagues. Neither of them was happy about the prospect of my leaving, but both encouraged me to do so. And so I did.

I settled into the Community Education Division on the second floor of the main campus building literally overnight. Another plus these new responsibilities offered was daily contact with the school's president, his cabinet, and members of the faculty. Alan Trawick was a key faculty advisor to President Harland Randolph, and Dr. Trawick valued my knowledge of suburban attitudes, my political instincts, a quick pen, and my ability to build rapport with community organizations. Before long, I, too, was a member of the small group of trusted aides President Randolph often consulted during routine meetings he held. The topics for discussion at these meetings included relations with specific Members of Congress whose support for, or antipathy toward, the school was important, and, pending congressional legislation that was potentially harmful to the school's long-term interests. Randolph spoke of problematic faculty members, budget priorities, and requests from actual and aspiring African-American politicians for FCC to serve as host for their training seminars and strategy sessions for upcoming mayoral and congressional campaigns. Also on the president's agenda were student demands and the issue of relations with the local police during a period of increasing student unrest in Washington.

As a member of the "kitchen cabinet" and crisis management team, my political education moved to the graduate level. Crafting solutions to the kinds of problems FCC's president grappled with often defined the length of a college or university president's tenure at that time in our history. The casualty rate among college and university administrators was high and growing. I now understood why. Within our group, we were determined that President Randolph not become the political casualty his predecessor became.

The District of Columbia, as a federal district, was unique because its affairs – even those of The Federal City College – were either administered by the House (of Representatives) District Committee, or held hostage by that same committee because of its chairman's influence over the District's budget. All previous land grant colleges were granted land when land was largely underutilized, except by local Indian tribes. The Morrill Act of 1862 established Land Grant colleges in an era when the national priority was to populate the country, particularly west of Missouri, and to develop the nation's agricultural base. The Federal City College, the first Land Grant College to be established in more than 50-years, did not receive a grant of land. Land for that purpose did not exist in the District of Columbia. In lieu of a grant of land, The Federal City College was offered a seven-million-dollar permanent endowment. The Chairman of the House District Committee often threatened that endowment when he did not approve of academic policies or programs the school sought to develop. Quite often, the Chairman was reacting to complaints from suburban residents, or to pressures from Washington's Consortium of Universities. After all, the FCC student body had vowed to make the school one of the premier institutions in the country, whose student body just happened to be African-American. The school, according to studies I had seen, had the potential to grow to 50,000 students, a student population larger than all of the colleges and universities in the city. The level of intellectual and physical threat FCC was perceived to pose was real to its detractors, and the Chairman of the House District Committee shared the fears of many whites in the area and those African-Americans who did not want Howard University's status overshadowed as the premier African-American, higher educational institution in America.

Harland Randolph shared with us the gist of a conversation he had with the Chairman of the House District Committee. He told Randolph that The Federal City College, if allowed to develop to its full potential, had the capacity to graduate 2,000 undergraduates four times a year. Since most of them were already in the federal workforce, that would upset the employment balance in the city and he could not allow that. Moreover, he said he had heard that Randolph's students had vowed to put a team in the Rose Bowl within five years and America was not prepared to accept an "all-Black" team at that level of college sports. He went on to say, according to Randolph, that this was the political reality of the college, but that he would deny ever having made those comments should they become public. President Randolph knew that the Chairman, himself from South Carolina, was in a position to act on this level of threat. He often did. He and his bigoted politics threatened the very future of the college; therefore, he had to be removed from office. We had a plan.

To many African-Americans, The Federal City College captured the spirit of Black political aspirations in 1968, and beyond. Some of the faculty and most students at the college understood the struggle being waged in America for political and social equality. Acting in concert, they naturally reached out to a rising generation of African-American politicians: Kenneth Gibson running to become the first African-American mayor of Newark, New Jersey; John Conyers, then a junior representative from Detroit; Fannie Lou Hamer of the Mississippi Freedom Party, and Gus Savage, vying for a House seat from Chicago. They were but a few of a new generation of Black leaders with whom we established rapport.

President Randolph, a man of commanding presence and towering strength, embodied a generation of leadership with the political will to forge links between The Federal City College and this new breed of African-American political leadership in America's urban centers, on Capitol Hill, and in the country's institutions of higher learning. "There has to be an intellectual and a programmatic tie between academic institutions and the communities that hosted them," he was fond of saying. His team understood his philosophy and Randolph became the vanguard for this new breed of Black urban college administrator. At least once a month, Randolph and our group would host strategy and planning meetings at FCC with African-Americans who were striving to salvage communities, local economies, and the lives of African-Americans, from the ashes of cities devastated by riots, a history of police misconduct, and corrupt white politicians. Had the Chairman of the House District Committee known of these meetings, he most assuredly would have moved aggressively against President Randolph's administration. To thwart clandestine attempts to monitor our discussions, we would often hold meetings in a conference room that had running water. The sound of running water would not suffice today given the sophisticated technologies available. This was the late 1960's. We could only take those precautions available to us and that did not involve major expense. We were not paranoid, just prudent.

We, the professional staff, encouraged FCC's students to avoid acting out their frustrations in the streets. I mention this because we, too, had our contingent of hotheads and rabble rousers whose only purpose was to agitate, confront, and make a name for themselves. Rather, we espoused learning the political process and acquiring skills as community organizers. We exhorted the students, especially their leaders, to work within the system to improve it. In other words, lead by example; take the long view, to survive and prosper, not be shot in the streets and forgotten. Kenneth Gibson's successful campaign to become Newark's first African-American mayor is due, in part, to student volunteers from The Federal City College, including those from my club, who cut their teeth on his hard fought campaign against Carmine Buzzardi, the gatekeeper to Newark's City Hall. Before allowing our students to travel to Newark, we held training seminars in which we told them how to work with designated community leaders in get-out-the-vote activities; how to position themselves when handing out flyers, how to cover each other when on the streets to avoid becoming casualties, and how to blend into the community to avoid being identified as "outsiders."

When the South Carolina Democrat, who was the Chairman of the House District Committee, and the self-declared Mayor of the District of Columbia, lost his bid to be re-elected, he could have extended his gratitude in part to the students from The Federal City College majoring in Political Science, Government, and Community Education who traveled to his congressional district to help African-Americans there organize a massive get-out-the-vote drive. Congressman John MacSweeney personified a generation of southern politician who believed in legal, second-class citizenship for African-Americans. Slavery was no longer possible, so second-class citizenship would suffice for his purposes. The rallying cry for his political opponents during his last campaign for re-election was "Johnny Mac ain't going back." When the election results were tabulated during that election, "Johnny Mac" did not go back. Our students were learning how to make the political process work to further their goals without running the risk of incarceration or becoming another statistic.

The first of two proposals I was tasked to complete for Dr. Trawick met the deadline and was funded the full $55,000. The funds we received allowed the Community Education Division to establish a program to teach community leaders, many of them single, female heads of households, how to secure federal funding for community-based projects important to the health of their neighborhoods. This was our biblical equivalent of "teaching a community to fish." This modest grant was important in our effort to establish a foundation within local communities for the concept of "self help." I should note that the community members we worked with in the evenings did not want welfare; they wanted to avail themselves of resources the federal government offered to individuals and community organizations interested in launching micro-enterprises e.g., small businesses, day-care centers, and training centers. The constant refrain from those community members we worked with during evening hours was "we want to do the work; you explain the process and provide the technical expertise...show us how to write the proposals." Proposal writing, by the way, involves special skills and these women wanted to learn. They were a joy to work with because they did perform the due diligence; they did write the proposals, and they did secure funding for the projects they conceived. Although I was exhausted by the time I arrived home on those nights, my exhaustion was tempered by an even greater feeling of personal satisfaction.

The extended deadline for the second proposal seeking $500,000 dollars offered a little more breathing space. I had a novel idea and the time was ripe to broach it with Dr. Trawick. Alan Trawick thrived on ideas and I knew the odds were in my favor. Here was my idea: Manpower utilization and development on the American frontier in the

19th Century was a simple proposition: farming and ranching. In 20th Century urban America, manpower planning, development, and training was haphazard at best. Unemployment among African-Americans, when factored out of national averages, was dangerously high, often double national rates of unemployment. This was an underlying cause for civil unrest in those cities devastated by riots. The country needed a plan and the U.S. Department of Labor was not exactly pioneering in this area. I saw a need to develop a graduate-level program in *"Manpower Research and Development."* The professionals it would produce would have the theoretical, analytical, and practical skills to assess the medium-to-long term manpower needs of America's economy, serve as advisors to Labor, to federal, state, and local governments concerned about skills' development with the American labor pool; and develop curricula at the college level to train future generations of labor leaders, labor economists, and manpower specialists.

Armed with an executive summary, I scheduled a meeting with Dr. Trawick during the winter term of 1970. If Alan signed on, Dr. James Williams, the Dean of Community Education, would support it because the programs under the direction of Alan Trawick were the heart of his entire program at FCC. Alan Trawick's office could easily have been mistaken for Grand Central Station West because it was west of the city's Union Station, and on most days, it was more congested with students and community activists than could have been accommodated at Union Station. I asked Julia, his secretary, to shut the door for two hours to give me time to make my pitch. Julia also disconnected the telephone on his desk. She was happy to accommodate me just to have some quiet time to work on the backlog on her desk that Alan rummaged through on a daily basis.

As I walked in, I got right to the point because I needed him to focus. "Alan, I need your undivided attention," I began. Over the next 30 - 45 minutes, I presented my idea. I walked him through the "What," the "When," the "Why," the "How," and the "Who." To complete my presentation, I added budget projections and political considerations. I took a deep breath and let it sink in while waiting for his reaction. It came. "Damn, George, this is brilliant" Alan declared. I don't know that I expected that, but it was a great beginning. Alan then talked about the natural link between extension programs he was developing at satellite centers around the city, and a first-of-its-kind degree program at the Lorton Prison Complex in neighboring Lorton, Virginia. Finally, he asked, "George, what do you need me to do?" In response, I said, "I need you to obtain approval from Dean Williams and approval from the faculty's academic program's committee." "James Williams, you can handle, George." "He and I, with support from the new Provost, Dr. Rafael Cortada, will present it to the faculty." As I prepared to go, I said, "Alan, I will need one more thing – a student research assistant." "You will have one within a week," he assured me. I was also given a new office, just around the corner from the Provost's Office and a dozen steps from Dr. Randolph's suite of offices. I met Dr. Cortada early in my tenure at the college. Ralph had prior experience as a desk officer at the U.S. State Department, and that gave us a lot to talk about. I also shared with him my interest in resuming a Foreign Service career. The question of timing was always complex because of my commitment to the college – stronger now than a year earlier.

On the way back to my office following my meeting with Alan, I was thinking, the easy part was done; now I had to build out the program. From prior research, I knew the University of Iowa at Ames, Iowa offered the only degree program anywhere in the country that remotely resembled the program I envisioned. I contacted the director of Iowa's program, described my project proposal, and asked if I could visit to meet with the program faculty and a current class of students. On a cold and snowy day in February 1970, I arrived in Ames, Iowa. The program director, teaching faculty, and the students provided a warm and gracious welcome. This new institution in Washington that I represented intrigued them, and it became an amusing struggle for me to keep them focused on the purpose of my visit. I was also a rare African-American presence on a campus overwhelmingly white and mid-western. To my surprise, the program there was not nearly as comprehensive as I had envisioned, but I came away with ideas about course offerings, degree structure, and funding options.

At the end of my first six months in the Community Education Division, I had met the two deadlines Dr. Trawick was required to meet. The first project had been funded, and I had completed a detailed plan for my proposed degree program for the larger fund request. A late-night, congratulatory phone call from a friend on the faculty, also an intimate of Alan Dr. Trawick, alerted me to a conversation she had several days earlier with Alan. In that conversation, he told her the Department of Labor was willing to fund the proposed degree program for $500,000, pending timely submission of information they required. I approached Alan the next day, but I was also wondering why he had not shared the news with me. I learned very quickly. The project was now in the hands of the chair of the faculty's academic programs committee.

This had been a challenging project of its own accord, however the greater challenge became the struggle to maintain the integrity of the concept: a stand-alone, graduate program. Had I been as familiar with the internecine politics of academia, I would have anticipated this next phase of the process. I was still the idealist, and I trusted Alan. Here is the context for what ensued. Since my project could receive a substantial infusion of funds, Alan sought to subsume my new graduate-level program under the aegis of a novel prison education project he was developing, thus providing greater visibility for his pet project. I argued that logic dictated a reverse order: his new baccalaureate program could function as a natural bridge to a graduate program offering his students an intellectual opportunity to build on their urban backgrounds. To my surprise, Alan was unmoved. My thesis was really simple: had my proposed program become an adjunct to his prison education program, it is very unlikely the Department of Education would have released the funds. Furthermore, there could very well be blowback from the Chairman of the House District Committee. I billed the Manpower Program as a stand-alone, graduate-level program with its own entrance criteria; criteria consistent with other graduate programs offered by the college. The only response Alan could muster was, "George, all I hear you saying is no." We had exhausted the limits of that meeting and we agreed to continue talking. I now had a major problem on my hands, one I could not have anticipated.

I continued to develop the program, and Alan and I continued our dialogue to identify common ground. The more we talked, the less ground he was willing to concede. Here you had the classic face off of the 1960s between the purists and idealists, and the political opportunists. Both of us had vested interests in the outcome of the debate. Alan needed the credibility my project conferred and the assurance of financing. He also had the upper hand as a member of the faculty, and he had begun to line up support for his position. A conflict was developing, one I assiduously sought to avoid, especially after the dust up with Whittaker in the Admissions' Office. This time, however, there was too much at stake. Although Dean Williams had initially approved the project in concept, his support was now more tentative, nothing specific, nothing material. I decided to continue my work on the project, but to secure all of my materials at night, including the annotated copy from the faculty's academic programs committee. That particular copy had been returned to me with comments and further required action. That copy was valuable and the key to any future progress for this program within the college. I could only conclude that Alan felt that a $500,000 funding commitment was too attractive to pass up, and that he would stop at nothing to gain access to it for his purposes. I also knew that Alan had staked his reputation on the prison education project he was developing.

I now had the ideal moment to take stock of my situation because, ultimately, I was going to have to make a decision about the direction of my future. It was the spring of 1970 and I was settled into a career earning a princely salary of $15,000 a year. I was also conflicted about giving up everything for graduate student status back at the University of Oregon. A former teaching assistant in the political science department back at Oregon had completed his doctorate and was earning just under $10,000 teaching at a college in Southern California. Resigning to resume work on a doctorate while losing several years of income and professional growth was not an option I could seriously entertain. Among the qualities Dr. Trawick, the College Provost, and President Randolph valued in me was that I planned. I was the consummate planner. Late in 1969, I had discussed the possibility of such a personal conflict with each of these men and, collectively, they helped me to formulate career options.

Another member of the President's advisory group, and a personal friend of Dr. Cortada, Dr. Mohammad El Khawas, counseled me to consider graduate school at Washington's prestigious Johns Hopkins School of Advanced International Studies (SAIS). El Khawas was a SAIS graduate and he offered to arrange an interview for me. SAIS administrators in 1970 were looking for good minority candidates. Concomitantly, Dr. Trawick and President Randolph knew John Richardson, director of a special program at Princeton University, who was in the midst of a nationwide search for candidates for the newly-created Martin Luther King, Jr. Fellows Program. Ultimately, there would be a total of 35 Fellows, and Drs. Cortada and El Khawas offered to support my candidacy. At the behest of Dr. Trawick and President Randolph, John Richardson agreed to interview me as a prospective candidate during one of his trips to Washington. Johns Hopkins, meanwhile, had committed itself to increasing the number of African-American students through a grant from the Rockefeller Foundation in New York.

I was an attractive candidate to both Johns Hopkins and to the King Fellows' Program. Both interviews went well, but it was spring 1970 and I needed to know if I was to be a recipient of the financial support each program offered to its successful candidates. I really did not want to return to Oregon, at least not yet. My prospects through FCC were bright and improving. I also had another idea, something I could only discuss with Chet, who was now back in Washington. That was the White House Fellows' Program. Chet thought it was a good idea, but advised me to talk to his old boss, the former chief of protocol at the State Department, James W. Symington. Jim Symington was the son of former United States Senator, Stuart Symington, himself the first

Secretary of the U.S. Air Force when it became an independent branch of the U.S. Military. Chet told me that Jim was closer to the White House Fellows' Program than he was, and that he would arrange an appointment for me to meet with him. Thus began a friendship with Jim Symington that endured for decades. From our very first meeting, I found Jim to be a warm, compassionate man with an infectious laugh and a great capacity to listen and to be helpful. He was not cut from that Washington political cloth most politicians wear: Let me get back to you, while looking over your shoulder to see who else might have entered the room. Jim makes things happen and he will candidly admit when he cannot. He traced his lineage to major figures in American history and can regale you with interesting anecdotes passed through his family about historical events in the founding of this country.

Jim Symington offered to contact the White House Fellows' Program for me to obtain the application forms. I had the forms in hand within two weeks, but as I reviewed them, I concluded quickly that I had two principal hurdles. One was a deal breaker. I was now one month shy of my 30th birthday, which was the age cutoff. Secondly, I would have been a stronger candidate had I already earned a graduate degree, or been a professional Foreign Service officer. I had great experience, but I did not feel confident enough to apply. Moreover, Republicans controlled the White House and I did not know any Republicans. Jim Symington brought this little fact to my attention. I recall spending a great deal of time with that application, and in the end, decided against submitting it. I freely admit I may have been guilty of faulty judgment, but I wanted to be a stronger candidate than I felt I was. In May of that year, I did qualify for the King Fellows' Program, and learned that I would be among the entering class of Johns Hopkins SAIS in the fall. These developments, taken together, meant that I had an alternative to returning to Oregon, and whatever opportunity I may have missed through the long shot of the White House Fellows' Program. Life was good and seemed to be getting better all the time.

Fall 1970 rolled around quickly. I had spent much of the summer on extracurricular reading that Dr. El Khawas had recommended in preparation for the rigor Johns Hopkins was know to impose. Thirteen African-Americans entered SAIS that fall, the largest group of African-Americans in the school's history. All, with one exception, were graduates of Ivy League schools and schools from the Big-10 and PAC-8 Conferences. One of the members of our group, an African-American female, was a recent graduate of Howard University. Several among us were older and already established professionally. The size of our class of African-Americans was a function of the school's success in securing a significant grant from the Rockefeller Foundation in New York City. SAIS had been willing to admit more African-Americans, but was unprepared to offer them financial support from the school's general scholarship fund. What is so ironic is that the average recipient of a general scholarship grant at that time was not in financial need. As we later learned, our group was an experiment with a built-in failure rate. The Dean of Students at SAIS assumed a 15 – 20 percent dropout rate, consistent with a national norm, thus freeing those funds to be reprogrammed for the class entering the fall of 1971. At our first meeting of the African-American students, our commitment to ourselves and to each other was a vow not to drop out. For us, there would be no attrition rate. Our commitment then became an enigma for a school administration that did not quite know what to make of us. We challenged professors' stereotyped views in several areas, one of which was African politics, sociology, and economic development. Most of us were proficient in a foreign language, a significant hurdle for SAIS students at that time. Proficiency in a foreign language was *de rigueur* to graduate. My prior knowledge of German and Italian would eventually satisfy this requirement. I chose to take my proficiency test in German.

Our intrepid test group thrived at SAIS. Courses and examinations were, to an extent, unstructured and research-focused. We understood the course requirements, practically lived in the school's library and were determined to succeed. Washington is a resource-rich environment, the Garden of Eden for the city's graduate student community. It is also home to several of the nation's premier think tanks and prominent members of previous administrations – both Democrat and Republican; dozens of non-governmental organizations (NGOs), national associations of every conceivable sector of business and professional activity, and the three branches of government. And then, there was the international corps of diplomats representing most of the countries on the face of the planet – with few exceptions. I was still a career employee at The Federal City College while attending SAIS full-time. I had a plan and, thus far, it was working.

In 1970, the year of my 30th birthday, I was convinced I had the Midas touch. The job at FCC was progressing reasonably well; I was a full-time student at SAIS; my wardrobe showed signs of prosperity; my savings increased, and like all of my professional colleagues, I was examining options, trying to assess my competitiveness whenever an attractive position opening crossed my desk. Moreover, I was now "plugged-in" politically, even entertaining the idea of running for the U.S. Congress from my hometown in Woodbury, New Jersey, the place

192

of my birth. Vincent Cream, my life-long friend planted that seed. On the downside, however, I was still inclined to trust those I admired, those I respected. It was this trait that opened the door for my departure from The Federal City College.

I was unaware of it at the time, but a power struggle for the leadership of the Community Education Division was unfolding and Dr. Williams was fighting to avoid dismissal. There had been allegations of misconduct involving Dr. Williams and one of his male student assistants. To wit, I looked up one day to see Alan in my doorway wearing one of his classical "I-need-to-talk-to-you-privately" expressions. "Sit down, Alan," I said. "What's up?" He said, "George, I want you to talk to one of the students, privately...he works for James Williams. Ask him if he is still comfortable working with James, and confirm that there has been nothing out of the ordinary." He went on to say, "if I call him in, it might alarm him, given my role here." A large red flag should have gone up in my mind immediately, but it did not. I still trusted Alan. More importantly, I respected him, our intellectual and programmatic differences notwithstanding. I owed him. He rescued me from the admissions' office. Innocently, I said, "sure, who is the student? And, how do I contact him?"

That afternoon, I contacted the student, called him in and had a brief conversation with him. I had seen him on campus before and he recalled our having met on an earlier occasion. We must have talked for about 10-minutes and he assured me nothing had happened out of the ordinary, and that he enjoyed his internship in Dr. Williams's office. I dutifully reported this to Alan and promptly forgot the meeting. Several days later, I learned the rest of the story. In a desperate ploy to save himself, James Williams told Dr. Randolph that the student had told him about his discussion with me, that were he, Randolph, to dismiss him, he would go public with an audio tape of my conversation with this particular student, during which I am alleged to have accused him of unprofessional, sexual conduct. "I have it on tape, Harland; I have it on tape," James Williams told Harland.

Harland convened a meeting with Alan and me, and when he shared all of this with us, I literally came out of my chair. "Are you serious, Harland?" I asked. I completely forgot that his title was Dr. Randolph. "I made no such accusation," I said. "I want to hear the tape!" As I recovered from my initial shock at hearing this, it dawned on me why Alan had tapped me for this delicate mission. For all of my political sophistication, this was new territory for me, and Alan suspected that was the case. Throughout that meeting, Alan did not face me squarely and I wanted to call him out on having set me up. "George, don't worry," Harland said. "This is a standard ploy under circumstances like this." "Someone says they have something on tape to avoid termination or sanction, particularly in these situations." That begged a question regarding James's sexual preferences, but I chose discretion and hoped that someone would enlighten me. Both Harland and Alan explained that this was a delaying tactic that had to play itself out. Again, I was outraged to have been set up by someone I trusted. I could only assume that my future relationship with both Alan and James would now be tainted by this incident.

Throughout the fall of 1970 into January of 1971, this drama with James Willians and Alan Trawick unfolded in many acts and thus effectively paralyzed the leadership of the School of Community Education, and those of us responsible for program management and direction. First, it was Jack Whittaker; now Alan Trawick and James Williams. I knew I would survive, but the schools, its programs, and ultimately the students, would be victims. Incidents of this type were distracting and an unproductive use of the talent we had assembled at the college in its early years. I had not become part of the professional staff to play these kinds of games, to engage in petty power struggles, or to wage internecine warfare with colleagues. This is what the school's growing legion of detractors hoped for to justify reducing the school's budget, enrollment, and program offerings. I badly wanted to inaugurate a new graduate program at the college, but in the end, I chose not to. While my erstwhile colleagues continued their struggle, I quietly removed the program proposal and all supporting documents from my office. As far as I was concerned, they were not proprietary. They were too distracted to notice. I decided the time was right to move on and I told President Randolph of my intentions. He implored me not to do so. Moreover, he assured me I was a valued member of his team, and was confident that this crisis would pass. Although I did appreciate his vote of confidence, and was momentarily hesitant about leaving, I did have an opportunity and I thought the better judgment was to seize it.

Midway through the academic year 1970 – 1971, I left Federal City College and rejoined the Foreign Service, this time with the former U.S. Information Agency, not the State Department. I felt the time was right for a change. My intent always had been to return to the Foreign Service; it was just a matter of timing. I am positive there were some misperceptions among some of my closest colleagues regarding my departure from the college because my leaving was abrupt. There were no farewell parties, collegial luncheons, a dinner. Nothing! I was there one day and gone the next! My reasons for leaving were crystal in my mind. Perhaps I had deluded myself into thinking that others saw me as I saw myself – and I did see myself positively. I had no reason not to. The experiment of The Federal City College was for me, a once-in-a-life-time opportunity to be part of something historic, something larger than myself: a mission led by African-Americans for African-Americans (largely) and of African-Americans, and I was exhilarated to be part of it. My specific responsibility in the Community Education Division, as I viewed it, was to design programs of legacy dimension, a challenge of its own accord. This was what the college was all about. As the graduate-level project I had been developing gained acceptance, I was completely unprepared for the larger challenge I faced in trying to maintain its integrity. I worked with men of integrity, but I made the fatal error of assuming that integrity of effort and purpose would extend to our work product as well. I further assumed we were all on the same team.

As the drama surrounding the last incident continued to unfold, I learned that Dean Williams was Gay, a fact that in itself would not have posed a problem for me. However, as someone still in "the closet" as it were, he found it necessary to seek validation of himself as a person through his work and the efforts of his subordinates. This was his preferred approach rather than exhibit his true personality and character more openly. Perhaps he felt he did not have that option. I do not presume to be judge and jury on this one; merely a victim that survived. I was disappointed, perhaps naively, but disappointed, nonetheless. Dr. Williams staked his very self-esteem on the success of the academic programs he sponsored, some of which were, at best, uninspired. When he and Alan became familiar with my novel project, rather than support it on its merits, they increasingly saw it as a cargo vehicle on which they could load the baggage that was their experimental prison program. I was then faced with a series of protracted negotiations with the two of them to arrive at a compromise position. Who knows, we may have been able to do so had their individual motives been more transparent.

Although I did not succeed in launching my graduate program as an independent concept, I did learn some valuable lessons about consensus building, patience, and the application of person-centered dialogue. Had James Williams and Alan Trawick been more forthright in outlining their plans for the project at the outset, there is every possibility we could have reached agreement regarding its relationship with the Lorton Prison Project. We could have redesigned the goals and program objectives. We could have "war-gamed" it to facilitate speedy acceptance by the faculty's academic programs' committee. The process would have been completely transparent. I also believe the program would have been successfully incorporated into the regular graduate-level course offerings within two years. This was a major, lost opportunity. The lessons I learned at this stage of my career proved to be invaluable in the years that followed. So, the experience at The Federal City College had been valuable, not always pleasant, but valuable.

The key to my return to foreign affairs was Dean Hassler. Periodically, he and I would discuss our mutual foreign affairs interests privately or over lunch. At his own initiative, he arranged an interview for me with an old friend of his, Ken Coffey, Director of Foreign Service Personnel at the U.S. Information Agency. I thought my meeting with Coffey had not gone well especially after he made derogatory comments about the college and I challenged him. Later, I told Hassler how surprised I was to learn how critical Coffey was about the college since he knew of our involvement with it. Hassler laughed and told me that Coffey had called him immediately that evening with a more positive assessment. He had enjoyed my candor and was pleased that I would be attending SAIS later that year. Moreover, he thought, should USIA be in a position to hire me, I would bring a new perspective to USIA's Minority Recruitment Program. With Coffey's support, and that of Lawrence Masterson, USIA's Director of Personnel, I was able to negotiate an understanding that should they hire me, I would be allowed to retain my status as a full-time student at Johns Hopkins SAIS. USIA accepted this condition because, in offering me the position of Director of Minority Recruiting, I would assume primary responsibility for mentoring a class of Foreign Affairs Interns pursuing graduate degrees in international relations at George Washington University. Each intern aspired to become a Foreign Service Information Officer (FSIO). This particular group of interns was unique in its ethnic and racial diversity. There were males and females, African-Americans, a Filipino, one Chinese American, a Mongolian, one Hawaiian and a Mexican. I was a natural for the position.

I felt good to be back in foreign affairs again. The demands of my role with USIA were considerable and my responsibilities did require that I travel to California to interview candidates for a new class of foreign affairs interns. At the end of my first year at SAIS, I was exhausted. USIA's 1971 summer recruitment program offered no respite and I still had another year remaining before I would complete my Master's Degree. I had to revise my game plan if I was to survive a second year. SAIS had its own culture and its own peculiar brand of politics. Several of my colleagues had begun to grumble about a work schedule that allowed me to pursue graduate studies on "company time." They conveniently overlooked the fact that several of my courses were evening courses, and that I regularly logged more than 50 hours weekly.

Early in the fall semester of 1971, Scott Thompson, another second-year student at SAIS, and I were having lunch, and he made a comment that piqued my interest. Scott was saying that he, too, was "tired of the games they play at SAIS to justify a two-year program they have not revised in years." He went on to say, "I think I am going to request an oral examination after three semesters, George. In certain circumstances, if your faculty advisor thinks you are prepared, they will recommend it to the faculty committee." "Is it possible to do that?" I asked. "Yes," Scott responded, "and I plan to give it a shot."

Here, perhaps, was the solution I was looking for. Dr. Robert Osgood, my faculty advisor, and I were on very good terms and I solicited his support for early oral exams. Dr. Osgood had served in a previous administration at the State Department, therefore he understood the pressure I was under. I worked hard that third semester to build a strong case for an oral examining board in early 1972, a full semester before my class was expected to complete all degree requirements for a Master's Degree. Scott and I were granted approval to meet with a board in January 1972. This was a one-shot deal for me. I had to succeed. SAIS nurtured its reputation for producing students well grounded in development economics and I concentrated my intensive review effort there. The day my panel met, I had 60-minutes to convince three senior professors that I had earned my degree in three semesters, rather than the customary four.

To prepare, I focused less on textbooks and more on my voluminous notes and selected articles from the early issues of Foreign Policy magazine. An old friend and colleague from my days at Embassy Bonn, John Franklin Campbell, was one of the intellectual gurus behind the launch of that publication. I am a charter subscriber and have every issue ever published. "Don't let them see you sweat," I told myself as I sat down before my panel in the Dean's office. "Do not bloviate... if I don't understand a question, ask for a clarification, a definition of terms," was my second piece of advice to myself. That second piece of advice saved the day for me. A tricky economic question left me to accept a vague interpretation of the question, or ask for a definition of a particular term. "Dr. Osgood, what do you mean by a 'watershed' event?" I asked. "That's right, George, make him define his terms. Dr. Charles Marshall chimed in." Dr. Osgood recast his question and I had an opportunity to expound on a topic I had studied almost *ad nauseum*.

With the international economics portion of the examination completed, I dared to breathe a little. Later, a ten-minute interpretation of Jefferson's Farewell Address stimulated an exchange with Dr. Marshall on one of his favorite topics. I was a little less sure of myself here, but I must have acquitted myself well. With Charles Burton Marshall, you knew where you stood during an exchange because he would cut you off in mid-syllable. I avoided that humiliation that day. At the end of the session, I was commended on my grasp of economic issues and, for the first time during the entire hour, I felt optimistic about the outcome. I thanked the panel, left the room, and returned to work. Dr. Osgood called me later that evening as I was preparing for a conference with a new group of officer candidates. He had good news: I had received favorable comments from each member of the panel and I was exempt from further coursework pending the graduation ceremony in June. All I heard was "you passed." I had done it again.

Although I enjoyed the challenge of mentoring a new generation of Foreign Service officer candidates, I, too, had to get back in the game. The position of Director of Minority Recruiting within USIA was not on the average Foreign Service officer's A-list of career-enhancing positions. It served to get me into one of the premier foreign affairs agencies. Now, it was time to position myself for the end-game. There is no foreign policy content associated with that position's principal responsibilities. Contact with other Foreign Service officers whose portfolios are issue-oriented is limited, and the position is career limiting. To be more precise, I was not competitive with Foreign Service officers serving in geographic bureaus in Washington, or at our embassies abroad. The fact that Foreign Service officers bear responsibility for recruiting, assessing, mentoring, training, and promoting officer candidates and other officers, carried little weight with promotion panels. It is for that reason I had to get back in the game.

Accepting the position as a Foreign Service Limited Reserve Officer (FSLR) on a five-year contract was a strategic move for me for the simple reason that it offered entree to a principal foreign affairs agency; the agency responsible for "Telling America's Story to the World." One of the first acts of the Nixon Administration upon occupying the White House in 1969, was to impose hiring freezes throughout the federal government. The President's decision dashed any hope I may have had about resuming my career with the State Department. The interview with Ken Coffey convinced me I had the experience and the program management skills the Information Agency required in this position. I could establish rapport with upwardly mobile, bright young people from diverse backgrounds and America's minority communities. I was familiar with the diversity in worldview they represented, and I could relate to their aspirations as young professionals in a foreign affairs agency. My Foreign Service background only conferred greater depth to my resume. It was on the basis of background and experience that USIA requested, and received, an exception from the U.S. Office of Personnel Management to bring me on board. The hiring freeze was lifted for one day for one position. That is how I was able to join USIA.

Within my first year at USIA, I was able to launch a sizable group of young foreign affairs interns and recruit a successor generation of new officer candidates equally as qualified as their predecessors. This was, after all, my primary mission. The success I achieved at Johns Hopkins was instrumental in effecting a major change in the Foreign Affairs Intern Program: the new class of interns would be earning their graduate degrees from Johns Hopkins SAIS, not from George Washington University. I was instrumental in effecting this strategic change. Once the new class of interns was on board, I had time to step back and assess the professional goals on my shortlist. Recruitment at the federal level was not only a unique learning experience for me, but it also allowed me to do something that fit with my experience, my temperament, and that thrust me into situations where the defense of ideas is a measurement of effectiveness. I knew that if I was to resume my Foreign Service career, I had to establish my candidacy soon.

The first step was to gain approval to recruit my successor. John Gravely, my counterpart at the State Department, was looking to make a change. He was a known quantity, African-American, and immediately available. The second step was to arrange a transfer to an office within the personnel division populated by career Foreign Service officers. This was the most practical choice because I was well established there. The office I selected was the training division where I was tasked to develop seminars for officers returning from abroad to assignments in Washington. My task was simplified by having a valuable Rolodex of contacts developed during the previous three years. Many of those officers in transition to stateside assignments had been out of the country during the late 1960s and early 1970s. While on assignment abroad, they had not experienced, nor could they adequately explain to foreign audiences, the social transformation of America e.g., urban riots, the Anti-War Movement, student protests, the African-American Black Power Movement, and Earth Day activities. I felt I could serve as the bridge between the America these officers remembered and the contemporary America they would now experience. The Director of Seminars, Jake Gillespie, asked me to revitalize "The Contemporary America Seminar" for returning Foreign Service personnel. I was able to tap into a rich vein of prominent African-Americans, noted academics, and reputable political activists to engage these officers on a variety of contemporary themes. Through this seminar, I helped my colleagues understand the contemporary America they and their teenage children would confront in the media, on college campuses, and in public policy debates.

Gradually, I altered my profile from that of a domestic officer responsible for recruiting Foreign Service talent to that of a Foreign Service officer with the ability, the perspective, and the motivation to tell America's story abroad. In my last performance appraisal as the Director of Minority Recruiting, Lawrence Masterson, the Director of Personnel and Training said this of me: "George Kennedy joined USIA to resume his Foreign Service career. He should have the opportunity to prove himself." I could not have been more in agreement. Shortly after my transfer to Jake Gillespie's team, I was assigned to the American Embassy in Rome as the Assistant Cultural Attache' responsible for economic programs and the Fulbright Exchange Program in Italy. The Rome assignment was not without an amusing twist. A colleague and collaborator from the Contemporary America program stopped me in the corridor the day I learned of my assignment. This colleague, Richard Ross, was visibly agitated. "How did you get my job?" he asked. "I wanted that position in Rome." In 1972, USIA did not enjoy the tradition of assigning African-American officers to the larger, more visible diplomatic missions in Europe. Africa was the beat for African-Americans even when many of them were qualified by dint of language proficiency, military experience, and academic credentials, to serve elsewhere in the world. I was the first African-American officer from USIA in 15 years to be assigned to Rome, and the ripples were beginning to reverberate among those officers who viewed European assignments as their exclusive domain. I could not know that a pattern for my future Foreign Service assignments, each of them, with one exception, a first for an African-American officer, had begun to form. Controversy was not new to me and my preferred solution to controversy, with race as its genesis, was performance-based success.

CHAPTER 10

ITALY REDUX – THE PURSUIT OF EXCELLENCE

When my TWA flight touched down on Italian soil at Rome's Fiumicino International Airport, it had a familiar and comfortable feel. It was late December 1972 and, although it had been a few years since my last visit to Rome, I felt good to be back in a country that had nurtured me into manhood as a young, inexperienced soldier just a few short years ago. Maybe it would be difficult for someone else to understand my emotional attachment to this country. It was the Italian people in all their elegant simplicity that had restored my faith in humanity. For the first time in my life, a people had welcomed me and accepted me not on the basis of race, but my humanity. Stated more simply, race was not a factor; at least I never felt it was – and that was important. I was an African-American, and acceptance on that basis was not easily forgotten, especially in the late 1950s and early 1960s. This was before the Civil Rights Act became the law of the land. While legislation did not guarantee equality, it at least opened the door to the possibility, and for the U.S, that would represent an achievement. Well, I was already living the promise of equality before I lived it at home. This particular arrival that December was important to me for another reason. This was the start of the career as a Foreign Service officer that I felt was my destiny. I also knew that, for me, the true test of my ability to cross that threshold was not in the personnel division back at USIA Washington. It was in the field. It was here in Rome that I would be judged on my ability to meet the standard by officers I did not know. It was their collective judgment I would have to shape. My purpose in Rome, therefore, was twofold: to earn career status and, second, to earn my first critical promotion as a mid-career officer.

As a rule, newly arriving personnel at large American missions in Europe then were not met upon arrival unless that officer is a senior officer, or has a large family. I was a single, mid-career officer expected to make my own way to Rome. I was apprised of this practice by telegram shortly before my departure for Rome. There is important context to this practice, however. The volume of official visitors at large missions like Rome severely taxes limited embassy resources. These missions simply did not have the staff or the logistical capability to meet and greet everyone – including officers like myself. My colleagues at USIS Rome had reserved a room for me at the Pensione Tea, a small family-owned hotel just two short blocks from the embassy on the Via Veneto. The entrance to USIS Rome's offices was on a side street behind the chancery building at Via Boncompagni #2. I should point out that abroad, and at America's diplomatic missions, the U.S. Information Agency was known as the U.S. Information Service, or the more familiar USIS. "Agency" when translated into many languages suggests a function analogous to the CIA when juxtaposed with "Information."

I checked into the Tea and, since it was early evening, I decided to unpack and take a walk. The brisk evening air felt refreshing after the long, trans-Atlantic flight. When I looked out the window of my room, I could see Rome's famed Via Veneto. At first glimpse, the street seemed deserted. There were a few souls on the street, but they were headed in other directions, not into any of the sidewalk cafes, most of which were empty. The "beautiful people" that attracted the city's famous paparazzi must have been vacationing elsewhere. They certainly were not visible this particular evening. I walked for almost an hour, wandering really, and then decided to call it a night. My room was small, but warm and comfortable. Feeling a little fatigued, I took a hot shower and rolled into bed. That night, I slept well.

The following morning, I was up early, had a typical European breakfast of a cappuccino, croissant, and orange juice. Following the directions in the welcome kit left at the reception desk for me by someone from USIS, I arrived at the entrance to USIS Rome around 7:30 am. I was the first American to arrive that day. The American Marine on duty checked my official passport and allowed me to enter. True to my nature, I was early.

Alexander Klieforth, the ultra-sophisticated, urbane Director of USIS Italy, with offices in Rome, Milan, Naples, Trieste, Genoa, and Palermo, welcomed me as the newest member of his team. Joe Townsend, his deputy, came in to join us for the few minutes Klieforth could spend with me. He was on his way to the ambassador's early morning meeting of his senior staff, also known as the "Country Team." I appreciated that Alec had made it a point to welcome me before that meeting. As he rose to leave, he said something totally unexpected. "We have work for you to do, George, but an officer cannot really function well if he is rushing around trying to get settled, checking on household effects, his car, and trying to find a place to live. Find a place to live, get settled, and come back when you're ready to work." Wow! I thought; what a magnanimous gesture. I would remember that act of kindness if the situation was ever reversed and I was the director of USIS at an overseas mission.

Joseph Townsend picked up on Klieforth's comment and told me that Vincenzo "Enzo" Mazzaglia, a senior Italian staff member, would assist me to get settled. "Do what Enzo tells you!" Joseph said. "He is very good at what he does, and he will not steer you wrong." He then took me around to meet the other members of the USIS Rome staff – including the legendary Vincenzo Mazzaglia. The most successful USIS operations abroad have at least one, often several, senior Foreign Service national employees whose range of contacts and institutional knowledge of the post's programs and host country is so extraordinary that he or she is irreplaceable. No American officer, regardless of years in country, could build the reputation of trust, integrity and credibility reposed in this one individual. Vincenzo Mazzaglia, I would soon learn, was our most valuable human resource. I never understood how it was that the State Department never lured him away from the U.S. Information Service. Mazzaglia was a legend at embassy Rome.

Townsend and I were still making our way around the building when Alec Klieforth returned. He pulled me aside for a few minutes to tell me he had asked the ambassador if he had a moment to welcome me as the latest addition to his team. Alec felt we should do this before I got too involved in settling my transition. He then took a few minutes to brief me on developments surrounding the ambassador. Ambassador Graham Martin had been named as the new U.S. Ambassador to Vietnam and would be departing post soon. Wells Stabler, his deputy, would remain through the transition and then depart for his next assignment. John Volpe, former Governor of Massachusetts and Secretary of Transportation during the first Nixon Administration, was recently appointed as the new U.S. Ambassador to Italy. Secretary Volpe was a major supporter of the President and this appointment was his swan song. That afternoon, Alec did accompany me to meet the ambassador. Ambassador Martin was quiet, soft spoken, reserved. He welcomed me to Italy, spoke briefly about how much he had enjoyed this assignment, and ensured me I would as well. Within ten minutes, we were on our way back to the office.

I was joining a solid staff of able American professionals, many of whom had developed an affinity for the Italian people, their culture, and life in Rome. Chief among them was Margaret Haferd, the Deputy Cultural Attache' and Chief Librarian. "Maggie," as everyone called her, was a living repository of knowledge about Etruscan culture, Italian history, and the structure of the Italian language. Dr. William Braun, the embassy's Cultural Attache', was of Alec Klieforth's class of seniority, education, sophistication, and charm. He was beyond the career concerns of many senior officers, including Joe Townsend. Only months from retirement, Bill Braun was an island of calm and self-confidence. Nico, a first-tour junior officer, and I, discovered we shared an interest in motor sports, good humor, social developments in the U.S., and my perspective as an African-American on these and a host of other topics. Nico also owned the most extensive private collection of Playboy magazines I imagined existed in 1972. I felt comfortable with this team, the one exception being Joe Townsend. Call it instinct, but Joseph's body language and tone said caution. Perhaps a better world is prudence. But now, it was time to get settled. I wanted to keep an open mind and not pre-judge anyone.

I knew from experiences in Germany and the Philippines that the pace of daily life at an embassy begins to wind down in early December. Christmas is just over the horizon and staff find it hard to concentrate. They, too, have families, obligations, and shopping to do. Add to that the excitement of being in a foreign culture whose approach to this most western of holidays may be different than ours. Therefore, I wanted to use that time to get settled, and quickly. I also wanted time to read-in on the economic programs I would have to manage. Above all, I wanted to be ready to go to work as soon as possible after the New Year.

As I looked at the embassy bulletin board and the local newspapers, all sources of information about available housing, a brutal fact surfaced that plagued most mid-level officers like myself upon arrival in Rome: the housing allowance is inadequate to defray the cost of decent quarters. And, being single, my allowance would be woefully inadequate, according to some of the monthly rental rates advertised. Utility costs in Europe are historically higher than in America. I also learned that many Italian homes in the area around Rome at that time did not offer the amenities, the complete kitchens and bathrooms that are customary in the U.S. So, there would be the costs of electrical fixtures, appliances, and bathroom fixtures. Any new occupants had to supply literally everything when taking possession and either sell everything upon departure or take it with them. Were I to live in Rome, I would have to resort to the use of personal funds just to pay rent, other expenses notwithstanding. Suitable housing within a reasonable commute from the embassy became less and less likely for me. The most likely option would involve a commute, but from what distance? Little did I know that a financially prudent decision to live within my means would result in mild criticism from other officers in the embassy. My new embassy colleagues would maintain that my low monthly rent lowered the embassy's average rent thus making it more difficult to request an increase in the embassy's housing allowances. I confess that particular concern was not on my list of priorities; I was not aware of the issue.

During my search, I also read the *"Daily American,"* Rome's English-language newspaper. I spotted an ad for a recently built, all brick, 4-story, 3-bedroom, 4-bath, villetta in Osteria Nuova near Lake Bracciano north of Rome. The owner was asking a monthly rent of $225, an amount even I could afford. Assuming the rent quoted was a typo, I decided to call just to satisfy my curiosity. The owner, Mario Pinzi, spoke very good English and he confirmed that the figure quoted was accurate. He also told me he advertised in the Daily American because he was hoping to attract Americans as potential renters. I had shipped my car, a 1971 Mercedes, 280-S sedan, and it was available, so I agreed to drive out to inspect the place. Enzo confirmed the location and agreed to accompany me on my exploratory mission. As we rolled to a stop at the address given, the property was even more spectacular than described in the ad. It was self-contained and part of a duplex, both of which were available. The grounds were neatly manicured and complete with a small garden and terraces leading from each room on all floors. Once inside, I discovered a wine cellar and a heated garage. The town of Osteria Nuova was small and practically isolated. In each direction from my third floor terrace was nothing but flat, fertile soil, scattered woods and some farms. Enzo was initially concerned about the commute. I did, however, like the house. Something clicked and I knew this was it, a bachelor's dream spot. To make a decision, I would have to make the commute during normal rush hour from that part of the Italian countryside.

The next day, I left the Pensione Tea and drove out to the house around 5:00 am and waited until approximately 7:00 am to drive in with the early morning traffic. I estimated I would be leaving home around that time, so 7:00 am it was. The 30-kilometer commute into Rome took less than an hour. The only real traffic I encountered was at the "Gates of Rome," the principal grouping of access roads into the city. Nino later told me there were alternate routes, therefore, my commute would take even less time. Two additional test runs on successive days confirmed that my daily commute would be an hour or less in both directions. Following another visit with the owner and an embassy inspection, I signed the lease. Our Executive Officer advised me that my household effects would arrive before the end of December, so it was safe to shop for appliances, light fixtures, and fixtures for four bathrooms. American appliances were more durable than those manufactured in-country, and it became necessary to travel to the U.S. Naval facility in Naples to order an American washer and refrigerator. I had an enclosed backyard with garden, therefore, I could hang my clothes out to dry. My landlord provided the clotheslines. During the winter months, I would hang laundry in my heated basement. I decided to purchase an Italian gas stove and that proved to be a major mistake. The oven exploded twice sending tiny shards of glass at projectile speed across the kitchen.

It was during the negotiations for the light fixtures and fixtures for the bathrooms that I began to appreciate Enzo's true value. No doubt I would have paid considerably more for these necessities had Enzo not negotiated the prices. As I became more familiar with my new community, I discovered I was the only American there and no one spoke English. Perfect, I thought; now I can perfect my Italian.

I had Christmas dinner with my immediate supervisor, the cultural attache', Dr. William Braun, and his wife Wanda. The balance of the evening I spent in my room at the Pensione Tea. This was to be the loneliest Christmas I had spent in quite some time, but there were larger considerations, and that took the edge off whatever I might have been feeling. Shortly after Christmas, I took occupancy of my new villa. I moved in quickly and within a week, I was settled enough to go to work. I have a rule whenever I move into a new place. I work around the clock and hang the pictures within 72-hours. When my pictures are hung, the house is settled, everything is in its proper place, and the trash has been removed. I lose several pounds in the process, but I am done. The place looks as though it has been occupied for years.

The reputation of USIS Rome and its countrywide public affairs program made it the perfect assignment for the young, mid-career officer I was who had a feel for international public diplomacy. I felt that for me, USIA's global mission was the better intellectual choice for me. It was the career suited to my gifts. Therefore, I would give this assignment everything I had. Success at this post could pave the way for assignments of even greater consequence. Although I worked for Dr. Braun, as the economic programs officer, I also reported directly to Joe Townsend. At the outset of my relationship with both officers, I had a clear understanding of the level of responsibility I accepted and the goals I expected to achieve. It was implicit in Townsend's initial briefing that he would monitor my progress very closely. Although he, too, was a SAIS graduate ('48) and understood the heavy emphasis on international economics SAIS required, I wondered early on if he trusted my ability to handle complex, bilateral economic and trade policy issues. I say this because he would speak to me as though economics was an arcane science, the intricacies of which, in his mind, may have eluded me. For example, when discussing a project and the policy message we intended to convey, he would way, "you may talk in technical terms." In my initial meeting with him, I did tell him that Rome's emphasis on economic issues was my principal attraction, the reason it was my first choice for an initial assignment. I think had I shared with him my experience while sitting for my oral exams at SAIS earlier that year, the hint that I was more than comfortable with economics just might have antagonized him. For the moment, I decided to endure his condescension.

Our post economic program, even above the other major project portfolio on East-West Security Issues, involved the active participation of the embassy's Minister for Economic and Commercial Affairs, and his staff at each American mission in Italy. Both Klieforth and Townsend agreed I would represent USIS at the economic minister's daily, early morning staff meeting. Therefore, I went over to his office to introduce myself. Michael E. C. Ely, the Economic Minister, was the third ranking officer at embassy Rome after the ambassador and the deputy chief of mission. Ely wore both hats with considerable personal and professional pride. Mike welcomed me as a full participant in his meeting. Furthermore, he let me know that he and his staff were fully supportive of our economic public diplomacy program in Italy. In our first meeting, he said, "your success, George, means that ours is a strong and effective partnership." "The other guy you will work closely with is Roy Eberhardt, my deputy. He is next door."

The contrast between the courtly Mike Ely and Roy Eberhardt was amusingly stark. Mike accepted me as a colleague; Roy, although pleasant, wanted to know if I was a "Mustang." A "Mustang" is State Department parlance for participants in an affirmative action program offered for promising minority officers, women, and Foreign Service staff personnel (as I had been previously at our embassy in Bonn) to assess their suitability for conversion to the Foreign Service officer corps. When he posed the question, I responded, "about as much as you are! No! I am not a Mustang." My response must have momentarily stunned him because there was this quizzical expression on his face as though someone had mildly insulted him. He recovered enough to affect a faint smile and welcome me to Rome. Later, I mentioned the exchange to Mike Ely to get it on the record in the event Eberhardt might register a complaint. "Roy is a captive of his personality; he is more insular and tends to have a more limited perspective on people," Mike said. I think I knew what he meant by "people." Mike assured me "Roy will not be a problem." I confess annoyance at the apparent ease with which white officers assume Black officers must be affirmative action hires and I wanted him to know that. I think Joseph Townsend embodied that same mindset. The initial reaction of both officers to my assignment to Rome supports the conclusion they did not enjoy the experience of working with African-Americans as professional equals. Well, they would now.

The other interested parties in our economic diplomacy program were USIA Washington and the European Bureau at the Department of State. There was a broader policy context that framed the economic outreach program in Italy. This meant that I had considerable latitude to develop a successful program, but not much latitude for error. There was logic to my reasoning. I knew from policy guidance that the American business community in the U.S., key supporters of the Nixon Administration, had extracted a commitment from the Nixon White House to mandate that America's diplomatic missions abroad take a more proactive approach to supporting American business in select overseas markets. Moreover, they were to accord higher priority to export and trade promotion, and protection of American investments abroad. We in Rome took that mandate seriously. The U.S. Information Agency was the program arm of American diplomacy. We were tasked to identify and build support among those individuals and institutions that shaped foreign public opinion, and that represented an emerging generation, in Rome's case, of Italian and European political leadership. The American business community in the U.S. and overseas wanted support for its global export programs, and USIA had a defined role it could play. We also had resources we could commit to further our policy and program goals. Meanwhile, Alec Klieforth and Joe Townsend had pioneered in defining and perfecting unique communication's tools through which American business and policymakers could engage an elite level of Italian society, and I was now the responsible officer. This was the basis of my attraction to an assignment at USIS Rome once it became clear that the assignment would hold. As an unproven quantity, my life, at least during the day, was lived in a fishbowl and Joe Townsend was content to keep the fishbowl practically on his desk.

I was to learn that Joe Townsend was a complex individual with a well-ordered sense of the world we occupied and, most importantly, his role in it. He felt undervalued as a senior officer who should have been the director of USIS Italy. I also felt I would not have been his first choice to fill the position I did. His preference was for a younger, more junior officer. I had experience, was comfortable with myself and the lexicon of our economic diplomacy programs. Moreover, I, too, was a SAIS graduate.

Throughout 1973, in close collaboration with Mike Ely and his team of economic, trade policy, commercial, and financial officers, I planned and coordinated a concentrated program of lectures, seminars, and special programs that gave Mike increased visibility as the embassy's principal spokesman on bilateral economic issues. Our program brought noted American policy figures from the Nixon Administration, business leaders, and prominent American academics into contact with their Italian counterparts and those Italians that actively supported, and opposed, specific policy objectives advocated by the Nixon White House. During the first six months of that year, through direct contact with Italian public and private organizations, I deployed all of the embassy's economic and commercial officers throughout Italy to discuss the principal economic issues facing Italy, the United States, and Western Europe. Prominent on our bilateral issues' agenda was tourist travel, one of the more sensitive topics with the Italians.

A cornerstone of the Italian economy in 1973 was revenue generated by tourist travel. We at embassy Rome were under pressure from the U.S. Commerce and State Departments to stimulate Italian tourist travel to the U.S. to improve our bi-lateral balance of payments account. The specific program vehicle to launch a dialogue with the Italians and to assess methods to reverse tourist patterns among Italian tourists was the newly created "Visit USA Working Committee." That working group was chaired by the newest member of the embassy's senior team, Commercial Counselor, Albert L. Zucca. Zucca, an Italian American, and a recent arrival from our embassy in Nairobi, Kenya, was a young, dynamic officer, possessed of an engaging personality, and prepared to offer real leadership to a high profile activity. He invited me to become the secretary of the committee and a partner in this high profile effort. Under Al Zucca, the committee cast a wide net and launched a new field of embassy cooperation with representatives of thirteen airlines serving Italy and the United States. I worked closely with Zucca and his team of commercial specialists and, as my effectiveness grew, prodded by Al Zucca, Joe Townsend expanded my responsibilities to include revising and enlarging the subscriber list for the embassy's Commercial Bulletin. This publication had been the embassy's primary program tool to support the Nixon Administration's trade initiatives in Italy. It was also the most effective means to reach the leadership of Italy's vast business and commercial sectors.

With strengthened confidence in my ability to translate policy into specific and measurable program objectives, I earned the confidence of the embassy's most senior officers. According to Mike Ely, Al Zucca, Joe Townsend, and the rumor mill, what I had going for me was high energy and motivation, strong organizational skills, an ability to communicate in Italian, willingness and the versatility to take on the less glamorous tasks to ensure success and, an ability to work well with American corporate executives.

Among my expanding circle of friends within the embassy community was Captain Robert Jordan, the Naval Attache'. Captain Jordan and I met at a farewell gathering for his predecessor, whom I did not know well. I am partial to the military as an institution because of my family's proud record of military service since World War 1. I easily struck up a conversation with Captain Jordan. I forget how I put it, but my point was, "why was he not in command of a ship at sea, as opposed to duty at an embassy, especially in Italy which did not have one of the strongest navies in NATO?" His response was simple. It was Navy policy that if a naval officer attains the rank of Captain without having commanded a ship and is over 50 years of age, that officer will not be promoted to admiral and is subject to an earlier retirement. For his last duty station, he chose a tour at embassy Rome. And thus began our friendship. Captain Jordan and his wife loved Italy, and decided to make it the swan song assignment of a lengthy career. Before long, I was a dinner guest at their beautifully appointed Rome apartment. As a student of American military history, I was a smooth and easy fit with many of his foreign military guests.

Captain Jordan called one day to ask a favor. The Undersecretary of the Italian Navy, his grandson, and a small coterie of aides, were to be his guests aboard an American aircraft carrier off the coast of Italy. The Italians wanted to observe flight operations. Jordan asked if I would serve as one of two interpreters for the aides accompanying the undersecretary. The captain also knew I would enjoy a visit to a carrier. "Absolutely!" I said. "I will take it up with Thornton Engstrom." Thornton Engstrom was the new Director of USIS Italy replacing the venerated Alec Klieforth. Engstrom drew a line between events of a social nature conducted during business hours (golf and tennis, for example) and those events or activities that advanced American policy objectives. My request fell into the latter category. In granting approval, he said something to the effect that he would have liked such an invitation himself. I had never seen the business end of an aircraft carrier before, so this would be another new experience. As an aside, I did observe from a distance the construction of an aircraft carrier in the shipyard in Camden years earlier. I think it was the U.S.S. Kittyhawk.

A week later, the Italian delegation, Captain Jordan, and I, landed on the aircraft carrier Midway. Approaching a carrier from the air can be unnerving. You notice the pilot is preparing to land, you know the carrier is down there, but it is not visible. And then, there is that tiny speck off in the distance, and your heart begins to pound. Landing on, and being catapulted from, an aircraft carrier must be analogous to astronaut training. Decelerating from 160 knots per hour to a standstill within 2 seconds and, conversely, accelerating from a standstill to 140 knots in 2.9 seconds is a physically jarring experience. As a novice, there is nothing that can prepare you for this. I understand why you are strapped so tightly in your seat that breathing can be a little difficult. They had provided us with earplugs for when we exited the aircraft and stepped onto the deck. I wanted the full experience. Without ear plugs, the howl of jet engines shrieking at full throttle being launched and recovered numbs the brain and your senses. The noise is so deafening, it temporarily paralyzes you as you try to comprehend what is happening around you. Without escort officers moving you along, some inner voice compels you to just stand where you are. Everything and everyone is in motion. Ordnance is being loaded on different types of aircraft in line to be launched while aircraft are being refueled; other aircraft are being parked. Crew decked in different colors are everywhere reminding you of a well-choreographed ballet. Every crew member on that flight deck knows where they are supposed to be, we were told later because, one misstep and someone could be seriously injured or even killed. In fact, a working flight deck is the most dangerous four-and-a-half acres of sovereign U.S. territory we own. It is a precarious place, especially for the uninitiated. Within seconds of our landing and after crossing 40-yards of flight deck, we were whisked up to the captain's quarters for a briefing, and to begin our tour of this veritable floating city.

An aircraft carrier is a mini-city complete with at least 5,000 sailors (crews were not integrated with women at that time), aviators, and marines, along with 75-80 aircraft of various mission capabilities. As we became familiar with the ship, the Italians were dumbfounded to learn that the average age of the deck crew orchestrating the delicate ballet of precision they bore witness to was between 19 and 22. I heard the undersecretary say, "Loro sono bambini" (they are children). The idea that "children" were launching and recovering multimillion-dollar aircraft and highly skilled pilots was unfathomable. He went on to say, "Questa non succede mai in Italia" (this could never happen in Italy.) The captain of the Midway explained there was a launch sequence involving the various aircraft. Nothing happening on the flight deck was random.

Everything was planned, evolving in a highly orchestrated fashion, and controlled. This did not mean that an accident was unavoidable; it meant that a working flight deck was too dangerous an environment not to have controls. Crews worked around the clock and fatigue and inattentiveness were the two things that could result in serious injury and death. What the captain told them just before we went below stunned them into silence. "This ship's primary mission is to project American power and when required, to launch our aircraft as quickly as possible. After that, we are expendable, if necessary." And so it went for the balance of the day as we learned more about the capability of this vessel to sustain itself at sea. During the return flight, I thanked Captain Jordan for the invitation and the experience. I also volunteered for any future opportunities that might arise.

Dr. Braun retired within the first 19-months of my arrival in Rome as had his principal deputy, Margaret Haferd. Alec Klieforth was now directing USIS Germany, an even larger program in a country with which he had history extending back to the final days of World War 11. I temporarily assumed Dr. Braun's responsibilities as the embassy's cultural attache', a very prestigious title; no mean feat for a mid-career officer. Meanwhile, other forces were in motion to redirect the outreach activities of USIS Rome, their policy importance notwithstanding. In the summer of 1974, Dr. William Castleman, the new Cultural Attaché, arrived along with his wife, herself a senior Foreign Service officer. She would now be assuming the role of a newly created position of Director of Programs. To make room for two senior officers, the post had to abolish the position of Executive Officer, a functional position, and create the new position she would now occupy. Unknown to some of us, this couple had a notorious reputation for fostering divisiveness to assert their control over programs at USIS offices overseas. Only posts of considerable size with large, complex programs could accommodate them. Rome was fertile ground for a variety of reasons; one of the reasons being their knowledge that Thornton Engstrom was not a strong manager.

Thornton Engstrom, soon began to experience a major effort by the new cultural attache and his spouse to undermine the economic outreach program, our most successful public affairs activity. I was, by default, their new target and I was exposed. Their point was that economic programs were not a traditional USIS activity and should be eliminated in favor of more "culturally-focused-programs." More specifically, visits by prominent American performing artists, cultural exhibits, recitals, and educational exchanges. Joe Townsend had also retired and his successor, Charles H. Royster, was now in the delicate position of managing an insurrection from more senior colleagues while trying to preserve the operational effectiveness of our most successful program. This was an internal war not of my choosing, but it was clear to the entire staff that I could become the most obvious casualty. The solution – firm leadership – was obvious, but elusive to Engstrom. My continued success was the equivalent of digging my own grave – in career terms. My new boss let me know unequivocally how opposed she was to my principal responsibility and, by extension, me. I was good at what I did. The more I tried to keep her informed about my activities and areas in which I needed her support, the more actively she opposed me. She even took issue with where I lived and how it impeded my ability to adequately represent USIS interests. It had not been a problem before, but it was now. I was not spending my own funds for representation even though my allotment from post resources was limited to $50.00 a year.

Dr. William Castleman, was unapologetically ruthless, smug, and inclined to describe the moral imperative of his effort to refocus USIS Italy. His treatment of me as the acting cultural attache' was brutal. Rather than benefit from my 18 months of experience in helping to create the success he inherited, he dismissed me on the day he arrived in the office. His words still ring in my ears: "I don't need you; I am here now, perhaps Thornton has something for you to do", all with a smile. What else could I do but leave his office? He asked not a single question about the programs of the cultural section, staff, budget, or operations. Castleman summarily dismissed me without having requesting a single document.

His wife, while determined to shape the activities of the program office, was not prepared to oppose her husband. She had staff, he did not. The program office teams were all former staff from the cultural section and our programs gave content and purpose to that shop. Castleman's staff consisted of an Italian secretary and a young, first-tour female officer, herself the wife of another first-tour officer at USIS Rome. He, therefore, saw it as his mission to exert control over the activities of the program office through his wife. Morale among the officers in the cultural section and among the Italian nationals was nonexistent. The Italian staff observed that they had seen practically every personality and management style conceivable over the years, but this new power couple was the most ruthless in the history of their tenures with USIS Rome. Several of the junior officers were quietly seeking transfers. My colleague and friend, Nico, was transfered to embassy Copenhagen as Cultural Attache'. While there, he received a promotion in each of the next two promotion cycles.

Thornton Engstrom was on the telephone daily with Washington management looking for options and emotional support. The new deputy, meanwhile, was feeling less appreciated while being buffeted between the forces of statism and the team of Castleman/Hinton advocating revolutionary change. Meanwhile, I was caught in the vortex of a storm with others prematurely drafting my obituary. Moreover, I was the one constant in both the cultural section and the program office, and the bridge between the old Klieforth regime and the new Engstrom team. Neither Bill Castleman nor his wife, Rebecca Hinton, knew that I had requested to be reassigned; that the European director from USIA Washington had visited Rome, denied my request for transfer, and directed that I remain in Rome as continuity for the new team. And, two of the new team had declared me persona non grata. What an ironic twist of fate. I should note that my request for transfer had nothing to do with the new team; I had achieved measurable success in Rome and was seeking assignment to a hardship post to mitigate the image of a mid-career officer seeking to extend for another two years in one of the more desirable assignments USIA had to offer. Negative perceptions once developed by career managers in Washington, can be difficult to overcome.

Months into this dark chapter of human behavior within USIS Rome, I learned from colleagues that Bill Castleman and Rebecca Hinton had decided that their success was partially contingent upon engineering my removal from Rome. Daily, they were exhorting Engstrom and Royster to get rid of George Kennedy, that I was a proponent of programs that were inconsistent with the traditions of USIA abroad. I recall one contentious meeting I had with both Engstrom and Royster in which the latter was playing the role of the heavy: he accused me of being uncooperative, not a team player. I heard that line from Rebecca every day. Royster was feeling the pressure and now I had to hear the line from him as well. My success notwithstanding, Royster's posture typified the white officer who felt he could not support an African-American officer without jeopardizing important social relationships or, more importantly, his career and the quality of his judgment.

In this particular meeting, I felt the ground shifting and I felt I had to do something. I took a deep breath, shifted just slightly and told Royster, "I am not the issue or the problem here! Rebecca and William do not support our most effective program and I embody that program!" My head was now firmly on the block so I continued: "Delay their request that I be reassigned and I will show you that my removal would open the door to their larger objective of destroying our economic diplomacy program; that the crisis they have engineered is one of their own making!" Well, there it was. I then turned and looked directly at Engstrom as if to say, "you're the PAO – make a decision." They agreed to monitor my interaction with Rebecca more closely.

I do not mean to blithely suggest a de minimus effort on my part could be the prelude to a successful outcome of the most divisive struggle the staff in Rome could recall. Ultimately, my fate was in the hands of Royster and Engstrom, thus they became the focal point of a meticulously planned, well-conceived, and coordinated strategy to outflank the "devils duo" of Castleman and Hinton. Daily, for example, I would prepare detailed briefing or background memoranda for both gentlemen, including Hinton, on each active project (of which there were many) with appropriate input from my embassy colleagues in the economic and commercial section. The project objectives I felt we could accomplish were well documented and the larger foreign economic policy implications were clearly delineated. On one occasion when I delivered a copy of a project memorandum to Rebecca, she passed me in a cold fury on my way to deliver copies to Engstrom and Royster. Daily, I would huddle with Al Zucca or the appropriate embassy participant in a given project to discuss possible venues, important Italian participants, logistics, costs, media interest, and follow up activities. I left nothing to chance.

Mike Ely and Al Zucca, the embassy's most senior representatives on economic and commercial policy, had a large stake in the economic diplomacy programs under my direction. After all, we in USIS provided them the wherewithal to advance U.S. economic policy in Italy where it mattered; we had the means they lacked. Naturally, they did not want to see this novel program scuttled. Official visitors to the embassy were briefed about the program and, as more senior officials in Washington became active participants in this transatlantic dialogue, they, too, became advocates with their counterparts at USIA Washington. Finally, their senior colleagues at the ambassador's early morning staff meeting regularly complimented Thornton Engstrom and Charles Royster for developing such a visible, well-targeted effort. This was not a frequent occurrence in relations between State and USIA officers. I could minimize my own role because everyone knew I was the responsible officer. Moreover, flattering press clips from Italian dailies and trade publications reporting on a timely, joint effort between the embassy in Rome and a major Italian entity were impossible for embassy officers to ignore. Often, I gave Rebecca the credit she did not deserve and I, too, activated a reporting channel with Washington colleagues who provided timely personal advice and policy guidance. They also shared in our success. To put all of this in some context, I was the victim of a war waged above my head, one that I could survive only by getting bloodied. I also had to win. The end game for me had not changed throughout the struggle: my twin objectives since arriving at post in December 1972 had been to build a record of accomplishment and to establish a track record strong enough to substantiate my quest for conversion to career status. My career was at stake and good options were few.

With wise counsel from Al Zucca, I was able to navigate the rocky shoals of this storm until the leadership of USIS Italy was forced by management in Washington to "knock some heads together." There were those days when the pressure within USIS Rome was so intense that Al would take me for a walk outside the embassy or invite me to dinner with his family. Rebecca was unsparing in her disdain for economic public diplomacy and I bore the brunt of that daily. I knew that part of her strategy was to force me into an uncontrolled outburst, or act of insubordination. I had been there before and I was not going to play that game. This saga had dragged on for five months, but in the end, I was able to persuade Engstrom and Royster to take a step back, observe the activities of the newly created program office and the officers responsible for specific programs, me included; to base program direction decisions on the basis of effectiveness and not philosophical differences regarding the mission of our public diplomacy programs. With the support of friends at post, personal diplomacy, a willingness to incur the risks inherent in challenging more senior officers, and the ability to make my case, I prevailed.

Before the change in leadership at USIS Rome, there was another, more pleasant, development. By July 1973, settled in and very much in command of my metastasizing responsibilities, I decided to do something I may never have the time or the opportunity to do again: invite my mother to Italy for an extended period. Mother had imbued in each of us the will to excel at whatever we did, even if it was no more than digging a ditch. "Make it the best ditch possible," she would say. Well, I wanted her to see me in "the ditch" I chose for a career. Mother would enjoy Italy and come to understand the part Italian I became earlier in my life. Italians and African-Americans shared more in common than was acknowledged by either group and I knew that. Bringing mother to Italy would give real meaning to the words of my maternal grandmother: "The success of getting old is having good memories." Why not give mother the memory of a lifetime? I could and so I did.

My mother's adventures in Italy would make for an interesting book, at least an expanded chapter. I tried for years after she returned home to record her impressions for family and posterity. Unfortunately,

I was not successful and she died in 2008. Mother was part of my motivation to write this book. But, let's not get ahead of the story. Watching my mother, she thrived in Italy. Her diabetes became less problematic. In fact, she did not take insulin for the entire eight months she was there. She debated whether to tell her doctor and decided against it. All of my Italian and American friends young enough to be her children became surrogate "offspring" to this pleasant stranger in their midst. In late summer 1973, I planned a trip to Taormina, Sicily. The former mayor of that beautiful resort for the rich was an old friend of my colleague, Enzo Mazzaglia. Through that connection, I had a standing invitation to visit Taormina whenever I could. Sicily was a region steeped in history and Italian folklore. I knew little about it, but mother and I could discover it together. We could enjoy the drive from Rome. Naturally, I drove and mother just enjoyed the ride. The first night, while crossing on the ferry to Sicily, mother began to cry softly and I thought, what did I do to upset her? "Mom," I asked, "what's the matter?"

She turned to me and recounted a story I had not heard before. "When I was a young girl studying geography," she began, "I saw a picture of Mount Etna in Sicily and I told myself that one day, I would go there. Between marriage, children, and life, that dream faded away. Here I am now with the child who was not supposed to live, on my way to see Mount Etna. This is something I never expected to do." This revelation came as a surprise because, of all my siblings, I thought I knew and understood mother more so than they did. I was the child that never slept, and who watched her on her knees praying during some of the most desperate moments we experienced as a family after my father abandoned us. I could not recall her ever having mentioned anything about Sicily or Mount Etna. In retrospect, I had seen that same photograph in those old encyclopedias my father brought home. In that instant, I felt a bond that only the two of us understood. Mother could not know how special I felt in enabling her to fulfill a young girl's dream. Up until her death in 2008, she spoke of her trip to Italy. Several pieces of volcanic ash from her trip up the mountain that day remained with her throughout the balance of her life. Our trip up Mount Etna that day seemed to have a narcotic effect on her. She did not say much; just gazed quietly and intently out the car window. I could only imagine what was going through her head: "I did it! I am here, finally!" This time, she did not cry, as she had done on the ferry crossing. She smiled softly and asked me to pick up several pieces of lava rock for her. My satisfaction came from being able to actually help mother satisfy one of life's personal, but forgotten, goals on a checklist I imagine most parents keep tucked away in the recesses of their minds. Those lists become a victim to the vicissitudes of life and the exigency of the struggle parents wage to obtain the means to raise and support a family. I knew this to be the case with mother.

And then, there was that time mother got lost somewhere in Rome. This was one of those priceless moments with my mother. None of us knew where she was or how she arrived at the location from which she telephoned us. Her voice during the call was calm and all she said was, "I'll find my way back; just wait for me." An embassy colleague from the Treasury Department, her visiting mother, and I spent several anxious hours waiting for mother to return. She did, and then she broke down. She and my colleague's mother were walking buddies, but on that day, mother was alone. All she could tell us was she had been walking, taking in everything and, at one point, she caught a bus. The hours passed and before she knew it, it was evening. That's when it dawned on her that she should return. Mother was not one to frighten easily, but, that day, mother's fear was palpable. What if she had said she needed help. What could I have done to help her? That was my real but unspoken fear. From that day, mother continued her Roman odyssey but never alone.

My landlord's mother developed a real attachment to mother and, many days, they would just sit in the kitchen with dictionaries exchanging stories about life, husbands, raising children. Mother said, "we mothers have a universal language." My landlord's mother spoke no English and mother spoke no Italian but they could spend an entire day together and, watching them, you would have thought they were lifelong friends. My landlord was pleased because his mother really enjoyed the time she spent together with mother. When mother left Rome, he had to take his mother away several days in advance because she would have become emotionally too distraught that my mother was leaving.

As my grandmother's health began to deteriorate, mother returned home in 1974 after eight months. She was now a "world traveler" among her friends. She had earned it through a lifetime of sacrifice for her children, family, and friends. Home leave in December that year was different this time because mother now understood my dreams, the world I embraced, and the life I had chosen. She had been entertained by my embassy colleagues, some of whom refused to believe she was my mother until she produced suitable identification. Mother, at the age of 52 still looked 20 years younger. Given our time together, my hope was that there would be less tension in our relationship. She and I did not always agree, but we agreed to disagree. Mother had new memories and a relationship with new friends and new "children" she would nurture for the next several decades. Every year around the Christmas holidays, she would receive small gifts from one of her Italian children.

In December 1974, I would complete a two-year tour in Rome, take home leave, and be examined by a panel of officers in Washington. The panel would assess my suitability for permanent career status. This was a major step and the outcome was unpredictable. In my last performance review before his retirement, Joseph Townsend wrote: "George has earned his spurs." While that may have been true, the reality was this review panel had the last word. They would be the final arbiters of that decision. In December, I flew home for a well-earned break, and to learn if I would be allowed to fulfill a destiny I now knew was mine. Home leave also had its obligations. Among them was the obligation to attend at least one Sunday morning church service with mother. The pastor of the family church in Woodbury, New Jersey, was now my old boyhood friend, Vincent Cream. Mother was living with her mother in the home her parents had built in the 1920s. It was on that bit of contested ground that I was born in 1940, the second of nine grandchildren, and the only one to be born at the family home there in Woodbury. This house was special to me and everyone in the family understood that.

It was early December 1974, when I landed at Philadelphia International Airport, just outside the city. The weather was unseasonably mild and it felt comfortable, even reassuring, to be back in Woodbury. Home leave was all of 30-days and I wanted to maximize my time. First on my list of "must do's" was to contact a young lady I had met in Rome during one of her group's European tours. She was lead vocalist in an all-female R & B group "The Love Machine." That December, they were scheduled to perform in San Juan, Puerto Rico, and she invited me to join them there. In our last conversation just before I came home, she called from Paris. "George," she said, "how would you like to make wild passionate love on the beach in San Juan?" What else would a young, virile, all-American male say but "Absolutely!" I just wanted you to understand why this was first on my list of things to do. During that call from Paris, I was advised by my friend to call her sister in Boston...She would have the name, address, and telephone number of their hotel.

After agreeing to accompany mother to church the second Sunday of my stay at home, I was on the phone to Boston. The plan was to spend that first weekend in San Juan. The anticipation of a fabulous vacation in Puerto Rico was dashed when my friend's sister said she did not have the information I sought. In fact, she had not heard from her sister. Her sister knew nothing. As I was about to terminate the conversation with the sister, I told her, "should you hear from Marvelle, please tell her to contact me at my mother's house...I will be there through the holiday period." What an inauspicious beginning to my vacation. Earlene, my younger sister, was to meet one of her best friends that afternoon and suggested that perhaps I would like to meet this friend. She was single, very attractive, and available.

My plans were now altered so I told mother I would accompany her to church the first Sunday, rather than the second Sunday. Everything happens for a reason. Mother and I were early arrivals that Sunday morning. I knew the ritual: greet each family friend, classmates I had not seen since childhood, see old teachers from Woodbury's Carpenter Street School, the school designated for the city's African-American citizens, preceding even mother's generation. Vincent was delivering the sermon that day and I knew he would make an event of my presence. Although I would have preferred anonymity, Vincent rose to the occasion. I knew getting away from there at the end of the service was going to take considerably more time now. At the conclusion of the service, Vincent took his customary place by the door to receive well wishes from the congregation. Mother had me firmly by the arm and I had to run the gauntlet of well-wishers from the well of the church to the door. Along the way, I shook hands with Ms. Brown, the second grade teacher I last saw in 1948, the year my parents moved the family to Mizpah. She was the daughter of our former landlord in Woodbury and the sister of the famed Hollywood actor, Roscoe Lee Brown. It was now 1974 and Ms. Brown was shocked that I recognized her. How could she know that I could forget a name in an instant, but possessed an elephantine memory for faces and most events? Slowly, we inched toward the door. Out of the corner of my left eye, I saw the door, Pastor Cream, and the last person I had to acknowledge before I would be out the door.

As I turned to greet him, Vincent said, "Alfred, here is someone I want you to meet...she is a lot like you." A tall, statuesque, brown-skinned, lovely woman with a captivating smile said, "Hi, my name is Diane...Vincent has told me a lot about you." Everything changed in an instant. We walked together from the church to the home of a mutual friend a few yards away. There, we talked for almost 30-minutes agreeing to meet later that evening. For the balance of my time at home that December, Diane and I saw each other practically everyday. Two days before my departure for Washington, I asked Diane to marry me. It just felt right, more so than my first marriage a decade earlier. Diane said yes. It was now time to tell her parents and mother. Everyone had reservations, except the two of us. The matter was therefore settled. I never did make contact with Marvelle, the young lady I had hoped to meet in San Juan, until after returning to Rome. I did, however, call Vincent to tell him of our decision to marry the summer of 1975. Vincent chuckled and let me know he expected to preside over the ceremony.

Before returning to Rome in January 1975, there was the appointment at the State Department with an oral examining board comprised of officers from the official Board of Examiners for the Foreign Service. I had done this before, only, this time, the stakes were higher. This was not about qualifying as an entry-level junior officer; this was the whole ball game. This was my command performance. The day of the interview began as any other day. The key for me was to take the advice I previously offered to aspiring junior Foreign Service officers a few years earlier: remain calm and focussed. That old bugaboo, my speech defect lurked nearby and I did not want to become so anxious that he would rear his ugly head and complicate, even derail, this opportunity. If anything, I wanted to look and sound like "them." I wanted this to be a conversation among colleagues, as had been the case so often at embassy Rome. Before entering the exam room, I inhaled deeply several times, said a short prayer, and strode into the room as though I was to administer the exam. In brief, I enjoyed the experience. There were the standard foreign policy questions: U.S. policy in Vietnam and a question about NATO. There were also the questions designed to test reasoning and judgment, not right or wrong responses. The test was about the quality of my reasoning in a complex situation. And then, about 45-minutes into the process, there was the question out of far left field.

"Mr. Kennedy," one of the panelists began, "In 1966, in response to a Letter to the Staff Corps from Walker Diamanti, (a director in the office of personnel at that time) published in the Foreign Service Newsletter, you wrote 'America can afford to listen more...' ' "What did you mean by that?" Wow, I thought, they did their homework. I was surprised that letter was still in my file since I did have a break in my Foreign Service career between 1966 and 1971. Taking another deep breath and shifting my posture as I had learned to do, I recalled the letter and took several minutes to review it in the context of the times, the increasing American involvement in Vietnam. I talked about the political and geostrategic context of an assignment to the Philippines in the mid-1960s, and why I felt our political leadership in Washington was acting more unilaterally in prosecuting the war and not availing itself of support and advice from our allies. I wondered if perhaps the Johnson Administration was tone-deaf to the concerns of the generation they committed to prosecuting the war. I also reminded my panelists that in 1966, I was a junior member of the Foreign Service without policy responsibilities, but concerned, nevertheless, about America's image abroad. In the event they had not retrieved a copy of Mr. Diamanti's letter urging junior staff to share their opinions, I pointed out that we were urged to be candid, that the Department wanted to hear from us. Well, I took them up on it, and that my letter represented a group effort. I was expressing the sentiment of many of us in the Foreign Service Staff Corps on duty in Manila. "The letter you read was my opinion at that time in history" I said.

My response must have satisfied them because there was an awkward silence that I broke by requesting a minute to visit the men's room. "Afterwards," I said, "I will be happy to respond to any additional questions for as long as they care to; that I was actually enjoying our conversation." When I returned several minutes later, the panel director asked if I had any questions for them? "Just one" I said. "Can you tell me when I will be notified of your decision? I have one year remaining on my five-year contract and I will need that time to make plans in the event you render an unfavorable judgment." "You will hear from us within 30-days," he replied. It was over. Although our meeting had been relaxed, it was impossible to know the outcome. The panels are designed to leave you guessing.

It was late January, early February 1975. Rome was chilly, but no snow. The embassy was abuzz because President Ford would be transiting Rome in late spring or early summer from a trip to Austria. Precise dates had not been established yet. Five months advance notice of a White House visit is customary because of the logistics and advance preparation involved. Henry Kissinger, then Secretary of State, was a frequent visitor to Rome and the impact of his visits was reminiscent of a presidential visit ten years earlier. Specific support roles had not been assigned within USIS Rome, so I resumed stewardship of our economic outreach program. My confidence had reached its zenith for several reasons: In late January that year, I received a telegram from the Department's Board of Examiners notifying me that I had passed my recent oral examination. On the strength of that accomplishment and my performance reviews for the past four years, the Board (BEX) had recommended my conversion to career status. I was now a career Foreign Service Information Officer (FSIO) at my current grade of Class 5 and entitled to that most prized of perks, the black diplomatic passport. Second, my confidence was bolstered even further after an internal USIS Rome review of the previous year's program in USIS Italy revealed that the economic outreach program under my direction had been our post's most successful public diplomacy program. Oddly enough, my immediate supervisor was not the one to share this news with me; it was the deputy director, Stanton Royster, during a brief meeting about the pending visit of President Ford. I momentarily savored the idea of dropping by Rebecca's office to congratulate "us" (she and I) on "our" success, but by the time I got to the elevator, it occurred to me that the outcome of an internal program review she had to have contributed to, must have been painful for her. I do recall that relations between us became even more estranged around the time this news became public knowledge within USIS Italy.

It was not long before the White House Interagency, Pre-Advance and Advance Teams began arriving to set the stage for the President's arrival, now scheduled for June 1975. Along with my regular duties, I carved out time to bring Diane to Rome during her spring break. She liked to say she was "the spice in my life." I could not deny that I enjoyed having someone special in my life to enjoy what I now took for granted: life in one of the world's most desirable cities. Diane was an instant hit with all of my friends. The Italians in my circle thought she was the most exquisite creature imaginable. They sensed that ours was a special relationship, so inquiring minds brought forth interminable questions about any future plans.

Spring break passed quickly, and once Diane was safely aboard the flight home, I was again consumed with the economic projects arrayed neatly across my desk. By April, two things were clear in my mind. The first was the setting of a wedding date in early June. The second was being named as project officer for the White House Press Center at the Rome Hilton. The wedding was to take place in Woodbury, but a pending presidential visit meant all vacation requests were cancelled for anyone involved in the Ford visit. I called Diane and explained why our plans had to be adjusted. She took the news like a good trooper, and we went to Plan-B: she would come to Rome and we would marry there. Enzo, whom she had met, would arrange everything, I told her.

Staging a White House Press Center is exhausting, meticulous work. The traveling White House press corps has a royalty complex and the sense of entitlement that accompanies such a complex. This is the one time the White House shows a keen interest in the care and feeding of the press that accompany the President. Attend to their needs and at least they won't generate negative press, so the theory goes. This was long before the advent of the Internet and the Blogosphere. Our own Charles Royster had the reputation of the Press Officer's Press Officer, the gold standard for USIA press officers. He had asked me to plan and stage the Press Center for the Ford visit. I believe I was asked to take on this assignment because I had been mildly, but constructively critical, of how we had handled the press arrangements for a recent Kissinger visit when Kissinger's press secretary dressed down our director, Thornton Engstrom in a very public manner. I would now be put to the test. The fishbowl existence I became accustomed to was now center stage with a spotlight that caught my every move. Royster was now a supporter impressed by my attention to detail and organizational skills. He was also putting me to the test because during our last performance review, I shared with him my interest in Press and Media relations as the basis for my next assignment.

White House Press Centers have evolved since 1975, as advances in communications technology increased the speed by which stories are filed. Presidential visits have the capacity to generate news and the Washington, New York, Chicago, Los Angeles, and Miami-based corporate offices of most major electronic and print media organizations have a voracious appetite that must be fed constantly. A Press Center, vintage 1975, had to anticipate every need of the traveling press: desks and chairs, electrical outlets, mult-boxes (to connect recording equipment), microphones and a public address system, platform risers for camera and TV crews, an office for the White House Press Secretary, and the spokesperson for the Secretary of State. If the Director of USIA was part of the President's party, there had to be facilities for him as well. There was also the matter of transportation, telecopiers, facsimile machines, daily schedules of the President and his principal aides, interview areas, directions to all principal events, and most importantly, catered food and beverages around the clock.

The General Manager of the Rome Hilton was amenable to his hotel serving as the venue for the White House Press Center, but space availability was the purview of the Food and Beverage Manager. Major exhibits and conferences are scheduled months, sometimes years, in advance at major hotels in many European capitols. Space, even for the White House, is not always available if the hotel's commercially available space is already under contract. Rome's Hilton was no exception. The remaining space available for my purposes was inadequate and I was advised to speak to the onsite representative of the New England firm that had booked the rest of the main ballroom, the space most in demand for press centers. The Food and Beverage Manager could only suggest that "perhaps she could be persuaded to relinquish some of the space her company has under contract since it would be to support the White House."

Seeking more suitable space at another location in Rome was not an option. The White House Advance Team had selected the Hilton location and that decision was too complex to revisit. So, I told the general manager I would give it a shot. My only hope was that the onsite representative would be amenable to a special request under most unusual circumstances. Jeannette Williams, the onsite rep, was Vice President of Marketing for the firm hosting the exhibit there at the Hilton. She listened as I described my dilemma. In response, she said, "Mr. Kennedy, this exhibit required two years to plan and all of the exhibitors have paid for their space. I cannot unilaterally curtail the space they have paid for. A presidential Visit, however, is a special event. Let me see what I can do."

For a week, I camped out at the Hilton and made myself available with detailed schematics of the space I minimally required. Several of the exhibitors wanted to meet with me. On each occasion, I described the importance of a visit by an American President abroad, the impact it has on bilateral relations, the goodwill inherent in the visit, and the commercial objectives American business is able to promote. The exhibitors were businessmen, but newcomers to the world of White House stagecraft and international public diplomacy. The subtle, but focused diplomacy bore fruit. Several days later, I was able to obtain the additional space; I was now in business. As a gesture of good will and appreciation, I promised passes to all affected exhibitors to the press conference should President Ford make an appearance. That last promise would have to have clearance, but I thought it was the least I could do under the circumstances. The response from the exhibitors could have been a polite thanks, but no thanks. While briefing Charles Royster on progress in developing the site, I made him aware of the promise made to the exhibitors and sought his assistance should he have to honor the commitment. I also felt relieved that I could describe a problem with a solution.

Diane, meanwhile, was making plans to arrive after the White House event. Friends in the Consular Affairs Office at the embassy were quietly preparing the documents required to apply for a civil ceremony in the ornate ceremonial office of Rome's mayor. A civil ceremony at Campidoglio, the Office of the Mayor, is every Roman girl's dream. Suffice it to say that deep family political or social connections help pave the way. The requests are too numerous. Everyone at embassy Rome stood in awe of Enzo Mazzaglia's connections throughout Italian society, and they also knew if anyone could make this a reality, he could. If he pulled it off, the civil ceremony would be his wedding gift to us.

President Ford arrived in Rome from Vienna on June 5, 1975, and I was standing by in the Press Center. The set-up there passed muster with Charles Royster. As the day's events progress, I received a call informing me that the visit would be abbreviated. Therefore, Ron Nessan, the White House Press Secretary would not be briefing at the Hilton. Moreover, there would not even be time for the traveling press corps to make the trek to the press center to file their stories. The visit was billed as a success. I disestablished the press center and thanked the hotel staff for their cooperation. Ms. Williams came by at the hour originally scheduled for a press briefing and I informed her of the change in plans. I thanked her profusely for her understanding of my special circumstances and her support. I also insisted that she allow me to host her at dinner and agree to a meeting with my embassy colleagues. They, too, were aware of her support and told me they wanted to thank her personally.

During the customary post mortem of any high-level Washington visit, Thornton Engstrom and Charles Royster were glowing in their assessment of the press center, itself the largest operation of the visit. Both officers were seasoned press officers and their appraisal was an important validation at this stage of my career.

Diane arrived on June 6. A week of intensive visits through the byzantine corridors of Rome's bureaucracy could not be avoided: a signature here, fees everywhere, a stamp for our documents, and a character witness – or two – by complete strangers only added to the flavor of the experience. The time of record within the embassy to complete this phase of the process was six months. With Enzo as our Sherpa (guide), Diane and I accomplished this monumental feat in six days and were married on June 14, 1975. It was a gorgeous day! Close friends, including Thornton Engstrom and Charles Royster, formed the wedding party. Enzo interpreted for Diane and the Mayor's Executive Assistant was on hand to present a special bouquet of flowers from the Mayor to the new bride. The next day, we were on the road headed north to Florence, Vicenza, Venice, and up into the Dolomite Mountains of the Veneto Region. Ours was now a partnership. What better way to begin this partnership than with a tour of the region whose people helped shape the man I had become. Apart from a mosquito attack in Vicenza, the ten days we spent on our motorized tour carried me into the halcyon days of my past and opened a window into the future for Diane. Each passing day, the sights, sounds, and smells of her new home captivated

Diane. I took a step back and enjoyed Diane's Italian seduction. In doing so, I was reminded of an old friend, Stanley Tillman, and how he had watched my seduction by the same people years earlier.

Life with Diane was the equivalent of greeting a fresh, gentle breeze on most days. She brought a youthful exuberance, eyes that spoke volumes when I would surprise her with a small gift, or when experiencing something for the first time. Events, people, activities I accepted as a natural part of my world, excited her and expanded her in ways big and small. Italy of the 1970s was the fashion center of Europe and its creations were the rage in America. One of the joys in my life was shopping for the woman in my life. Diane was tall, statuesque and with a posture and regal bearing fit for the runways of Europe's finest fashion houses. I indulged her and enjoyed every moment of it. As she often said, "Giorgio, I am the spice in your life." That is why I enjoyed the experience. Falling in love with Diane as quickly and as easily as I did was easy. There was a void in my life not easily filled by just anyone. There had been opportunity for that. Diane's was a special blend of youth and beauty, determination and talent, charm, and an infectious laugh that I wanted in my life. She seemed to know what she wanted and was prepared to incur the risks involved in pursuing life and the success she sought. The principal difference between my approach to this marriage and my earlier marriage to Cassie was the desire of my heart and the rhythm we created together. I felt this the very first day we met. I wanted this woman and I let her know it. And then, there was the strictly male ego thing that came later. We frequented Rome's many delightful restaurants, the outdoor cafes on the Via Veneto, the piano bars along the Tevere, and the upscale boutiques of the city's famed Via Condotti. With Diane on my arm, our reception was the equivalent of the parting of the Red Sea. Italians adored her, I adored her, and she was mine. If I appear slightly effusive in describing my feelings for her, it is intentional. Most guys I knew wanted a woman that others could admire, perhaps even envy ever so slightly. It's a guy thing. We were living in one of the planet's most desirable cities. True to their character, Italians have finely tuned aesthetic sensibilities: food, wine, fashions, automobiles, design, and beautiful women. Italian women, including several on our staff, used to say that a woman has not been courted until an Italian man has courted her. Well, Diane was an object of their fascination and their affection. I enjoyed that. She was not a trophy, she was my wife and she brought out the best in me. Life for me was now more complete than it had been.

Advancing the American economic policy agenda in the U.S.-Italian dialogue presented frequent opportunities to showcase my substantive and organizational skills during the balance of 1975 and into the New Year. The success of the press center operation strengthened my relationship with Charles Royster. By now, even my boss, the program director, had adjusted to new realities. While she did not change her views on economic outreach, she was less overtly hostile. I had my eye on a regional economic post in Brussels or Paris as my next assignment. Charles Royster's imprimatur on my request, (as USIA's most successful press officer and spokesman on East-West economic and security issues) was worth its weight in gold, or so I hoped. The transatlantic stream of American officials from the Ford Administration, Honeywell Corporation, Harvard and Georgetown Universities, as well as the Chairman of the U.S. National Commission on Manpower, Eli Ginsberg – among others, projected me into the center of the dialogue with one of our closest European allies. I honestly felt well positioned to further my career goals. In a previous conversation with Charles regarding career choices, he said, "in this business, you have to decide whether you want to be a conduit of information for others, or someone in a position to contribute to the policy dialogue. If you are interested in becoming a press officer, then you are choosing the latter." Charles was exactly right: contributing to a policy dialogue offers greater professional satisfaction than carrying out mechanical arrangements for a program – their complexity notwithstanding. Staging and managing a White House event abroad, however, is not for the faint hearted. That would be an exception.

The responsibilities I shouldered that last year in Rome, and my familiarity with the details of U.S.-European Political Military/Security issues, as well as bilateral and multilateral economic and trade issues, provided the depth that would serve me well throughout the balance of my Foreign Service career.

It was now time again to begin the negotiations for my next assignment. The assignment process in 1976 was neither transparent nor rational, particularly if you were overseas. In fact, the process militated against the officer who did not have someone back in Washington safeguarding your career interests. Here is how it worked. You expressed your assignment preferences to your career counselor back in Washington, and he or she became your advocate, not always enthusiastically during the negotiations between other career counselors and the geographic bureaus that often advanced their own candidates. While the geographic bureaus ostensibly did not wield a veto over assignments, they really did. Why would a career counselor force a confrontation with a bureau when that officer might be looking for an assignment in that bureau as well? This is where the process worked to the disadvantage of most African-American officers. You needed to know someone back in Washington willing to advance your candidacy for the more competitive assignments. Often, you did not. The African-American officer who negotiated my assignment to Rome paid a heavy price. He retired shortly thereafter. Let's just say he felt that was the better option for him. He was the rare officer with that kind of integrity. USIA did not enjoy the tradition of assigning African-Americans to Europe and he was determined to bring some degree of equity to the process. I was always grateful to him for that.

Eugene Kopp, a former deputy director of USIA once said, "you can be old at age 45 or young at age 45 if you do not have the right mix of rank, age, and experience." The successful officers were part of a network of mentors, those willing to advocate for you, nurture you, steer you into the right enrichment opportunities at strategic points in your career, and facilitate introductions. Barring this, it was not unusual as a field officer to be in competition with the same person you depended upon back in Washington as your advocate and not be aware of it. This was my dilemma in 1976 as I was attempting to position myself for an assignment to our Mission to the European Communities in Brussels. I did not know if a vacancy existed there, or would in the near future. You bid on your preferences and depended on your advocate to advance your candidacy for an appropriate opening at a particular post, a similar position at another post in Europe, or another geographic region important to policymakers in Washington. It is important to understand this bizarre process.

On the strength of my 1975 performance, my name appeared on the promotion list in early spring 1976. The second of my two goals had been attained. Rebecca Hinton took credit for my success in a small champagne ceremony at the Hotel Excelsior next door to the embassy. I went along with this brazen act of self-aggrandizement. I knew that the lion's share of the credit was Charles Royster's because of the Review Statement he had written to her assessment of my performance that year. I immediately factored the promotion into the assignment possibilities I forwarded to my career counselor. After several months of frustrating exchanges with my career "mangler," as they were affectionately called, I was advised of my options: Director of USIS Pusan, or Director of USIS Medellin. Ironically, I must have asked a dozen of my officer colleagues, but only Al Zucca knew that Medellin was in Columbia, South America. I was reluctant to bid on this position because assignments to regions in inverse order of our geographic foreign policy priorities have been known to be fatal to a promising career; in this case, my own career. Unfortunately, Latin America ranked just above Africa, and both of them ranked below Europe, East Asia and the Pacific, and Near East-North Africa. Learn Spanish and you could be shunted from one mediocre assignment to another for 30 years and disappear into oblivion. Latin American specialists would take a different view, but I could not afford to.

An assignment to South Korea, on the other had, would necessitate learning one of the world's most difficult languages, and becoming intimately familiar with the cultural mores and social structure of a complex society. Pusan was also considered a hardship assignment. A future "fair share" policy would mandate that all officers take their fair share of hardship assignments. Everyone cannot be assigned to the more desirable posts. Well, I saw this as a strategic move after having served in one of the most desirable assignments in USIA. I had career status and I had been promoted. What better time to go then now? I explained to Diane how our lives would change; that Korea was a traditional, male-dominated society, and that her access would be more restricted socially than was the case in Italy. "I signed on with you Giorgio, so, let's go to Korea...I'll deal with it!"

Sitting in my office that last week offered a little quiet time to reflect on the events of the past 43 months. I felt accomplished, seasoned, and wiser. The Foreign Service was a viable career option, but it was not going to be easy. I knew the career I wanted would take me into uncharted waters more often than not, that the barriers to access were institutional, and that race was going to be a major factor. The key topics on our agenda of bilateral and multilateral relationships with important European allies made sense to me. Moreover, I was comfortable translating issues into specific programs to advance our policy dialogue. I knew I could play on a stage when the other actors were the White House, cabinet officials, corporate executives, and their foreign counterparts. Italy, however, had been easy for me – the perfect assignment to "earn my spurs." To be more specific, I am referring to the Italian people. I knew the culture, the geography, the politics, and the language. The greater challenge had been my senior officer colleagues. At the end of the day, however, I did pass muster with senior officers considered among the best in the service. This bolstered my confidence for what ever might lie ahead.

Throughout the balance of 1975, up until our departure from Italy during the summer of 1976, Diane continued to add a new dimension to life as I knew it. I was no longer a bachelor and thus another social level of Italian society was opened to me: The Italian economic and political leadership important to the embassy. Business relationships now evolved into social relationships because I had a partner. A network of friends embraced Diane as they had me. Often, when she was not discovering Rome on her own, one or more of these friends would show her the Rome of the Romans; those delightful and inexpensive locales rarely seen by tourists. Possessed of an effervescent personality and a self-confidence belying her youth, Diane, on one occasion, convinced a local radio producer that she could substitute as a disc jockey on his nightly broadcast. It is interesting how she set me up for this one. One evening, she told me she would be arriving home late; that she had a surprise for me. I was not sure what she was up to, but I went along with it. I was not enamored of the idea that she would be in Rome alone while I was at home. I am protective by nature and she was new to living abroad. Diane told me not to worry. She knew that I would be tuned into a particular radio station. So, that night, while going through my nightly ritual of shining shoes while listening to the radio, I heard her voice as the evening's host for easy listening music. I was thunderstruck, but also awed by her ingenuity. Another part of me was proud of her ability to create opportunity in unfamiliar circumstances, the hallmark of someone adapted to life in the Foreign Service. I stopped worrying as much after that when we were apart. The station manager brought her home and we had a drink to this latest coup on her part.

In retrospect, Italy nurtured Diane as spring rain nurtures the soil. After one year of marriage, we had amassed a lifetime of memories: shopping for jewelry on Ponte Vecchio in Florence; feeding the pigeons in Saint Marks Square in Venice; marveling at the breathtaking vistas of the Dolomites in summer; lunch on the Isle of Capri in the Bay of Naples; people-watching on Rome's famed Via Veneto; countless nights arguing Italian politics over dinner with my landlord at his restaurant on Lake Bracciano north of Rome, Christmas in Rome; Sunday afternoons at Valle Lunga not far from home, watching Ferrari test new Formula-One prototypes; and memories of early married life in an Italian villa. Who could build a better castle of memories than that? It was time for the next adventure – South Korea. The next stop for us was Washington for intensive Korean-language training.

CHAPTER 11

THE ULTIMATE CHALLENGE – *KENNEDY WONJANGNIM*

The fall of 1976 was the culmination of the quadrennial preoccupation with the next occupant of 1600 Pennsylvania Avenue. "Jimmy Who" from Plains, Georgia, had captured the Democratic Party's nomination, and the big question inside the Beltway was, "can he win?" President Ford was laboring under the burden of rising inflation (remember the infamous WIN – Whip Inflation Now – button?) and his pardon of President Nixon. I do not think the country was quite ready for a pardon of one of the most controversial presidents of the 20th century. Along the Washington-end of the Potomac, the political landscape was threatened with real change after eight years of Republican rule. The man from obscurity did not fit any mold that comforted official Washington. Washington's social mavens, and other Democratic loyalists, tittered that he carried his own garment bag and frequently quoted from the Bible. This latter quality would have endeared him to the GOP's emerging, religious conservatives but, alas, he was the "other" candidate.

A plank in candidate Carter's foreign policy platform was a promise to withdraw American forces, the U.S. Eighth Army, from South Korea. The Democratic nominee's campaign was now personal because this was an issue I was going to have to deal with. For the first time, there was a direct connection between presidential politics and my immediate career. Pusan was the surrogate capitol to Seoul, and, concurrently, home to the largest commercial port in South Korea; a port of tremendous strategic importance to supplying American forces and sustaining a war effort in the event of hostilities on the Korean Peninsula. Pusan was also going to be my home for at least two years; perhaps longer.

South Koreans – facing a volatile, unpredictable Communist neighbor – feared the worst if candidate Carter became president of the country they most relied upon to guarantee their security. Korea has the world's most heavily armed border and the-then South Korean President Park Chung Hee was dumbfounded that an American presidential candidate would advocate such a questionable policy. American media were reporting a rumor circulating in Seoul to the effect that President Park might launch a pre-emptive strike against Pyong Yang to forestall the possibility of a crippling attack against Seoul. Alarm bells were ringing in the Pentagon and at the National Security Council. A bilateral crisis of confidence was rapidly developing and both sides had to actively contain the situation before it got out of hand. This was the political backdrop on Korea as Diane and I settled into an apartment within a stone's throw from the State Department the summer of 1976.

Individual language instruction for both of us was to begin almost immediately at the International Center for Language Studies at Dupont Circle in Washington, D.C. The early morning, fifteen-to-twenty-minute walk from our apartment was actually pleasant, that is until the winter of 1976/1977 when temperatures dropped below zero degrees Fahrenheit.

Korean is considered a "hard language" requiring 44 weeks of intensive instruction. That was State Department policy then and now. The U.S. Information Agency, however, had not standardized its policies and that affected the length of the language instruction the two of us could expect. While meeting with my career counselor, I was told simply to "get as much language instruction as you can...44 weeks is not possible...maybe 24 to 28 weeks. Seoul would like you to arrive in January" (1977). Adapting to the routine of student still left time for me to indulge my passion for politics. After all, it was a presidential election year. First, I called my old friend and mentor, ambassador C. Cheston Clifton. We had remained in touch since our first encounter in Bonn some years back, but he did not know that Diane and I were back in D.C. Cheston had been an appointee of both the Kennedy and Johnson Administrations; perhaps he was campaigning on behalf of Carter. I had to know what was going on. At any rate, he and his wife, Claudia, had not met Diane. My second call was to the Office of Congressman (D. - Ga.) Andy Young of Atlanta. While in Rome, I had served as the embassy escort officer during the Italian leg of a foreign trip involving Andy and Mrs. Coretta Scott King, the widow of slain Civil Rights leader, Martin Luther King, Jr.

My involvement with Congressman Young came at the specific request of an African-American colleague from USIA, Horace G. Dawson, a senior career officer who also accompanied the Congressman and Mrs. King. Andy Young was an early supporter of Governor Carter and was instrumental in galvanizing African-Americans to support Carter's presidential quest. The day I met with Andy in his Capitol Hill office, he expressed concern that members of the Ford team might, at the last minute, put in place policies that would have the effect of mortgaging a new administration. He thanked me for my assistance in Rome and asked about my current plans. I told him of my assignment to Pusan, and that I would be in Washington for at least five-to-six-months studying the Korean language. I also volunteered to be helpful to him in any way that I could. He then invited me to attend a meeting of several members of his team to talk specifically about some issues on his agenda.

Cheston was thriving as the owner of the Capitol City Liquor Company in Northwest Washington. Black Enterprise magazine on several occasions noted his success as one exemplifying America's new breed of Black entrepreneur. In response to my questions about his involvement in the Carter Campaign, Cheston said he was not interested. "These past five years have been good for business. I am a Democrat, and while Republicans' domestic and social policies are abysmal, they are friendly to business." He was, however, in frequent contact with friends within the campaign, but chose to remain at the periphery. Business had to come first. I could not quarrel with that logic. It was also Cheston's familiarity with Korea that interested me. Although some time had passed, I did want to learn more about his experience in that largely Buddhist country while serving there during the Korean War. I had already heard enough to know that African-Americans could expect a different, more negative, reception from Koreans, something Cheston may have dealt with as an Army officer. Let me expand on this. The only other African-American Foreign Service officer I knew with service in South Korea was Michael Braxton. I had called him in Belgrade while still in Rome.

In response to Claudia Carter's question, "why Korea, George?" I said that I wanted the ultimate linguistic challenge and a Korean assignment offered that. Furthermore, the assignment was potentially more career enhancing than a comparable level assignment to Columbia. Continuing, I went on to tell her that earlier in my tenure with USIA, "I volunteered for an assignment to Moscow because I wanted to learn Russian, another hard language. My request was denied at that time on the basis of my marital status. Single officers were deemed security risks, and therefore not assigned to Moscow." Still on the assignment to Korea, I wanted Claudia to understand that I had a real interest in the Pacific Rim. An assignment to that region earlier in my career would help me decide just how ephemeral or permanent my interests were. There is one other observation I offered Claudia. "If Carter wins in November, Korea is going to be front burner and I will be there! Someone from the new administration will have the unpleasant duty of either aggressively advocating Carter's Korea policy, or walking it back. If possible, before I go, it would be good for me if I could meet someone from the new team responsible for our Asia policy."

Washington and the world went to bed on November 4, 1976, aware of a tectonic shift under the political structure in Washington. The plainspoken, former governor of Georgia was now the 39th President of the United States. Jimmy Carter was the new "Alpha Male" and the District's real estate agents were scrambling to update their lists of available housing. Cheston was away on a business trip to Europe when he received a call from the President-Elect." "Cheston, I need you," the new president said. "You were the Chief of Protocol during the Johnson Administration and I need you to guide us through my inauguration and our transition to the White House." The request temporarily changed the rhythm of life in Cheston's household. He could not say no to the President. "When a president makes a request of you," he later told me, "you have to consider it seriously and have a good reason to say no."

Cheston immediately returned to Washington and took up temporary residence at Carter's Transition Headquarters in Southwest Washington. The last thing he had on his mind at that time was an appointment to the new administration. He was, however, committed to recommending the names of capable African-Americans for consideration by the new team. I was among those whose names he would forward to the new team, but I could not reveal this to anyone at USIA. Even the remote prospect of an appointment with the Carter Administration was worth serious consideration. I was young, ambitious, and understood the advantages of a quantum leap in responsibilities, albeit at a political level. White officers felt a duty and obligation to advance their careers in a similar manner. Why not myself?

Meanwhile, Cheston was shuttling between his business and Transition Headquarters, while concurrently planning the President-Elect's inauguration. Cheston was the Interim Chief of Protocol and Diane and I were to be his guests at a private reception for foreign ambassadors to meet the new President and Mrs. Carter. On January 20, 1977, Diane and I took our assigned places among the dozens of foreign ambassadors assembled in a special room at Union Station to greet the new president. Diane, as always, looked stunning in a beautiful black dress more than suitable for the occasion. As diplomatic functions go, this one was a staid affair. Places were assigned on both sides of the room and the din, or noise level, was lower than might have been expected. Normally, you hear at least a dozen languages being spoken, lots of laughter, and the mood is lighter. All of the invitees were on their best behavior since they were meeting the new president for the first time.

Shortly after everyone was in place, we could hear the roar of escort motorcycles coming to a halt followed by the staccato of car doors closing. As the President and First Lady entered the room with their entourage, they momentarily stopped just inside the door and the President whispered something to the First Lady while pointing in the direction of the assembled guests. Rather than greet his guests as a couple, he directed his wife, Rosalyn, to take one side of the room and he would take the other. I forget whether it was his hand we shook or that of his wife. The fact that they split up caused a mild stir in the room. I, for one, was disappointed. I was also struck by how small in stature they both were.

That evening, Cheston also shared some personal reflections about the new administration. He pulled me aside before the new president arrived and said, "we have bought another pig in a poke." I thought I knew what he meant, but, reflexively, I asked, "what does that mean?" "Carter is already denying that Blacks are responsible for his victory." I knew the press had been "buzzing" about that issue, but no one could have had any real doubt that Blacks provided Carter's margin for victory. It was obvious to the most casual of observers. Cheston was disappointed. Oddly enough, the one box containing the resumes of qualified African-Americans to serve in the new administration was the one carton misplaced during the transition from Transition Headquarters to the White House. I had been holding out hope for an appointment, but with this latest development, my hopes sank like a lead balloon. Cheston was even more adamant that evening that he did not want an appointment. In fact, he had refused an offer to become the Chief of Protocol for Carter, pointing out to the President that he had already held that position. His priority now had to be to his business and to guarantee the financial security of his family. Diane and I mingled a while after the President and First Lady departed. Cheston's words were ringing in my ears and I told Diane what he had said. We thanked Cheston for inviting us and let him know we were leaving. His parting glance told us he understood.

True to his character, Cheston did aggressively support the candidacy of several people he thought could, and would, serve the new administration, if given the opportunity to do so. At Cheston's urging, I had been delaying my departure for Pusan. It was now March 1977, and still no word from Cheston regarding the likelihood of an appointment. The new team in the White House was conducting a pogrom of Nixon and Ford holdovers and "it would be a while," Cheston said, "before I, or any of the outside candidates, would come up for consideration."

Seoul was beginning to query me about my arrival date. My predecessor in Pusan, Blanchard Parsons, had died and Clawson Ridgeway, the Director of USIS Korea, wanted me there to ensure continuity. Pusan was home to the second largest diplomatic mission in South Korea and he, Ridgeway, felt that a prolonged absence of the new director could be misinterpreted. His concern was not without merit given the promise of President Carter to withdraw American forces. There were other special circumstances surrounding my assignment that he would apprise me of upon arrival in country. When I could delay no longer, Cheston said, "go to Korea... should the situation here change, they can always bring you back." Several days later, Diane and I settled in for the long flight to Korea. As the Northwest Airlines flight prepared for touchdown at Seoul's Kimpo International Airport, all passengers were instructed to pull down the window shades for reasons of security. Although a strange request, everyone complied. At touchdown, Diane opened her shade only slightly and we were able to glimpse anti-aircraft batteries along the runway. A stewardess rushed to our seat, leaned over us and sternly, almost defiantly, closed the shade with a stare that would have withered ice. This was Korea at first glance in March 1977. Diane and I looked at each other as if to ask, what have we gotten ourselves into?

Transpacific flights affect my biorhythm and this one was no different in that respect. Diane managed to sleep a few hours during the flight, but I could not. Following an expedited clearance process with Korean immigration, we were taken to our hotel. The next morning, while Muriel Ridgeway hosted a welcome for Diane, Clawson and I huddled very briefly in his office before being introduced to the rest of the staff. I did not know Clawson Ridgeway, only of him. His "corridor reputation" was good: bold, aggressive, charismatic; one of the premier USIS directors in the Asia-Pacific region. Unfortunately, he would be reassigned shortly after my arrival in country. On this particular morning, it was obvious something grave was on Clawson's mind. "Let me introduce you to the staff," he began. "I have a Country Team meeting and, following that, you and I need to talk." By mid-morning, Clawson and I closed the door to his office. He, again, welcomed me, told me he had spoken to several people in the Office of East Asia and Pacific Affairs back in Washington about some of the questions I had regarding my predecessor, Blanchard Parsons, and the Seoul-based Field Program Coordinator, Vernon Thompson. Thompson was a devout Mormon and, frankly, I was concerned about how effective he and I could work as a team since he would bear responsibility for ensuring I had the resources to conduct my program in Pusan.

"There are several things I need to share with you. First, we have a real problem in Pusan" Clawson began "and I intend to deal with it quickly and publicly. I needed you here before I could initiate any remedial action. When the staff there learned you were Black, they immediately interpreted that as a further downgrading of relations with Korea and Pusan in particular." Well, you can imagine how that intrigued me. I had dealt with matters of race all of my life, but this was a new one even for me. "Clawson," I said only half amused, "I assume you are going to explain this." He began, "the staff in Pusan is insular; they have never dealt with African-Americans and are captives of their own ignorance. This is the only way I can reason this situation. They have been saying that African-Americans are second-class citizens in America and, by extension, they and the program in Pusan are of lesser importance to the United States. The Mayor, the Provincial Governor, the President of Pusan National University (second largest in Korea), and the heads of all the media organizations have called me personally. All of them have expressed deep concern about the climate of fear the staff is creating."

"I have already let the staff know," Clawson continued, "how I felt about what they had done. To save face, they subsequently put out the story that African-Americans were the key to President Carter's victory; that assigning an African-American officer to Pusan is an indication of the importance the new president attaches to America's relationship with Korea." Clawson went on to say "it is important to me and to your effectiveness as our representative that the political, civic, and military leadership in Pusan know that you have my full confidence and that of Ambassador Tipton. Therefore, I will host a reception for all of your principal interlocutors at your office when we arrive tomorrow. Moreover, I am personally escorting you and Diane to Pusan. Normally this would not be necessary, but this time, the situation calls for my personal intervention. Second, as you have already heard, I will be leaving Seoul soon and my replacement is Matthew Price. Price is timid, complex, and not very decisive. I will stick my neck out and tell you something: from our brief conversation here, I can tell you and he are going to have a difficult relationship. Hang in there and try to make it work. I wish you and I were going to work together because I have some ideas about the program in Pusan."

Continuing his briefing, Ridgeway said "Vernon Thompson is struggling to give content to his job and weighs in often on discussions about program content and direction about the posts in Taegu, Kwangju and Pusan. I don't have much use for him, but I can't fire him. Although my deputy, Lawrence Nichols, is your first-line supervisor, he is inclined to defer to Thompson far too frequently, and that complicates our relations with those of you at our branch posts outside Seoul." "I am leaving so you will have to wait and see how Matthew realigns things, if at all. Third, we have a major public affairs problem in this country because of heightened Korean concerns about the possibility of an American troop withdrawal. Ambassador Tipton is concerned and I am short on ideas at the moment. Do you have any ideas? You have met some of the new Carter team; what are they like?" Before I could respond, he interjected to remind me that newly arriving officers are offered the opportunity to visit the Demilitarized Zone (DMZ) north of Seoul. I immediately accepted. "Since we were leaving for Pusan tomorrow" Clawson said, "you will have to make the visit in the morning; that he would arrange our transportation." "Now, back to my question."

In response, I said, "reach out to Andy Young. He is the new UN Ambassador and is very close to President Carter. The team at State is still undefined. Before Andy's agenda is consumed with other issues, consider asking him to come to Korea...I realize you have to run this past Ambassador Tipton, but it may be worth consideration. I can give you the telephone numbers of his chief of staff, Stoney Cooks, and others who will be part of his team at State." Clawson looked at me for a moment as though light bulbs were going off. He clasped my hand thanking me for the suggestion saying, "you've given me some ideas; I'll take them up with the ambassador." Clawson and I emerged from that meeting to be on time for a meeting with the ambassador and his team. Phillip Harrison, the Political Counselor, and I had served together in Bonn. David Twining, one of the economic officers, was an old friend from the Philippines. I was reassured to know there were at least two familiar faces in Seoul. My emerging concern, however, was with the impending change at the country director level. I had just left a post where strong, charismatic leadership was replaced by weak and timid leadership. It was about to happen again. My experience at The Federal City College and at USIS Rome taught me that I respond well to strong, focussed direction, and less well to those who are unsure of themselves. My only consolation this time would be the 500 kilometers separating me from headquarters in Seoul.

That evening over dinner with Clawson and Muriel, I told them

I was not completely surprised at the reaction of the staff in Pusan. There is almost an inevitable undertow of resistance that occurs during a leadership change; that resistance can take a particularly virulent form if the new leadership is African-American. That said, I wanted Clawson to know that I would work hard to earn the staff's respect, and that I wanted to develop an official presence in the city consistent with the economic and commercial importance of Pusan. He and I were in full accord. We were up early the next morning to make the trip to the DMZ. Clawson had arranged for an embassy sedan to make the short ride to the DMZ. The DMZ, as it is commonly known, is the world's most heavily armed and most dangerous border separating two sovereign nations. I was interested in seeing it because it is also a "flashpoint" in the geostrategic calculus in that region. If you serve in Korea and are part of the perennial debate about Korea's future, it helps to have been there. Both South and North Korea maintain a constant military vigil at that contested border. I understand there is very little room for error. The atmosphere, if you can call it that, is almost surreal. It is what I would call the ultimate "faceoff." The slightest offense, the most innocuous of gestures probably could be misinterpreted with serious consequences for both sides. The visuals are sparse. Several spartan looking buildings, one astride the border within which meetings are held, and another more elaborate structure used by the North Koreans as an observation post. Within the hour, we were in the car headed back to Seoul. The situation has changed, but in the 1970s, few South Koreans were allowed to visit the DMZ.

Once back in Seoul, we finished packing in time to meet Clawson for the flight to Pusan. The three of us landed in Pusan in the afternoon to be taken immediately to the American military compound at Hialeah, not far from center city. The expatriate community then was small, thus practically eliminating a substantial demand for western-style housing in the city and its environs. Diane and I moved into official quarters on the base. I knew this would be a culture shock for her, but, to her credit, she tried mightily to make an undesirable situation tenable. That evening, Clawson hosted a reception in my honor for Pusan's illuminati in the USIS building, itself quite spacious. The presence of women at a function at that time automatically made it social, according to custom. However, Clawson set the tone early with the following statement following the customary greeting: "George Kennedy is our representative in Pusan and the Kyung Sang Namdo Province. If there is any aspect of our relationship with Korea you wish to discuss, take it up with him! My purpose tonight is to convey that message." Clawson rarely traveled to Pusan except on special occasions. That was not lost on the staff, or the leadership in the room. The invective of the staff had rippled throughout the city and Clawson's presence put a halt to it. Now, it was up to me. The next day, Clawson was on a flight back to Seoul, but before he left, I did thank him for his support and expressed regret that we would not have the opportunity to create the kind of synergy each of us felt was achievable.

While my staff was digesting the change I represented, my imperative was to give that change direction and focus. During the initial meeting with my Korean staff, I picked up on the theme Clawson had mentioned the night before. "Mr. Ridgeway has given me the mandate to broaden our program and policy emphasis to include economic and commercial objectives, not just educational and cultural. I will seek your ideas because you know the city. A new direction, however, is inevitable. The question is, how creative, innovative, and aggressive, will we be in embracing change?" There were no questions; just blank expressions.

As the early weeks turned into spring and summer, I noticed that life at home was undergoing a gradual facelift. My concern was less for myself than for Diane. She was new to the regimentation of military life – even for spouses and family; I was not. We had exchanged a modern, four-story, brick, Italian villa for a Korean War-vintage, one-story, 3-bedroom, cinderblock, rambler-style bungalow on a military compound, less than one-hundred meters from the quarters of the base commander. The base was small, but it was home to the Army's logistical support units at the military port of Pusan. On that first day, as we walked through the modestly furnished house, I kept thinking that this would be home for the next two years. A quick tour of the base revealed how sparse the amenities were beyond the traditional Base Exchange, the commissary, and the officers' club. We had been married less than two years and it was difficult for me to predict the impact this radical change in lifestyle could have on our relationship. I knew from my own military experience how difficult the adjustment could be for military families. I could immerse myself in my new job, but how would the professional women's groups, both among the American military spouses and the larger Korean community, receive Diane? Well, I would soon find out. I planned to brief her as thoroughly as I could before she ventured out on her own.

There was a protocol list on my desk of important civic leaders, American and Korean military commanders, my diplomatic counterparts in Pusan, leading figures in the local business community, and government officials at both the city and provincial level, I needed to call upon. High on the list were the two senior American military commanders in the city: Colonel King, the Hialeah Base Commander, and Colonel Bristow, Commander of the Joint U.S.-Korean Military Assistance Advisor Group (JUSMAAG). I decided to meet with them first. The courtesy call on Colonel King was to have been perfunctory; to acknowledge his command, to extend the embassy's appreciation for housing the Director of USIS Pusan, and to continue the cooperation expected between the major military commander and the embassy. That was the purpose of my visit. We got through the protocol and then he adjusted his posture ever so slightly and wondered aloud if I would be comfortable in Pusan's more limiting social and cultural environment. "This is not Rome," he intoned, suggesting that my tailored clothing and vest pocket watch might overwhelm the Koreans. In other words, how dare I bring a level of sartorial elegance that offended his homegrown preference for khaki, camouflage, and occasional polyester? Surely, I had not noticed that the Quonset huts on base bore no resemblance to the fading majesty of Rome's Coliseum. Little did he know that Koreans' taste for high fashion was flowering just beneath his blinders. I smiled and let the comment pass because they were unnecessarily personal and gratuitous. I rose to leave and thanked him for receiving me. The hairs on the back of my neck tingled and I knew I had not heard the last from him.

Colonel Bristow, on the other hand, enjoyed semi-diplomatic status, and welcomed both Diane and me; offered to work with me and hinted at a shared status that might be the envy of his Army counterpart. I sensed a rivalry that I did not want to be part of, nor did I want to be perceived as having fostered any social distinctions by aligning myself with Colonel Bristow. He was not my host, Colonel King was. Shades of Rome and internecine warfare seemed to be emerging and I was on guard from that day forward.

The early days of my tenure in Pusan were painful for my senior Korean assistant. Apparently, he had established the practice of limiting the American director's access, therefore effectiveness, because of the language barrier. He, in effect, decided who it was important for the American director so see and why. He was a high school graduate in a status-conscious culture. His social access was, therefore, limited and he lacked the intellectual depth and range to engage influential members of the community on issues of concern on the policy agenda we sought to advance. The new direction I sought was a direct challenge to his authority among our staff and, ultimately, control over program direction. It was not long before he realized change was inevitable. I made a surprising discovery during my initial round of introductions within the Korean civic and business communities: my comprehension of the language far exceeded my conversational ability. Many older Korean professionals shared this circumstance: they understood more English than they could use conversationally. It did not take long for my interlocutors and me to realize we could use this to our mutual advantage, particularly in private conversations when U.S. policy or Korean Government practices were the topic. We now had a mutually acceptable solution.

Where I thought staff input was helpful, I accepted it. In large measure, I charted my own course, engaging a stratum of leadership previously ignored by my American predecessors and my senior assistant: the business community. Many of the city's most prominent business leaders were surprised, but pleased at my approach. They shared with me a long standing interest in building a relationship at other than a military level with the American base commander at the Port of Pusan and at Hialeah. Economic growth, developing export markets, building strategic partnerships with foreign partners, and strengthening the Korean economy were the topics uppermost on their minds. These topics headed my agenda and I was determined to engage business leaders as frequently and as productively as I could. I could be an effective sounding board for their ideas, complaints, suggestions and a conduit to share same with my colleagues at the embassy in Seoul. I was also prepared to attempt a dialogue on these new issues without my senior assistant as interpreter, but that would have meant a serious loss of face for him. In Korean society, loss of face had to be avoided at all costs. Although he was uncomfortable with this change in program direction, an opportunity did arise to reduce my dependence on him. While visiting a local manufacturer of export-quality footwear, I was questioning the long-term efficacy of maintaining a competitive advantage through harsh labor practices, low wages, and an unsafe work environment. My assistant must have felt the question too direct because he altered it during translation. Before the president of the company could respond, I said, "Mr. Chung, you did not translate my question accurately." "What did I leave out?" he asked. When I correctly identified the missing phrase, he smiled and said "good, very good." At that point his days as my interpreter were numbered. From that day forward, he would accompany me only on select occasions. I helped him save face by explaining how important it was for me to have him man the office while I was away; that I needed him to maintain the continuity in the relationships I sought to build. I was not sure if he saw the transparency of that argument, but he accepted it graciously. Having solved that problem, I soon learned I had another, more sensitive, problem to address: the reputation of my Korean program director. It was rumored throughout the community of those I was meeting that he was a KCIA (Korean Central Intelligence Agency) informant, that no one would speak in front of him should he ever accompany me. I immediately shared this with my colleagues in Seoul and, without confirming this to be the case, they did not deny it. I understand the language of non-committal when I heard it. Several members of my own staff also believed this to be true and they, too, kept him at arm's length. I believe the feeling in Seoul was that he was not harmful enough to eliminate. In Pusan, however, they took him far more seriously, and that I could not ignore.

Before I continue, I should elaborate on another decision I made that places the question of how I use interpreters in a broader context. Michael Braxton, the other African-American that had served in Korea, shared a personal perspective with me. He made the point that I would have to decide whether I wanted to spend a great deal of my time perfecting my command of the language, or pursuing a more fruitful program and policy dialogue with my Korean interlocutors. He suggested that on a two year tour, I would find it very difficult to accomplish both. I could have structured relationships with Korean academics who would cherish the prestige of working with the American director of USIS Pusan to perfect his knowledge of the language. It would have been easy to spend several hours a day at the local universities and cultural centers with English-speaking academics; socializing with them more frequently than I would, without consequence to my assignment. There was another consideration I could not ignore. I frankly did not know if I wanted to be viewed as a Korean-language officer. My colleague in Kwangju did take the latter approach and he told me years later that was a career mistake. His subsequent assignments for the next dozen years were in China or Korea. He wanted a more diverse geographical experience but he had been tracked as an Asian language specialist. I was fortunate in that many of my Korean interlocutors understood English well enough that I could have a dialogue. They were never comfortable at having an interpreter in the room because it inhibited the candor of the dialogue they sought. Gradually, as I achieved acceptance within the business community, the mayor and the President of the Pusan Chamber of Commerce expressed their gratitude at my willingness to work with them. I was given high marks for a new, refreshing approach that opened doors unknown to even my more senior colleagues at embassy Seoul.

On a monthly basis, outside routine social occasions, I would meet with a business group I had organized early on. The members included the Japanese Consul General, the Honorary Consul from Taiwan, the Austrian General Manager of the Chosun Beach Hotel, and the resident American President of the Bank of America. This would be our time to compare notes, to problem-solve on occasion, and to discuss opportunities. We were all members of the resident expatriate and diplomatic community and many of our interests did converge. Often, we would have as our guest the Mayor of Pusan, the Provincial Governor, the President of the Pusan Chamber of Commerce, or the President of Pusan National University, among others. Our meetings with the mayor were particularly fruitful. He always found our informal style and candor a refreshing change from the more formal relationships he was accustomed to. I was careful to avoid any issues that fell within the program or policy purview of the American commander at Hialeah. That was quite easily done because there were so many other non-military topics of interest. In private conversation, I learned a great deal about Colonel King: that he was a proud man, accustomed to a certain deference within Pusan society, and that my success was problematic for him. It soon came to light that he and his wife resented having to share social prominence with Diane and myself, and that he had never found himself in equal social and professional standing with an African-American. (He was from Louisiana and the product of an era when this would not have been an issue) Although relations between the colonel and myself were correct, I decided his problems were his, not mine.

When Diane and I were not engaged with Koreans, exploring the Province, or unearthing the shopping treasures or culinary delights of Pusan, we were at Hialeah. Given our status, we automatically became members of the base Officers' Club. We quickly discovered that the club was often empty; officers rarely used it to socialize. Perhaps that was a form of silent protest against the base commander. I frequently enjoyed a game of racquetball with one of the few African-American officers there and, he, too, rarely used the club's facilities. As he put it in response to my question about why officers did not support the club, "I have to work with many of those officers during the day; why would I voluntarily choose to socialize with people I do not respect. Moreover, I am not alone in that respect. Like many other officers in this command, I would prefer to be among Koreans."

In contrast, the Enlisted and Non-Commissioned Officers' Club, or commonly referred to as the NCO Club, by reputation, had the best food, the best music and entertainment, and it was frequently crowded. We could attend this club as guests of a member, but not on our own. During the evenings, most officers were at home. Gradually, we began to meet some of the African-American soldiers and civilian contractors there. That is when our real education began. Since most of them were NCOs, they were prohibited from the officers' housing area. It gets worse. On several occasions, Diane and I had extended invitations to African-Americans we met casually and only once did the invitees respond favorably. Naturally, we wondered why. When Colonel King learned that African-American NCOs had visited our home, they were told to respect his order to refrain from entering that area of the base, unless it was for official military business. Attending a social function at our home did not meet that standard. Now we knew! It was not us, as one sergeant and his wife told us one morning in the commissary. "If the two of you are comfortable visiting with us in our homes, you will be welcome with all of us here. We would love to visit with you, but you must understand that we are still in uniform." He laughed slightly and went on to add, "you two are the worst thing that could have happened to the colonel. Whatever you do, do not let him bully you the way he did your predecessor." Thus, our circle of friends on the base expanded significantly. The two of us were often at the NCO Club where the friendships were warm, the music was straight from Motown, and the food was great.

I learned something else from many of the African-American military stationed in Pusan: the only reason they reenlisted to remain in Korea was to avoid duty in Germany, the likely alternative for many of them. Having served in Italy years earlier, I understood that sentiment. As difficult as duty was for those of us serving in Italy, everyone except some of the hardcore NCOs wanted to avoid duty in Germany's famous line outfits. Life in the States, even on military bases, was too expensive, they said. And no one wanted to be assigned to a base in the southern states. Korea became the preferred choice by a process of elimination. Surprisingly, I met a Master Sergeant I had served with 18 years earlier in Italy. Although he did not recognize me at first, I reminded him of several adventures involving the two of us while stationed there. The expression on his face said everything. He just found it difficult to believe that we could meet under our current circumstances. He had married an Italian, which came as no surprise. Normally, his family would have accompanied him, he said, but an unaccompanied tour was shorter; that was his preference. "I have 15 months to complete my eligibility for retirement; that's why I am here by myself. I stay away from the colonel. All I want to do is complete this tour, retire, and get back to my family." That is precisely what he did.

Diane, meanwhile, had found her niche, even within the confines of Korean society as it existed in 1977. A weekly article under her byline appeared in a daily called the Pusan "Ilbo." Her articles would describe current fashions in the U.S., something of considerable interest to the local fashion industry and, naturally, Korean women. She was also invited to become President of the Korean-American Women's Club. Moreover, as a consequence of my contacts in the business community, she also was asked to teach English to middle managers responsible for American accounts. We entertained frequently since Koreans were very much at home in the informal atmosphere of *Chez Kennedy.* These occasions would prompt a level of dialogue often impossible to conduct in someone's office. Everyone was rightly paranoid about expressing an honest opinion either publicly or semi-publicly – even in the privacy of their offices or chauffer-driven automobiles. Dinner and drinks at our home provided the zone of security that made the difference.

My geographic area of responsibility, my "beat" if you will, was the Kyung Sang Nam Do Province. What distinguished it from other provinces in the country was that it is home to the infrastructure the Korean economy depended upon e.g., manufacturing, shipbuilding, export industries, iron and steel production, ports, Free Trade Zones and industrial complexes. Restlessness became my middle name. Several times weekly, I was on the road, visiting every factory with an export division, every shipyard building tankers and other large bulk carriers for foreign owners; and the large industrial complex that offered tax incentives to the foreign investors their complex was designed to attract. In addition, I met with the administration and faculty of each college and university in my district engaged in dialogue with students interested in their country's relationship with America. Moreover, I was a regular at graduation ceremonies held by the Korean Naval Academy at Chin Hae. Often, I sat less than 15-feet from then Korean President Park Chung Hee.

I was one of three American directors at regional posts in Korea and would submit weekly reports to my boss and new country director Matthew Price. In my reports, I would describe the political-psychological climate in Pusan and the Province at large; topics that rippled among my contacts, irritants in our bilateral relationship best communicated discreetly to the embassy in Seoul. I would cover new investments by the Japanese, then a major presence in my district; programs I hosted; and, developments surrounding American and European investments in Pusan. Matthew would share highlights of my reports with William Melton, the new ambassador, and others on the Country Team. The strength of my reports and the ambassador's interest in developments outside Seoul, compelled him to spend three days with me within six months of his arrival in country.

His visit was my show and I prepared meticulously for it. It was important to me that he see and experience the economic and commercial vitality of this district; not just the gracious, unlimited hospitality Koreans were prepared to lavish upon him. During the day, he and I were on the road. A power generating facility using generators supplied by the General Electric Corporation; Pohang Iron and Steel Works; a ship builder who had just launched the world's largest Very Large Crude Carrier (VLCC) - one million deadweight tons; and the Changwon Industrial Complex, also the world's largest, were among our stops. For three days following a major site visit, the ambassador would utter the four-letter expletive - Shit! The meaning was not clear until the end of his visit. We were returning to his hotel at Chosun Beach when he said, "I had no idea this district is as vibrant as it is and offers American investors the opportunities that have been described to me! From now on, we in Seoul will pay more attention to our regional posts and the activities in their districts, especially here in Pusan. Your reporting is useful to me, keep it up! And, let me know what you need from us."

The ambassador's visit was punctuated by an incident that had serious consequences for a member of my staff. My Korean driver, Mr. Lee, performed yeoman duty for the entire visit, without missing a cue. However, on that last day, he failed to meet us at a pre-designated location. In 1977, we did not have radio communications in Pusan; therefore it was impossible to contact him. I was disguising a rising level of irritation, and about to summon a taxicab, when the ambassador said, "it's a pleasant day; can we not walk back? How far is it to the hotel?" "About a mile" I said. From outward appearances, ambassador Melton was a modest man and predisposed to accept that my driver had simply missed a cue. So, he said, "let's walk back." We set off in the direction of the hotel whereupon we spotted Mr. Lee sitting in the car. Mr. Lee was mortified at his misunderstanding and apologized profusely. The ambassador took it well, told me not to mention it to my boss, and that he had enjoyed the walk.

As instructed, I did not report the incident to Matthew. Given his nervousness and timidity in the face of authority, had I done so, he might have suffered a cardiac arrest on the spot with the telephone in his hand. The ambassador must have mentioned it in passing at his senior staff meeting because I did receive a call from Matthew early the day after the ambassador's return to Seoul. When my secretary told me Matthew Price was on the line, I picked up saying "good morning, Matthew " and that is as far as I got. "George, why didn't you tell me? he asked. "Tell you what, Matthew!" "About the incident with your driver." In response, I said, "ambassador Melton took it in good humor as an honest miscue, told me he had a good visit. Moreover, he expressly instructed me not to mention it to you." "Well, he mentioned it at senior staff this morning and I was embarrassed." "Did he complain?" I asked.

"No, everyone had a good laugh, but I was embarrassed." "I want you to terminate Mr. Lee," he instructed. "Are you serious?" "Yes!" "Roy Tidwell (the executive officer) will be in touch with you." That was Matthew's sole purpose for calling. He offered not one word about the ambassador's extended visit. I did hear from the ambassador's deputy, and the economic and political counselors. Now that I recall, I heard from every member of the senior staff. Each of them offered positive comments reflecting their own views, as well as impressions shared by ambassador Melton. They also had good questions. I was now on their radar and I took considerable professional pride in that.

Ambassador Melton's visit underlined my leadership and my effectiveness in Pusan while cementing several key relationships. It also was a mixed blessing. Every officer in Seoul with an economic or commercial portfolio now wanted to visit with us. Before the ambassador's visit, the mantra among embassy officers was, if it did not happen in Seoul, it was of no consequence to them. If it happened down country, it could not be important. That myopic view of the world changed overnight. Some of my embassy colleagues were helpful to me in advancing a dialogue on several specific issues. The commercial attache fell into this category. Others merely consumed time, but it was important to them that they appear sensitive to developments outside Seoul. I suppose it became necessary to "play the game."

President Carter's promise to withdraw American forces from Korea was the key topic in most of my private conversations with influential Koreans in Pusan and throughout the Province. The concern they expressed was real and troubling to people accustomed to the security trip-wire American forces represented. Often in private, I tried to make the point that campaign promises become policy only after they meet the "real world test," a test this promise likely would not survive. On this highly salient, but emotional issue, Koreans were not to be mollified. The new administration finally dispatched noted Georgetown University academic Jean Kirkpatrick to Korea for extended consultations with national and provincial leaders. Geopolitical and geostrategic imperatives on the Korean Peninsula had to be addressed in some detail. Her public mission was to explain President Carter's Korea policy, without saying publicly our American forces would not be withdrawn. Reality prevailed over rhetoric and the Koreans, at least in my district, understood that this was President Carter's attempt to say that he had seen the "real world."

The pulse of Pusan was business, competitiveness, and exports, and I tapped into the rich vein of opportunities each sector provided to advance American commercial objectives. I worked hard and was fortunate enough to be seen by the right people. For example, Wang Sang Eun was one of the city's most respected businessmen, advisor to Korean Presidents, a member of the South Korean Senate, owner of a major shipping company (Hyopsung), and a friend of the United States. He became my most consistent supporter and, ultimately, a close friend. He widened the network of people I had access to. It was he that ensured I could approach the leadership of the industries within my district that formed the backbone of the Korean economy. When the President of the American Can Company flew into Pusan on his company's corporate jet, something most Koreans there had never seen, Wang Sang Eun made sure I had identified the local companies operating at comparable levels of efficiency, who were therefore, of interest to our American visitors. The relationship I was able to nurture with Mr. Wang, who became a true Korean partner, involved a process extending well beyond my two-year tenure in Pusan. It was to endure almost 20 years. I derived considerable personal and professional satisfaction from being the man on the ground at that time. In the eyes of my Korean interlocutors, there was no daylight between the audio of what I said and the video of my behavior.

A decision early in my tenure as Director of the Pusan mission contributed to the success I subsequently enjoyed, and that was selecting a personal assistant/secretary. Although my staff grudgingly accepted the change in program and policy direction, they still were determined to slow down the transition. I needed an assistant loyal to me, who would not report my every move and conversation; and, someone who would not work at cross purposes with me to ensure the primacy of my staff in defining our new mission. I needed someone loyal to me. Among the several candidates my staff brought forth for an interview was a former staff member of the United Nations Development Project (UNDP). She was the atypical Korean female because of her range of professional interests, experience, and contacts within the city's business and development communities. She was pleasant, competent, diligent, and spoke English at a high level of proficiency. To my great fortune, I hired her. My Korean program director, alas, did not favor her selection for this sensitive position. It was unfortunate, but I had to have eyes and ears during my frequent absences because my senior Korean assistant was determined to regain his standing within a more narrow spectrum of academics and second-tier officials at the expense of the program I had begun to build.

Korean society at that time was vastly different than it is now. Assistants to Korean executives and senior government officials functioned as mere receptionists then. Frequently, a secretary to an executive would sit at a small desk outside his door. When the telephones rang on the desk inside, they got up, entered the office to respond to the telephones on his desk. Often, there were multiple instruments. Somehow, prestige was also a function of the number of instruments on your desk. My important contacts quickly learned, and accepted, to speak to Mrs. Lee during my absence. I was able to build on her already considerable skills. My Korean contacts reasoned Americans were different. Assistants are vital to them. Interacting across cultural boundaries, they could justify discussing business arrangements with someone at a lower social level. Nothing was simple; everything had to be accommodated within an established mindset. Mrs. Lee quickly gained their confidence given her UNDP background. Eventually, I had to tell her she would pay a price with our staff for breaking the mold. She understood, but preferred to build on her prior experience rather than stagnate.

One evening, Mrs. Lee invited Diane and me for dinner at her home as an expression of gratitude for offering her a position on my staff. We instantly fell in love with her son, and only child, JiYub. He became the child we did not have. Her family became our surrogate family. Her contacts also included lesser known, but highly talented, members of Pusan's fashion and design community. In addition to her articles, Diane was now able to collaborate with a local designer, thanks to Mrs. Lee, destined to develop Korea's most successful fashion house: Bae Young Fashions. He prevailed upon Diane and she often modeled his latest creations, thus ensuring maximum media and Korean industry coverage. Bae Young Fashions thrived with this exotic brown beauty on its runways. With the collaboration of the general manager of the Chosun Beach, the city's newest luxury hotel, Diane and I, working with Mrs. Lee, staged the city's first Fashion Disco Ball in the spring of 1978, featuring fashions by Bae Young.

The social context for this event is revealing of the social climate in Pusan in the 1970s. Koreans were exhorted by their political leadership to refrain from attending lavish social events, especially those with a western character. President Park Chung Hee desired that the nation remain serious in purpose, focused, and anti-decadence. Technically, he said, the South was still at war with the Communist North. A daily nationwide curfew was still in effect from midnight until 4 am, except on the Island of Che Ju Do. It might seen strange to anyone else, but many Koreans were simply afraid to have a good time, especially in public. The political and social leadership of Pusan responded well to our attempts to solidify the bonds of friendship between our two societies and sanctioned support for what was to become the social event of the year, "The First Annual Fashion-Disco Ball." The night of the Ball, Pusan Mayor Choi (pronounced Che') and the Provincial Governor were seen actually dancing with their wives, something no one had ever witnessed. Rather than return to their homes before curfew, many Koreans took rooms at the hotel to stay and have an old-fashioned good time. The event was a glittering success and it united elements of the local community in a fashion that most events did not. Mrs. Lee helped to make the difference.

Several days after the Ball, I received a call from Mayor Choi asking me to visit with him. Mayor Choi was a staunch supporter of my business outreach program and naturally I scheduled an appointment for the following day. When his executive aide ushered me into his inner office, the Mayor rose and walked toward me. He clasped my right hand with his while placing his left hand just above my right wrist – a true and sincere gesture of friendship. "Mr. Kennedy," be began, "the people of Pusan and I really appreciate all of your effort on our behalf. Your outreach to the business community, and the activities you conduct at your center and within our universities, distinguishes you from many of your predecessors...We have never had a director as active as you are; the Ball was the first event of its type in the city." "Koreans are hardworking people and they need to have some fun on occasion," I said. "I hope I have not complicated your job." The Mayor laughed and added, "my wife might expect a little more from me, but I just wanted to say how much we appreciate having you here."

Clawson had told me to revitalize the program in Pusan and I was doing just that. I thrived on my independence away from the stifling atmosphere I knew existed within USIS Seoul. This particular meeting with Mayor Choi also marked my first anniversary in Pusan. I felt a part of the city's fabric, a feeling derived from the confidences many senior contacts frequently shared with me that I was not at liberty to discuss. I had my finger on the pulse and I felt on top of my game. Now was the time to launch an idea I knew would ignite intense interest in Seoul: upgrade our diplomatic presence in Pusan by establishing an American Consulate there, or at least building a strong rationale for upgrading our presence there.

Before I could do so, however, a major controversy erupted between USIS and Colonel King, one that reverberated in Seoul with the ambassador and with Colonel King's superior, a two-star general in the city of Taegu. As the commanding officer at the Hialeah Military Compound, Colonel King was the de facto equivalent of a small town mayor, a role no one could have been more ill-suited for than he. It would have taken more than a complete facelift to improve the physical appearance of the collection of Quonset huts, cinder block ramblers, and post-Korean War, wood frame huts that housed the several thousand Army personnel assigned to this small, but important command. Morale on any given day was in the tank. Colonel King's dictatorial and ubiquitous presence, according to his troops, was the consequence of a mediocre officer who felt he was destined for larger responsibility. He patrolled the community and would often stop someone to inquire about their destination, particularly if the individual was an enlisted person and seemingly headed in the wrong direction. That was interpreted to mean destinations not generally frequented by enlisted personnel. His Louisiana background manifested itself in ways that constantly irritated the African-Americans and some whites. In large measure, he seemed to be underemployed.

Seven months after our arrival, Colonel King decided to paint every officer's house white with black trim. The pastel-colored buildings, which previous families appreciated because it broke the monotony of military uniformity, must have offended the colonel's aesthetic tastes. This was a decree from on high. The resulting disquiet was of little concern to him. When we received our notice to this effect, we contacted the responsible officer to request that our quarters be exempt, citing our status, personal preference, and ease of recognition for Korean visitors. Initially, our request was granted and Diane was visibly relieved. Several days later, I was in my office when the telephone rang. It was Diane and she was quite upset. That morning, the housing officer had called to inform her that Colonel King's "no exception" would apply to us as though we, too, were members of his command. In an earlier conversation, I pointed out that under the terms of the agreement between the Command and the embassy, all maintenance costs on our residence were the responsibility of the embassy, another basis for our exemption. To Colonel King, this was an exception to his authority, and that he would not countenance. He wanted uniformity, our residence included. Diane asked me if she could make a personal appeal. I saw no harm in that.

We rehearsed what she would say and I went back to work. Shortly after lunch, my telephone rang and my secretary, Mrs. Lee, said it was Colonel King. Diane had called after her meeting and this was a call I was expecting. In a calm, steady voice, he proceeded to characterize Diane's visit as a high-handed intrusion, during which she imperiously demanded an exception. I was mystified by this characterization and went on to explain in some detail the background to our request, the fact that an exception had been granted and subsequently revoked.

Moreover, I supported Diane's effort to make a personal appeal. I told Colonel King that Diane had called me after the disappointing visit. This time, she was even more distraught. What disturbed me was the contrast between her characterization of the meeting and that of Colonel King. According to Diane, he had consented to see her, allowed her to explain again, why we sought an exception. To that point, he had been gracious and even offered her a cup of coffee. In response, he reproached her for "coming in my office with your little tin pot on demanding an exception." That was not Diane's style and I knew it. I pointed this out to Colonel King. I expressed concern about the outcome of the meeting and took issue with his characterization of my wife. Moreover, I wanted him to know that I was unsettled by the capricious and arbitrary process by which he made this decision. "Diane," I said, "was not one of your troops."

Meanwhile, Colonel King's wife had been actively expressing her unhappiness over Diane's presidency of the Korean-American Women's Club. Elections were on the horizon and she would not support a second term for Diane. As the wife of the ranking military officer, she "wore" the rank of her husband over the subordinate status of each member's military spouse. This is military culture: hierarchical, rigid, and undemocratic. The Korean members acquiesced and, contrary to the desires of the membership, Diane did not stand for re-election. Diane resigned from the club because several members told her what was going on and how they felt about it. Diane, by now, was well known within the Pusan media establishment and the business community. She had more than enough opportunities to compensate for this "tempest in a teapot." The convergence of these two events, however, was unfortunate, unnerving, and psychologically debilitating. For the first time in our marriage, we had a crisis, one I had to get involved in. The Colonel's ire was focussed and I knew it. What infuriated me was the coordinated, cowardly attack on my wife.

It is standard practice with me to fight my own battles and involve those I deem it right and proper to do so. The decision point was whether to call my boss, Matthew Price or the ambassador. Diane was insisting that I do so. Matthew would have panicked whereas Clawson Ridgeway would have resolved it in a manner that respected the autonomy we enjoyed while acknowledging the command authority of Colonel King over his military personnel, but not us. That is what the situation called for. After some discussion, we decided that the better outcome would flow from a call from Diane to the ambassador rather than from me. The issue was domestic and not program or policy. I may have erred in judgment on this particular occasion, but that was a calculated risk I was prepared to take.

My immediate supervisor was the Deputy Director of USIS Korea. Therefore, I briefed him on this development including Diane's call to the ambassador. "Never blindside your boss." The ambassador meanwhile, called USIS and, more importantly, he called Colonel King's boss, a two-star general in Taegu. The avalanche continued to gather force. The general, as related to me by Colonel King in a subsequent conversation, called him, stood him at attention, took several large bites out of his generous posterior anatomy by reminding him that George Kennedy has equal standing in the Kyung-Sang Nam Do Province and is responsible for everything non-military. Well, there it was, the reality Colonel King sought to insulate himself from: equal status with an African-American.

As the debris began to settle, Lawrence Nichols, became the designated hitter to deal with Colonel King. Nichols told me this was not a new development with embassy personnel outside Seoul; that frankly, he was not surprised at Colonel King's behavior. To avoid reoccurrence of similar treatment by military authorities at the U.S. Eighth Army's sprawling housing complex at Yongsan Army Base in Seoul, embassy personnel lived in a designated section of the base, outside the jurisdiction of standard Army maintenance directives. Nichols said that I should avoid further direct contact with the Colonel, that he would resolve the issue. I let the matter rest.

Nichols, who was to explain the policy to Colonel King, capitulated to assuage King's wounded psyche, and our house was subsequently included in the latest base "remodeling scheme." My ensuing conversation with Nichols was not one of our more productive. What was essential for me during my conversation with him was to record my disappointment over the outcome he negotiated without expressly stating that he had betrayed us. The Colonel's behavior had contradicted the spirit of the agreement between our two offices. More narrowly, his behavior revealed the limits of his willingness to coexist with a non-white equal. Entrenched feelings were aroused which he obviously could not rise above.

Diane was an emotional shell by now, and I was concerned for her and our relationship. This was an unnecessary degree of stress that could have been avoided. Now, I had something else to add to my list: could my wife survive in that environment? I grappled with this daily. She had handled herself well considering her lack of experience with military culture. I also knew I was unwilling to risk her emotional health by keeping her with me. The light in her eyes began to flicker and that hurt. We decided that she would return home and join me at the end of my tour.

Over the summer and fall of 1978 while back at home, Diane would avail herself of the opportunity to complete the few remaining course requirements for her Baccalaureate degree. I notified Matthew who suspected nothing other than what we revealed to him. And, suddenly, I was alone with a house that no longer rang of Diane's laughter, busywork, and time spent with JiYub and Sam, the daughter of our neighbor across the street. Sam was JiYub's co-model for some of Diane's photo projects. Diane arrived home safely and I plunged into my latest project: documenting voices of support to establish an American Consulate in Pusan. I had the support of every key local and provincial official, including the growing American private sector; leading Korean industrialists, the banking sector, and the Korean Chamber of Commerce. I performed the due diligence and forwarded my report to Seoul. I am not sure what I expected beyond a discussion with Matthew during which he would ask, "George, what's this? What are you up to?" Change, or the prospect of it, frightened Matthew. He was a staunch proponent of maintaining the status quo; eschew innovation in program development. Avoid bold new ideas. Do not stretch the proverbial envelope; put it back in the box.

My proposal excited every officer in both the economic and political sections who suddenly viewed himself as the likely candidate to become a Principal Officer (Consul) in Pusan. Of course, the ambassador would have to request that the Department of State enter into a formal dialogue with the Korean Government to upgrade our presence in Pusan. My telephone began to ring more often than usual. My colleagues in Seoul either wanted to visit or pump me for information. On the serious side, my proposal did generate considerable interest and was forwarded to Washington for review. Although I never received any formal response beyond an acknowledgment of a well-developed proposal, I was told months later that budget considerations were a major factor militating against a positive response. That could have meant anything since "budget considerations" is a favored catchall response when a more definitive response has political or other sensitive elements to consider. The political counselor did suggest that it was just a matter of time before we would elevate the level of our diplomatic representation in Korea's second largest city. Within five years, a consulate was established and I take considerable pride in having contributed to that important change.

Concurrent with these developments, USIS Korea was undergoing a Post Inspection. Matthew feared the outcome because he knew he did not have the respect of his staff. The inspectors came, they saw, and they published their findings. I responded candidly to all of their questions. My whole approach, as I explained to them and, later to Matthew, was to bring credit to USIS and its Country Director through an aggressive, innovative program with strong local support and the interest of the ambassador. Is that not what was expected of good officers? Matthew, the super cautious administrator that he was, thought his image, whatever he perceived that to be, would suffer, that his judgment would be questioned if he supported me. Whereas I had been able to convert Charles Royster in Rome, Matthew lacked the strength of character of a Charles Royster.

The final report was so damaging, Matthew would only allow one copy to be produced. Moreover, he directed that Roy Tidwell, the executive officer, personally travel to each of the three constituent posts to allow us to read it in Tidwell's presence, only; that no copies of any portion be copied. The report was damning. It began by condemning the lack of leadership from Matthew and then explained in meticulous detail the effect that had on our program in Korea. It is not unheard of for a staff to rally around a director if he or she is respected, but has other flaws. In Matthew's case, the staff was not reticent about voicing well-documented leadership deficiencies. One of the inspectors noted somewhat sarcastically that the Director of USIS Pusan aspired to become a Principal Officer – as though officers like myself should not have such lofty ambition. My operation, however, was in overall good shape.

Diane and I exchanged letters several times weekly. She did note that many of her female friends felt strongly that she erred in returning home; that she should have remained in Korea. Her difficulties, they suggested, were the "stuff" of the life she had chosen. Diane wanted to know what I thought about their comments and her decision to leave. I was torn between supporting her and acknowledging the veracity of her friends' observations. In the end, I decided to allow time to lapse to see if Diane would rise above her seeming ambivalence and conclude that either she was prepared to live with and defend her decision, or do as they suggest and return to Korea.

In December 1978, I had my answer: she completed the requirements for her degree and decided to return to Pusan in time for Christmas. I did miss her along with the many friends she had made in the city. JiYub was certainly happy that "Oh-mon-ee" (phonetic Korean for "aunty") was coming back. Diane's return had a pleasant and unusual twist to it. When my delegation of friends and I went to the train station to meet her, there was a slight delay before she emerged, even though the train had arrived on time. When she did emerge, the delay was delightfully obvious. She had wrapped herself in a giant, red Christmas bow with a card attached that read, "Merry Christmas, Giorgio, from your wife Diane." That was Diane, the spice in my life. She was back. The other change in both our lives had been the arrival of a new base commander.

In January 1979, the usual waltz with the USIA Personnel Division began: my next assignment. I knew I could not depend on Matthew for support. Here, I should elaborate. Matthew visited each of his regional posts before Christmas and our dialogue was truly extraordinary for what it revealed about his lack of integrity and character. Even I was surprised this time. Matthew knew how inbred my staff was and that they did not believe in our expanded mission. He also knew I had a green light from Ambassador Melton to develop a more aggressive outreach effort to civic and business leadership in my region to support larger embassy objectives. I was in the trenches and he did not trust my judgment – judgment validated by our ambassador and USIS Inspectors. Toward the end of our meeting, he did acknowledge that although my ideas initially did scare him, ultimately, my effort was designed to energize the country program and make him look good. He even offered an apology for his lack of support. I thought I had a tailored opening to solicit his support for my next assignment. After briefing him on the state of my negotiations with Washington, I asked him as straightforward as I could, "would you be willing to help me now?" To which he responded, "No! You can make it on your own. You have a strong character, you're aggressive and you don't need my help." When my boss could have been supportive, he again chose not to. That was Matthew, one of USIA's "golden boys." He fit the mold; I did not. Therefore, for my next assignment, I was on my own. There was nothing else I could accomplish in Pusan without greater support from Seoul. I was emotionally in conflict about severing some relationships, but, professionally, I knew I had to move on. Had Clawson Ridgeway remained as Director of USIS Korea, not only would I have had a different experience in Pusan, there is the added possibility I might have redirected my focus from Europe to East Asia and the Pacific.

This chapter is not yet complete. Something else happened which offered Diane a task she relished as a re-introduction to Pusan now that she was back. The First Annual Fashion-Disco Ball had been such a success, pressure had been building for an encore before our March departure. Several influential friends had approached me the previous November and quietly broached the idea. "If you organize it, Mr. Kennedy, we will support it" they said. "Do not worry!" To fit my timeframe, it had to be in late January or February if we were going to avoid colliding with arrangements for our March departure. I made quite a few telephone calls and a date was set for February. On this occasion, I partnered with the Pusan and Taegu chapters of the F.&A.A.Y.M. Masonic Lodge at Hialeah. Its African-American members were active, well organized, and in search of an opportunity our Ball presented to showcase their organization, and possibly to recruit new members. Once the word went out on base, I had to put a lid on ticket sales to ensure a balance with the Korean community. This time, the Koreans knew what to expect and the event was a greater success. They really got into the spirit of having a great time. Remember, this was 1979 and Korean men did not dance publicly. Every table was sold. Bae Young Fashions with Diane as their lead model graced the runway. John Esterhazy, general manager of the Chosun Beach, told me the occupancy rate for that one evening was beyond expectations for a cold night in February. This was the perfect antidote for the brutal experience Diane had suffered months earlier. Once again, she sparkled, she laughed, and she left no detail unattended as we made preparations for what would be our farewell to a city we loved and a people who welcomed us as family. There could not have been a more fitting tribute for all of the goodwill she brought to Korea. As our final gesture before departure, we sold our car and donated $7,500, the amount over the original purchase price, to the city to finance the purchase of an incubator for one of the local orphanages. We chose an orphanage we had visited on several occasions. The City of Pusan would not soon forget us.

A large measure of the success I achieved in Pusan is attributed to my relationship with Mayor Choi Suk Won. We forged a partnership that reaped mutually beneficial dividends. My departure, generally a non-event for the political and business leadership in the region, did not go unnoticed. Mayor Choi hosted a farewell luncheon that rivaled my reception two years earlier. I deeply appreciated the gesture; it spoke volumes about the man and what he felt we accomplished together.

In retrospect, the assignment to Pusan had represented a pivotal point in my career. There, I was on my own; my hand was on the tiller. A medium-sized tiller, but a tiller, nonetheless. It was my responsibility to develop a program, define objectives, and justify the resources to achieve them. For other projects, I had to marshall independent resources. In Pusan, I was accountable at a different level. Moreover, I learned the value of good leadership to the directors of constituent posts within a country. In Rome, I was a direct report to mission leadership. The contrast between Matthew Price and Alex Klieforth can be measured in the degree of respect accorded by their staffs and colleagues. Matthew was the classic study of leadership mistakes to avoid. Korea is a true Asian society, different than Western Europe, and even the Philippines. I had navigated one of the world's more difficult languages and social systems, and achieved something that fit well with my interests and goals. My experience reinforced my conviction that I can make a difference in the realm of people, diplomacy, and ideas. Again, this was not Italy. For the first time, I liked the feel of the ground under my feet. The senior ranks of the Foreign Service were only one promotion away, which made my next assignment a matter of crucial importance. The process of securing that next assignment continued to be frustrating, but I was committed to it. Before I left Rome, Charles Royster, the Deputy Director of USIS Italy, wrote in my final evaluation that "Mr. Kennedy had the potential to make a significant contribution to the Service if his assignments were chosen with care." The next assignment was also key to my goal of an assignment to one of Europe's important regional economic posts in Brussels or Paris. I could not appreciate that the process of shaping that next assignment would almost cost me my life on the eve of my departure from Pusan.

Just before 5 pm on a Wednesday evening, while sitting in my office preparing for a meeting with a group of academics from local colleges and universities, I developed a headache, possibly from tension. I innocently took two Bufferin and, a short time later, plunged into a lively discussion about American values, a favorite topic of Korean academics. My headache subsided; I went home around 8:30 pm. Just before dawn the next morning, around 5 am, I awoke experiencing difficulty breathing. Diane was asleep as I went into the bathroom. Switching on the light, I looked into the mirror. My own image shocked me. My face had swelled to twice its normal size. Trying not to panic, I dressed quickly and quietly and ran to the military infirmary on base. Although the junior enlisted man on duty sensed the urgency of my situation and called the duty physician immediately, it was two hours before the doctor finally arrived. While waiting, I called Diane, told her what had happened, and that she should not worry. I was doing enough of that for the both of us. Oddly enough, the physician, a captain, was decidedly unconcerned that I had breathing difficulties; told me that I had had an allergic reaction, gave me an injection, and sent me home. I thought allergic reactions were serious business. His cavalier attitude did unsettle me, but raising my concern to a higher level, given that I was not military, would only have made matters worse. The previous base commander was from Louisiana and many of his personal views regarding African-Americans were widely known within his command. The new commander was still fairly new and it was unclear to me how he was perceived by his troops. Their perceptions affected their relationship with you; this I knew from experience.

Somehow, I felt I must have had a reaction to the Bufferin. I have no evidence to support that conclusion, but on a gut level, I believed it. I was an allergy sufferer of long standing, but had never experienced a massive swelling like this. My predecessor had died at Post because of inadequate medical care and the possibility of a reoccurrence set off alarm bells in the Kennedy household and with our director in Seoul. There is a serious note to all of this. Routine health issues in the Foreign Service can become life-threatening because of our nomadic existence and the unevenness in the quality of medical care available to us around the globe.

The proposed change in our lives was dramatic. After a frustrating and confusing long distance dialogue with Washington, I was to be assigned to the American Embassy in Nepal as Director of USIS. This was an assignment I had not sought. It was a position that had not been advertised worldwide, as all positions were 1979. This also was an assignment not in my best career interests, particularly now in light of a heightened concern about my health. As an interesting footnote, what I did not know at the time was that reorganization at Washington Headquarters resulted in a more complex assignments' process. An officer's Career Counselor ("mangler") was no longer that officer's principal advocate. Each officer now had an Area Personnel Officer who was that officer's advocate for an assignment within a designated geographic bureau (Western Europe and Canada; Near East and North Africa; Latin America and the Caribbean; East Asia and the Pacific.) My Career Counselor was new, someone I did not know. I was later informed by my Area Personnel Officer that my new Career Counselor "does not like you, George. I don't know why, but he will not advance your name for any of your stated assignment preferences. He was determined to send you to Nepal."

Without agreeing to accept the Nepal assignment, we returned to Washington on March 29, 1979. Korea had presented new challenges and I looked forward to even greater change. Nepal did not fit the equation. That would have to be sorted out in Washington. After an emotional round of farewells, we headed east. Leaving the Lee family and their son JiYub was more gut wrenching than watching Solange depart from my life.

CHAPTER 12

CHANGE – STANDING ON THE THRESHOLD

My first overseas assignment as an independent director of a USIS mission in South Korea had been a clarifying experience for me. I thought a lot about this on the flight home. Coming out of Korea, I now knew and accepted a defining quality of my character: I do thrive on change, taking risks to make positive things happen, and assuming leadership. The greater the challenge, the harder I work to develop bona fide solutions to problems. I like building relationships and my creative juices flow more readily when innovation might be the most effective way to achieve an objective. While I did not know what to expect back at USIA Washington, instinct told me I was going to be tested no less than I had been in Pusan. In a perverse way, I almost looked forward to it. Perhaps I was steeling myself psychologically; a survival mechanism.

I also felt it would be good to be back in Washington for other reasons as well. There were small fissures in my marriage that could only widen had I readily accepted the assignment to Nepal. The more research Diane and I did on this "backpacker's paradise," the less enamored we were of accepting it as the next chapter in our lives. Perhaps it would be a fun adventure for a week or two, but three years! The reality of that just did not register with either of us. At this point, I did not have the right answers to the questions I had regarding this assignment. Our marriage could be in jeopardy. More research and contemplation was necessary; there was just no way around that.

A major, but related consideration had to be a better understanding of why I had such a negative reaction to Bufferin. In all of my years of coping with a serious allergy condition, I had never suffered an allergy-related attack as grave as this most recent one. Sinus and nasal congestion, severe headaches, antibiotics and other prescription drugs were just part of my regimen to manage my condition. However, the image I saw in the mirror early that morning at home in Pusan was frightening. I could not help but think, had I been in Nepal rather than Pusan, the results really could have been fatal. I do not know this to be a fact, but soon came to understand that the health risks inherent in going to Nepal were unacceptable.

The challenge I faced now was to address my health problem while trying to keep my career on track. The two were inextricably intertwined. The first item then on my agenda, once back at USIA, was to meet with my career counselor. He and I had never met even though we had corresponded frequently. Our first meeting was cordial and professional, but it was all too apparent he was not prepared to respond to any questions I raised regarding my other assignment preferences. The decision to assign me to our embassy in Kathmandu was final, at least it was in his mind. I could see that it was futile to press the issue in that first meeting so I resolved to revisit it at a later date. My real purpose was just to introduce myself and begin a dialogue about my assignment preferences and the reasons I felt qualified for them. Under normal circumstances, we would have begun that dialogue before I departed Korea. I don't recall why that exchange did not happen. Following the meeting with my career counselor, my next stop was the medical unit at the State Department for an emergency ENT (ear-nose-throat) referral.

Two days later, Dr. Fairbanks, of the Washington-based ENT Group, delivered the grim news: a severe case of nasal polyps. He described my options in this order: a) to have radical surgery to remove them; b) a one-time cortisone treatment to relieve the pressure within my nasal passages; or, c) to do nothing and run the risk of developing an asthmatic condition. My first question was, "what are nasal polyps? And, how did I develop the condition? As I reasoned it, following his explanation, my only real option was surgery, to be preceded by a period of treatment. That was the remedy I chose and it probably did not come as a surprise to Dr. Fairbanks. Surgery was not imminent, but he did recommend that I not delay for an indeterminate period. When he learned the mode of travel I employed to return from Korea, he leaned forward across his desk saying, "Mr. Kennedy, you could have suffered an attack en-route and died. You should have been properly diagnosed in Pusan and advised not to fly under any circumstances; obviously you were not!"

That remark then led to a discussion about my pending assignment to Nepal. "Mr. Kennedy," Dr. Fairbanks continued, "you cannot fly in your condition. You are prohibited from flying pending a final medical evaluation, therefore you will not be going to Nepal." Although I was delighted at that bit of news, I confess a certain unease.

Here is why. I had been misdiagnosed in Pusan and that could have resulted in my being the second director of USIS Pusan to die on duty. That was frightening. The really good news was Nepal. I did not want that assignment.

Earlier, I had placed a call to the USIS director in Nepal to gain a sense of what we might expect were we to move there. The conditions she described were so harsh at that time that I elected not to tell Diane about it until the assignment was settled. I decided then I would do what it took to break the assignment. Fortunately, I was now declared medically ineligible to travel to Nepal. The issue, therefore, was moot.

My focus now was on the future and that meant another round of talks with my career counselor, Howard Roswell, about a desirable Washington assignment. I did not look forward to it but it had to be done. Upon learning that I would not be going to Nepal, Howard, according to his colleagues, became enraged. I, however, did not have the option of negotiating an assignment with anyone other than Howard Roswell, therefore, I arranged to meet with him. To me, the only issue was available assignments for which I was competitive. That was my agenda for the meeting when I walked in to meet with him. He was abrupt and hostile. I was more than a little perplexed because this was our first extended meeting. Remember, I did not know this officer. His comments bear repeating: "I heard you were not satisfied with your assignment, that you felt you were being treated unfairly." And then, he really got ugly: "I guess guys like you think the system doesn't work for them. You probably refer to me as whitey or something like that." Nothing I had said before justified his last comment. And, yes, I was angered by this gratuitous assumption on his part. I told him I did not have to tolerate his behavior and immediately left his office.

I then scheduled a meeting with Carmela Menendez, the Director of USIA Personnel. At my request she did agree to review the background of my assignment, including the exchange of correspondence with my counselor, Howard Roswell. I was still mystified by his hostility toward me, therefore my only recourse was to seek her direct intervention. When we did meet, I did say "it is impossible to have a constructive dialogue with someone openly hostile and disinclined to act in a manner supportive of my best career interests." A week later, Carmela Menendez and I met again. At that meeting, she agreed that I had been "treated unfairly," but, surprisingly enough, she was not prepared to take remedial action. "Go home, George, until you hear from us. There are no vacant positions at the moment." Imagine that level of response from the director of personnel! I knew better than that; I had served in personnel. I knew how the system could work. But at that moment, I was not in a position to play a stronger hand.

Home for us temporarily was a spare bedroom at the home of my good friends, Jim and Sylvia Nance. They had just recently purchased a new house in Clinton, Maryland, several miles from the old Nance homestead in Southeast Washington. Life for us changed because an overseas assignment was not medically possible. I was to be assigned to Washington and this meant having to find more permanent housing. At that time, I did not own a house in the Greater Washington Metropolitan Area.

As the days and weeks became months without an assignment, I became increasingly concerned about my competitiveness during this promotion cycle. Given that I was an unassigned officer, I spent my days walking the corridors at USIA in an attempt to advance my candidacy for possible openings. I also checked bulletin boards for available housing. Washington can be clannish and, since I had been abroad for the past seven years, I was an unknown quantity and I had to re-establish myself. I lacked a "Godfather," someone who can make things happen for you. Through an acquaintance, I re-established contact with Gordon Hill, an African-American officer currently serving as a special assistant to the Secretary of State. Gordon was seeking a qualified replacement due to a pending assignment at our embassy in London.

Gordon Hill and I had served together in Rome during the 1970s and he asked me if I would be interested in interviewing as his replacement. My star at USIA had dipped below the horizon, so I naturally said I would. Although Gordon supported the Secretary of State, his duty assignment was headed by the immensely popular, and well-respected Hodding Carter, the Assistant Secretary of State for Public Affairs. Through Gordon, I met Hodding. Among the 33 candidates he personally interviewed for the position, I became his first and only choice.

I thought an assignment to the Department of State would be well received at USIA since they could not find a suitable job for me and I had solved their problem if I could be detached to fill this new position. When Assistant Secretary Carter made a routine request to assign me from USIA to the Department, I suddenly became indispensable to USIA. This was an interesting turn of events.

The Director of Personnel at USIA refused to release me, but she could not find a job for me. I was spending each day within the Bureau of Public Affairs at the State Department learning a job I wanted and felt I would eventually have. I had nothing else to do. Meanwhile, the impasse between USIA and State grew wider. I had now become a "cause celebre," according to William Dracht, Hodding's principal deputy. That was never anyone's intention. I was looking for an interesting job and had found one, only to find myself in the vortex of another storm.

Hodding Carter was naturally mystified by USIA's resistance to *my* assignment, but not the assignment of any of the other USIA officers assigned as public affairs officers in his bureau. His was the principal bureau for press and media affairs within the Washington foreign policy establishment. That is what USIA's officers did. At one point, my "case" reached the office of Louis Martin, Special Assistant to President Carter, and a good friend of Hodding's. Martin called John Reinhardt, the Director of USIA. According to Hodding, the call went something like this: "John, I don't understand this situation. Hodding tells me you are not able to offer George Kennedy a position. He is currently sitting at home, has a good record, according to Hodding, and he is Hodding's preferred candidate for a position that provides public affairs support for Secretary (of State) Vance. John, you well know that one of my responsibilities is to try and place competent Blacks in this administration. I assume you are taking a similar posture in your shop. If you cannot offer George anything at this time, let him go!" John Reinhardt did not need that call.

I was at home the day of that conversation. My day was made memorable by two calls: one from John Reinhardt informing me that "we have been working diligently to find you a good job" and that "you will be hearing from the Office of Personnel, possibly even today." The second call was from Howard Roswell asking me to come to review a list of position vacancies. "A list," I thought! Yesterday, they had nothing; today they have a list of vacancies. Howard's call only confirmed what most officers already knew: Personnel does not always reveal all job vacancies. Some are held in reserve for contingencies and for officers fortunate enough to have a "Godfather." I suddenly became a contingency with two Godfathers.

The next day, I dutifully reported to USIA's Office of Personnel to review the list. Howard was, again, overtly hostile. The hostility he exhibited at our last meeting did not compare with what I encountered at this meeting. It was immediately clear he did not approve of this latest turn of events. Each of the positions on the list he handed me was desirable, and I immediately selected the dream job of "Director, Office of Policy, Planning, and Evaluation in the Directorate for

Educational and Cultural Affairs." "You should go down and meet with Dr. Alice Ilchman," Howard advised. Interestingly enough, none of the six positions on the list I held in my hand had been advertised at the time I submitted my earlier bids for an assignment – domestic or foreign; a contravention of stated USIA policy. That was of little to no consequence at this point because I was pleased to have a job. By now, I thought bizarre was behind me. But it, again reared its ugly head. Stay with me!

I immediately headed for the office of Dr. Ilchman, the Associate Director of the Bureau for Educational and Cultural Affairs. Dr. Ilchman was a prominent scholar appointed by the Carter Administration to manage one of our most important programs: the U.S. government's global network of professional and scholarly educational and cultural exchanges. Exchanges of scholars and civic and government officials are essential to telling America's story abroad, and to fostering the introduction of democratic elections, free market principles, and the rule of law. This program has had an illustrious roster of alumni including the heads of state or government of most of the sovereign nations around the world. My first meeting with Dr. Ilchman went well; at least I thought so. It certainly was the most pleasant encounter I had had with a USIA official in the three months since my return from Korea. She briefly outlined the purpose of the Office of Policy Planning and how it related to her program and policy objectives. She then directed me to the policy staff a few steps down the hall from her office. Bizarre was now about to re-emerge. While introducing myself to the other four members of the policy staff, Dr. Ilchman called central personnel, apparently to remind them that she had promised the position of Director of Policy Planning to another officer. In fact, the officer she was referring to was en-route to Washington. My meeting with the policy staff lasted approximately five minutes, whereupon I returned to Dr. Ilchman's office. This time, however, the content and tone of our dialogue was vastly different. Although gracious, she was apologetic. "I'm sorry, George," she began. "The position you selected has been promised to someone else. Personnel must have meant the position of Policy Officer, Western European Programs, which is also a position on the policy staff."

I tried to mask my confusion because the position she now made reference to was not among the list of six presented to me by Howard Roswell less than 30-minutes earlier. "Alan Dodds has been promised the position of Director," she said. "I do apologize for the confusion." "Alan Dodds is a friend and trusted colleague," I replied. "I can work with him." "Thank you, George," Ilchman responded, visibly relieved.

"As a member of my policy team, you will have the largest portfolio of Western Europe and Canada, an area you know well," she continued. Frankly, I was not prepared to make an issue of yet another bizarre personnel snafu. Alan was a known quantity. He and I had served together in Italy, and I would need his support in the European Bureau. He was a charter member of that bureau's "Old Boys' Club."

Alan would be arriving within a month, time enough for Diane and me to get settled in the townhouse in Southwest Washington we had managed to find. I would also have time to introduce myself to the desk officers in the European Bureau, and schedule an initial round of meetings with the bureau's leadership. It was important to me that I be up to speed by the time Alan arrived.

My immediate future now secure, at least for the next three-to-four-years, the normal length of a Washington assignment, I arranged a meeting with Assistant Secretary Carter to let him know of my new job. He had, after all, refused to fill his slot until USIA resolved the problem of my status. His willingness to champion my cause became the catalyst for the intervention of Louie Martin at the White House. Hodding shared with me the details of his conversation with Louie and Louie's conversation with John Reinhardt. One of the more amusing details regarded the role of Carmela Menendez, the Director of Personnel. She was apparently in Reinhardt's office during his conversations telling him not to capitulate, to keep me at the Agency even though she was not prepared to assign me to more career-enhancing positions she knew were available. Reinhardt could not afford to do that because he would need the intercession of Louie Martin to further his candidacy for the position of Secretary General of UNESCO in Paris. Hodding and I both had a good laugh, but lamented the fact that it took this much effort to find a good job. I owed Hodding and I wanted to express my appreciation for his support and to build a friendship. We ultimately developed a friendship that endured beyond his tenure at the State Department.

The next priority was my allergy condition, by now progressively more uncomfortable than ever. Although I was still under treatment for my condition, surgery could no longer be avoided. I had spent many a night walking around my new neighborhood in Southwest Washington unable to sleep and trying to breathe through congested sinuses. Diane knew to look for me outside near the house should she awaken and not find me. I also wanted to brief Alan, since I would be on medical leave for approximately two weeks.

As I said earlier, a Washington assignment was not just about resuscitating my career and recovering my health; it was also common ground for Diane and me to reevaluate our four-year-old marriage. Four years is not a long time, but ours' had not been a typical young marriage. Korea had taken its toll. I was older than Diane and, while I was there to cushion the impact of colonel King (the base commander who presided over the military community where we lived in Pusan) and some of the other challenges inherent in adapting to a traditional Asian culture, some of the damage was psychologically debilitating. After all, we were not part of a military culture with the regimented lifestyle that all military personnel must accept. Now that Nepal no longer loomed on our horizon, conversations about the future – which is a constant in the Foreign Service – were less strained. Korea had offered Diane opportunities to stretch her wings, to understand her potential, and, define more clearly, possibilities within her grasp; especially now that we were in Washington. Even though her focus shifted from international to domestic prospects, I remained one of her more ardent supporters. I knew that her success could mean a "diminished" us. I say this because Italy and Korea were defining experiences for Diane as a new Foreign Service spouse. We all have our baptism of fire and Korea was that for Diane. The price of the successes she achieved in Italy was less dear than success in Korea and Korea was not considered a hardship assignment. Pusan, for example, was classified as a "differential" post: ten percent to compensate for the lack of amenities that would have contributed to a greater quality of life.

Just to place our assignments in context, some are classified as hardship, others are classified as greater hardship. And then, there are the assignments to which dependents do not accompany the Foreign Service member. Nepal would have been a hardship, and both of us wondered how well Diane would have adapted to the hardships that assignment presented – and they were considerable. The greater hardship in these assignments devolves to the home bound spouse, devoid of the gratification one derives from mastering a new role in a new country, but who is expected to cope with the linguistic, social, and cultural challenges inherent in sustaining life. The doubts Diane entertained were real and for either of us to ignore them now could have been catastrophic later. We both saw the handwriting on the wall.

Following a radical, six-hour surgical procedure (nasal polypectomy) at George Washington University Hospital in September 1979, a week in the hospital, followed by a second week of convalescence, I was anxious to get back to work. I had been in a state of limbo since my March return from Korea. What I had endured the first few months back in Washington was the all-too-frequent peril that befalls an African-

American officer in his or her quest for a career-enhancing job. I was a staunch believer in the first rule of career management: get involved in the process, stay involved, and become an aggressive advocate for your interests. Leave nothing to chance! From that first day in this policy job, I knew the struggle had been worth the effort.

What set this position apart from my previous responsibilities was the essential nature of a policy job: no operational responsibility and none of the unique pressures and obligations that accompany staff supervision. The allure of the position was the inherent freedom to explore new ideas and to question old policy assumptions. My specific task was to reflect on the scope, effectiveness, and funding levels of the professional and scholarly exchange programs sponsored by the American government for West European governments and a vast network of academic and professional organizations throughout Europe and Canada. Talk about a dream assignment for someone interested in the Agency's ultimate policy job of a multilateral mission.

I was part of a team, each member of which had had an impressive resume and operational experience. Under the direction of Alan Dodds, I looked forward to a period of stability in my career and change in the direction of Agency policies. Alan had settled into his new role as director of our policy team and quickly realized that the European "account" was his largest and most complex. That was my account. Following one of our early morning staff meetings, Alan suggested we have lunch that day. Alan was coming off an assignment as the Cultural Attache' in Bonn, a city and an embassy with which I was quite familiar. When Alec Klieforth, my old boss in Rome, was appointed as Director of USIS Germany, Alan was one of the senior officers he chose as part of his core team.

Over lunch, I shared with Alan details of my most recent experience with the Office of Personnel and the bizarre screw-up leading to my assignment as one of his policy officers. Alan listened intently and thanked me for sharing the background with him. Apparently, no one had deemed it necessary to brief him. Alan also said, "you have the largest portfolio, and both Alice and the Director of USIA have a keen interest in Europe for all of the obvious reasons. You know the game with political appointees! As a policy officer, you will not travel as much as your colleagues will be traveling to their countries. When Alice and the USIA Director travel, I will be traveling with them." He smiled and said, "that is your peculiar cross to bear...now, what we have to do is get you promoted." That was music to my ears. I was more than willing to give up travel in favor of a promotion. Alan and I had reached an accommodation, and now I had the motivation to get deeply engrossed in my job – and I did.

The convergence of timing, pre-election period in our quadrennial past-time, and job responsibility, could not have been more propitious. By the fall of 1979, we were on the cusp of President Carter's campaign for re-election. Little did we know that a Reagan-led revolution was just a few months away from engulfing Washington. As I settled into the job, Alan and I knew that my real focus had to be on anticipating change in our relationship with West European institutions in the event of a change in the White House. Program shifts would be inevitable if Carter lost, but the real battle would be about resources. I made one fairly simple assumption as a guidepost: resources undergird policy; policy papers and analyses justify priorities and allocation of resources; and, the nuance of politics shape the outcome of decision making.

The Bureau of European and Canadian Affairs historically housed the largest embassy operations abroad. Therefore, in a period of scarcity (resources), its budget would be under continuous assault by the other geographic bureaus seeking to justify more for their operations, inevitably at Europe's expense. I stepped into the fray by convening a series of intra-agency planning sessions to evaluate project proposals from 32 European posts, developed a Europe-wide priority list of essential programs, and prepared a bureau-wide budget that anticipated policy and program changes, according to geopolitical factors of a new Administration (Reagan).

Within six months, I was a respected advisor to the leadership of the European Bureau. I had to earn respect if I wanted a major assignment in that part of the world. It was not going to be easy because the "European Club" had a rigid practice of not accepting African-American officers at a management level. I was going to need not only Alan's full support, but that of Alice Ilchman as well, if I was going to be even remotely within range of consideration by the European Bureau for the positions I had in mind.

My passion for politics was by now a family affair. Diane became involved at a local level with the campaign of Washington's Sterling Tucker in his bid for the chairmanship of the City Council for the District of Columbia. Hard work, a cooperative spirit, and a willingness to do what it took to succeed earned her the coveted position of press advisor to the Tucker Campaign. It was also during this campaign that Diane came to the attention of Ben Brown, Campaign Director for the Carter reelection effort. Ben wanted her for his team – an offer she could only accept. At that point, our lives seemed to change dramatically.

While I was settling into a new job, Diane was juggling the requirements of graduate studies at Howard University and the increasing demands of the Carter Campaign. Often, the inherent conflict in meeting conflicting demands meant according the higher priority to her graduate program. She learned to function on much less than the routine eight hours of sleep she was accustomed to. Diane's involvement with the Carter reelection effort did have one tangible benefit: periodic invitations to the White House when President Carter was receiving a foreign visitor on the South Lawn, or when he was trying to mend political fences with various African-American groups. On these occasions, I was able to spend valuable time with some of the African-American officials sprinkled throughout the Carter Administration and on his campaign team. Meanwhile, a well-placed source within the Kennedy Presidential Campaign was a useful conduit for ideas I sought to bring to Ronald H. Brown, a senior advisor to Senator Kennedy. Chappaquiddick notwithstanding, Kennedy was my preferred candidate that year. Carter had been a major disappointment for African-Americans, even though we made the margin of difference in his election four years earlier. This time, he faced an uphill struggle, and deservedly so.

I recall one humorous incident involving the President at a major White House reception he hosted for some of the most politically influential African-Americans in the country. President Carter was slipping in the polls and Ben Brown was feverishly trying to "energize the African-American base." Many of the attendees did not want to attend a blatantly political event, and had made that known to Ben Brown. The reception was billed as social and Carter would not "pitch" them as he often did. Everyone was enjoying the event and waiting for the President to make his appearance. Carter appeared, welcomed his guests to the White House, spoke briefly of his administration's record, as expected, and went on to offer a progress report on his bid for re-election. Had he concluded his remarks at that point, he could have avoided a major "faux pas" that cost him politically.

At the conclusion of his remarks, he added, and I am paraphrasing even though I was there: "With your continued support and me as your president, we can accomplish even more during a second term." Some in the audience groaned audibly; others were upset, and I overheard several people say, "He's taking us for granted again." One very influential politician from the mid-west, I was later told, predicted out loud that Carter would not make it this time. He spoke with an air of authority I found difficult to dismiss. President Carter was in deep political trouble and I don't think his advisors appreciated the depth of the disenchantment among African-Americans, if that day's events was a harbinger of things to come. The next day, I described the event to Alan Dodds because of his interest in anything that might signal a change in November.

By the fall of 1980, both Diane and I were managing a full menu of daily activities that kept us intellectually stimulated, even physically exhausted on occasion. We did, however, miss our Korean family, letters, cards, and long-distance telephone conversations notwithstanding. While I have not mentioned her before, there is someone without whose love, support, and total dedication to the two of us, life in Pusan would have been starker than it became. I am referring to our housekeeper, Chae Min, Mrs. Lee's older sister. A widow with two small children and living with her parents, Chae Min was God's gift to us and we loved her dearly. I survived as well as I did during Diane's absence because Chae Min ordered my life so well that I merely needed to show up whenever I could and did. A widow with no prospects for marriage, or real employment in Pusan, we wanted to bring Chae Min to America. There was a real need for her in our lives..

The townhouse we occupied at 808 Third Street in Southwest Washington was now an even more temporary spot for us since we were moving to settle on a new and larger townhouse in the Northwest quadrant of the city just off North Capitol Street and Florida Avenue. In our new home, there would be room for Chae Min if we were successful in securing temporary worker status for her requiring an H-1 visa. In December 1980, we moved into our new home at 22 Bates Street. The Lee family agreed to take care of her two children should her visa be granted. The success of that quest brought her back into our lives. The newest member of our small family did not experience the isolation other foreign visitors in her status felt because of ties we forged to the local Korean community when we were Korean language students three years earlier.

Within weeks, Chae Min was as comfortable in her new surroundings as those of longer tenure in the city. The inherent risk is always that your guest will meet someone that appreciates them, perhaps even falling in love with them. Eventually, that happened to our dear Chae Min. We could not, in good conscience, deny her a chance at happiness. The man she met, and concluded he could not live without her, came to our home to plead his case. I felt awkward because he was an older gentleman, much older than I. Chae Min said it was right for her, that she could be reunited with her children, and, together, the four of them could become a real family - an outcome beyond her reach in Pusan. She departed our household with our blessing slightly more than a year after her arrival. Although no longer with us, she was within reach, an acceptable consolation. Although today again a widow, she is also a proud and doting grandmother. Sadly, she did lose her teenage daughter to a terminal disease and never fully recovered from her loss.

1981 was also the year in which the fabric of our marriage was torn to its breaking point. We disagreed more frequently and more acrimoniously, and arguments seemed out of proportion to the weight of the issue we were incapable of dealing with rationally. Talk of separation became the instant remedy. Later, the dreaded "D" word was added to the mix of options. From there, it was a short leap to shorter conversations and greater estrangement. Although the Tucker Campaign was now history, Diane still maintained a grueling schedule, returning late at night, at times the next day, and increasingly remained out of sight and contact for several days at a time. It was not until a late night telephone call from Diane's closest friend in New Jersey that I learned the real reason for her absences. She was not studying with friends, or visiting family in Virginia, or just being angry with me. I now learned she was also involved in a romantic relationship of long standing.

When I confronted her with this, I confess I was not prepared for her response. Instead of showing some degree of contrition, her attitude and posture was unapologetic, almost indifference. She felt that now that I had found out about this relationship, somehow I should be mature enough to understand and move beyond her behavior. It is true that I did love her, and that she had made me very happy during the earlier years of our marriage, but I was totally unprepared for what Diane had become. I was home every night but, more often than not, she was away. Perhaps she had always had this disposition and I simply never really knew her. Friends in my hometown of Woodbury certainly tried to make this point on several occasions. By this time, I simply felt it impossible to countenance her infidelity and her attitude about it. After months of gut wrenching disagreements, weeks of unexplained absences on her part and, finally, a separation, I decided to terminate our marriage. Oddly enough, months into this, Diane began to object to my decision to end our marriage and made an attempt to forestall the outcome I sought. My emotional salvation at this point – at least I thought so – was my job and its emphasis on political and social developments in Europe.

Europe of the early 1980's was in the throes of change; a

274

generational shift in political leadership. Young Turks, that post-World War 11 "Successor Generation," had arrived near the apex of the career ladder. Educated, ambitious, and impatient to sit at "the table," they were clamoring for a change in Europe's overall relationship with the United States. Our political and military defeat in Vietnam assured that they were not inclined to accept American leadership of the Atlantic Alliance as readily as the current generation of European leadership had. Intellectual products of Europe's finest universities, but estranged from the U.S. throughout the Vietnam War years, many of this new generation's political views of American government and society were not tempered by extensive travels in the U.S., or having attended an American college or university.

We had a natural opportunity to begin building relationships for the future. This was my thumbnail assessment of the mood among an emerging generation of leadership in Europe and I took it to Alan for further discussion. I said, "It is time to identify several members of this current successor generation in each major European country and bring them to the U.S. for a structured program of high-level briefings and visits with Americans at all walks of life. Including the Executive and Legislative branches of government...In addition, the national political conventions will be held this year. Why not invite a group of these young leaders to attend both conventions; to see the American political process up close?" Alan agreed and assured me I would have the full support of the European Bureau.

Nico, my old colleague from Rome controlled the purse strings for projects like the one I proposed. He, too, liked the idea and enthusiastically provided a grant to the Washington-based American Council of Young Leaders and U.S. Youth Council to develop the project, identify participants, and bring them to the United States.

If there is one political event that most epitomizes the American political process, it is a national political convention. Conventions are raw, high energy, raucous, emotional, fun, confusing to the uninitiated, and deadly serious to the delegates. The Democratic and Republican Conventions of 1980 reflected the clash of social culture and political philosophy dividing America at that time. Jimmy Carter and his challenger for the Democratic nomination, the late Senator Ted Kennedy, represented the Liberal Left, and Gerald Ford and Ronald Reagan were their ideological opposites. My ten European and Japanese guests (all Parliamentarians) and I were honored guests at both conventions. Their initial reactions were priceless. In a word, they were thunderstruck. They were witnessing a national political event as few Americans do

– up close and personal. My guests watched in spellbound silence as the Democrats' convention became transfixed by Senator Kennedy's "Dream Shall Never Die" oration, but nevertheless chose Carter as their candidate.

At the Republican National Convention in Detroit (July 14 – 17, 1980), they wondered how a co-presidency between Ford and Reagan would work. Confusion seemed to reign. Several of my guests wondered aloud, where is the decorum, the deference to leadership? The scripted outcomes they were accustomed to in Parliamentary systems of government did not seem to prevail here in America. This was raw: ordinary Americans as delegates deciding who their Party's candidate was to be. I am convinced that that two-week experience shaped their views about how the American political process works more than any other experience we could have offered them. I'm getting ahead of myself. The point is each of them departed the United States profoundly grateful for a rare, once-in-a-lifetime experience.

On a personal level, I was prepared to bet the "farm" that Ronald Reagan would become our next president. The words of that influential African-American politician from the mid-west haunted me: "Carter won't make it this time." All of my Democratic friends, African-American and white, Liberal and Conservative, consigned me to the loony bin as a heretic or simply naïve. But quietly, I factored the priorities of a Reagan Presidency, as I could best define them, into my budget, policy, and program proposals for the European Bureau. My gut told me change was riding the crest of the political wave about to engulf Washington, the foreign policy establishment, and the country at large. I did not relish the thought of playing catch-up. On a policy level, I wanted to be the pitcher in the starting lineup, not fielding ground balls in the outfield. These guys were coming and we were not prepared. When Carter lost, many of my colleagues were in shock and worried about the future of USIA under a Reagan Administration. They had legitimate cause to worry.

I wondered why several of my colleagues in policy planning were stunned by the success of Ronald Reagan that year. For the unknown that Jimmy Carter was in 1976, he did capture the mood of a country looking for more integrity in their White House and more stability in their lives. He did not meet their expectations. What the electorate sought made sense, but for people like myself, that level of need was more remote. I needed something more visceral, more tangible, that would personify the disaffection many felt with the Carter Administration. Attending the Republican National Convention in 1980 filled the bill for me. Here was a visible manifestation of the failure many Americans attributed to Carter, rightly or wrongly. Someone had to be guilty and he was it.

Driving in from the airport in Detroit and our commute to the downtown Joe Louis Arena, the convention site, provided the optic I needed. Detroit was one of those iconic cities that sustained confidence in the uniqueness of the American worker, the strength of our manufacturing sector, and the future for American competitiveness. That was all in the past now. Block by block, all you saw were boarded-up, middle-class homes of workers who powered the industrial base in the heartland state that Michigan was. Here was a visual manifestation of frustration and disappointment. Whole communities that once resonated with hope, the promise of tomorrow, and the laughter of children, were desolate. These communities were the stuff of Norman Rockwell and now they were hollowed out shells of despair. People wanted change, Here was a part of the "Rust Belt" that did not generate the pride in manufacturing output and community cohesion Carter needed to win. Explaining his defeat was going to be relatively easy. This project was a useful experience for me as well.

My friend Nico made this experience possible and I wanted to share some of the more humorous aspects with him. Nico loved a good laugh. He, too, was going through a divorce and, to economize, he would "brown bag" his lunch on occasion. We were sitting in his office having lunch and a good laugh about an experience I had had at the Republican National Convention. As always, we spoke of promotability, assignments and, Howard Roswell's name came up. Nico knew of my earlier travails with Howard. Nico apparently knew him fairly well. He went on to tell me that "Howard doesn't just dislike you, George, he dislikes a lot of people for reasons other friends and I don't understand. I know it does not make sense, but let me sum it up this way: Howard is complex, erratic, and now, unpredictable. I think he will probably give up his Foreign Service career and revert to the Civil Service. Something is going on with him that he is going to have to resolve." For the first time, I understood what had happened to me. Nico was a valued friend who "had my back." He would also provide an endorsement that helped earn my next assignment.

Meanwhile, I was coping with change. The Reagan Administration, and the revolution he promised, hit Washington with the impact of a Tsunami. Symbols of impending change were visible everywhere. For example, the General Aviation Terminal at the Washington National Airport, according to an article in the Washington Post, reported gridlock with the influx of private jets, more than collective memory could recall. Also, every privately-owned limousine from New York City to Virginia – a six-state area – had been rented. I just happened to see at least 50 of them occupy four lanes of Connecticut Avenue in front of the Mayflower Hotel just after the Inaugural that year. Many onlookers just stood on the sidewalk and gawked.

On a more visceral level, and closer to home, change could be measured in the words of Charles Z. Wick, a personal friend of the Reagans, and the newly appointed Director of the renamed U.S. International Communication Agency (USIS abroad) when he told an assembled group of policy officers (myself included) and managers, "your job is not to tell me what I cannot and should not do; your job is to help me do the things I want to do." We were headed into uncharted waters, butting up against our charter as an independent agency while remaining under the policy direction of the Department of State. Life was going to get interesting very quickly and the focus of Mr. Wick's efforts, at least initially, was Western Europe.

I was now into the second year of an assignment I hoped would have strengthened my bid for an assignment to our Mission to the-then European Community in Brussels. Budget cuts and changing program priorities dominated most discussions between my office and the USICA European Area. Alan Dodds had approved a prototype, a matrix, for a Resource Planning Model (RPM) I had developed to help the director of the European Area form a basis for resource allocation. Here was a new tool for resource management that had a comfortable fit with Mr. Wick's design for program change in an important area of the world.

My second major success, on the eve of my departure for a year of academic study, was an analysis of the new Reagan Administration's policy directions in Europe; directions that were being formulated to achieve a consensus among our ambassadors in Europe on key issues of multilateral concern. Part of the recognition I earned came in the form of a commendation for my RPM (Resource Planning Model) from the USICA European Area Director. He used my RPM to prepare himself and Mr. Wick for his first official trip to Europe. Moreover, the RPM was now being used by all of USICA's geographic areas as an important tool for analyzing USIS resources in each country we maintained an official presence.

The broader success I sought to achieve included taking full advantage of enrichment opportunities: executive-level training through the Mid-Career Executive Development Program – an important "notch on the belt" for consideration as a senior manager. To strengthen my policy background, I completed the Foreign Affairs Interdepartmental Seminar, a two-week intensive course of study of the foreign policy process and current issues in the formulation, coordination, and execution of foreign policy. And then, there was a two-week course – World Views and Ideology - emphasizing the interaction of ideology, nationalism, and development to improve our ability to respond effectively to critiques of Western values. A close friend and colleague in personnel had tipped me earlier in the year that promotion panels were paying close attention to training as an indicator of an officer's fitness for senior level responsibility. Dr. Ilchman and Alan endorsed my request for an assignment to one of the universities in Washington for a coveted year of academic study under the Pearson Fellows Program. I chose to spend a year studying U.S. national security policy at Johns Hopkins SAIS culminating in my second graduate degree: Masters of International Public Policy (MIPP), in 1982. It is important to understand that every major decision I took was designed to enhance my prospects for promotion and to earn a shot at a specific job in Brussels.

The Counselor of the Agency, and "Dean of the USICA European Club," career FSO Ambassador John Shirley, had become aware of my work on behalf of the European Area through my friend Nico. Rarely would I have an occasion to interact with ambassador Shirley. Therefore, I arranged for him to meet with my study group at SAIS. I planned his visit as thoughtfully as I would have for a more senior official. I knew I might have possibly 45-seconds-to-a-minute to respond to the question "what do you want to do after this assignment? Another favored question from political appointees from the private sector is "What is your current project?" That question from ambassador Shirley would come during the walk from the curb outside SAIS to the elevator. It substitutes for the small talk if your escort officer is relatively unknown to the more senior officer. You do not get to say "I am not sure, but I would be pleased to follow up with you!" They really are not interested, so it pays to hit them between the eyes with exactly what you want. I greeted ambassador Shirley at the curb and escorted him into the building, and up the elevator to the conference room. He did ask, "what do you want to do after this?" Without hesitation, I replied, "an assignment as Deputy Director of USIS at Brussels USEC (US Mission to the European Communities). If anyone could make that request happen, he could – and he did. My recent success on behalf of the European Area notwithstanding, my candidacy never would have emerged from USICA Personnel at that time in my career without Jock Shirley's intervention. I also say that because the principal deputy in the European Area, Jack Williams, a great guy, was opposed to an important assignment in Europe and told me so. He argued that I would need more experience, a standard that did not apply to other officers he and I both knew and discussed. Jack was a gatekeeper.

Several days later, I received a call from the Director of Foreign Service Personnel to the effect that my "interest in an assignment to Brussels had been duly noted. He went on to say that he had received word of my interest from ambassador Shirley." Ambassador Shirley had made the call. I relaxed at that point because I would not have received the call if my candidacy had not been well received. By the way, Jack Williams also called to congratulate me; he knew I was going to get the Brussels job over an objection I am sure he wisely chose not to register.

Let's rewind the clock a little. At the age of 41, I was, again, a graduate student at Johns Hopkins. This was familiar territory. Dr. Robert E. Osgood, Christian A. Herter Professor of American Foreign Policy, agreed to serve as my faculty advisor. I had been a student of his while pursuing my first graduate degree at SAIS a decade earlier. This time, I brought more to the relationship because I now had specific areas of inquiry that made sense to explore. Dr. Osgood and I spent many hours in his office examining my questions regarding the efficacy of American security policy on the Korean Peninsula and within NATO. He would give me books to read to broaden my historical frame of reference on many of the topics we would discuss. I thrived during that academic year; it was practically a vacation without the insistent demands of the job while having unlimited freedom to probe into the intellectual foundation of the strategic policies being promulgated by the new Reagan Administration.

While I did anticipate receiving a second Master's Degree in the spring of 1982, the taste of that achievement was made even sweeter by a promotion elevating me to a Class One officer. Alan Dodds had made it happen. I did the work, but he wrote the performance evaluation. Alice Ilchman's deputy, David Nalle, provided a strong endorsement. As Alan had predicted, I did not travel to any of my countries the previous two years. I think among Director Wick, Alice Ilchman, and Alan, they must have made close to ten trips during my tenure as the policy officer for Europe. But this critical promotion meant that I could become a candidate for the Senior Foreign Service. Brussels was my future and, if I stood a chance of being selected for the senior service, it would come from success in my next assignment.

When I returned to Washington in March 1979, I made a wish list: reach a mutual understanding about the future of our marriage;

restore my health; land a good assignment in Washington; spend a year at either the National War College or an academic year; earn a promotion to Class One, and negotiate an assignment to Brussels. It was now June 1982 and I was batting a thousand. Quietly, I celebrated with my old friend Nico. Following a mid-May graduation, I spent two months with the State Department's Board of Examiners, the office that has as one of its responsibilities the requirement to assess the suitability of career-conditional candidates for permanent status as career officers. I now sat on the other side of the table – a change since my own assessment back in early 1975. This assignment was short lived. I requested to be transferred from BEX because I was expected to endorse "practices," not policies, to reduce the number of African-Americans in career-conditional status. The term for them was "second orals." There was the initial oral examination which was part of the intake process. A second oral examination was required to determine if their subsequent performance met the standard required to earn career status. The practice was to offer the second oral, deem them unfit, and process them out - a de facto revolving door.

During this second oral, the process for most examiners was pro-forma: ask a few perfunctory questions and avoid any that might provide insights into the officer's experience but, when necessary, ask them to defend against negative comments in their evaluation reports. I was asking the candidates to assess their performance, to explain their actions on specific responsibilities; tell us why there were disconnects between a Rating Officer's evaluation and that of the Rated Officer. I would ask, for example, why the Foreign Service should retain them? Since this would be their final review before a judgment was rendered, I asked them to make their best case for a career opportunity. We were still their judge and jury. My colleagues were not happy and word filtered through BEX very quickly. I am sure it was intentional. "George is saving second orals." I did not interview a candidate with a judgment already rendered. This was just more of the discrimination the Foreign Service was noted for and I was expected to condone it. I called ambassador Shirley, explained the situation, and asked to be transferred. A week later, he summoned me. Since I was destined for Brussels, he asked me to serve as acting deputy policy officer in the European Area, pending the November arrival of a permanent replacement. "In November, you will enter language training, and they need someone now." I couldn't accept quickly enough. Now, I would have the timely opportunity of an important domestic job, in his favorite region, to vindicate his faith for having advanced my candidacy for Brussels. He did not just advance my candidacy, he made it a reality.

Judy Jamison, a colleague I would encounter at regional briefings in Brussels during my earlier assignment to Rome, was the acting policy officer. On that first day, I told Judy I was willing to undertake any assigned tasks, even the most mundane, to get the job done. She and I were the first white female- African-American male team to run the policy shop and I wanted her to know I recognized the significance of our partnership in a critical office. We were under the microscope and success was the only acceptable route for us. Judy never tired of telling me how much she appreciated my attitude. Here is a snapshot of what we were up against.

The European Area Office pace, hectic at the best of times, had reached rare heights of frenzy when I arrived in early July. Almost five months later, as I prepared to depart the policy shop, that pace had not abated. Serving as the desk officer for the Brussels Mission in the policy shop had been one of my daily tasks. Meetings, policy drafts, and deadlines were handled on the fly. Projects included taking over a conference organized by the Brussels Mission with the British Foreign Office (the equivalent of our Department of State), shepherding plans to strengthen the Agency's Radio and Television broadcasting capabilities in Europe, and making arrangements for Director Wick to participate in a major European film festival. Late in the afternoon, when Judy and I could steal a breather, we would take on some of the more cerebral tasks: position papers, the USIA Director's weekly report, telegrams, and correspondence. Working with Judy had been that rare pleasure one experiences occasionally in our profession. Many officers are good, but Judy was a breed apart: broad experience, a quick wit, decisive, a dynamic and creative genius with a pen in her hand, and, one of the most compassionate human beings I have yet to meet. For example, during that time, I was going through my worst moments with Diane; moments when I needed to be at my best. Judy recognized the pain and helped me through it. I did not know it but she had been there before. One awful morning toward the end of 1982 when I walked into the office, I was practically a walking shell, Judy said, "George, I recognize that kind of pain when I see it. Take a walk, come back later! I'll cover for you." I will always love her for that. She and I made a great team and we never missed a beat, my tumultuous home life notwithstanding. By November, I was ready to go to Brussels. However, French language instruction had to come first.

The fall of that year, I started French-language instruction while still engaged in divorce proceedings. Diane and I had separated over a year earlier. The evening prior to the final court appearance, Diane and I had a bitter telephone conversation to the extent I looked forward to the meeting the following morning with the judge. I was through! The details are less important than sharing with you a sense of my mindset.

The collapse of a relationship that initially began on love, hope, and promise can be emotionally and psychologically devastating. It was for me. There had been those interminable moments when nothing seemed familiar or friendly, when your life's axis seemed permanently out of balance. I think it was the primordial instinct to survive that anchored me during this time to avoid giving in to more base desires. I was considered to be pretty good in a crisis, but there was so much shit breaking with Diane, I could not keep up. I had no control. On that fateful, but final, day in court, my attorney and I were there; Diane was not. She did not show! In early 1983, following almost eight years of marriage, Diane and I put an end to the pain, the confusion, and the disappointment that had become my daily companions. My "wish list" was now complete.

French language consumed my life and I was a willing captive. Career success came at a cost and I needed a demanding distraction. Eight hours daily, and three-to-four-hours every evening were devoted to French. In May 1983, I attained the requisite proficiency in French and began to focus on preparations for my departure. There was, however, one last assignment: the May 28 -30 Summit of Industrialized Nations in Williamsburg, Virginia.

The G-7 Summit brought together the Heads of State or Government of France, Germany, Italy, Japan, the United Kingdom, the United States, Canada, and the head of the European Commission (now, European Union). Russia recently had become a member of this prestigious club. The annual meeting offers the principals and their senior advisors (for the U.S, the Secretaries of State and the Treasury) a unique moment to review and agree upon those policies that sustain economic growth, expand global trade and investment, and promote free markets among the non-industrialized nations. The United States Information Agency in Washington, augmented by USIS language officers from our embassies in the G-7 countries, assumes a major support role whenever the American President is the host, as President Reagan was in 1983. My predecessor from Brussels USIS, Jack Lawrence, was on hand as White House Press Liaison to the EC Delegation, and I was to join him. I would now have an inside view of one of the roles I would be expected to play in London in 1984, the site for the next G-7 Summit. My other roles would encompass deputy spokesman for the U.S. Mission; press and media support officer for the Annual US-EC Ministerial; Mission advance officer for G-7 Summits, and media liaison for White House visits (President and Vice President) to Brussels when the European Commission was involved. Brussels hosts three American Missions accredited to NATO, the EC, and the Kingdom of Belgium.

Among these three Missions, high-level visitors are an all-too-frequent occurrence (12 to 13 thousand annually in the early 1980s). The value of these visits for officers is they offer an opportunity to showcase skills, judgment, and creative problem-solving ability at the highest level of government. Important people get to see you and relationships are built. The hours are long, the pressure relentless, the responsibilities are complex and demanding, and the rewards in the short-term are more psychic than real: the reward of having done something well. Over the long term, however, the ability to perform at this level improves markedly an officer's chances for promotion and assignment to career-enhancing positions both in Washington and at certain overseas posts. The value of "executive rub," of working in close proximity with senior White House staff and members of the President's Cabinet is incalculable. Rarely did African-American officers of that era have these opportunities. And they routinely were not selected for European assignments at a policy or management level. To make this happen, you had to get involved in the assignment's process – and not leave it to the administrative equivalent of Adam Smith's benevolent hand. Your value as an officer is, in the final analysis, as good as the system that assigns you. Often, you have to add that value and become your most effective and aggressive advocate.

Jack Lawrence and I drove down to Williamsburg, picked up our myriad U.S. Information Agency and White House credentials, and proceeded to USIA's full-service media center. Our specific role was to function as media liaison between the EC Delegation and the White House Press Office: attend briefings (in French) by Gaston Thorn, President of the European Commission, and briefings by his principal advisors. In addition, we were to provide written summaries of those briefings, particularly on sticky trade issues, to the White House to ensure that the American team was fully apprised of the thinking of their European Commission counterparts. Second, we met with English and French-language journalists covering the US-EC dialogue on trade and agricultural policy. This was a more substantive role than mechanical support for a White House visit. In this role, you had to know the arcane' of "Eurospeak," a language unto itself. Four months in the European Area Office and six months of French paid off handsomely as Jack and I sat through a series of EC briefings and responded to questions from European journalists. Initially, I was a bit hesitant to trust my ability to field questions on our steel policy and agriculture, but Jack assured me that I would be up to speed by the December 1983 US-EC Ministerial in Brussels.

CHAPTER 13

SUMMITS, TRADE WARS AND OTHER
MULTILATERAL ISSUES

The Williamsburg Summit of 1983 was my formal introduction to the world of multilateral stagecraft and I liked the fit. The scope and the complexity of a summit, and the skills required to stage an event of this magnitude intrigued me. I knew then that my next assignment would test me differently than had been my experience to date – and I looked forward to that.

"Be careful what you wish for," my maternal grandmother often said. "Your wish might be granted." It was no secret among my small group of friends that I had long desired an assignment to one of our most important multilateral missions and, now, my wish had been granted. I gazed out the window and I recognized the familiar coastline of Northern Ireland and a European landscape I had seen on countless flights since 1959. Brussels, also the headquarters of NATO, was only a few hours away. The most important detail you need to absorb about the European Communities is this: it comprises our most important trading partners (Japan excluded) and security allies. With the exclusion of China, that is still as true today as it was in 1983. Paradoxically, at that time, it was the only major multilateral organization in which the United States did not enjoy the benefits and responsibilities of membership. Therefore, that set this particular grouping of countries apart from NATO (North Atlantic Treaty Organization), the OECD (Organization for Economic Cooperation and Development), NAFTA (North American Free Trade Agreement), the WTO (World Trade Organization), the United Nations, the World Bank and the International Monetary Fund, and the WHO (World Health Organization), to name a few.

Our Mission to the European Communities (USEC) represented this country's economic, commercial, and agricultural interests before that body. This assignment was center stage as Foreign Service assignments go and, as an African-American, I felt damned good about being there. Why? You ask. Careers were made in Brussels, including for military officers. Success there would put "paid" to our assertion that we have the intellectual capability, the desire, and the skills to handle complex economic, financial, and trade issues as competently as anyone else for whom, by the way, there was never any question. Stay in the context of the times. As far as I was concerned, USEC was just another stage upon which we could play. I was well accustomed to life under the microscope; to succeed or fail on my merit, unnatural scrutiny notwithstanding. Failure, again, was not an option because this assignment was a dream come true. Now you understand the mindset I carried into this latest chapter of my journey.

Jack Lawrence, the officer I would succeed, and Dwight Pendleton, the Director of USIS at the mission, met me upon arrival at Zaventem, the international airport in Brussels. I recall how unusually warm it was that day; out of the ordinary for Brussels. In fact, Jack did say on the drive into the city that they had been experiencing unusually warm weather. "Enjoy it while it lasts," he said. My transition on this assignment would be painless because I had agreed to take Jack's conveniently located apartment, sight unseen. He convinced me of that in Williamsburg. This proved to be a wise decision for a variety of reasons. As I said, the location was great: I could walk to work on a beautiful spring or fall day. His Filipina housekeeper had also agreed to a trial period with me, and his landlord was a gem. My car was due within weeks as were my household effects. The day following my arrival, I was in the office. Jack gladly surrendered his office, the briefing book, and several files on key projects I had to pick up on quickly. "It's all yours, George, I'm out of here."

I knew Dwight from his previous position as the policy officer for the European Bureau at ICA Washington. An officer of totemic opinion, Dwight was bright, had a keen policy sense, and one of the quickest pens of any officer in the Foreign Service. He could generate a 25-page policy position after dinner and have it ready for the typist the following morning. Dwight also assumed an intellectual superiority that earned him a small legion of critics among his agency colleagues. On my last day in the European Bureau, I met briefly with Jack Williams, the deputy director. His parting words to me were: "George, we would appreciate anything you can do to balance Dwight's reporting. There is too much description of the problems; not enough prescription...we need options," he said. On another level, I had a personal quest I could not ignore. On the eve of Dwight's departure for Brussels two years earlier, he circulated another of his famous missives: "A Policy Officer's

Last Will and Testament." In this paper, Dwight offered interesting observations about a broad range of Agency practices. In that same paper, he also questioned the Agency's recent practice of assigning African-American officers beyond the "African" box to which most of us had been consigned. I imagine to avoid being labeled insensitive, Dwight went on to question our "dubious linguistic skills" as part of the recruitment, selection, and assignment process. Fortunately for him, the paper did not receive wide internal circulation. The European Bureau was my beat so, naturally, I heard about and requested a copy of it. His views, however, did mirror those of many officers in that bureau. A particular point of contention for me was his comment about our dubious linguistic skills. I had achieved proficiency in three European languages (French, German, and Italian) by this time and was quite comfortable with European contexts, having lived on the continent for seven years. As an aside, I personally counted among my friends, African-American officers proficient in every major European language and others proficient in Vietnamese, Russian, and Korean. The African-American officer proficient in Vietnamese was my supervisor in 1971 when I entered on duty with the-then U.S. Information Agency. My assignment to Brussels had been earned the hard way: I worked for it. On a personal level then, I vowed to climb this "totem pole" with a mild prejudice.

From prior European experience, I knew that most Europeans were already in vacation mode by June. It was now June and I was looking forward to a relaxing summer in one of the continent's iconic capitols. Both Jack and Dwight departed within days of my arrival: Jack to another assignment and Dwight back to Chicago for eight weeks of home leave and return to Brussels for another two years. My relaxing summer hit a snag before I was familiar with the materials on my desk. Within 48 hours of their departure, I experienced first hand why Brussels had the reputation it did: difficult, demanding, and clamorous. This is what happened. The U.S. and the European Communities' often fractious relationship plunged into crisis over our action against the EC's specialty steel exports, an action that inflamed European opinion so soon after the recent Williamsburg Summit. The large and specialized EC press corps smelled blood and my telephone started ringing. They were looking for headlines and not perspective. One of the calls I received was from the European Bureau back in Washington. With only seven hours notice, I was told to organize a tele-press conference with the U.S. Trade Representative. With the assistance of my small and competent staff, we mobilized the most important Brussels-based print media and wire service organizations that cover the EC beat. They had questions and fortunately for our side, we had the right official with the answers. According to my betters back at home, the event was a complete success. According to the Director of the European Bureau in ICA, the trans-Atlantic tele-press conference we organized, was the fastest any European mission had ever organized. His complement became an early testament to my substantive and organizational skills. I confess it did give me considerable satisfaction to handle my trial by fire so successfully on an issue of this import so soon after my arrival. I was off to a good start.

Dwight would be away until mid-August, time to build a relationship with the ambassador and other members of the mission team. Ambassador George Dimon had a sterling reputation. He had been a spokesman for Henry Kissinger, therefore, he understood the public dimension of policy, the pressures we faced as public diplomatists, and how to deal with an aggressive press corps. In short, this particular ambassador was a strategic asset for Dwight and me. In the weeks that followed, I familiarized myself with the myriad topics and issues that were often flash points in the US-EC dialogue. At night, I explored the city, most often its great restaurants. I soon learned that the challenge there was to find a bad restaurant. Apart from steel, there were several agricultural issues, (pasta, agricultural subsidies) and the emerging dialogue on high technology, according to Dwight's notes. The EC and we had not reached a common definition on High Technology. Here was something new, an area in which I could carve out some space on the ground floor. When Dwight returned in mid-August, I was familiar with the GATT issues that consumed much of everyone's energy on a daily basis, the important policy documents (most of which Dwight had authored) that framed our dialogue with the European Commission, and the specific programs we managed that gave content to policy. Programs were my specific bailiwick. The Annual US-EC Ministerial in December was just months away and I had begun to develop a specific proposal to advance our common dialogue on high technology. I commandeered the high technology issue because it was new, interesting, and it offered me the opportunity to establish a substantive role within the mission. I always appreciated Dwight's confidence in my ability to manage our High Technology portfolio.

The EC bureaucracy is large, specialized and highly competent in the technical fields with which it deals. My approach was to work with contacts at the EC and in Washington to agree upon the language of a high technology program that would serve the delicate balance of both American and European policy interests. The next step was to give real content to a project whose participants would bear major responsibility for ironing out our respective differences and forging consensus whenever serious differences arose. We now had an agreement on terms and the kinds of participants we felt should be the focal point of the project. The most effective tool we had in the mission was an exchange visitor program (earlier referred to as the Leader Grant Program) to bring key European officials to the United States. I carefully negotiated an agenda, working with our ambassador, other mission colleagues, and senior European Commission officials to select those participants whose portfolios centered on high technology issues and who would be the Europeans likely to engage us in a dialogue on high technology issues. To deepen my own background on high technology, I read a mountain of materials and was briefed extensively by my mission colleagues and several of the journalists who reported on specialized technology themes. I then volunteered to travel with the group to the U.S. There is always the public dimension of policy formulation and it was important that I share this unique experience with those officials whose future public comments would condition policy reflexes on the American side of the Atlantic.

Over the course of two weeks, I accompanied a group of eight EC officials on a round of high level consultations in Washington and onsite visits with those American corporations essential to building our high technology industry. My extensive preparations were serving my group. Through my research, I was familiar with new developments in each of the companies we visited and the dialogue they were conducting with official Washington. Their lobbyists ensured that the media was well briefed on a company's desire to bring maximum pressure on either the Executive Branch agency involved or specific members of the Legislative Branch responsible for legislation of interest. As our group came to understand the role of lobbyists in shaping legislation, they recognized that the EC was going to have to play a more strategic game in negotiating with their American counterparts.

In each of our briefings, and on every site visit around the country, an amusing pattern would emerge. A senior government official, a vice president of marketing or operations, would ask who developed this innovative project? Or, they would ask, "Who is Mr. Kennedy?" That an African-American had conceived this project came as a total surprise and that surprise registered on their faces. By the third day, members of my group noticed a dynamic that became a humorous topic of conversation during mealtimes. I wanted to say, welcome to race relations 101 but discretion prevailed. Again, this was the early 1980s. AOL, still years away, was not part of the high technology landscape.

The enduring, tangible benefit of my effort - this project - was not only that we now knew who the EC's high technology experts were, but, also, that as members of the next generation of policy makers within the commission's Directorate for Technology, they had a new recognition of high tech's role in US-EC relations. Each side now had a counterpart with whom relationships could be built and crises managed before they reached flashpoint. At least that was the idea. Politics often took precedence over reason and logic whenever the EC was the other half of the policy dispute.

My first of five US-EC Ministerials beginning in 1983 was an exciting learning experience in which speed and accuracy, fueled by an adrenalin rush, were the ingredients for success. Our Secretary of State, as head of delegation, accompanied by his counterparts from the US Treasury, Commerce, and Agriculture Departments, and the US Trade Representative, descend upon the Belgian capitol for a full day of intensive dialogue with their EC counterparts and a summary, joint press conference. I had a two-fold role: provide a tape of the actual press conference to the Secretary of State's spokesman before they left the press conference (literally two minutes lead time), and a verbatim, literatim transcript to the Secretary of State's aircraft within three hours after his departure from Brussels. Dwight, the staff and I would return quickly to the office after the press conference and spend the next several hours transcribing from four audio tapes to produce an accurate rendering of the press conference. That transcript was in demand by the Secretary of State within hours of his departure (who wanted to review his comments, those of his delegation, and the question-and-answer session), official Washington, the press corps, and the White House. We consistently provided the fastest, most accurate transcript of any American mission on the Secretary's circuit abroad.

Toward the end of my first year in Brussels, I could fully appreciate how important USEC and its role were to the American embassies accredited to the governments comprising the EC's membership. On any given day, our colleagues in those capitols valued our ability to take the EC's temperature on an issue of bilateral importance to them, but represented only one of myriad issues on our agenda. On occasion, Dwight or I would travel to an EC capitol to brief the ambassador there and our embassy colleagues on EC issues important in that capitol. This opened the door to policymaking – itself a rare occurrence.

The British were the hosts for the 1984 G-7 Summit of Industrialized Nations at Lancaster House in London. The USICA (U.S. International Communications Agency) Policy Bureau and the European Bureau were soliciting our views for a comprehensive public affairs strategy they were developing for the White House. They were seeking our views and we were not bashful about offering them. When the final strategy document was presented to all of the missions in Western Europe, it did contain several of our recommendations. I took personal pleasure from this achievement because the recommendations chosen from our mission were my own. On June 7th, I was dispatched to the London Summit, my second. Williamsburg had taught me the drill. At this summit, however, my relations with the EC Delegation did reap dividends for the White House. The story, in brief, is that during G-7 Summits, the most prized possession is access, access for the press accredited to a delegation; in this case, the American Delegation. The traveling press writes the stories, the opinion pieces, the editorials that frame public opinion in EC capitols, and in the U.S. on the policy stance of the American president. The accredited press to each delegation needs to be in the room when the host head of government or state briefs the press corps covering the summit.

The then-British Prime Minister Margaret Thatcher, had a particular disdain for the press corps and, for this summit, at one of her briefings, an American journalist posed a question she apparently did not want to deal with and in a manner she felt was contemptuous. My liaison colleagues with the UK Delegation told me that her icy stare, without responding to her questioner, would have withered steel. To show her contempt, Prime Minister Thatcher withdrew the press passes reserved for the American press at the June 9 Reading of the Joint Declaration by the Heads of State/Government and summary press conference. This was the single most important public event of the summit, especially for the thousands of journalists covering the event. That Prime Minister Thatcher made this decision on the eve of the final event only underscored her fury. The White House Press Secretary, under siege by its traveling press, was frantic. A senior White House aide called a meeting of the USICA liaison officers assigned to each country's delegation. We were informed that the American press would be denied access to the press pools covering this event if they did not have the proper press credential. Could we help? Each delegation was allotted a finite number of press passes by the host government and, according to my colleagues working with those delegations, none of the other participating delegations would be willing to surrender any of its passes to the Americans. The one hope was the EC Delegation. I made no promises but said I would try and make the case for us. For most of that last evening, I huddled with my press contact on the EC Delegation to explain our dilemma. He, in turn, huddled with the Press Spokesman for the EC. Late that night, I received word from Nicholas Van Der Pas, assistant to the EC Spokesman, that they would be willing to surrender their passes to help the White House. Bear in mind, they could have refused, and justifiably so, had their own press corps objected to this unusual request. They did not and I earned the plaudits of a grateful White House Press Spokesman. For the rest of the night, he had the delicate task of deciding which American news organization would receive a pass. That was one assignment I was pleased not to have.

The next day, before the Final Communique', I was offered one of the special passes given to the White House for a military ceremony in honor of the Queen's birthday. This highly ritualized military spectacular is one of the most prestigious, annual events in the City of London. Each of the thousands of attendees is selected by a national lottery. For this officer, the fact that I could attend represented a once-in-a-lifetime experience. I had witnessed military tattoos in the past, but nothing approached the level of precision of some of the formations we saw that day. Nicholas Van Der Pas was a valued contact, destined to become the next EC spokesman, and I intended to repay his act of generosity.

If there were any doubts about my fitness for the position of deputy director of USIS/USEC, I had dissolved them by the following spring. I gave myself completely to the job because, as a bachelor, there were no familial demands from home. You might say that my career was the singular focus of my life at that time; a price I was willing to pay. The climate within the mission was perfect for my development and that of any new officer. The presence of ambassador Dimon ensured this. I had autonomy over my areas of responsibility, over new projects, and the benefit of Dwight's guidance when needed. I was briefing visitor groups to the mission from other European posts interested in our point of view on matters of concern to the U.S., developing projects on "Job Creation and Telecommunications", hosting discussion groups of Stagiares (Interns) at EC Headquarters, and assuming a larger liaison/support role for White House visits involving the EC or EC institutions. I was constantly on display to those in a position to affect the direction of my career after Brussels. Naturally, I developed more than a passing interest in Dwight's successor due to arrive the following summer of 1985. Personnel assignments at that level would be announced by summer 1984, a full year in advance. In the tradition of any good deputy, I made discreet inquiries through friends in Washington. I wanted to know who was on the short list to succeed Dwight.

In late June, I traveled to Washington in connection with the Inaugural U.S.-European Commission Student Exchange Project (part of President Reagan's Youth Exchange Initiative.) As I emerged from a taxi at USICA Headquarters, I saw an old friend, Theodore "Ted" Boyd. He was exiting the building as I was going in. Before I could say anything, he said "Congratulations, George." Surprised, I replied, "for what?" He smiled and continued on his way. I imagine he was going to lunch. I proceeded to the European Bureau to consult with the executive officer regarding our budget, several staff issues, and new Wang computers destined for our post. This time, our desk officer offered his congratulations. Now I was really intrigued. They obviously knew something I did not. Within minutes, Marvin Rostoc, the bureau deputy director, came in as I sat waiting in his office. Marvin was a straight-shooting, no-nonsense senior officer from the old school. He set exacting standards for all of his directors, abhorred excuses, and was known to strike fear in the hearts of anyone that did not measure up.

"Good to see you George." "You've had a great year in Brussels!" he said. "You have been selected by Mr. Wick (USICA Director) to succeed Dwight as the new Director of USIS/USEC next summer." Now I knew! Marvin knew I was shocked, but doing an adequate job of containing my surprise. Deputies are not promoted to the top job at overseas posts. I had been promoted from within after less than a year on the job. I had achieved the extraordinary: the first African-American director of USIS/USEC, and the only African-American director of an important European mission. This appointment was a timely, important psychological stimulus for my motivation because it was completely unexpected and it occurred at a time when my role within the mission was expanding substantially. Meanwhile, I thanked Marvin for his support and, together, we went up to see the director of the European Bureau. I knew that only they could have advanced my candidacy for this promotion. Mr. Wick did not know me from his chauffeur. When the congratulations had petered out, I met with the European Bureau's executive officer – a friend in court, so to speak. He and I agreed on the significance of this move not only for myself but for the Bureau's image. I knew I could handle the job, especially after being an understudy to Dwight for the past year. My challenge, and goal, was to perform at the level required for promotion to the senior Foreign Service. My mind was already two steps ahead of the game. With this appointment, I now had a new concern: who would become my new deputy? I wanted Judy Jamison or Crescencio "Cris" Arcos, if they were available. Cris would be a long shot because he was Mexican-American and a rising star in the Bureau for Latin American Affairs. Judy, on the other hand, was a European hand and a known quantity. The one option I did not have was to request the deputy of my choice.

My promotion from within represented the second opportunity

that came along at the right time, and both materializing at the same post. How truly extraordinary. God, did I feel blessed. On the return flight to Brussels, since I cannot sleep on planes, I tried to outline two sets of plans: objectives I wanted to achieve before assuming direction of the Brussels office, and changes I knew would improve the program there. I would have a year to refine that second set of plans so I could approach it with less urgency. During that second year, my work continued on an even keel. It was important to me that I set a standard against which I would measure the performance of my new deputy. How often would I encounter a similar set of circumstances in a career?

I had been back about a week and was enjoying a quiet dinner at home when the phone rang. It was a call from Mrs. Lee in South Korea. "When are you coming, George?" she asked. "JiYub always asks about you!" Her call was a not-so-subtle reminder of a promise I made months earlier to visit them that August. I had become so absorbed, I simply forgot. Thinking quickly, I said, "Tell JiYub and the family to look for me around mid-August." The fall calendar was already full; Dwight would be relinquishing more of his responsibilities and a real vacation next year was probably impractical.

If you ever wanted the ultimate in economy class, intercontinental airline travel, treat yourself to a flight on Singapore Airlines. The level of service they provide the economy class traveler, even then, was the best I had ever experienced on any airline. My 14-hour flight to Seoul, and on to Pusan via Korean Airlines, was the pleasant interlude the airline promised. While I did not sleep, I certainly did feel more relaxed than on any of the American flag carriers we were required to use when on official travel. I could only imagine the comfort and service offered to the business and first class passengers on my flight. As expected, most of the Lee family was on hand at the airport and I was delighted to see them. It had been five years since my departure in 1979. Time passed so quickly. There had been a major change in my life and Lorraine was not with me. I would need to explain that to JiYub. He was not familiar with divorce. There would be time, and for the moment, we just hugged, kissed, and even cried a little. It just felt so good to be with my family again. JiYub was now the typical, gangly 12-year old; handsome, computer literate, still mildly conversant in English. I had missed him terribly. For two weeks, I replenished my wardrobe, all tailor made, at prices I could afford; spent hours languishing in the local hot baths, eating the finest seafood at the Lee's favorite restaurants, walking on Haeundae Beach, sitting up late at night eating Korean pears with the family while teaching JiYub the American card game UNO. Before long, he was beating me at will. Commercial development and urban modernization had transformed the city I once knew well into a modern metropolis. Familiar routes had been altered and I was too often lost. I preferred the old Pusan: easier to navigate, better environmental quality, less traffic, and a lot less commercial.

I believe in the healing and restorative power of traditional medicine so, daily, I took Chinese herbal medicine. During one of my early visits to the Chinese doctor Mrs. Lee had arranged for me to meet, he took my pulse and began to describe my medical history. It was as though he had access to my medical files back in Washington. I was truly amazed at how accurate he was. The medicine he prescribed was to strengthen my organs, something I needed. Two weeks were a blur and I was saying goodbye again. It had always been my intention, with the family's concurrence, to adopt JiYub; to give him a broader formal and worldly education, something even his teachers wished for him. I also visited with his teachers while there. Mrs. Lee had told them so much about me, they knew who I was and they said, "if there is a way you can take him out of Korea, you should do so. He is too sensitive a child for our system." Korean law then forbid foreign travel by male children who had not completed their military obligation. Even then, it was still a matter of family status that determined who received passports and who knew not to apply. My old network of friends was still in place and, had it been possible to get a passport, they would have expedited the process for me. Departing this time was even more difficult because JiYub was older now.

Once back in Brussels after a rejuvenating two weeks with family in Pusan, my focus shifted to the dialogue between the US and the EC on high technology trade. We had not settled on a common definition of "High Technology" thus increasing the likelihood of another impasse. Within the mission, we understood that one of the most effective ways to soften the rough edges of bias and misunderstanding among EC policy makers is to strengthen their understanding of American society through direct exposure and contact with Americans: policy makers, industrialists, the American workforce; Americans developing innovative and creative solutions to social ills, and those developing new technologies to enhance America's competitiveness. Through our contacts at the Commission, we had identified the Chefs de Cabinet, senior advisors, products specialists, and office directors who advised EC commissioners, and those likely to succeed their principal. They could become tomorrow's leadership and we had the perfect vehicle to reach them.

We in USIS/USEC were recognized as having one of the most

well managed and policy-focussed visitor exchange programs in the Agency. As the driving force behind this program, I created a tailored American experience for 57 exchange visitors from EC headquarters and the Brussels' press corps during that second year, more than four times the level of the program before my arrival. Again, our program and policy goals converged: soften the rough edge of probable bias in future disputes between the US and the EC.

The political context to future trade policy on high technology was uncomplicated in the mid-1980s, but it has evolved since then. The United States was emerging as a high technology powerhouse in biotechnology, information technology, and telecommunications. Trade disputes with our EC partners were inevitable because they are economic competitors in many fields, and because they lagged behind the U.S. in investments in these sectors. Yet, the European Community represented a major market for our technology exports. Protecting nascent industries would have been Europe's obvious initial response as our technology exports increased. The American experience we offered through our exchange visitor program exposed them to innovative job creation programs, policies, applicable legislation, and new developments in the telecommunications sector. Our programs had a practical program objective: shape a generation of leadership within the European Commission with whom we could negotiate our policy differences as trade policy evolved giving rise to the inevitable disputes.

Although I could not accurately predict the outcome of future trade disputes involving our exchange visitors, and any role they might play in dispute resolution on a broader policy level, I could guarantee that each of them returned to Brussels with a healthy respect for the dynamism, the energy, and the resilience of American society and its people. I know because I was with our EC visitors. We spent many hours over drinks and at mealtimes discussing each day's events and their impressions. At night, they wrote reports in preparation for the briefings they would conduct once back in Brussels. Again, if we could narrow the margins of dispute, that in itself, was a victory. More concretely, as European strategies emerged at that time in job creation and telecommunications, according to internal EC reports, it was evident that our investment in our exchange visitor program had reaped dividends.

In early 1985, we received word that President Reagan would be visiting the European Parliament in Strasbourg in late spring. This would be the first visit of a sitting American president to this tier of the European Community. At a two-officer post, there is an inevitable blurring of responsibilities. Since Dwight would be departing post in June, literally weeks after the President's visit in May, I knew for this visit, I would be largely on my own. Whenever an American president visits for the first time, other high-level visitor experience notwithstanding, there are challenges the host cannot anticipate. Even though royalty, the Pope, and other heads of state and government had visited the European Parliament, the arrangements for each of those visitors pales in comparison to the full impact of a presidential visit. This is not a value judgment, just a statement of fact. Apart from those arrangements surrounding the President, there is also the First Lady. Nancy Reagan was unique in her requirements when she accompanied the president. And then, there is the traveling press. Accommodating the White House traveling press on such an historic visit posed other unique challenges. Therein was the basis for my involvement.

Although I could not relinquish my other responsibilities, between February and May, I travelled to Strasbourg on five occasions – twice with the White House Pre-Advance and Advance teams – to meet with the Parliament's spokesman and his staff, local press, and other officials increasingly alarmed by the growing requirements for President Reagan's visit. My visits were to ensure that arrangements, once negotiated, would not be arbitrarily changed. Regularly, some local official would decide that a particular requirement was not essential or that it was precedent-setting, therefore, unnecessary. On the occasion of my second visit, the Parliament's spokesman met me in a highly agitated state. "Monsieur Kennedy, je ne' comprend pas...Nous von accueilli les chefs d'etat, Sa Saintete' le Pape, mais jamais nous avon eu a' repondre a ces exigences imposee par la visite de Monsieur Reagan...Pour quoi et tout de ce necessaire?") (Mr. Kennedy, I do not understand...We have hosted heads of state, His Holiness The Pope, but never have we had to meet such requirements imposed by the visit of Mr. Reagan...why is all of this necessary?")

His reaction was expected and my usual approach in these circumstances was to walk the individual through all of the stages of a presidential visit e.g., logistics, security, staffing, press and media requirements, communications, the first lady's itinerary, and staging the president. I wanted my host to understand the larger context of the visit and how the process came together; not just the more limited perspective they were given. I had to do this for each of my visits to Strasbourg because the closer the date of the visit, the more visible the impact became. On the fourth visit, I put on my amateur psychologist's cap and employed a line I often use when trying to get a harried official to focus. On this occasion, I tailored it to Strasbourg. I recall saying something to the effect that "by the time President Reagan is on the ground, the City of Strasbourg will have sunk four inches under the weight of it, but, we will get through it." Implicit in my statement was the reality of the moment framed with a little humor. The incredulous expression on his face and my smile usually softened the impact. In the end, we survived another successful visit. Officials in Strasbourg talked about that visit for months afterward. They had never seen anything like it. The European Parliament was now a member of an illustrious club: hosts of the President of the United States. In the future, they would know what to expect should another American president come calling.

In becoming the Director of USIS /USEC the summer of 1985, I was living a dream and occupying a job in great demand. I also moved into larger, more spacious quarters more appropriate for the expanded representation responsibilities that came with the new title. The new apartment on Brussels' famed Avenue Louise occupied one half of an entire floor of a building constructed for the city's elite early in the 20th century. I should note that I rarely ever saw another African-American or person of color in that neighborhood the entire three years I lived there. In fact, on one occasion, the city police actually stopped me less than a block from my home and asked for my identification. I could tell by the way their vehicle approached that I would be stopped. They were polite, examined my diplomatic identification card, saluted and went on their way. It happened again when my assistant and I were on a site visit to the City of Bruges. Only this time, the police were so gratuitously rude and insulting that my female assistant, a Belgian of French descent married to a ranking EC official, was practically beside herself with rage. Ultimately, the mayor of Bruges offered an official apology to our ambassador. The police behavior in Bruges on that day was reminiscent of what I had endured back home in the states.

We were five months into the second Reagan Administration and awaiting the arrival of Wilhelm N. Masterson, the new ambassador, and my deputy. Since there had been considerable turnover among mission officers, several new economic and trade policy officers would be arriving to return us to our full complement of officers. Life for me was about to change radically and within the mission at large. Gone were the halcyon days with Ambassador Dimon. Not only did everyone in the mission function as a team; people liked and respected each other on a personal basis. Dimon was admired, even loved, and, for that reason, USEC was one of the most cohesive and effective embassies in the world. Marvin Rostoc had briefed me and the news was not encouraging. Masterson was a "torch bearer" for the Reagan Revolution. A former secretary of the Navy and ambassador to the Organization of American States (OAS), Jack Masterson was a "darling" of the ultra conservative wing of the Republican Party. Rostoc told me Masterson often referred to Senator Jesse Helms as the most courageous man in America for the principled stands he took in the Senate on issues dear to conservatives and on appointments of staunch conservatives to the Executive Branch. A deeply religious man, Masterson also owned the world's largest private collection of art by the Dutch masters. In his spare time, he wrote martial music in the best traditions of John Philip Sousa.

Franklin Edgewater, his public affairs advisor at the OAS, now my new deputy, arrived with him. During a round of farewells in Washington, ambassador Masterson would introduce Franklin as his public affairs advisor and announced that Franklin would be accompanying him to Brussels. Masterson may have blurred the distinction between Franklin's current duties and those he would assume in Brussels, but Franklin did not. Franklin was a career USICA Foreign Service officer who basked in Masterson's shadow. It was unfortunate that he arrived in Brussels prepared to act as my co-equal. Franklin had a reputation that I was not prepared to advance at my own expense and that of the post. I made everyone aware of my concerns. Relations between the U.S. and the EC were beginning to fray over specialty steel and crises always energized the resident press corps. What I did not need then was a conflict with a new deputy.

From the beginning, Ambassador Masterson waded into the fray with unabashed enthusiasm. I, of course, was with him as were my opposites from the Agricultural division and the head of the mission's economic section. Ambassador Dimon was effective because he was thoroughly briefed on policy, knew the history of our relations with the European Community, and could hold his own discussing or fielding questions on pasta, citrus fruits, hormones in beef production, agricultural subsidies, or specialty steel. We discovered early in his tenure at the mission that the new ambassador had little patience for reading his brief. Issues this complex could not be reduced to a paragraph. He was disinterested in technical discussions, but always prepared to forge ahead on the basis of the imperatives of his conservative philosophy. "George," he would often say, "I want to meet with the press...we've got to get our message out!" "I agree, sir...let's work on the message and discuss timing," was my instinctive response. "We will develop some talking points for you and set up a meeting with your senior advisors (the Country Team)." This was standard procedure for every senior official from the president to the lowest level official in the Executive Branch with a mandate to meet with the press.

Masterson was new and the resident press corps also wanted to take their measure of him. If he came across as prepared, rather than another Reagan ideologue, they could prove useful allies to him in a crisis. Following a detailed, two-hour briefing with members of his team, Ambassador Masterson sat down for his first press briefing, made no opening comments outlining the American position on specialty steel, but asked the journalists if they had any questions. Momentarily silenced by this unusual approach for an American ambassador at this mission, they opened up on him. He forgot his brief and presented himself as totally unprepared for one of the most demanding, substantive positions an American ambassador could aspire to. I had to contain the damage – the reporting in tomorrow's press. For 30-minutes after Masterson's departure, my colleagues and I tried to give the briefing some context. Today, it's commonly referred to as "spin control."

Once the press had left the building, we scheduled a few minutes with the ambassador - the customary practice whenever he meets with the press. It is called a post mortem. Ambassador Masterson was thoroughly pleased with his performance and dismissed all constructive suggestions from any of us. He did not grasp that the press could have savaged him but, in the end, did not do so. They would simply ignore him and us. All of us had enough experience to know what was coming. My phone rang incessantly for several days after and the questions were: "Who is this guy?" "Why did Reagan appoint him to this sensitive position?" Or, "This is not the job for a political lightweight." It was all true, but the deed had been done. Masterson was now a reality. This was our first problem. In his initial round of consultations with the EC's infamous trade commissioner, Masterson did not present himself as a serious interlocutor, rather an ideological lightweight. My mission colleagues later told me of the calls they received from their contacts at the EC. What they were reporting were the impressions of the EC's more influential commissioners. This was our second problem.

It is often that Washington's political transients do not appreciate that the effectiveness of USEC is a function of the respect the EC and its president have for the American ambassador and his team. In the best of times, but certainly in the worst of times, it is important to the health of our relationship with the EC that they call the American ambassador before the press, that they initiate a dialogue before they initiate a public dispute, that they forewarn us if a policy shift on a contentious issue becomes politically necessary, and that they ask us for a Washington reaction to blunt criticism when necessary or, decide to put a decision on hold. Lacking the respect of a George Dimon, the EC chose to bypass the mission and employ direct contact with Washington. This was our third problem. We were now, in Washington parlance, "out of the loop." The immediate consequence was an increase in the number of "fire brigades," delegations from Washington. Internally, we had a problem for which all solutions resided in Washington. Privately, I wondered how long the business and trade policy community at home would tolerate this new state of affairs.

On an average day, I could not depend upon my deputy as an alter ego. He had hitched his career wagon to Masterson's star thus compromising his value even as an advisor to the ambassador he slavishly served. I had to appear supportive of Ambassador Masterson's requests for greater public and media exposure while trying to install safeguards against potential embarrassment to him or the mission. With the exception of Seth Lipsky, the Brussels Bureau Chief of the Wall Street Journal, representatives of the major wire services, specialized publications (Business Week), and print media were reluctant to meet with him. Managing my relations with the press, drafting speeches for the ambassador, traveling with him to London, Copenhagen, and SHAPE (Supreme Headquarters Allied Powers Europe) Headquarters in Mons, Belgium; and mitigating the effects of my deputy on the staff and the ambassador were the ingredients of my 15 – 17-hour day.

As senior staff, we met daily, primarily to discuss damage control. At one meeting, I confidently predicted that Masterson would not last more than 18 months in his current role. The trade policy community within the State, Commerce, Agriculture, and Treasury Departments, and the Office of the Trade Representative, noticed the change in Brussels; how less effective we now were in managing the relationship with the EC. Trade policy specialists and product and commodity experts in these departments were also in daily contact with the responsible officer at the mission. In an unusual turnabout, we now had to rely upon feedback from Washington on EC issues to keep us informed when the reverse should have been the norm – as in the past. In November 1985, amid our dispute with the EC on a growing list of issues, President Reagan visited NATO to address a Ministers' meeting. Ambassador Masterson saw this as a unique moment for "face time" with the President. There are limits to the ability of a staff to "advise" an ambassador in certain circumstances. This was one of them. He was beyond our control. Although there are three American missions in Brussels, their missions are uniquely different. We respected that uniqueness as career officers. Masterson was distracted with the impending visit of President Reagan. Perhaps that was a blessing.

I now had a press advisor's worst nightmare, something my

predecessor never had to confront: an ambassador who refused to learn his brief, our protestations to the contrary. Our most effective weapon had consigned himself to the margins of our dialogue with the EC when he could have made a difference. Daily, I would be on the phone with my boss, Marvin Rostoc. He understood the problem, but could only offer that I "make it work, just don't kill him," the latter point in jest. I did have a plan to convince Ambassador Masterson of his need for a special assistant and that Franklin Edgewater was the logical choice given their close relationship. Franklin did not want to be the deputy I had been and, frankly, expected. Now that Rostoc was on board with my plan, I could approach our deputy mission chief of USEC, who understood the problem I confronted and its impact on the staff. Within six months of his arrival, I had Franklin ensconced in a newly created office next to the ambassador. Of course, this just gave him a new perch from which to snipe at my operation. That, however, was preferable to having him in direct line of authority.

Given the travails of the previous six months, I looked forward to having a real deputy. I was scheduled to take home leave the summer of '86 and I wanted to be well represented during my first extended absence as the director. There were several very competent officers I would have recommended for the position had I been asked. The solution, however, was being forged in Washington. Unfortunately, for those of us at post, a bad situation was about to become worse. I soon learned that the solution to my problem was the Foreign Service spouse of the new Press Officer at our Mission to the North Atlantic Treaty Organization (NATO). Claudette Packwood was eager, aggressive, full of ideas, but impetuous. She was also too junior for the responsibilities she was now expected to assume. It soon became all too apparent to me and my senior colleagues that more field experience would have strengthened her standing with the ambassador, his deputy, and among my colleagues; but I needed someone at once. The real truth is I also did not have a choice. I was prepared to offer her every opportunity to succeed. Early in her tenure, I did just that. By the spring of that year, however, her performance was more uneven. Although somewhat ill at ease with her, I prepared to depart post for home leave. There were no immediate crises brewing and I was just going to have to have confidence in her ability to cope in my absence. That is what any competent deputy should be prepared to do. As my departure date drew close, she would say, "relax chief. You've earned a break...we're in good hands here." Claudette's words rang in my ear as I headed for the airport. My exhaustion was real and the damp Brussels climate had aggravated an old shoulder injury from an earlier automobile accident.

Woodbury, New Jersey in the summer was exactly what I needed: hot. Brussels averaged 266 days of rainfall annually and I felt old and arthritic. It was difficult to raise my left arm above my shoulder with limited articulation. I needed some sun and lots of it! For six weeks, I visited a fitness center daily, entertained friends visiting from Brussels, and hung out in Atlantic City on the boardwalk. Intellectual stimulation was not a major priority for me during this home leave and I did not charge from one newsstand to another looking for copies of the New York Times, or issues of Time, Newsweek, or Business Week magazine. I had forgotten how refreshingly limited a small town newspaper could be. International news was often reduced to a few paragraphs. Home leave had been pleasant. I was feeling rejuvenated and wishing I could have extended another 30-days.

In mid-August, I headed to Washington for the customary consultations prior to returning to Brussels. Josh Wilson, the Executive Officer in the European Bureau at USICA handed me a telegram from my office asking, "Did you approve this?" The telegram from my deputy proposed resource shifts I had not authorized for purposes I had not approved. "No, Josh, this is news to me" I said, handing him the telegram. "Well, we thought so...the sooner you return, the better we will feel here. Your deputy chief of mission said he had attempted to reach you. Apparently, Ms. Packwood's behavior has alarmed Ambassador Masterson. They are awaiting your return before any action is proposed." I knew Claudette well enough by that time to know that a transAtlantic query on my part would not produce any concrete results, even for the benign situation I initially thought the telegram portended.

Upon arrival in Brussels, I decided to get a good night's rest and deal with the situation the following morning. It had already been six weeks; what difference could another day make? The following morning, I attended the ambassador's senior staff meeting, not Claudette. She protested, the first sign I knew the situation was more complex than I had imagined. She said, "this is our office and I should be there also!" After the meeting, I met with Ambassador Masterson and his deputy, Nelson Swaggert. Each described a series of bizarre events in evidence almost immediately after my departure. "Had I been able to contact you, George, I would have asked you to return immediately, postponing your home leave until a more convenient date," said Mr. Swaggert. "Bob," I said, "let me talk to Claudette, my staff, and everyone that has dealt with her in my absence...I will then call Washington for further guidance... Within the week, I will apprise you and the ambassador of steps I am authorized to take towards a remedy...I apologize for any discomfort you and the ambassador may have experienced."

My meeting with Claudette produced very little beyond an aggressive defense of her actions, for most of which she offered little in the way of explanatory detail. My Belgian staff met with me individually, each expressing not only confusion, but also a genuine concern regarding Claudette's mental state. Other meetings with our embassy colleagues at our bilateral embassy up the street (accredited to the Kingdom of Belgium) revealed a similar concern. The looming question to me was naturally about Claudette's health. If she had a medical condition that was beyond my purview, our regional medical advisor in Vienna would best address it since none of the three embassies in Brussels had a resident American physician. It was now time to consult with colleagues in Washington. Questions addressing an officer's emotional, physical, or psychological well-being involve privacy issues beyond a field director's competence and scope of authority. I needed guidance regarding a remedial course of action. With approval from Washington, I approached Claudette with a choice: agree to meet with Dr. Rigamer from Vienna or, I would have to relieve her. To preserve her career, I urged her to meet in private with Dr. Rigamer. She reluctantly agreed to do do.

I soon learned that Claudette's illness required constant medication and strict adherence to a diet. Two immediate consequences of failure to maintain discipline on both requirements are mood swings and erratic behavior, apparently a daily occurrence with Claudette. Relations between Claudette and myself, and with all of her colleagues, deteriorated rapidly, to the point that her performance suffered demonstrably. As often as I would attempt to work with her, she would rebuff me almost reflexively. I suppose her reaction was more of embarrassment than anything else I could think of. Her housekeeper, also mine as well, threatened to quit; my staff refused to take direction from her; she defied me on a daily basis, and her presence in the office was by now disruptive. My remaining option was to request that she be reassigned to Washington. Within a span of nine months from her arrival in Brussels, what could have been a career-defining assignment evolved into an ignominious transfer with the full concurrence of her direct supervisor and the chief of our mission. I had waged an uphill battle to be assigned to Brussels; was several grades her senior, even in my previous position as the deputy director, and had more experience. She, a white female, with considerably fewer arrows in her quiver was deemed suitable for a job more senior officers would have fought for. To salvage herself, Claudette filed a formal grievance against Ambassador Masterson and me by alleging we had accessed her medical records and were unfairly using privileged information in a manner detrimental to her interests. The World Wide Web did not yet exist, neither did the Internet. It was only recently that we had received our first Wang computers. It was never made clear to me how I would have been able to access her private medical records.

Resolving Claudette's status was one of the most unpleasant chapters in my tenure as director of public affairs at the mission. If anything, her assignment was a graphic reminder of what can happen when important personnel decisions are not handled with care. But, then, her assignment was not precedent setting; this happened on a regular basis, but not for officers that looked like me. Why could we not be given equal opportunity to demonstrate competence or inability to perform? Where was the meritocracy I had heard so much about?

Home leave seemed a distant experience within a month of my return. It was now October, a new program year had begun and I needed help. One of the junior officers assigned to our Brussels' embassy just a block away performed yeoman duty until a permanent replacement arrived in early January 1987. Ambassador Masterson and Franklin Edgewater departed Brussels that January – 19 months after arrival and within the time frame of my earlier prediction. Nelson Swaggert assumed charge pending the spring arrival of his replacement, Michael E. C. Ely, and the new ambassador, Aldridge Kepler. Stability, a hallmark of the mission to the EC, was shattered and the consequences were reverberating in Brussels, other European capitols, and Washington as well. Within a span of 19-months, I would have three different deputies while working for my third ambassador. The Brussels-based Mission to the European Communities has many masters in Washington and it was only the professionalism of the officers and staff at post that enabled us to manage a series of escalating crises with the European Communities while simultaneously coping with our internal leadership crisis.

I was now in the fourth year of my four-year assignment. The prospect of transfer had been very much on my mind when USICA announced a policy change that had a direct impact on my life. Two overseas missions were to be exempt from the four-year transfer rule, especially at the director level: USIS/USEC and another specialized post in Vienna. The new assignments' policy established a five-year tour at both missions, but only with the concurrence of the ambassador. The rationale for the policy change was the substantive knowledge required for each position. Naturally, I requested to be extended for a fifth year. My performance reviews were consistently outstanding. Moreover, I did not see any of the more career-enhancing assignments on the vacancy lists that year. So, why not remain where I was? Before their departures, Nelson Swaggert and Ambassador Masterson supported my request for a fifth year.

Washington's approval offered a quiet, poignant moment to step back and reflect on what I had achieved over four years. The recent personnel and management challenges were part of the job. They occurred on my watch and it was incumbent upon me to address them. This was different. In addition to being the first African-American director, and to have been promoted from within, I would now establish a third precedent by becoming the first director ever approved for a five-year tour because of the substantive knowledge and skills required for the position of director at USIS/USEC. This was the validation I sought. I may have been the first African-American director and now I knew I would not be the last. Generally, all of us are judged by the failures of one and the foundation I now stood upon was one of achievement. I could lay that burden down – and I did.

1986 and 1987 were years marked by particular and unusual challenges in our relations with the EC. A new ambassador was still months away and my new deputy had not arrived. On substance, we lurched from crisis to crisis with repeated risks of action and counter-action that would touch off a trade war. Our confrontation with the European Communities followed an increase in the number of countries comprising its membership, and the resultant impact on a billion dollars of American exports to Spain and Portugal. More specifically, any enlargement of the Communities' membership and the terms of that enlargement may not have an adverse impact on American exports to those countries that become new EC members. Unfortunately, the bilateral agreements governing American exports to Spain and Portugal were abrogated to meet the terms of their accession to the EC. The U.S., under GATT rules, was entitled to full compensation for the value of its exports (one billion-dollars) adversely affected by the abrogation of trade agreements in force at the time of the accession of Spain and Portugal to the EC. There were important principles of fairness at stake.

I had the difficult and sensitive task of explaining to several European policymakers and to European publics that despite the fact that we supported European integration and the European Community, and despite the fact that we favored the entry of Spain and Portugal to the EC, America's rights with the General Agreement on Tariffs and Trade (GATT) had to be respected. Our demand for adequate compensation for the value of our lost exports was, therefore, just. This was a hostile environment for those of us in press and media relations as well as our trade negotiators because the prevailing view in Europe was that we were being unreasonable; that we Americans should be prepared to accept trade disadvantages in return for the political and security advantages accruing from enlargement of the EC. My public affairs campaign with the Brussels' press corps had one consistent theme: U.S. public opinion would not accept the prevailing European view; that with a $170 billion-dollar trade deficit, the Reagan Administration had to insist on full compensation. I noted that the consequences, otherwise, would have been a field day for the protectionists in the Congress – something the EC consistently feared.

Gregg Kinnear, my new deputy, arrived in February 1987, just as European opinion gradually came to recognize the merits of our position which allowed EC negotiators to offer us a politically thin level of satisfaction, and just barely at that. I briefed Gregg on this crisis, outlined two major projects I was developing, which he would have to manage, and asked him to follow up with our other EC missions on the "Enlargement Crisis." I turned immediately to the next brewing trade crisis – the EC's proposed Fats and Oils Tax which would jeopardize America's three-billion dollar soybean trade with Europe. To advance American obligations in this latest crisis, I called an important contact at EUROPA TV who I knew would be interested in providing media coverage. I was offering an insider's view, something she would seize immediately. I told her I needed an influential platform from which my new ambassador could make our case on this and several other key issues: the question of U.S. trade policy and the new GATT Round, and America's policy on East-West Trade. In a timely, wide-ranging interview conducted by my contact, our new ambassador was able to reach an important audience of five-to-seven million Europeans. We needed to get our message out to the broadest audience possible, and quickly to mitigate the effects of a counter effort by the European Commission.

To strengthen the high technology dialogue with the EC, I had developed two new exchange projects that would give added focus to a specific process in high tech manufacturing and, secondly, offer insights into the evolution of America as a post-industrial society. The first was "Computer Integrated Manufacturing: The U.S. Experience." The second project was "Information, New Technologies and the Information Needs of a Post-Industrial Society." Both projects delved into areas of importance to US-EC relations; areas in which the American experience had relevance and trade potential for European developmental needs.

We now had a new ambassador; as I said, my third. I had a plan, a strategy, which if implemented, would prepare him for the public dimension of his assignment. At night, I had drafted a rather extensive and comprehensive public diplomacy plan that would integrally and prominently involve him immediately upon arrival – provided he was as inclined to wade into this fray as enthusiastically as his predecessor had done. My goal was to effect a different outcome: success rather than ineptitude. Kepler endorsed the proposed plan with minor changes. He could now proceed at his own pace now that he was in country.

Ambassador Aldridge Kepler brought a unique set of credentials to this assignment as the most recent American Ambassador to the European Communities: Cabinet Secretary and Deputy Assistant to President Reagan; former Assistant Secretary of the Treasury for Policy Planning and Communication, and Assistant Secretary of Commerce for International Economic Policy. While living in New York City, he had been an editor-in-chief of *Financial World.* The combined public/private experience equipped him with a keen grasp of trade and monetary issues, and of the potential for public diplomacy to positively affect US-EC relations. While being briefed by my boss in Washington before taking up this new assignment, Kepler remarked, "My director of public affairs will have to be the best there is in the business...that he would have to measure up to a rare standard." In response, my boss, Ralph McConnell,said, "You are fortunate to have a man of Kennedy's caliber on your staff."

Ambassador Kepler and I did form a productive relationship. He understood my role and its importance to his success. Kepler was a man obsessed with greater political ambition, and success in this demanding assignment would burnish his credentials for the cabinet post he aspired to should the Republicans recapture the White House in 1988. This ambassador, like his predecessors, shared a common flaw: like many politically appointed ambassadors, they harbored the illusion that relations between the U.S. and the European Commission began the day they arrived. What was there to learn from the past when what mattered was today and their ability to play onstage tomorrow? Ambassador Masterson would not read his brief. Ambassador Kepler, to his credit, did not commit that fatal error. What mattered to both men, however, was appearing competent to their political betters back in Washington,

My senior colleagues and I moved quickly to repair the "communications bridge" between USEC and EC Headquarters, with leaders of the Brussels' business community, and with the Brussels' press corps. While each of these groups was initially pleased with Ambassador Kepler's White House and private sector experience, they quickly began to grumble privately about his tendency to lecture, to admonish, and to have a tin ear regarding others' points of view. He also had the annoying tendency to go on and off the record multiple times in the same response to a question. In the best tradition of his immediate predecessor, he clamored for public and media exposure beyond Brussels in other EC capitols. Creating media coverage in other EC capitols was delicate since there were other higher profile ambassadors in those capitols who expected the courtesy of a request and statement of purpose for a visit by their Brussels-based colleague. "You are the president's representative to the European Communities in Brussels, not to each of the member countries" we would delicately point out. Kepler's view was that as the American representative to the European Communities, he had carte blanche to travel within each of the member countries as he deemed it necessary to do so. We would obtain the customary approval from our colleagues in those EC capitols Kepler felt it important to visit e.g., Denmark, the United Kingdom, the Federal Republic of Germany, France, and Spain. Generally, Ambassador Kepler was well received. On each trip, I was able to arrange press interviews or press conferences that resulted in good coverage of his remarks on television, radio, and in the press. We communicated major U.S. policy objectives on sensitive trade and economic issues in key European dailies in Paris, Copenhagen, Stockholm, and Brussels, as well as Munich, London, Bonn, and Madrid.

It was the spring of 1987 and I was again asked to submit a public diplomacy strategy for the G-7 Summit to be hosted by the Italians in Venice. Venice represented my third G-7 summit, seventh or eighth White House visit, and countless ministerials. Communications strategy was my forte and a hallmark of USIS/USEC. Our recommendations, therefore, were useful to our colleagues back in Washington and their counterparts in the White House Press Office.

Venice in June is delightful under most circumstances, but the impact of a gathering of the leaders of the world's most industrialized nations and 3,000 members of the international press was transforming. Most of the city, including the most noted museums, the Island of San Giorgio Maggiore, the Piazzetta di San Marco, Marco Polo Airport, the Lido, the Palazzo Ducale, and the Grand Canal were wrapped in a tight security blanket. Tourists were discouraged from entering the city and barred from each of these locations. Residents of some restricted areas were similarly encouraged to visit friends or relatives. I had never seen the city so devoid of tourists, for example. Everyone on the streets, in a restaurant, on a gondola, or on a ferry was either security or a member of a delegation. This I can say was a unique life's experience for someone who was as familiar with the city as I was. Unlike the '83 Williamsburg

Summit, the '84 London Summit, or the '85 Bonn Summit, the Venice Summit took place at a time of escalating tension in the Persian Gulf. The economic goals these leaders pursue at each summit remain essentially the stability of the international monetary system, preserving open markets, and eliminating regulatory impediments to global commerce.

I returned from Venice and several weeks later, embarked on a vacation to visit family and friends in Pusan. This time, I could relax in the knowledge that my able deputy was in charge. What a difference competence makes! Pusan was now a teeming metropolis replete with frustrating traffic congestion, an expanding population, new industries, and in full preparation for the aquatic events of the 1988 Summer Olympics. The Olympics the following year was to be the equivalent of Korea's international debut, and they were determined that it would be the best organized, the best managed, the most secure, and the splashiest of any Summer Olympics on record. Koreans are a proud, hard working people and, while I would not be able to return the following summer, I never doubted that theirs' was destined to be among the more successful Olympics in modern times. JiYub had blossomed into a 15-year old teenager, a source of great pride to his extended family, to me, and to his teachers – most of whom knew me and of my interest in giving him opportunities unavailable in Pusan. For this visit, his parents and I avoided talk of adopting him, raising false hopes. We all understood Korean law regarding male children. I did resolve to visit often and take him out of Korea at the first opportunity possible.

My fifth and final year was now into its third month and my agenda resembled that of a first year director. No White House visits had been announced and my fifth and final US-EC Ministerial was still several months away. Before beginning an earnest dialogue about my future after USEC, I had to complete a project I initiated with the EC's Directorate-General for External Relations. This exchange project was dubbed "Competitiveness: The Global Challenge." The project was designed to address the competitive challenge from the Pacific Rim nations. My purpose in designing this project was to stress the point that the European Community needed to attract capital for real investments in EC countries and to demonstrate that the strength of the American economy was the foundation on which the United States would continue to fulfill its obligations to the Atlantic Alliance. This exchange project and its predecessor projects in high technology, competitiveness, information, telecommunications, and job-creation focused on two consistent themes in US-EC relations: improving the economic and industrial competitiveness of EC member states, and reducing EC anxiety that the U.S. might retreat behind a wall of protectionist legislation.

The second project on my drawing board was an analysis of the talks between the European Community and the Council for Mutual Economic Assistance (CEMA – the old Soviet and East European counterpart to the EC.) The report detailed the Eastern European drive to "normalize" relations between CEMA and the EC. Marvin Rostoc was an old Eastern European hand, thus he made extensive use of my analysis. The December 1987 EC Ministerial was my farewell to ministerials, at least in Brussels. Five ministerials, more than any of my predecessors, had been a great experience. I thought of the friendships built, the crises we had endured, and the many small success that were the notches on our belts.

There was another new development. I was now a member of the senior Foreign Service, having been promoted to the rank of Counselor in early December. I appreciated the many congratulatory messages from colleagues around the world, especially those in Brussels. They, among all, had shared the turbulent times with me and knew I had earned it. My litmus test for USICA now was my next assignment. Brussels had the reputation of a career-enhancing post. All of my predecessors had moved on to some of the Agency's most prestigious senior management positions in Washington and overseas. It was now my turn; would the magic continue for me? And so, the negotiations began for my next assignment. Another rare African-American officer had cracked the "glass ceiling," but would I, too, be destined for Africa or a marginal, but senior, position in Washington? I did wonder.

And so, the ritual began. I lobbied each honest contact I had throughout the Agency. From one good friend at NATO, the message was, "you are competitive for New Delhi, but it is being held in reserve for the current director of USIS Italy should he not be named as an ambassador." Well, that was not the way the process was designed to work, but it did for senior white officers, the most critical opponents of affirmative action within our organization at that time. The attractive senior vacancies were few, New Delhi representing the most attractive. The same valued friend advised me to bid on Director, USIS/Bogota. "Narco-Terrorism is a front-burner issue...high visibility, high risk, but important." Having few attractive options, I bid on Bogota. Several weeks later, the phone rang on my desk. It was a friend advising me informally that Bogota was a "done deal." "Official notification is forthcoming but do not announce it until then." As the days went by without the official notification, word leaked out. Everyone knew, but I remained tentative when queried about my future plans.

In February '88, my boss, Ralph McConnell, called me from Washington. "Has anyone from personnel called you regarding your assignment to Bogota?" "No, they have not, Ralph. I am still awaiting official notification." Ralph then shared with me his experience the previous evening at a social function for the new and departing Director of USIS Bogota, Howie Lane. Both Ralph and I knew Howie Lane and this came as a surprise to both of us. "Call personnel, George. They owe you an explanation." I promptly did, only to be advised that someone would call me. The call never came. I was adrift, without an assignment, and Washington was playing their games again. It was obvious now that a major assignment was not in the cards for me, my success in Brussels notwithstanding. In March, the word came: Director USIS/USOECD (U.S. Mission to the Organization for Economic Cooperation and Development) Paris. This was at best a lateral move on a slightly descending plane; larger organizational membership but only one support staff. Was I disappointed? Absolutely!

My farewell from Brussels was a continuous affair, emotional, many poignant moments with testimonials from many friends and colleagues who credited me with everything from single handedly rescuing US-EC relations, to having provided an American experience for more EC officials than anyone in the history of the US-EC relationship, to having had an impact on individual lives and careers. For the first time, I did not feel the urge to move on.

The US/OECD Ministerial convenes each spring. This year, they were without a USIS director for press and media relations, and I was asked if I would go on temporary duty to Paris to help them out given my extensive experience in Brussels. "Why not," I said. That was the extent of my enthusiasm. The few days I spent in Paris were not particularly memorable. There was the usual flurry of media activity surrounding the presence of several members of the Reagan Cabinet; a few press scrums, the gratitude of the American ambassador, and back to Brussels. I took home leave shortly thereafter. Bob Shryock, a reporter for my home town daily *"The Woodbury Times"* had been contacted by USICA to ascertain their interest in an interview since I was on home leave. They were, and Bob and I met one particularly hot afternoon at my mother's house. The resulting article "He Keeps the World on Understandable Terms With The U.S." was about my most memorable experience that summer. A framed copy hangs in my office at home.

Before reporting to Paris that fall, I spent several days at USICA Headquarters in Washington. I felt a need to understand why my assignment had been derailed. Why had I not been treated more professionally, with the level of courtesy any officer had a right to expect? I naively believed that I had earned at least that much. Again, a friend and colleague in a position to know the background of my assignment, offered to have a closed-door with me with the proviso that I not reveal our conversation to anyone. His career would be in jeopardy. The details, when revealed, confirmed my view of the Agency at that time. In essence, this is what happened. Final decisions on all of the positions I had bid for were deferred until I had been selected for the Paris job. They needed someone to go to Paris for the express purpose of terminating the one staff assistant position, scaling back the program, and to maintain a "presence." That assignment would have been more suitable for someone on the verge of retirement having just completed a hardship tour and needed a quiet, comfortable perch from which to transition into retirement. I could legitimately be advised by personnel that the only foreign vacancy was in Paris, leaving it to me to accept that position or request an assignment in Washington, which I did not want. Once the Paris slot was filled, the candidates for the other jobs I sought were selected. African-American success was an anomaly not subject to the same considerations as that of my white colleagues. Racism was still alive and well. The real question is, why should I have expected fairness? Was I still that naïve? Undoubtedly, yes!

CHAPTER 14

PARIS AND THE UNEXPECTED

The position of director of Press and Public Affairs at the American mission to the Organization for Economic Cooperation and Development (US/OECD) was not in considerable demand in 1988 among many senior officers at the U.S. International Communications Agency, its Paris address notwithstanding. I suppose a legitimate question then is, had Paris lost its appeal as one of the more desired Foreign Service assignments? To the contrary! Conversely, the counterpart position at the larger bilateral embassy across the city was reserved for the most senior white officers, primarily those whose careers consisted of assignments to Europe, Moscow, and the larger posts in the old eastern Europe. The director's position at the OECD had been vacant for almost a year. That was the telltale sign the position was considered by many in the "European Club" as a "pass." You know, "pass" as in, what else is there?

The previous incumbent was an African-American – friend and colleague – who had died at post and, now, the very existence of that office was precarious. Only a locally hired American secretary/program assistant stood between USICA and the decision to close the office. Now that I was to become the director, the leadership in the European Bureau proposed that I terminate the program assistant, in effect, becoming a one-officer post with no staff. As a newly-minted senior officer, my preference had been for greater responsibility, not location. I would readily have given up Paris for a more challenging assignment in Latin America, or out in the Pacific. Remember, I had already served in Brussels, Bonn, Rome, Pusan, and the Philippines. I was not asking for another tour in Europe. I was available for assignment on a world-wide basis. My morale was in disrepair and I seriously considered serving 18-months in Paris and applying for retirement at age 50; perhaps retiring in France or Italy. The idea of retiring in Europe had titillated me since the age of 19 when I fell in love with Italy of the 1950s. My friend and Rome mentor, Al Zucca, retired at the age of 50 and I never heard him express regret at having done so. Al had set up shop with a trusted friend and, together, they had built a thriving consulting business on "N" Street, N.W., a stone's throw from Dupont Circle in Washington, D.C.

Success in the Brussels' assignment was to have been my ticket through the glass ceiling and, although I heard the door slam before arriving in Paris, I could not help but wonder anew what it would take for equal consideration. I was not yet prepared to abandon the idea that fairness had to be a reasonable expectation. Each of my assignments had been a struggle. I personally knew white officers who were known alcoholics, racists, mediocre in the extreme, public adulterers, linguistically challenged in assignments that required foreign language proficiency, and all of them had directed our largest, most important programs in Washington and our most prestigious posts abroad. Plum assignments were also reserved for them. The process that ensured continuity in this practice surely can be no other than affirmative action. My last two assignments validated my skills and I knew it. To even think that, skills aside, affirmative action could only apply to officers of color and a few white females is the height of arrogance. That attitude was, and remains, the prevailing view. I do confess a lack of enthusiasm as I headed for Paris that summer.

My forte is not managing low morale, especially my own. Moreover, I did not have a track record of presiding over defeat or the inevitability of defeat, and that, in my estimation, was what this assignment appeared to represent. There was, however, another option available to me. Why not have some fun and do the unexpected: turn the Paris operation around; revitalize it; give it real content! In addition, justify the continued employment of the program assistant by giving her real work to do; develop one of the most visible, effective programs of any small mission in Europe. I well understood that if I was going to rescue that operation, I could not accomplish that on my own. Although I had a few ideas, I needed allies. Fortunately for me, I garnered critical support from our ambassador, Nelson Lambert. During one of my early conversations with him shortly after I settled in, I learned that what we shared was an interest in putting the OECD on the map. To begin, what is the OECD?

The OECD is the premier research organization for the world's industrialized economies. Its membership in 1988 included all the western European countries plus the United States, Canada, Japan, and Mexico. As an organization, its influence, especially within Europe, is quite significant. The OECD's value to the U.S. is that it represents an important forum for the promotion of specific policies. The fact that ICA or, more accurately, my new boss in the European Bureau, failed to appreciate the unique role of the OECD and the continuing value of an Agency presence was, frankly, mystifying. No other institution is positioned to perform the intellectual "heavy lifting" required for G-7 (later G-8) Summits as ably as the OECD.

Well, there was Paris. In August, the city is a newcomer's dream, and I was a new arrival. Parisians were on vacation, traffic was negligible, and I had a few weeks to find an apartment and decide just how best to pump myself up for a less-than-desirable assignment. Make no mistake; I was drawing upon every ounce of psychic motivation I could muster. I did not have a family that would have been delighted at living in Paris. I was practically a workaholic. The management team within the European Bureau back at the Agency had changed and they were not inspiring the degree of confidence among its field directors as had previously been the case with Marvin Rostoc and Ralph McConnell. The new crowd appeared hesitant, halting, and unsure, almost overwhelmed. In a briefing memorandum prepared for a meeting between ambassador Lambert and the new management team, they took the position that the OECD did not rank on their list of priority posts; furthermore, that USIS/OECD's meager resources could not be augmented. Their attitude seemed to be, "we have a presence there, make the best of it!" I would not rank even as a rescue operation. I do believe that had I chosen to close the post, the European Bureau would have welcomed my decision. Again, I could only play the cards I was dealt. What a stark contrast with the same bureau's approach to my previous post. This assignment was going to be an uphill battle; one that could effectively derail my career at a time when I felt my greatest achievements could lie ahead. I set those concerns aside just long enough to find an apartment. A friend from Brussels, herself a Parisian, came up to help me negotiate with the local landlords. She knew the games they could play with a foreigner like myself. We looked at four apartments over several days, only to settle on a delightful spot across from the Russian Embassy, and within 10-minutes walk from the OECD complex. I would avoid the dreaded Paris commute. Moreover, I could park my car in the OECD garage, walk to work, and have my car at hand and available for use on the weekends. While I may not have been very excited about my job, my living arrangements were a bright spot, something I could appreciate daily. Restaurants were an obvious choice, but what I came to enjoy were the neighborhood shops where I could shop daily, as Parisians did. My favorite was a local rotisserie: you stopped by early in the morning, order a quarter, half, or full roast chicken, gave the proprietor the time you would return, and went about your day. At the appointed hour, you returned, claimed your order, added a few extras to make a fresh and delicious dinner and I was home sitting at my table within 10-minutes.

I sat in my un-air conditioned office one hot September day and began thinking out loud with my program assistant. Alice Pembrooke was a tough American transplant from Iowa who spoke fluent French, was thoroughly familiar with the OECD bureaucracy, and I wanted her reaction to what was emerging as my game plan. My immediate task, I told her, was multifaceted: define a new role for USIS/US/OECD (U.S. Information Service at the U.S. Mission to the OECD); identify the audience I needed to reach; articulate for ICA Washington my goals and priorities, and put in place a plan to devise and implement my program. This, as I explained, was my management challenge and, one by the way, Alice enthusiastically endorsed. She also thanked me for my willingness to keep her knowing Washington had suggested I terminate her position. She understood the career risks for me. The new leadership of the European Bureau wanted a caretaker director and I did not fit the mold. Alice, I soon discovered, had a solid grasp of OECD programs and policies, the French telecommunications sector, and how to work with the French media. She already knew what would have taken me at least a year to learn. There was no rational reason I could terminate someone this valuable to us.

Meanwhile, on a policy level, I worked with ambassador Lambert to identify the important policy themes, an approach to deliver our message and, finally, the message itself. Unlike the European Community, U.S. relations with the OECD are less contentious and, therefore, irritants and disputes are not the stuff of daily headlines in European capitols. The level at which the ambassador and I interacted with the OECD Secretariat was more cerebral. Policy conflicts were "de riguer" in Brussels. For example, a debate about economic reform takes a different shape than one about specialty steel, durum wheat, or pasta. In the late 1980s, a principal American objective was advancing the cause of structural policy reform in OECD countries i.e., promoting deregulation and the greater opening of economies to the influence of market forces.

The economics of the argument regarding structural reform, as ambassador Lambert often said, made perfect sense to everyone. The difficulty was in persuading national political leadership and their representatives to the OECD to muster the political courage to advocate a reform agenda when political suicide was a probable end result for some of them. Ambassador Lambert knew and understood what I knew and understood: there was a need for our mission to devise a strategy and a program to shape public opinion within those capitols where opposition militated against cooperating with us. "I need ideas" he said...I know your resources are limited, but let me know what I can do to help you." To move public opinion in Europe would involve changing the mindset of senior Eurocrats at both the EC and the OECD, and the journalists who evolve in their orbit. A timely leak or strategically placed idea from a senior, well-placed Eurocrat could sink or elevate an idea.

I had due diligence to perform before the OECD's fall activity schedule shifted into high gear. For practically a full month, I met with several of the OECD Secretariat's senior economists, representatives of other delegations accredited to the organization, and those American and European journalists whose bylines hold sway over public opinion where it mattered. The ambassador needed ideas and I was trying to rescue a program. Structural reform framed the policy debate and I had an idea, which, if accepted, would bring the policy goal posts closer together. People exchanges increase the likelihood of bridging the last six inches in the communications process. "Structural Adjustment: The American Experience" was the theme for an exchange project I designed to send ten European journalists from several OECD member countries to the U.S. to gain a better understanding of the reform process, acceptable levels of political risks to advocate for reform, and the benefits that accrue to a society and its economy from structural reforms. My project and political goals were to generate a series of articles by prominent European journalists about structural reform, to take the sting out of the dialogue in European capitols, and within the policy debate at the OECD; and, to offer political cover to the European politicians bold enough to take a public position in support of reform measures. In addition, I persuaded my USIS colleagues at our missions in Europe on the merits of inviting ambassador Lambert to meet with skeptical press and political leaders in their capitols to talk about U.S. policy and our success with structural adjustment policies. Nelson Lambert was a known quantity to most career economic officers having been a deputy assistant secretary in the Bureau for Economic Affairs at State.

Project post mortem press reports from my colleagues who recommended the participants for my exchange project were the most balanced they had seen from these journalists on this topic in years. Now we had begun to have an impact on the policy debate on this particular issue. Nelson Lambert moved the goal posts even closer during a round of policy briefings in select European capitols. As word of his effectiveness spread throughout OECD capitols, we were able to arrange visits to the Far East and Sub-Saharan Africa. We broadened his message beyond structural reform to include U.S. economic and trade policies, and the implications of an integrated European Community by 1992.

Paris at that time was home base for COCOM (Coordinating Committee.) This was the organization that monitored and controlled the transfer of strategic technology to the former Soviet Union, eastern Europe, and China. The head of our delegation to COCOM, Nelson Swaggert, and I had worked together in Brussels and he, too, needed some help to demystify and clarify U.S. policy objectives within this organization. Our policies at that time represented an area of our multilateral economic diplomacy generally prone to misunderstanding. My press contacts were well developed by fall 1988, and I was able to arrange eleven interviews that enabled ambassador Lambert and Nelson Swaggert to clarify and, where necessary, defend in depth U.S. concerns about transfers of strategic technologies when many European dailies had become critical of our policies. Again, our goal was more balanced media reporting when it was American policies or actions under the microscope.

My programs were reverberating in ICA Washington because the Program Bureau there augmented my meager exchange budget with its own resources, thus enabling me to increase the number of OECD officials and journalists I could send to the U.S. for extended consultations. Oddly enough, there was never a second suggestion from Washington to terminate my program assistant. I now had a program, despite the unwillingness of the European Bureau to increase the resources they could have made available to me. My success did create some tension but, frankly, I enjoyed it. Ironically, my future was in the hands of a management team with a dubious commitment to my program and to my success. Frankly, I welcomed the tension; they could not ignore me. Success has many patrons and the only other legitimate patron of my success was ambassador Lambert. To sustain our momentum would require institutional support from the OECD Secretariat, more specifically, their Office of Personnel. With ambassador Lambert pointing me in the right direction, I sat down with senior Secretariat officials and made my case for their continued participation in our exchange programs. "This is how your staff will benefit," I would point out to each of them. "I will work with you and your team to identify specific policy issues, develop the most useful program of briefings and site visits, and identify the appropriate participants." Good staff people are difficult to spring loose, even for short periods, and, if I could persuade OECD management to "buy in" to our program, success was practically guaranteed. Within a year, 20 Secretariat officials traveled to the U.S. through my exchange program.

In the spring of 1989, Alice and I took on the annual, four-day OECD Ministerial. George Herbert Walker Bush was now the president and five members of his cabinet, most of them new to the OECD game, made their debut at the spring ministerial that year. Normally, an operation considerably larger than mine would have been on hand to ensure continuity in support. ICA offered no support and I did not request any. Perhaps I was taking advantage of another opportunity to highlight my success in spite of their best effort to ignore me. For four days, my assistant and I staffed and arranged press conferences for all five cabinet officers and responded to their requests for one-on-one meetings with both foreign and American journalists. In addition, there were dozens of "photo-ops" and television coverage. Our reward was a sincere "job superbly well done" from ambassador Lambert.

By this time, I was beginning to feel a level of gratification from my role within the mission. The ambassador gave me credit for contributing to his success as our representative to the OECD. That was huge! Moreover, he had directed that all contacts with the press by any of his team be handled through my office to avoid the unintended consequence of misspeaking on important policy issues. In addition, I had built considerable support within OECD's central personnel office for our exchange programs. I had a solid record of achievement and it felt good, once again, to be part of a team with a new sense of the public dimension of the mission's work. In the recent past, it had been neglected in the insular atmosphere of that office.

There were other events of historical dimension just over the horizon. I had been attending the planning meetings hosted by my USIS and embassy colleagues at the bilateral embassy for American participation in the French Bicentennial (1789 – 1989) and the G-7 Summit, also hosted by the French that year. For the first time since the Williamsburg Summit in 1983, I did not have a direct responsibility for the EC delegation, but since the Summit would be preceded by the celebration of the 200th anniversary of the French Revolution and the Declaration of the Rights of Man, this was destined to be a more labor-intensive effort than your average G-7 Summit. I volunteered to assist my cross-town counterpart, Bernard Krassman, who expressed his appreciation for my offer to augment his team.

President George H. W. Bush would be making his first Summit appearance following trips to Poland and Hungary. Bernard asked me to assume press and media responsibilities for the Secretary of State, James A. Baker lll. The complicating factor for me, according to my USIS colleagues on Bernard's staff, was that I would be coordinating with a new public affairs team from the State Department whose operating style contrasted sharply from that of their immediate predecessors. This was the word from colleagues at other embassies with direct experience with Baker's press staff. My ability to coordinate with the Secretary's team was complicated further because the Secretary and his Assistant Secretary for Public Affairs were traveling in eastern Europe. Summit preparations in Paris were taking form and the Secretary's team had not responded to any of my requests for details regarding the Secretary's schedule, or his reactions to any of the arrangements that would govern his life once he arrived in Paris. What should have been an uncomplicated task on my end was already more frustrating than in any previous Summit.

I was not the only one feeling frustrated. Negotiations between the White House Advance Team and French authorities were frequently acrimonious. We were bumping heads with the French on even the most minute details, according to the head of the White House Communication Agency (WHCA) team in Paris. Those negotiations often involved daily changes that could not be easily communicated to the Secretary's team, and decisions were often required that could not be approved by the Secretary within the strict headlines imposed by French officials. Under normal circumstances, I would not have been concerned, but I had reason to on this occasion. Press officers at the embassies on the Secretary's schedule had informally briefed my embassy colleagues and they were warned to expect considerable difficulty with the Secretary's public affairs team. Bernard had been told by his counterpart in Copenhagen that "this team will not give you the latitude we customarily expect when scheduling media appointments for the Secretary." Furthermore, "they insist that we not commit the Secretary to any event until they are on the ground..." As professional officers, we were accustomed to managing corporate-size egos and complex personalities. The standard "operational procedures" telegram that precedes any visit by a Secretary of State finally arrived, and it was obvious that not only had it been completely redrafted; it was personal, even admonitory in tone, with an edge. My embassy colleagues knew what I was in for, I did not. I later learned that they chose not to tell me out of fear that I might say "thanks, but no thanks."

My motto for White House and cabinet-level visits is "be prepared." My specific responsibility was press and media. However, I erred on the side of caution and "walked the Secretary's schedule" from "wheels down" (arrival) to "wheels up" (departure) e.g., logistics, security arrangements, local travel by motorcade, major network interview sites, accommodations, routes within event locations, communications, even the location of holding rooms prior to an event or appearance. Every fact, every detail was contained in two briefing books; one for myself, and one for my assistant. When the Secretary's plane landed, I was on hand to greet them. His principal press logistician was the senior deputy to his press secretary: tall, blonde and curt, with a serious game face. She moved to establish her position very quickly. "Well, Mr. Kennedy, thank you for your effort to keep us informed about developments here in Paris. I am sure you have other duties. I now have to ensure that the Secretary has a successful visit. You may have the driver take me to the hotel. Leave me your telephone number in the event I may need to call you."

Actually, I felt I was being dismissed, but I was in this game and a summary dismissal would not suffice. "I have no other duties, Ms. Hartman," I responded. "We have in common the responsibility to ensure that the Secretary has a successful visit in Paris." That was our introduction. Once at the hotel, I escorted her to the Secretary's control room whereupon she began to make telephone calls, introduce herself and inquire about press sites and location of network media organizations. Her questions focused on details already meticulously negotiated with the French; details the Secretary's team could not control. Invariably, as her conversations progressed, she would be asked, "have you talked to George Kennedy?" "We have discussed all of the arrangements with him." As the first day progressed, Ms. Hartman gradually came to appreciate the work we had done. To each of her questions, we had the appropriate response. My assistant spoke French and that made it easy to confirm details with the appropriate French officials. We were being tested and we knew it. By the second day, following visits to each site on the Secretary's schedule, Ms. Hartman felt a greater sense of relief about the amount of work she thought she would have to do. I think I even saw a faint smile. "Mr. Kennedy, what's on our agenda this afternoon?" she asked following the last site visit. I suggested that if she was satisfied with all of the arrangements, she might take a few hours off, that everything is in place. To my surprise, she agreed. "This is the first time I have ever been able to take time off on any of our visits. Just let me know what we have to do, when and where." Alice and I breathed a sigh of relief and began to reconfirm the schedule for the evening and the next day. I had been assigned a vehicle and driver so, that night, I retraced the principal motorcade routes for what must have been the tenth time. If a sign had been moved, or if the French construction crews at the plenary site had forgotten to clear away some debris, I wanted to know about it.

I thrive on the supercharged atmosphere of a White House visit. This was probably the most fun I would have in Paris so I logged 20-hour days checking and rechecking not only the Secretary's schedule, but that of President Bush as well. He and the Secretary often moved in tandem, but not in every instance. Were the Secretary to ask where the president was on any given moment, I wanted to have the answer. When the Secretary moved, I moved, and, on the third day, he motioned me to his car. He opened the door, extended his hand and said, "George, thank you for the great job you've done helping me with my schedule." Grasping his outstretched hand, I responded, "thank you, Mr. Secretary. I am pleased that everything went well. I am available at all times."

"That was a first for him" according to Kathryn Hartman. She then shared with me anecdotes regarding several unpleasant experiences they had had on overseas trips involving USIS officers and the resulting embarrassment to the Secretary. I then understood why they chose not to rely upon us for the press and media support we customarily provide all visiting Secretaries of State. Kathryn said, "George, our instructions are that we are to arrange and control all press and media contact for the Secretary and, if that means we have to begin from scratch once we are on the ground, that is the way Maureen wants it (Maureen S.M. McTaggert, Press Spokesman for the Department of State.) At the moment, Maureen prefers to trust only her own team. You are the rare exception."

On the last day of the Summit, Kathryn was late for the Secretary's motorcade and I was concerned because French security was moving motorcades on the minute; no exceptions granted other than to Heads of State or Government. The motorcade would be crossing the "dead zone" which was restricted to Heads of State and Government and their motorcades. Without the proper escort and a blue light on the roof of her vehicle, Kathryn would be unable to join the Secretary. Perhaps she had decided not to attend the afternoon session, as unlikely as that was. She finally appeared and identified herself to the embassy dispatcher, told him she needed transportation to join the Secretary at La Defense, principal site for meetings of the principals. The dispatcher politely and firmly told Kathryn that the motorcade had departed. The conversation became heated and quite public and my gut told me I was going to land in the middle of this one. I heard my name, "George, I have to be with the Secretary; make this happen!" I thought I saw a resolution to a potentially ugly and escalating situation. Ms. Hartman was accustomed to prevailing when the Secretary was involved and I did not want this situation to escalate beyond a polite disagreement. The French dispatcher was a local national employed by us at the mission to the OECD. "Pierre, Ms. Hartman is a senior advisor to Secretary Baker and she was unavoidably detained on his behalf" I began. "What can we do to accommodate her?" "Monsieur Kennedy, je vous connais tre bien, mai, j'ai en petite problem" (Mr. Kennedy, I know you well, but I have a small problem. "Alone, she is not authorized by the French authorities to cross the dead zone." "Let's get creative" I said. "Monsieur Kennedy, I could get in serious trouble if the French police stop the vehicle with her as the sole passenger." I then asked Kathryn if she could step outside the office for a moment. "Pierre, I'll take the heat, but we've got to get her across town." For a half moment, he looked at me and then he reached into his desk drawer and pulled out a blue light while motioning to me to follow him. In short order, we had a vehicle, complete with blue light and an escort. With Pierre at the wheel and Kathryn and I as passengers, we were ready to go. He told the escort driver, "Whatever you do, do not stop under any circumstances; flash your lights and blow your horn, but keep moving."

Center city Paris was already in lockdown with concentric circles of security zones increasingly restricted as you approached La Defense, the summit site in the western sector of Paris. As we rapidly picked up speed, we began the most harrowing ride any of us had experienced, or possibly ever will in this life. A trip that takes 45-minutes-to-an-hour in traffic took five-to-seven-minutes; perhaps less. Pierre was right; as we approached a checkpoint at breakneck speed, security responded favorably. Was it a rush? A visceral thrill? You bet your ass it was! This was the adrenalin pumping experience usually reserved for royalty, heads of state and government when shots had been fired. Anyone would have been impressed by that accomplishment and our passenger was. Kathryn had a crisis and Pierre and I found the solution. Her smile spoke volumes as she stepped out of the car. Even at the mission, Pierre was our principal "go to" guy and he came through again.

After this adventure, I was looking forward to the conclusion of the Summit, a successful visit, and "wheels up." (Our customary parlance to mean that Air Force One, or the Secretary's plane has lifted off the tarmac.) At Summit's end, the president and the Secretary of State meet with the American press and all embassy officers and staff at the American ambassador's residence. Kathryn and I had developed a productive relationship by this time; she trusted my judgment, but I had mixed emotions as we approached the hour of their departure. The anti-climax of a G-7 Summit is unique unto itself. Imagine the preparatory phase of an event involving the world's most powerful leaders; the build-up to the arrival; numerous highly choreographed movements throughout a city that you helped to organize. Overlay that with our experience of a Steve McQueen-styled car ride across Paris with lights flashing, horns blaring, and security scrambling to ensure you are not impeded; a final departure and, then, it's over. The silence of the next day is deafening and the predictability of life dulls the senses and you are still trying to climb down from a major adrenalin rush.

For two weeks following a summit, most of us involved in the event try to decompress, follow up on requests generated by visiting officials, and to restore normalcy. I had tentative plans to visit a friend in Brussels. At a senior staff meeting several days after the summit, we learned that Secretary Baker would be returning to Paris for a meeting with his French counterpart. I called Bernard Krassman, my USIS colleague at embassy Paris and, again, offered assistance. He graciously declined saying "thanks, but I think we will be fine."

During the interregnum between the president's early July visit and Secretary Baker's scheduled return in early August, I received a late night call from Mrs. Lee in Pusan. "George, do you still want JiYub?" she asked. An odd question, I thought, but, in response, I instinctively said "yes, I do! But why do you ask?" "Mr. Kim (her friend and contact at Pusan City Hall) told me yesterday that the Blue House (Korea's White House) had relaxed the rules prohibiting male Koreans from traveling abroad before they had completed compulsory military service," she said. "He must be mistaken," I responded. "Mr. Kim also believes it is a mistake and he said to tell you, if you still want him, complete the sponsorship application immediately and JiYub's passport application would be approved...to do it now because once someone discovers this, the ban will most likely be reimposed."

I immediately drafted a letter guaranteeing that I would sponsor JiYub's travel abroad and forwarded it to Mrs. Lee for Mr. Kim. JiYub's passport application was approved in record time and he was the proud owner of a rare document at that time in Korea for a young man: a passport. I still expected something to derail his travel; some bureaucrat at Pusan City Hall would disagree in principle and raise an objection. Mrs. Lee said she would accompany him to Paris and remain with us until JiYub was settled in school and reasonably well adjusted. Her offer was an unexpected bonus on top of the last thing I expected would happen until JiYub had completed his military service. Within a week from that fateful call, Mrs. Lee called again. "We will depart Seoul on July 19 and arrive at Charles DeGaulle Airport tomorrow morning ." The realization flashed through my mind that I was now a guardian.

ICA had approved my request to assume legal responsibility for my new dependent. My first thoughts were of school, English-language proficiency, French classes, and the daily needs of a 17-year old teenager outside his country for the first time in his life. Then, there were the changes in my own life. Wow! This was going to be different, but it was something I had long wanted to do.

When JiYub and Mrs. Lee emerged from French customs and immigration on that fateful July morning, they appeared overwhelmed by the rapidity of this life-transforming change. I think they were still in disbelief. We embraced, laughed, and cried in one emotional moment. I had arranged an interview for them with the director of admissions at the International School in Paris. Although a second semester junior at home in Pusan, JiYub would have to repeat his junior year. The new school year was still a month away and Mrs. Lee and JiYub told me, "Don't worry about us. Give us a map and we'll find our way... you don't worry." I walked them through our neighborhood to give them reference points, keys to the apartment, and directions to the Paris Metro. It was not until I saw the photographs of their daily trips that I realized they had seen more of Paris in two weeks than I had seen in a year. They were truly on their own and literally absorbing every delicious detail of life as they discovered it. I enjoyed having them around because on weekends, I could play host, introduce them to my world, my friends, and life under the diplomatic looking glass. Unlike my previous tour in Pusan a decade earlier, they were now part of it, especially JiYub.

On the eve of Secretary Bakers return to Paris, and before JiYub and Mrs. Lee arrived in Paris, instinct, or an inner voice, told me not to go to Brussels; to invent a pretext to visit with the Secretary's party. Find Kathryn Hartman and say hello. I knew she would be in the control room. As I walked in and greeted her, her first words were, "George, I sure wish you were handling this visit; everything is screwed up and I am not getting much help from your embassy colleagues." Although I could not lend any assistance, we did have a few brief moments to talk. Before leaving her, she agreed to join me and one of her executive assistants for dinner. The assistant happened to be a friend of mine extending back to my first US-EC Ministerial. Over dinner the next evening, I let Kathryn know how much I enjoyed working with her; that Paris was great but I was bored, and that under the right circumstances, I would be prepared to leave Paris. Startled by my comment, she said, "I thought all FSOs would kill for any assignment to Paris, and you're telling me you would give it up and come back to Washington." "Yes, I would." Her comment provided the two-minute opening I needed to summarize the background to my assignment to the OECD. She and the Department Spokesman were still assembling a team in the Bureau of Public Affairs and I wanted to throw my hat in the ring. The worst that could happen was another year of living graciously in Paris, so why not let her know of my interest in becoming part of their team.

A week later on a hot August afternoon, my telephone rang. My assistant said it was "Kathryn Hartman, Senior Deputy Assistant Secretary of State for Public Affairs." I picked up the telephone: "Good afternoon, George, it's Kathryn Hartman," said the voice. "Hello Kathryn, what a pleasant surprise; how are you? What can I do for you?" She continued, "Maureen and I plan to completely reorganize the Bureau and we need a strong deputy assistant secretary with management ability and who understands public affairs. The position will have unprecedented authority and responsibility to implement the reorganization plan we have devised." "We have selected you as our candidate. Would you be willing to come back to Washington?" Honestly, I thought she was "yanking my chain" so I responded in the spirit of what I thought was a light moment. I knew they were building their team and I felt comfortable enough with Kathryn to believe that she was not serious. "Sure, Kathryn, I can be there tomorrow! What do you need?" I asked, thinking the real purpose of her call was to follow up on something from the recent G-7 Summit. Such a request would have been normal. "George, I am serious, would you be interested? She continued. "Yes, Kathryn, I am also. What do you need?" There was this deadly, silent pause on her end and then it hit me. She was serious. "Kathryn, are you serious?" I asked again. "Yes, I am." "Kathryn, I have been through this before with State Public Affairs. ICA will never approve the transfer" and I explained why I thought they would respond negatively to such a request. "What does Maureen need to do?" "She will have to personally call the Director of ICA, Bruce Gelb, not the director of agency personnel, and put the request directly to him. "Is that it?" "Yes, that's it, he can make it happen." "Alright, I will get back to you."

To me, that was the end of it. I was convinced that ICA would deny this Assistant Secretary for Public Affairs as they had denied Hodding Carter's request a decade earlier. Once around that ring was enough for me. I promptly forgot about the conversation. Two days later, the phone rang again. It was Kathryn. "George, the Director has approved Maureen's request. What else do we need to do?" she asked. I was completely taken aback. Without thinking, I asked, "How did Maureen manage this?" "You don't know Maureen. How much time do you need?" Give me two-to-three weeks" I said. "That's fine, I'll have our executive officer, Leon Ramey, contact you to work out the details. I'll see you in two weeks." For a moment, I sat there stunned; almost in disbelief. Alice's reaction was mixed, pleased for me, but concerned about the future of the office and her status at the mission. She and I had infused that operation with a level of energy that even Washington had to recognize. Would my departure render the office vulnerable again? Probably.

That night, I told Mrs. Lee and JiYub the news: "guys, we are moving back to Washington... Does that present a problem for you, Mrs. Lee?" She was prepared to help JiYub settle in Paris, but I could not assume that she could extend her travel to an extended trip to the U.S. "No," she responded. "I will call Mr. Lee and tell him...JiYub will now need to settle in an American school. You have a new job and we don't want you to worry. And don't forget, my sister is there, she can help us." I did not feel too badly about uprooting JiYub because he had not actually started the new school year, therefore the disruption would be less traumatic. They would certainly not soon forget their brief, but pleasant, stay in Paris.

Ambassador Lambert and my colleagues at the OECD were delighted over my appointment, a rarity in itself. My USIS colleagues at the embassy and in Washington could not have been more indifferent. Call it professional jealousy or thinly veiled racism; it was obvious even to the ambassador. He and I had lunch just prior to my departure and he made a surprising confession. "You and I have had many conversations, George." "We've talked about racism in the Foreign Service and, honestly, I could not really appreciate the impact of it until your appointment." He had occasion to pay a return visit to ICA's European Bureau following my appointment and he sincerely felt they would be pleased that one of their own was now in the rare position to strengthen the relationship between ICA and State's Office of Public Affairs. It was a natural relationship. "I was truly amazed at their indifference, George." The more we talked, the more I felt he began to understand some of the issues I had raised with him in previous conversations. "I don't know how you do it," he said. "It must be demoralizing, but I do admire your attitude and commitment. I think you will do well in Washington."

I can think of no single phrase that adequately conveys the psychological impact of my year in Paris. My destiny had been charted by a power greater than myself. The transition from disappointment at my assignment to Paris, to success on the job, to assuming the responsibility for the content, scope, and direction of someone else's life;

and, ultimately to a quantum leap in career advancement beyond even the most successful officers, was breathtaking. A door was now opened through which I would stride with purpose and with a commitment to acquit myself well. Although my responsibilities were yet to be clearly defined, I had no doubt in my mind that I would be up to the task. Once again, I could dream of a future.

I suppose that you can say that accepting the responsibility awaiting me at the next stop in my journey marked my debut on mainstreet as a federal executive in public diplomacy. I would be making a transition from career staff and an Agency line manager to that of a federal executive. The political dimension of my role would be in sharper relief. Congressional oversight of bureau operations would add a new dimension to decisions I would make on behalf of Kathryn and Maureen. Moreover, my career prospects would be contingent upon the support of presidentially-appointed leadership and not career officers like myself. The consequences of failure at this level would be greater. In addition, I could not help but wonder if race would be a factor in assessing my performance. It had thus far.

By shattering the "glass ceiling" I disturbed an active minority of "gate keepers" who delighted in minimizing the candidacy of African-Americans for executive level responsibility. The sound of breaking glass also energized a silent majority of those at ICA who appointed the "gate keepers" and they were asking, "How did this happen?" Their response was classic. If an appointment is a "fait accompli," minimize its significance. I not only had my old enemies, but some new ones as well. You could ask, "how do you know this scenario was playing itself out? Are you not impugning the motives of others." In response, I would only say, "you would have to have been an ambitious Black officer at that time and suffered the slights, the indignities, and the racial comments directed at Black officers by no less than the USICA director – within earshot of others who reminded him that you could not use the N-word." I was optimistic and pleased to have been tapped for greater responsibility. Moreover, I did not harbor the illusion I would escape an attempt by ICA officers to downplay the strategic importance of my assignment to the Department. I would take the approach I customarily do in these circumstances: co-opt those I could and manage, or out-maneuver, the rest of them. Those bridges remained to be crossed. For now, though, it was "Mr. Secretary."

CHAPTER 15

MR. SECRETARY

When I accepted the position of Deputy Assistant Secretary of State for Public Affairs (DAS), I well understood the political dimension of the appointment. I also felt the better part of discretion was to reveal to both Kathryn Hartman and Maureen McTaggert that I was a registered Democrat. There is a reason for this. Washington is intensely political and all political appointments – even if the appointee is non-political – are subject to someone's scrutiny. I was a deputy to the Secretary of State's most trusted advisor, Maureen S.M. McTaggert, and my appointment was not going to go unnoticed. Although my position did not require Senate confirmation, it was to be intricately connected to policy formulation and execution at the highest levels of the Department. Moreover, as a DAS, I would be a first line executive manager within the Executive Branch of government. A career Foreign Service officer is by definition a-political, sworn to uphold the Constitution and to carry out the policies of the President of the United States. Now, however, I was to be part of the policy process and I did not want my loyalty to a Republican administration cast in doubt by anyone because of my political affiliation were they to gain access to that information. I certainly did not intend to broadcast it. Kathryn and Maureen appreciated this full disclosure, but both assured me any concerns I may have were without merit.

The cavernous expanse of my sixth-floor office at State was symbolic of the responsibility I agreed to accept and the authority riposted in my position. On an operational basis, the Bureau of Public Affairs was "terra incognita" and, to some of the staff there, I must have resembled red meat about to be fed to the lions. On a more personal level, I knew this appointment did not represent normal career progression. This was a quantum leap outside the norm for most officers and for African-American officers in particular. Mine was also the type of appointment that engenders intensely held, even retrograde, views; enormous hostility, professional jealousy, even the need by some to justify my appointment in terms that made it easier for them to understand why they were not considered: affirmative action. This twisted thought process exists even today. The Bush Administration must have needed a "Black" face, the reasoning goes; it was surely not about competence or experience. This primitive, but widely held, view enables many white officers to accept an African-American, Asian, Spanish-speaking, or female in a policy position to which they may be subordinate.

I was soon to be charged with managing the bureau's relationship within the State Department, and occasionally, the bureau's relationship with other Executive Branch agencies. The trajectory of my career was now established in a very public fashion and I knew the road ahead was going to have more than one bend in it.

During my first meeting with Maureen in mid-September, shortly after my arrival, she talked about leadership, her management style, and her relationship with the Secretary as advisor and Department Spokesman. She also talked about the nexus between domestic and international affairs; the need to merge domestic political concerns with foreign policy. I dutifully took notes.

"Secretary Baker takes seriously his role as the president's foreign policy advisor and he also recognizes the need to build public support for the administration's priority policy initiatives" she said. She went on to say "there is a natural support role for our bureau, but not in its present configuration. We have the tools, the staff, and the resources. The reorganization I envision will streamline operations, combine overlapping responsibilities, and expand our domestic outreach around the country." "Secretary Baker maintains an active travel schedule and Kathryn and I will be on the road with him most of the time. We are depending upon you to manage the bureau and implement the substantive reorganization changes we want to make." "As Kathryn as probably told you, you will have unprecedented responsibility within the bureau and the authority that accompanies it." Maureen did not underestimate the challenge and went on to add, "there is one more thing: you will also have to prepare the bureau for its first inspection in five years by the Office of the Inspector General." Frankly, I did not look forward to this last task because, in many instances, the inspection process focuses too intensely on personalities, as ours initially did. Gripe sessions frequently supplant constructive dialogue; personal agendas shield mediocre performance, and the natural rhythm of an office is often disrupted for extended periods.

My conversation with Maureen was broad, yet specific enough to provide the direction I sought. I learned much earlier in my career to make sure I understood the responsibilities I accepted and to be reasonably comfortable that the means sufficed to achieve the objectives I was given. At the end of our meeting, I came away with a healthy respect for someone growing into a role she had not sought, and who wielded awesome authority as one of many assistant secretaries. Her instinct was not to be well liked among her peers at the expense of providing leadership and unvarnished advice. This was refreshingly contrary to the approach of some of her male counterparts. Politically, she was untouchable and often regarded as another "political lightweight." I now had an opportunity to take a measure of her and I was impressed. She was simple, earnest, and direct. Furthermore, she understood how to effectively deploy the tools and resources she controlled to shape the public policy debate in the country at large. That was her mandate; one I now shared with her.

Initially, I was concerned that the physical separation of her office (adjacent to the Secretary on the seventh floor) and her frequent travels with him would impede communication between us. It did not. Kathryn, whose office was also on the seventh floor, and I quickly forged a strong working relationship that kept us in constant contact, even when she was on the road. She chaired the bureau senior staff meeting every morning and, when she was on the road with Maureen and the Secretary, I filled in for her. The six senior office directors under my direct supervision were an interesting brew of domestic and Foreign Service. They represented in varying degrees dynamism, statism, the future, and a reverence for tradition. Most of them were accustomed to more detached oversight but were now expected to keep the new management team far better informed of their activities – voluntarily. This was by far the most unsettling requirement for several of them. My mandate, they came to learn, was to challenge bureau orthodoxy; the commitments, customs, and habits of these senior managers unaccustomed to management oversight. With the assistance of Saundra Parkinson, a bright, young and extremely able civil servant as my executive assistant and bureau sherpa, I reviewed our organizational plan and budget. Next, Saundra and I began to develop an action plan for the reorganization and the OIG inspection; timetables, contact lists of key personnel within the State Department and on the congressional committees with bureau oversight responsibilities. In addition, we met with our legal advisor, my counterpart in State's office of Congressional Affairs, and with the senior staff. Another valued resource was Tony Darwin, one of the office directors and certainly one of the most creative individuals I have ever had the pleasure to be associated with. We called him Tony. What

I appreciated about Tony was his unstinting support, a willingness to work under some of the shortest, most demanding deadlines we could impose and without attitude. Tony never took rejection personally; with him, it was always a professional willingness to get it right even if you rejected the first nine of his ten ideas. More often than not, Tony got it right and was recognized as one of the Department's more able managers.

As I became immersed in detail, my appreciation for the analytical skills and prodigious work habits of Saundra Parkinson grew. Saundra was the daughter of a career Foreign Service officer and was herself a career public affairs professional. She knew the bureau and its problems. At the conclusion of each of those early organizational and strategy meetings, Saundra would summarize action points, decision items, and prepare the responses I needed to follow up with office directors, other Department officials, and a growing list of contacts within the Executive Branch. Very quickly, I came to recognize how effectively I could manage the bureau with just one assistant. Although this was the largest management position I had ever held, I was comfortable with broader responsibility. The principles of management were the same, just applied to a larger organization with more personnel, but with challenges similar to those I had encountered in both academia and throughout my Foreign Service career.

Meanwhile, as I was getting up to speed in my new role, my son JiYub was making great progress in school. He was accustomed to long hours of intense preparation for each of his classes and therefore I was spared the added burden of a a distracted, unfocussed, unmotivated teenager. Mrs. Lee had reunited with her sister living in Virginia. Together, they established a very comfortable home life for JiYub and for me. I could not have survived as well as I did without them. Moreover, they were JiYub's cultural and linguistic bridge between life in Korea and his new life in the United States.

The reorganization of the Bureau of Public Affairs meanwhile was engendering the unpopularity, the push back, I had expected from several of the most affected office directors and their staffs. In fact, one of my early detractors, an office director of the largest unit within the bureau, confidently predicted, "Mr. Kennedy will last six months." That prognostication proved a bitter pill for her to swallow. The omnipresence of the OIG inspectors was a double-edge blade: it exposed inefficiencies and the need for reorganization, while providing the aura of respectability some staff sought to complain about the new management team, namely, one Mr. Kennedy. I knew this and accepted it as part of the process. At the end of the 90-day review, most bureau personnel recognized that the reorganization was overdue and on the mark. The advantage for me was that Saundra and I could step back from close monitoring of better-performing offices while concentrating on the one shop whose director confidently predicted my early departure.

I do not mean to minimize the scope and impact of a comprehensive review of a large administrative unit. An inspection conducted by the Office of the Inspector General of the Department of State is a complex, layered process that also includes an "exit interview." The senior inspector, customarily, a former ambassador, meets informally with bureau management to review their findings (the draft report), respond to questions, and to offer unpublished advice regarding personnel, budget, morale, bureau policies, etc. Maureen and Kathryn were traveling with Secretary Baker, therefore Ambassador Rankin, head of the inspection team, and I met in my office. I was encouraged by his initial comments when he said, "you'll be pleased with the results of your inspection...there are fewer formal recommendations than you were probably anticipating." To help you – the reader - decipher this, the formal recommendations are of greater consequence because they represent major deficiencies, attest to the quality and efficacy of management, and require a formal response. Every manager wants to minimize the number of formal recommendations. I felt relieved simply because there were some tense moments on several occasions with some of ambassador Rankin's team. Maureen McTaggert was a political lightening rod within the State Department and a convenient target for everyone, including inspectors. They had a favorite but unflattering appellation for her which I did not share. During several, quite tense discussions with one particular inspector, I found it necessary to insist that we separate legitimate areas of inquiry from actions that resembled political revenge. I, too, had been a target; a more convenient target because I was career and therefore more vulnerable than either Maureen or Kathryn. They were political appointees ("Schedule – C") and generally beyond reach of civil service complaints. Often, the slings and arrows pointed in my direction were intended for them. This was a consequence of the job I had to accept, as unpleasant as it was. However, at the end of the day, ambassador Rankin and I narrowed our differences to the point that the draft report he would present to the Inspector General represented a balanced, accurate assessment of our bureau. He told me I would receive a final report within two-to-three weeks of our exist interview.

This experience in particular has a humorous postscript. Within a week of my exit interview with ambassador Rankin, he called.

"George, can we meet soon?" he asked. "Yes," I responded since I assumed the inspection was to be the topic under discussion. We met the following morning and to my great amazement, I was told "our report is too positive, too favorable towards bureau management." "Mr. Peters (the Inspector General) refused to accept the draft report. He said that no bureau is that well managed; that there have to be more formal recommendations." Reflexively, I laughed asking, "are you serious?" This was a rare and unique development for me. Rankin went on to say that, according to Mr. Peters, "no management can be that good." I thought about that for a moment and decided I did not have a large enough dog in that fight, even though that last comment was quite personal. Rankin and I worked out a compromise we both could live with, while not compromising the integrity of the real outcome of the inspection. I held my breath pending receipt of the final report. On my part, there would be no further compromise, but I did not want to get into a pissing match with the Inspector General. When Rankin handed me the report, he simply said, "Ms. McTaggert owes you big, George." I knew what he meant. The day would arrive when I would know if she appreciated my value to her and the bureau.

Phase two of my approach to this assignment involved becoming more engaged in broadening the bureau's national outreach to regional organizations and previously untargeted groups; recommending new and creative approaches for the format and style of the bureau's publications; focussing more resources on domestic constituency building; increasing contact between the Department and state and local community officials across the country, and strengthening the bureau's relationship with those responsible for domestic constituency strategies at other Executive Branch agencies.

The State Department has the premier public affairs shop among all Executive Branch agencies that looked to State for guidance on certain domestic policy issues and certainly the international dimension of strategy to advance the White House policy agenda. That was the world I came from. While I enjoyed the daily challenges of managing and reorganizing a major functional entity within the Department, policy issues gave the assignment greater flavor. The activities of a reorganized bureau accomplished three important goals for the new administration: a) enhanced Maureen's efforts to communicate policy from the Department's podium through daily press briefings, b) supported Secretary Baker's foreign travel and speeches which formulate policy, and c) enhanced administration foreign policies through major speeches by President Bush.

1989 is best and more accurately characterized as a watershed in the annals of 20th Century global diplomacy because it saw the demise of the former Soviet Union and its hegemony over the states of eastern Europe. The Cold War was effectively over. The Bush Administration stepped forward with a bold outreach effort to communicate with, and build domestic support among, eastern European communities in the United States for policy initiatives targeted for an eastern Europe now willing to chart an independent course from its former Soviet masters. Drawing upon experience gained at my most recent posts in Brussels and Paris, I recommended a public affairs strategy to deploy senior Department officials to articulate administration policy before eastern European ethnic communities in key Midwestern states. Maureen and Secretary Baker accepted my recommendation and, before long, our footprint in the Midwest was larger than ever.

That same year, another milestone in modern history was unfolding: the release of five members of South Africa's African National Congress (ANC) Party from years of incarceration. Their release was only the prelude to Nelson Mandela's eventual release in 1990. Nelson Mandela, the most generally admired man of our time, would be invited to visit the United States upon his release. I had been around long enough to know that any visit to this country would involve a visit to Washington. Secretary Baker's State Department would plan the visit and my goal was to have an opportunity – by any means necessary – to at least shake the hand of Nelson Mandela. To my generation of African-American, he was an icon, a symbol of resistance to the dark forces of apartheid. Mr. Mandela and his then-wife Winnie M. Mandela arrived at the Department of State on a grey day in 1990. I had strategically positioned myself inside the diplomatic entrance in the dead zone between the entry and the express elevators that would whisk him and his entourage to the Secretary's office on the seventh floor. My press staff, working with Diplomatic Security (DSS), controlled the dead zone, therefore I was accorded the luxury of position. Nelson and Winnie Mandela would have to pass directly by me to arrive at their designated elevator.

Right on schedule, the Mandelas, with their security escort, entered the diplomatic lobby (the flag entrance) and headed in my direction. Both of them radiated pride, hope, and enthusiasm. As they approached, I stepped forward, smiled, and extended my hand to him. Mr. Mandela clasped my right hand in his as I said, "What an honor and a privilege to meet you, sir. Good luck!" Brandishing his trademark broad smile, he responded, "Thank you, sir!" My day was made at that point. I returned to my office having accomplished what I sought.

Several days later, I happened to see the Department's photographer in the main cafeteria. He was also a friend. "Mr. Kennedy, I have something for you," he said. Continuing, he went on to let me know that he would come by my office that afternoon. "Sure," I responded..."Give Gracie a call." He knew Gracie was my secretary. That afternoon, he handed me something I cherish to this day: a photograph depicting the moment I extended my hand to Mr. Mandela. I admit, the photo rendered me momentarily speechless. For an instant, my eyes watered because that photograph, for me, was history. I never thought in my lifetime I would have the chance to meet the Mandelas. They were icons in history, just other larger-than-life personalities that registered in my memory; like Martin Luther King, Jr., for example. I could only say "Thank you, this means a lot to me." He sensed the impact, looked at me for a second, shook my hand and walked out. I did not expect this; in fact, I had not seen him in the lobby during the Mandela's arrival. I knew a photographer would capture the arrival because someone always did. The Department of State is so good at capturing the visual of an important visitor's arrival on the South Lawn of the White House, for example, that they can mount a full visual display of that event in the diplomatic entrance by the time the visitor arrives for a luncheon that same day hosted by the Secretary of State for their counterpart. The photograph of my meeting the Mandelas hangs on the wall of my office at home.

Perhaps the most unusual task I undertook early in this assignment was to coordinate a department plan of action to modernize the Foreign Relations of the United States series (FRUS), the sole U.S. government publication documenting the historical record of U.S. foreign policy. The Office of the Historian of the Department of State is one of the least publicly known, but more vital functions within the Bureau of Public Affairs. A very sizable staff of professional historians under the direction of the Historian of the Department compiles, reviews, edits, and publishes declassified historical materials for use by the Congress of the United States, the Executive Branch, academic and research institutions, and the general public. I might add another point. Policy, especially foreign policy, often has historical antecedents and it is to the Historian's Office that policy makers turn to to prepare policy-supportive historical research for the Secretary of State and the White House.

I am more accurately a history buff than historian and the challenge I faced was to persuade, cajole, even threaten, a group of academics to accept change in their modus operandi and the continued leadership of someone many of them were determined to remove: the then-office director, Walter Slattery. The parallel with situations

I encountered at The Federal City College two decades earlier were striking. To his credit, Walter Slattery also chose not to retire, as some wanted, but rather chose to remain in his job and implement plans that would have more profound impact upon the Foreign Relations series and the scholarly study of U.S. foreign policy than any other actions or events of the past half century. That notwithstanding, it is an axiom in Washington that every major function in government has a constituency, including the Foreign Relations series, and our efforts to bring forth critical reforms would have to be protected. Bill performed yeoman service in preparing Kathryn and me for numerous encounters with his staff and congressional oversight committee staffs, raising questions about the necessity for change in the process by which the FRUS was compiled, edited, and published. In the end, Walter Slattery, Kathryn, and I prevailed over the obstructionists. By the summer of 1991, we received word within the bureau that our action plan would be reflected in forthcoming congressional legislation.

Although I was the principal management executive within the bureau of public affairs, I was not afforded daily possibilities to showcase substantive public diplomacy skills. Those opportunities were the exclusive domain of Maureen and her deputy spokesman, Rodney Barnwell, also a career Foreign Service officer. Yes, I did yeoman duty moderating roundtable discussions and introducing the Secretary and his principal deputies to the Executive/Diplomat Seminar, and numerous conferences of executives from the public and private sector. My appearances, however, were episodic, lacking continuity. I kept the bureau's "trains running on time," but I was looking for other more visible ways to support the Secretary's policy goals. This, I later learned, was a mistake. They did not want me to have a public face. That revelation in itself was more than ironic. Among Maureen 's three deputies, I was the only career public affairs officer. However, the 1990 buildup to the conflict with Iraq and the Gulf War in 1991 changed everything. In December 1990, John Sununu, the White House Chief of Staff, formed the White House Gulf Strategy Working Group. The group's members included the senior public affairs official or spokesman from each of the principal executive branch agencies e.g., State Department, Defense, Armed Forces, Justice, Commerce, and others. Maureen would have been the obvious representative, but she asked me to sit in for her. The purpose of the group was to develop and coordinate all executive branch public affairs activities in support of the president's emerging Gulf strategy. The meetings were held daily during December 1990 and the early months of 1991, a particularly sensitive period during which Secretary Baker and President Bush labored to build the formidable military coalition that would ultimately engage Saddam Hussein in

"The mother of all battles" (Saddam Hussein's formulation, not ours). The agenda was simple, but our task as a working group was slightly more complex: coordinate public affairs activities government-wide to build domestic and international public support for the administration's strategy to remove Saddam Hussein's military from Kuwait.

President Bush was unequivocal in his conviction and public statements that "Iraq's clumsy attempt to annex Kuwait shall not stand." Each agency had a role to play, a unique or shared constituency with another agency, and each was eager to contribute. As the lead public affairs shop among Executive Branch agencies, Maureen was justifiably concerned that we of the working group not step on ourselves, and that each of us recognizes the "comparative advantage" a disparate but unified group offers to the formulation of strategy. I kept Maureen, Secretary Baker, and a small group of the Secretary's trusted aides fully apprised daily of those activities viewed by Executive Branch agencies as essential to building public support for the coming encounter with Saddam Hussein. Ours was a collective and collegial effort. Without exception, we understood the president's goals and, while there were moments of great levity, I can assure you we took our responsibility seriously. The work of the committee concluded in March 1991 following a successful prosecution of the war against Iraq. The president's Chief of Staff and his National Security Advisor visited us at the end and commended us for our success in communicating the president's Gulf policy to both American audiences and to publics abroad. And, then, suddenly it was over! As I reflect on that brief but heady experience, representing the Department of State at the White House level was a high honor for the kid from Mizpah.

Mine was a world away now from that hot Sunday afternoon in church four decades earlier.

Another equally important event captured my attention in 1991: JiYub's graduation from Montgomery Blair High School. For months, JiYub, his mother, and I talked about his future. We never doubted the inevitability of college; the questions were, where? And, at what cost? With their approval, I had been exploring an idea with my first cousin, Navy Lt. William "Butchie" Elam, an instructor at the Naval Academy in Annapolis, Maryland. My cousin had facilitated an introduction to one of the academy's recruiters. Since each of the four service academies accepts foreign candidates, I thought perhaps JiYub met their criteria for admission. The recruiter, Lt. Krill, was interested and requested a meeting with JiYub. The three of us met a week later in early February 1991. Although JiYub was not an American citizen, Lt. Krill felt he was attractive enough a candidate to present his candidacy to his superior officer, the academy's director of recruiting.

JiYub was in excellent physical condition, a prerequisite for survival in Korea's public schools at that time. The physical examination tested him, but he passed. His combined transcripts from his high school in Pusan and Montgomery Blair revealed a strong background in advanced mathematics, physics, and chemistry. With the support of his former instructors and my colleagues from State and American academia, we completed the application process. To prepare JiYub for oral interviews, he and I would spend at least an hour most evenings in mock interview sessions; sessions designed to test his reasoning and verbal skills, judgment, and the maturity you could expect of a 19-year old high school graduate. We made four or five visits to Annapolis to meet with Lt. Krill and, on each occasion, he would refer to the fact that JiYub was not a citizen. He would then resolve to press forward suggesting to us on several occasions that the issue of citizenship could be dealt with by the academy. We, of course, remained hopeful. We understood and accepted that were JiYub accepted into the academy, he would spend his first year at the academy's prep school primarily to improve his command of English. From there, he would begin his plebe year the summer of 1992 – the Class of 1996. Just the idea that this young man, whom I loved dearly, could earn a commission and receive an education at one of this nation's premier institutions, sent shivers up my spine. In the spring of 1991, Lt. Krill called and I held my breath. "Mr. Kennedy, your son has been accepted. Congratulations!" "Are you absolutely sure?" I asked. Lt. Krill then went on to tell me what we had to do to prepare JiYub for admission to prep school. I immediately called each individual who helped us advance his candidacy. Each was elated; Ms. Lee was ecstatic, and Jiyub, too, began to accept the idea that it could really happen.

Early the afternoon of the same day, my phone rang. This call, however, was from the academy's director of admissions, Commander Williamson. "Mr. Secretary, I regret to inform you that we will not be able to accept your son's candidacy for admission to our prep school... Please permit me an explanation, if you will, sir." "Please continue" I said. "Your son is the kind of candidate we are looking for, but he is not an American citizen. While we were preparing to assume the responsibility of that, the risk is too great." "Competition for a limited number of spaces is intense. If a parent were to discover that we had accepted your son, thus denying an American a vacancy they may otherwise have qualified for, we would be subject to a level of scrutiny we prefer to avoid." The commander was profusely apologetic, but he was also correct in his analysis of the risk inherent in the earlier, more favorable, decision rendered on JiYub's behalf. He went on to say, "If we did not have that hurdle to overcome, JiYub would have been a perfect candidate, a candidate we would have wanted to be part of our program here at the academy." "Thank you, commander" I responded. "We always felt it was a long shot, but one worth pursuing. Thank you for your consideration of my son! Thank you for your honesty and your candor!"

JiYub had been admitted for approximately five hours. Now, I had to convey the disappointing news to each person I had called just a few hours earlier. Not surprisingly, everyone understood the academy's decision. Each person I called was delighted to have been able to support JiYub and would do so for application to other colleges he may select. Our second choice had always been James Madison University (JMU) in Harrisonburg, Virginia. Independently of each other's review process, JiYub and I had selected JMU as our first choice for a non-military institution. And so we applied for the September freshman class of 1991, the Class of 1995. Although JiYub would graduate in 1995 with a degree in computer science, we still remember with considerable pride of accomplishment that eventful day in 1991 when for a brief period of five hours, he had been accepted as a candidate at the U.S. Naval Academy in Annapolis, Maryland. My son embodied the kind of candidate the academy sought. Boy, did I feel good about that.

While reflecting on our good fortune in securing JiYub's future, I could not help but reflect for another brief moment upon my own. I reached a very simple conclusion: Somewhere in the vastness of the universe is a chorus of angels assigned to each of us, who guide us through our preordained destiny upon earth. I believe this. My abilities aside, how else could I explain my extraordinary good fortune thus far? Among the chorus assigned to the kid from Mizpah was surely the spirit of ambassador C. Cheston Clifton, my early mentor from Bonn. Clifton was the first African-American deputy assistant secretary of State I had ever met and he was the first to express confidence in my ability to achieve the highest levels of the Foreign Service. I would have given anything to have him walk through the door to my office. My only act would have been to thank him for his confidence in someone he did not know. Our meeting in 1963 was truly fortuitous. I recall vividly him sitting on my sofa, relaxed, telling me, "What I have achieved is not beyond your reach, George." He spoke of the value of "executive rub," proximity to senior officials and opportunities to showcase skill, ability, and good judgment under pressure. He also stressed the importance of having a mentor, someone who wants to see you succeed. "Ability is not the whole ball game," he pointed out. My recent White House experience anchored me and it anchored my self-confidence as no prior experience could have. I, naturally, looked forward to the possibility of greater responsibility, perhaps my own mission after my current assignment. This was a natural expectation since I was a senior officer and a DAS (deputy assistance secretary) with executive-level responsibilities. I certainly would not have set a precedent, even within the bureau of public affairs. In harboring this expectation, then, I was no different than any other DAS in the Department with a similar experience profile and level of responsibility. Sure, Maureen could have erased any concerns I might have regarding my future, but that was not a card I could gamble upon. Everyone, including ambassador Rankin, knew that a word from Maureen would have secured my future as a chief of mission. I could however, discuss my future with ambassador Edwin Parsons, the Director General of the Foreign Service.

Ambassador Edwin Perkins, the first African-American director general of the Foreign Service, and mentor to those few of us who were senior officers, was the next person I called upon after my initial meeting with Maureen. Edwin Perkins had an impeccable institutional pedigree, was revered by a legion of supporters in both the domestic service and the Foreign Service alike, and was known to be honest, forthright, and of unquestionable integrity. Moreover, he was a product of the Department's administrative service and he knew how to get things done. I knew I would need his support to implement the reorganization of the bureau. Major personnel issues had to be addressed: transfers, promotions, and retirements. Some of the personnel actions would be delicate because one in particular would involve the involuntary retirement of a contentious member of the Senior Executive Service (SES) and Edwin and his capable staff could shepherd me through the minefield on SES retirement. There were other issues on my agenda with Edwin Perkins. At that time in the Department's history, there were seven African-American deputy assistant secretaries, but only two were career Foreign Service officers. One was a career member of the SES and the other four were non-career political appointees ("Schedule C"). The demands on our time were not confined to our respective bureaus. Ambassador Perkins was in constant demand as a speaker, as a Foreign Service recruiter at Historically African-American Colleges and Universities (HBCUs), and as a panel participant. He needed help to respond to myriad demands on his time and I wanted to let him know that I would make myself available as a surrogate speaker at local events when possible.

Meetings with ambassador Perkins were always an enlightening experience. You emerged from them wiser and enriched personally. If you were smart, you took advantage of the time to listen, take mental notes, and interrupt as little as possible. In our first meeting, he let me know that he was "pleased to have me on his team." "Maureen has spoken to me about you. She is demanding, but you are up to the challenge. Let's stay ahead of the problems you will encounter and let me know how we in personnel can help you." That initial conversation, and those that followed, also dealt with ideas he had to increase my visibility within the Department. He rightly saw the need to "get my name in circulation," primarily because in September 1989, I was not a State Department career officer, but rather a career Foreign Service officer from the International Communication Agency. There should not have been a distinction made before my actual transfer from ICA to State two years later but, to the corps of senior officers from the State Department, I was another "outsider," another contender for positions they tried to guard zealously: principal officers, deputy chiefs of mission, and the all-important chiefs of mission/ambassadorships. Ultimately, I did transfer to the State Department because of ICA's refusal to consider my competitiveness for senior-level positions there. State is the larger of the two foreign affairs agencies and, bias notwithstanding, I was prepared to explore my career options with State. In addition, I was now a known quantity within State's bureau of personnel and, therefore, my position was relatively stronger. Ambassador Perkins made me aware that "periodically, you will see your name advanced for ambassadorships I think are appropriate. Again, the purpose is to establish name recognition within the building."

It was not long before I came to understand the full impact of what it meant to be considered a candidate for selection as a principal officer, a deputy chief of mission, or a chief of mission. At that level of consideration, your life and career have another dimension over which you have absolutely no control. Thus began one of the most emotionally wrenching experiences ever for a senior officer aspiring to this level of career achievement. It is gut wrenching because every Foreign Service officer's dream is to be considered for an ambassadorship. Well, maybe not every officer, but a goodly number do harbor the dream. I was among them. By the time one reaches that phase of a career, you have developed preferences based on performance, skills, and experience. It is only natural because you share in the process by which you are evaluated for greater responsibility. There are also the impressions derived from negative experiences along the fault lines of a career. And, for a variety of reasons, family and health included, there are locations deemed less desirable. It was now decades into my career and I wanted the impossible: to become part of the consultative process leading to such an appointment. Only a few officers are accorded the luxury of consultation; most are not, and for African-Americans, there is simply the notice of an appointment that we accept. For two years, I rode this roller coaster. Some of the posts attached to my name required research to ascertain their precise location on the continent of Africa. Although I had never served in Africa, I was now the "perfect candidate" for some of that continent's most remote locations. Early on, I made the mistake of indicating my lack of interest in serving in a particular West African country I shall not name. I should note here, I did not say I would be unwilling to accept the assignment; just that I was less than enthusiastic. You'll appreciate my naivete in communicating my lack of interest. Later that same day, my phone rang, as it did a hundred times daily. My secretary, Gracie, said "it is ambassador Perkins for you." "Yes sir, how may I help you?" I asked. "Can you come around to my office?" he asked. "Yes sir, right away," I responded. Ambassador Perkins and I were on opposite ends of a sixth-floor corridor. As I entered his office, he motioned to me to shut his door.

"George, you are new to this process" he said with a slight smile. As he spoke, I was uncertain where this conversation was headed. Normally, our conversations are quite specific and I come prepared. "Earlier today, you expressed a lack of interest in possibly serving as ambassador to a particular country if offered." Instantly, I knew what was on his mind. "Yes sir, I did and I would like to offer an explanation, if I may." Ambassador Perkins, ever patient, allowed me a brief explanation. "I understand", he said upon hearing my explanation but, "appointments as chief of mission, theoretically, come from the president and it is impolitic to decline. The White House suffers embarrassment, theoretically, and you may never receive another offer..Always respond in the affirmative when you are asked...That is very important if you are a career officer." "Moreover", he continued, "although all candidates recommended are thoroughly vetted before their names emerge from the building, you do not want to become known as someone that feels he has the luxury to decline a recommendation, even though you may not be the preferred candidate for position, or that the appointment may offer less responsibility than you currently have." Perkins went on to say that "my reaction was not atypical for someone new to the process"; that "I will always know if you are the preferred candidate for a particular mission." I was grateful for his wise counsel because he could have simply chosen to eliminate my name for future consideration of a senior assignment. "Thanks, Edwin," I said. "My real concern was how it would appear to Maureen if she thought I was shopping for an ambassadorship. She needs to feel confident that I am committed to serving a full three-year tour in public affairs. While this is a difficult assignment, I do appreciate that she chose me as one of her deputies when my own agency was not prepared to offer me anything at the senior level." "Should the right opportunity arise for you", Edwin remarked, "I will take it to Maureen myself. She will decide if she is prepared to release you." He understood my concern and that offered me a measure of relief.

Walking back to my office, I reflected on my conversation with Edwin. One thing was obvious: I would never commit such a faux pas again. The difficulty I experienced from that day forward, as did so many other officers, was I never knew which phone call would change the course of my life: a post on my wish list, or a less desirable location, both of which I would have to accept, the latter choice reluctantly. All too frequently, my name appeared beside small, sub-Saharan African countries, missions of limited geopolitical, economic, and geostrategic importance to the foreign policy priorities of the Bush 41'Administration. There was that one odd occasion when my name appeared on the list for Moldova, but, the preferred candidate, I later learned, was a female officer. I did have a sense of my ability to handle larger responsibility and I feared being shunted aside for three years in mediocre splendor and isolation and, then, lacking an onward assignment of comparable responsibility, to be forced into ignominious retirement. I knew the pattern. This had been the fate of so many senior African-American officers before me. Some of them might be reluctant to admit this for reasons of pride, but the record speaks for itself.

Eventually, the call did come from Edwin Perkins informing me that I had been selected as the Department's candidate for Namibia in Southwest Africa. Edwin knew that region well having served as the first African-American ambassador to South Africa. Moreover, he had travelled frequently to Namibia. I was not enthusiastic about the assignment but I could only share that with him. Following a long conversation with Edwin about his experiences in that region, including Namibia, common sense prevailed and I deferred to his superior judgment. His instructions were to take no action until the official announcement of my appointment. Meanwhile, he advised me to pay a courtesy call on Ambassador Harry Crankman, the Assistant Secretary for African Affairs. My purpose would be to express my willingness to work with him to advance the African bureau's program in that region. I knew Harry Crankman since we had socialized on several occasions at the home of a mutual friend, Bernard "Barney" Coleman. Barney Coleman, an African-American, former Foreign Service officer with the Agency for International Agency (AID), was a member emeritus of a small group of vocal supporters of Africa within Washington's constituency for Africa. He was also a personal friend and mentor to many African-American Foreign Service officers, myself included.

Barney's advice regarding a possible appointment to Namibia was to accept it, should I be confirmed. What made Barney Coleman so unusual was that he was on a first-name basis with practically every African of any importance in sub-Saharan Africa and would prove invaluable should I be confirmed as our next ambassador to Namibia. These factors would ensure a smooth transition to an African bureau under Harry's leadership if Namibia became my future.

In the midst of this uncertain time in my life, Edwin Perkins was nominated to become the next American ambassador to the United Nations. In a matter of two weeks, he was gone. My appointment to Namibia had not been confirmed and my "Godfather" ceased to exist when I needed him most. In a word, I was adrift, floating towards the shoreline of career oblivion at a critical point in my career. As if the sea around me was not turbulent enough, Kathryn Hartman chose to resign as Maureen 's principal deputy and return home to her husband in Australia. Kathryn and I had developed a strong partnership and she was a friend in court. If ever I needed the continuity of our relationship, her link to Maureen, and her support for my future, it was now. Ginger Maxwell, Kathryn's replacement was another political friend of Maureen's. She, unlike Kathryn, was less sure of herself, hostile, and difficult. Within the Department, she became known as that "hysterical woman" in public affairs. Ginger questioned both the authority and responsibility I had and began to undermine both from her first day on board. Maureen had hosted a luncheon for her to meet her deputies and office directors and, it was during that lunch while we were introducing ourselves, that she referred to the number of office directors reporting to me. There was something in the way she phrased that remark that made the hairs on the back of my neck stand up. I had been here before. Further confirmation about her effort to undermine me came from friends in the bureau. Ginger talked a lot and staff asked me in private why she does not like me? On several occasions, I was advised to be careful; that she would not be a friend in court. The last thing I could do was discuss this with Maureen. Meanwhile, Namibia was awarded to another officer. In this process, you need a guru and mine was now in New York. Maureen could have interjected herself in the process on my behalf but, for reasons that mystified many, she remained silent.

The isolation I felt had an air of verisimilitude because I had been there before. Once again, I had to become an aggressive advocate to resuscitate the future I had earned, whatever that was destined to be. I sought the counsel and support of an old friend, himself a former ambassador who understood how to play the game at that level. He also knew how to survive and prosper during the "out years," that period of time when those favorably disposed to employing your skills are out of power. He, too, had been a victim. A member of State's "European Club," ambassador G. William Porterhouse had his finger on the pulse of the Department from his modest sixth-floor office. Moreover, he understood the delicacy of my status within Maureen's bureau. William was not astonished to learn that she "had not taken care of me." "They are not what you think they are" he said. "The Baker people do not reciprocate loyalty. In fact, it is safe to say that they are contemptuous of career civil servants. To them, your reward is you have a job."

"How can I help?" he asked. I leveled with him. "I do not have ambassador-on-the-brain disease," I told him. "What I seek is an interesting and challenging set of responsibilities with a degree of autonomy." For example, I pointed to a "number of consuls general appointments that offer significantly greater responsibility, prestige, and challenge than a goodly number of ambassadorships." That remark elicited a response: "I am pleased to hear you acknowledge that because it is true." I was signaling that I was not another African-American officer seeking an ambassadorship, any ambassadorship just to have the title. That is an unfortunate stereotype prevailing within the Foreign Service; at least it was at that time in history. As William and I talked, I identified the American consulates general in Frankfurt, Germany and Toronto, Canada as posts for which I felt competitive. "Let me talk to Roger Jackman (Principal Deputy Assistant Secretary for European and Canadian Affairs) in EUR. I'll let him know of your interest," he said. "You have a strong European background and I'm sure he and his team would be interested in you as a candidate." That very afternoon, Roger called me to acknowledge my interest in both Frankfurt and Toronto. Porterhouse had not wasted any time. Several days later, Reginald Melton, a DAS in EUR, and I met at the behest of Roger Jackman. Reginald and I had served on several panels together and therefore I felt at ease explaining why I felt competitive for an European assignment. "We would like to have you on our team...Frankfurt needs a strong manager. With your success in public affairs, you would be a strong candidate for us. Toronto would offer more cerebral satisfaction. NAFTA (North American Free Trade Agreement) needs shoring up with the Canadians."

When I left Reginald's office, for the first time in several months, I felt grounded again. Obscurity was not in the cards for me; at least I hoped not. I called ambassador Porterhouse to thank him for his support. "You earned your reputation," he said. "I was pleased to be able to support you." The final decision would rest with the "Deputy's' Committee," a small group of senior Department officials chaired by the Deputy Secretary of State whose responsibility it was to review and select candidates for deputy chiefs of mission, consuls general, and other senior level positions.

It was now August of 1992 and my assignment in public affairs was about to conclude. I was anxious to leave because life with Ginger Maxwell had become untenable. I recall how I felt at the time. Departing a bureau that had practically become my identity was a bittersweet moment. On my last day, Maureen had arranged a farewell but she was traveling. She had, however, asked Walter Slattery, the Historian, to present on her behalf, a Superior Honor Award as an expression of her appreciation for my contributions to the bureau and to helping the Department build public support for the Bush Administration's foreign policy objectives. That surprise gesture caught me completely unaware. I departed the bureau secure in the knowledge that public affairs was in better shape than I had encountered that first day three years earlier. Had it been rough sledding? Yes, but I did enjoy the challenge. My preferred approach as a manager was to inspire, but to those determined to resist the changes I was tasked to bring about, I had to instill fear and grudging respect. It is an axiom of management and also of human relations that people work best when they are happy and appreciated. That is equally true for managers. On far too many occasions, I felt neither happy nor appreciated. Because my mandate from Maureen was the equivalent of "cleaning the pool without disturbing the water," there were those moments when the staff was neither happy nor did they feel appreciated. Change is hard to accept under those circumstances, particularly among those devoted to resisting the inevitable. I tried to be fair, to be truthful, to be effective, and to bring integrity to the bureau's administrative processes. Most of the staff told me I had succeeded. In the end, I turned the page and moved on.

As an interim one-year assignment, I was detailed as Special Adviser to the Acting Director General of the Foreign Service, ambassador Joseph Manning. Through Perkins, I knew Manning well. He was a "diamond in the rough," brusque, direct, and one of the senior, more knowledgeable administrators in the Foreign Service. He is also someone whose counsel the Clinton foreign policy team should have sought before their ill-fated military excursion into Somalia. Manning knew that region well and practically predicted the outcome of our military objectives as he understood them. I was a known quantity to him because over the past three years, the director general's senior staff had been frequent collaborators during my effort to reform the bureau of public affairs. Manning was the senior deputy to ambassador Perkins and a frequent problem solver for me.

My first meeting with Joseph Manning in his capacity as acting Director General was pretty much what I expected: devoid of formalities and very much on point. "You're completing a rough assignment; I'm surprised you are not taking some time off. I am pleased to have you because I need your help. Here it is in brief. Our Mid-Level Program for minority hiring is in disarray and I need you to take a hard look at it. Tell me what we need to do to fix it. Talk to anyone in the Department in a position to offer ideas. That's it, George." That was our first meeting. In the inimitable words of that famous American lexicographer, Yogi Berra, "This is de' ja' vu all over again." The Mid-Level Program for minority hiring had been my exclusive domain at U.S. Information Agency in 1971 and 1972 when I was hired as the Director of Minority Recruiting. The program there had produced female and minority Foreign Service officers who, by 1992, had risen through USIA's ranks to serve as ambassadors, directors of public affairs, cultural attaches, program directors, and press attaches. Internal department politics and a lack of resources and other institutional support combined to thwart real progress in State's Mid-Level Program. State personnel knew what to do; they just lacked the will to do it. After all, the program was designed for women and minorities. A priority label low enough to accord this program had yet to be developed.

Lacking any support staff, I settled into my modest office on the first floor. Joseph Manning had given me my marching orders and I knew what to do. The immediate task beyond screening a few boxes of historical files was to identify anyone in the building that knew the history of the Department's program. I needed to know who could be counted on for support and how critical their support was. Conversely, I also needed to know who the program's critics were, whether I could mitigate the harm they could do, or convert them to our cause. This process was more time consuming than any other aspect of my task during the first month. By mid-September, I had presented a 12-page draft proposal to Joseph Manning and the other DASes in his front office. Once assured that my proposal was politically airtight, Joe and I established a deadline of November 1 for a final proposal. The new Director General, Ambassador Grace Manning-Rockwell, would be arriving at that time and Manning hoped to get this proposal on her agenda before too long. Meanwhile, I learned from Roger Jackman in EUR that I was one of four officers on a list of finalists his bureau would submit for consideration as the next consul general in Frankfurt. I was in the mood for good news and that made my day. Little did I know that I was again to be the subject of an hour's debate within the Deputy's Committee. Bizarre had to give way to the macabre on this part of the story. Keep reading.

There had been significant legislative changes since 1972, my last year managing a mid-level program, so my sessions with representatives of State's legal division to discuss the 1991 Civil Rights Act and its applicability to the Department's recruiting, hiring, and tenuring policies were illuminating. Other conversations with supporters of the program and its most severe critics offered detail I would need for the final proposal. By the third week of October, I had a final product. The briefing book I presented to Joseph Manning included: a) a plan to revise the Mid-Level Alternative Entry Program, b) a new design for the State Department's Mid-Level recruitment brochure, complete with two Fact Sheets, a handy Fact Sheet on the "Nuts and Bolts" of recruitment and screening; c) a legal analysis of the 1991 Civil Rights Act as it affects the new Mid-Level Program, d) a statement of suggested qualifications for the proposed Program Director, e) a five-year cost projections analysis I developed in consultation with the Director of the Director General's Resource Management Division, and f) a file of potential candidates that offered the qualifications the Department sought at that time. I accomplished this with minimal supervision, no staff, and little in the way of guidelines.

My proposal to revamp the Department's Mid-Level Program was a labor of love and, although I questioned the State Department's commitment to its implementation and success, I never doubted ambassador Manning's willingness to get in the right peoples' faces about the need for the program. In my performance evaluation, Joe wrote, "I am pleased with George's concept of the program because his ideas demonstrate a grasp of what the Foreign Service must become if we are to meet the challenges which will confront us during this decade. George represents the caliber of officer capable of senior leadership either in Washington or heading up one of our missions abroad." Joseph Manning had affirmed the competence I had demonstrated consistently over the past decade, but, would I receive the endorsement of the "Deputy's Committee?" That nagging question was my constant, unwelcome companion at that time. It was then that the macabre I referred to earlier, came crashing through my door and demanded a place in my life – again. I think by now, you can appreciate the detail.

Ambassador Manning-Rockwell arrived shortly before the "Deputy's Committee" meeting that would rule on my candidacy for

Frankfurt. It was toward the end of the October 1992. As Director General, she was a member of the committee. Meetings generally did not exceed an hour. That was also the day we hosted a "welcome" for her among those that would be her front office staff. We scheduled an hour that would coincide with what we assumed would be the conclusion of the committee's deliberations. On a personal level, I looked forward to celebrating my assignment to Frankfurt at the same event, particularly with a new director general present. Ambassador Manning, of course, accompanied ambassador Manning-Rockwell to the meeting. When the first hour passed and they had not returned, I knew without doubt that I was at least partially the reason why. By the end of the second hour, all of us assembled for the welcome were beginning to wonder. Within minutes of that, we heard voices in the hallway. Ambassador Manning-Rockwell entered her office followed by Manning. His expression spoke volumes. He looked tense, irritated, even frustrated. As he strode past me into his office, he said, "George, forget your German; you're going to Toronto!" Toronto was a great mission. It was, however, my second choice. I sensed a story behind that decision and I had to know the details. At first, Manning would only say, "forget about it...Toronto is a good assignment...look forward to it." I must have badgered him for almost an hour before he consented to meet with me privately. "Joe," I began, "that meeting lasted two hours. I am convinced that I was part of the reason why, perhaps even THE reason." "You're right, you were. Maureen had not weighed in on your behalf, as some expected that she would, therefore no one felt compelled to support you other than myself. The new Under Secretary for Political Affairs chaired the meeting...he did not know you and was non-committal."

Manning went on to describe the dynamic of a meeting in which it was not possible to settle on a consensus candidate for the Frankfurt job. The then-ambassador in Bonn, Jack Trimble, (the most recent under secretary for political affairs) had signaled his intent to support his current minister-counselor for economic affairs for the Frankfurt position. In the end, the Committee decided to set aside the current list of candidates for Frankfurt. A decision would be made at the next meeting with a fresh slate of candidates. Manning also made it clear that the debate had heavy political and veiled racial overtones. In the end, his arguments on my behalf carried the day. I was going to Toronto. For the first time in three years, I was stunned, outraged, bitter, and feeling betrayed by the very people I had supported at great personal cost. I now knew, "at what price, loyalty?" I could not let this go and Manning sensed my total sense of emotional devastation. These people had kicked me in the gut! Manning had been there himself. "George, get over it, move on!" he counseled. "The game at this level is rough; it is dirty, and there are always casualties. This is what you signed on to. I have been in your position and there is no healthy way to reason your way through it. We knew the kind of people you worked for; you didn't. They are loyal only unto themselves."

Manning was right! I had to put this behind me but, before I could, months would pass and many conversations would be held with others in the Department who had suffered the same fate. They were people I had assumed were part of the Baker-McTaggert axis, people who served with them while Baker was Secretary of the Treasury. Oddly enough, some of them only felt comfortable enough to talk about their experiences with them after Baker and Maureen had been called to the White House to manage the re-election effort of Bush '41. Although I now realized that there were other walking wounded, the pain of their betrayal endured for months to come. I will sum up my experience in the bureau of public affairs this way. The political content of my experience there can not be exaggerated. I shared it because it was a slice of the life, the career I had pursued. It was a valuable, but life altering, experience for me. I still had a future and it was important for me to move on.

Ambassador Manning-Rockwell was settling in and selecting her team. Manning was out; I was out of sight five floors down and the new director general was content with that arrangement. I was never invited for any of her meetings even though my title was Special Adviser to the Director General. Perhaps she felt that since I would be moving on next spring, why develop a relationship with me. I do not know what her thought process was. Whatever it was, it did not matter much to me. I was still in recovery mode. Manning and I would meet and I got to know the man that Edwin Perkins admired and respected. This was the real Joseph Manning. Once the new director general had settled in, Manning decided to retire. He was exhausted. Through my relationship with him, he offered sage advice on how to succeed as a consul general. The man was a goldmine of information and I mined that reservoir of knowledge as often as I could.

I must confess a perverse elation at the outcome of the 1992 presidential elections. In a narrow, more personal way, I felt revenge had been meted out. The Clinton team was an unknown, with the lone exception of Ron Brown. What mattered was that the Bush crowd had been defeated. My only point of contact with the new team was Lori Francine-Post, a former Foreign Service colleague who had resigned from USIA for the private sector. She was a member of Ron Brown's inner circle of advisors and supporters. Like everyone else, I scanned the Washington Post daily for news of appointments. What was in store for Ron given his pivotal role in elevating William Jefferson Clinton to become the nation's 42nd president? Well, I was about to learn. The telephone rang within a week of November 4th; it was Lori. "George, we need your help!" "What's up? and who is 'We'?" I asked. "Ron has been asked to consider the UN post and we need someone to brief him. You are the only one I would trust with this request. Would you do it?" "Yes, but what does he need to know?" "Ron knows nothing about the position, where it fits within the State Department, what it offers him." "I'll call you back with a date, time, and location." Right away, I pulled together some material I thought would be helpful to me. I had had a similar experience with Andy Young and his team as they prepared themselves for the same role back in 1976.

One evening several days later, I met Lori in Ron's office at the lobbying firm of Patton Boggs. I reminded Ron he and I had met in 1979 while he was advising Ted Kennedy's presidential run. Ron took an urgent call after which I said, "I understand you have been asked to consider becoming the next Permanent Representative to the United Nations." Ron nodded and asked, "should I consider it?" "I would consider it provided several key conditions were met" I responded. To begin, I described the role of the UN Ambassador, the structure of the New York mission, the perks of the job, including the desirability of cabinet status, the relationship to the Bureau of International Organization Affairs in Washington. I talked about the importance of selecting his own team, staffing in both New York and Washington, influence in the policy process, and budget discussions. My presentation was broad, yet specific enough to address issues a non-career appointee might have questions about. Ron listened intently, occasionally jotting down a point that interested him and, then, he asked, "would you take the job?" "Yes, if it had cabinet status," I replied; "if I could select my own team, and I had operational control over the Bureau of International Organization Affairs in the Department. Autonomy and access to the Secretary of State and to the President are non-negotiable. No, if these conditions, at a minimum could not be met." Ron thanked me and said, "the President and I are still talking. I'll be in touch."

The next morning, Lori called to say how much Ron valued my candid appraisal, but that a new offer is now on the table. She, too, said she would be in touch but, before she hung up, asked, "whatever it is, would you be willing to spend 30-45 days with him to ensure a smooth transition?" "Absolutely!" Within the Beltway, everyone knew Ron had wanted Secretary of State but Gore, Warren Christopher, and Mickey Kantor were in lockstep opposition to this. Jim Baker had delivered the presidency to George Bush and was rewarded with State; so had Ron for Clinton. Ron was no less qualified than Baker had been. Brown was a master politician, a skillful negotiator, and a respected businessman. He had built a national legion of supporters, knew how to navigate Capitol Hill, and did have access to the new president. Warren Christopher argued entitlement to become Secretary of State. Gore feared Ron's ambition, as did Mickey Kantor. Clinton owed Ron and could not afford a public spat early in his administration and possibly alienate African-Americans, his most loyal constituency.

I heard the news about Ron's selection as the first African-American Secretary of Commerce before Lori called to confirm that this was true. Ron and the president had reached an agreement shortly after my meeting with Ron in his office at Patton Boggs. The news of this historic appointment electrified African-Americans and stunned the business community. Within Washington, the impact was cataclysmic. Commerce was one of the big five cabinet posts along with State, Defense, Justice, and Treasury. Ron was now a player and obviously unwilling to accept one of the second-tier domestic agencies e.g., Transportation, Education, HUD, Energy, Veterans Administration, etc. Although I was pleased that we finally were going to get into the game, I tried to remain detached from the paroxysm of activity that is characteristic of any new administration settling in. In five months, I would be in Toronto. My attention thus shifted to managing my boredom until then. The Christmas holidays were the perfect antidote for the pain I still felt. I do not recall doing anything eventful that holiday season.

In January 1993, I received another call from Ron. He wanted to know if I would be willing to spend a month with him as he settled into his new role. No one in his immediate circle of advisors who would accompany him from the Democratic National Committee had served in government before. "What do I do with an agency of 38,000 employees? Where do I begin? How do I communicate with them?" he asked. He genuinely did not know and he would need help. I explained that he would have to secure my release from ambassador Manning-Rockwell. Apparently their paths had crossed previously and Ron said he would call her personally. The new director general agreed to make my services available for the period the new Secretary of Commerce had requested. Between the date of the request and the date I actually appeared at Commerce, a full month passed. Ron's team was beginning to understand how slowly the wheels of a bureaucracy could turn when it lacks motivation to turn quickly.

I was about to embark upon the most fascinating journey of my life. A 30-day detail lasted until June and it was now January. During the period that I call "Travels with Ron Brown," I came to know, love, and admire, and respect a man that African-Americans, other Americans and many abroad felt was qualified to be president. He would eventually earn the respect of the business community as the most effective Secretary of Commerce in history. He also earned the intense antipathy of a legion of detractors who feared the kind of change he had begun to generate. This African-American man had become too powerful, too influential. I know because I was there at the creation.

CHAPTER 16

RON BROWN – A NEW ERA FOR COMMERCE

Each of us reveals details of character by the choices we make, especially choices that shape the content and direction of our lives. We all know that exercising choice follows a pattern influenced by our early socialization to family and community. Moreover, we are all guilty of establishing patterns of behavior that offer insights into who we are as others see us. My choice of the Foreign Service as a career had enriched my life and that of members of my family beyond measure and, setbacks and disappointment notwithstanding, I harbored no regrets. On this journey, I appreciated once again that equally as important as the choices we make about career are the choices we make, or have made, about friends and role models.

I was an admirer of Ronald Harmon Brown because, as imperfect as he was, he was the unconventional man, a man of bold choices, a risk taker, and a staunch believer in his ability to prevail when others saw risks that created timidity on their part. Ron Brown's quest to become chairman of the Democratic National Committee in the late 1980s was a perfect example of this latter point. He dreamt when others slept and his latest, not penultimate, dream was to engineer the election of a Democrat to the White House in 1992. While others were digesting that success, Ron had selected a new battleground: to become the most successful Secretary of Commerce in this nation's history. He accomplished this by earning the grudging respect of detractors and an initially skeptical business community. I was a fellow traveler during that first six months of his tenure as Secretary of Commerce, the period that is generally omitted from the chronology of his travels and success. The formation of the man many Americans – and his foreign counterparts – came to admire, respect, and champion began shortly after his confirmation. This chapter offers another view on the Ron Brown I knew during the early days of his tenure at Commerce.

On a brisk, sunny day in January 1993, I walked east on Constitution Avenue from the State Department to the Department of Commerce to meet with Ray Steinhouse, Ron's chief of staff. Ron did make the call to my boss, Ambassador Grace Manning-Rockwell, at the State Department, requesting that I be detailed to his office for 30 – 45 days to assist him in his transition. I must admit I was intrigued by the possibilities inherent in becoming part of something really different. I was familiar with the "Manual" on cabinet-level transitions. By early 1993, I had Bonn, Manila, Rome, Pusan, Brussels, Paris, and, most recently, a stint as a deputy assistant secretary at the Department of State, under my belt. If I learned anything from those experiences, it was that an early barometer of success for cabinet officers is the quality and professionalism of the staff that accompany them. It really is simple: the quicker that staff learns that government is not the private sector and adapts accordingly, the less painful the experience is for them and the bureaucracy they are expected to assist in managing. The staffs in turn are the foot soldiers of the chief of staff. He or she has to assess quickly each individual's ability to grasp change, assimilate the new and different, and understand where and how the policy and program objectives of the new agency head can be accomplished. This latter quality distinguishes great cabinet officers from those whose accomplishments are as ephemeral as footprints in the desert sands.

My initial meeting on January 28th was with Jack Turner, himself African-American and acting counselor to the new Commerce Secretary. When I arrived, Ray and the Secretary were at the White House. Ron's transition team of approximately 12 – 15 senior and junior-level staff had arrived just days before my meeting with Turner. Jack and I had met at Patton Boggs when I briefed Ron on the UN job, so there was no need for introductions. When I asked Jack how I could help, he said, "whatever you want to do"; a puzzling response, I recall thinking. It had been my experience that requests for assistance under these circumstances are well thought out. "Ray and the Secretary will return this afternoon," he continued. Pointing to a box of resumes on his conference table, he said, "take a look at those and identify anyone with skills you feel we can use." It would have been helpful to know what they were looking for, but what the heck! Lacking any specific guidelines, I applied my own criteria. As I began to peruse the resumes, it quickly dawned on me that they were the "minority candidates" for positions at commerce. Don't ask me how I know; you just know what to look for. When I suggested this to Turner, he confirmed what I suspected. I recall that a majority of the candidates had impressive backgrounds. I even found my own resume among them; how it got there, I will never know.

My meeting with Jack Turner became more focused after I completed the minority candidate review, and after I had selected several they might want to interview. As an aside, one of the candidates I selected for review, I hired the very next month as deputy press secretary. Charlene Haskins, a New Yorker and race car enthusiast was among those on that fateful day who perished on a mountain in Bosnia with Ron Brown. On this January day, Jack addressed the broad sweep of Ron's vision for the commerce department and some of the early public appearances the White House had scheduled for him. As commerce secretary, Ron would propose themes that advocated the need to revitalize our economy while strengthening America's competitiveness as the world's most dynamic engine of global growth. "Ron," Jack said, "has ideas and he is eager to engage in a public dialogue." As Turner talked, a role, my role, began to take shape but, again, I needed to meet the rest of his team. Later that afternoon, around five pm, I was invited to participate in the first of countless strategy sessions. This meeting, chaired by Ray Steinhouse, was to discuss communications strategy. The team was finding its sea legs and a natural first step at an institutional level is to define your constituency, the message, and strategies for delivering the message. Another key activity was to develop a mission statement, that succinct statement of purpose that would define Ron Brown's commerce department. "Nuts and bolts" meetings were standard fare for those first several weeks in February. In addition, we prepared Ron for press interviews on all major networks, numerous public appearances, roundtable discussions, and meetings with congressional oversight committees. Ron Brown was the newest, and hottest phenomenon in the Clinton administration and everyone was anxious to size him up – and not always favorably.

Two important things happened for me during the flurry of activity that first several weeks at commerce. First, I was invited to participate in most of the early organizational meetings with Ron's team and all of the in-house press briefings because I knew and understood how government worked. I also knew how to stage press and media events for cabinet officials. I knew all too well that people from the private sector, including the Democratic National Committee, abhor the lumbering pace of government; they chafe under the restrictions, the rules and requirements imposed by myriad, complex, even overlapping, regulations. Later, however, the fortunate ones appreciate that the same rules prevented them from violating federal statutes that carry federal penalties.

Second, I got to know each member of Ron's team, their work habits, and why they chose to be with Ron at the commerce department at that time. Understand this and you can predict the success quotient for that agency head. Several members of his senior team were bad news and I began to fear for the impact they would have on any goals' agenda the new Secretary might establish, perhaps even the Secretary himself. Well, who were those in Ron's immediate orbit?

Seven individuals were the core of the Secretary's transition team: Ray Steinhouse, chief of staff; James Turner, counselor; Melvina Maxum, director of finance; John Singleton, deputy chief of staff; Jack Shaeffer, policy and strategic planning; Ron's secretary and executive assistant; and, myself as senior advisor. The contrast between the Baker team and this team, for example, was striking. The Baker team was intensely loyal to him personally and to his success as Secretary of State. Ron's team was not as cohesive. Several of them saw the new commerce secretary as the vehicle to achieve personal career objectives. A few of them wanted to be him, while one in particular, John Singleton, doubted Ron's ability to be an effective secretary of commerce. John was bold enough to author a memorandum explaining his views and circulated it among those who had accompanied Ron from the Democratic National Committee. He also outlined the steps he felt, if implemented, could contribute to the new secretary's effectiveness, provided the secretary had the intellectual capacity to grasp them. Frankly, I was aghast at his boldness and the fact that not one of the recipients questioned the premise of his ideas. I heard about the memorandum from someone who had seen it and had heard John discussing it on the telephone. This individual was arrogant to a fault. I obtained and kept a copy of this particular memorandum because of the political reaction it might engender were it to become public. Remember, we are talking about the first several weeks of Ron's tenure. Some of his team had not ventured beyond the fifth-floor executive suite and already they were plotting against the emperor.

The question I grappled with was, who is protecting Ron's flanks? Ray Steinhouse was the master conductor, but no one among the senior staff, with the possible exception of Jack Shaeffer, approached the level of personal loyalty that typified the Baker team. Rightly or wrongly, that was my litmus test because that was the level of staff commitment required for Ron, or any cabinet officer, to succeed. Ron was already navigating in uncharted waters and, somewhere, the sharks must have been sizing up their prey. Since I was one of two African-Americans in the management core (James Turner being the second), several of the career civil servants (African-American) approached me early on with concerns about some of the comments made in their presence about Ron Brown and some of the activities they knew were in contravention of federal regulations. I kept an open line to them and they and others kept me informed. What I have described thus far occurred within the first several weeks of my arrival. I had to decide when and how to use the information shared with me by professional staff genuinely concerned about the integrity of some of the people around the new secretary. A lot would depend upon the role he envisioned for me.

My specific role became more defined in a meeting with Ray Steinhouse and the secretary on February 5, 1993. Ron took the lead with a simple question: "Where do politics, program, and message converge in the Department of Commerce?" That question told me he had come to grips with the enormity of the management and policy task ahead. "How do I communicate with 38,000 employees?" He continued: "I am told there are 14 separate public affairs' offices within commerce. I want a centralized public affairs' operation that coordinates message with the other press offices to ensure that we speak with one voice." "In the past," he went on to say, "each of the separate entities within commerce acted independently of this office, thereby confusing public understanding of policy. I cannot have that. Moreover, the White House will not accept that from commerce." "Let's look at how your office is organized. I suppose the place to begin is with a review of the management systems available within the Office of the secretary," I said in response to the Secretary's questions. "For example, does commerce have an executive secretariat? If so, what are its principal functions?" I asked. Ray spoke up saying "it is no more than a correspondence unit... it needs to be reorganized." I agreed to design a plan to upgrade the role, the functions, and the staff of the existing secretariat immediately. What I envisaged was the secretariat as a management tool for Secretary Brown, the deputy secretary (not yet on board), and the chief of staff to assimilate and coordinate policy, essential programs, agency processes, and policy messages. Concurrently, I would work on a plan to reorganize the office of the Press Secretary to the Secretary and improve coordination among the other 13 press and public affairs' offices. The meeting then shifted to Ron's international role. "What should my role be within the administration to advance the president's economic agenda?" Ron asked. "How do I differentiate myself from previous secretaries of commerce?" "Where do I begin my international travel?" During that conversation, I learned that Thomas Thackery, Deputy Under Secretary of the International Trade Administration, was chairing a group to address those questions. Both Ron and Ray asked me to join the group. My role now had content, direction, urgency, and a real sense of purpose.

Kim Hartstein, a young, beautiful and politically ambitious

African-American who hailed from New York via Atlanta, volunteered to work with me. She had come to commerce via the California campaign in 1992 as deputy political director and a stint as assistant director of the office of public liaison for Clinton's first presidential inaugural committee. Daily, new faces appeared which only added to the excitement everyone felt about "being on the team." Controlled chaos was also rampant because every new face invoked the same refrain, "I am a friend of Ron's," not "the Secretary." That was another problem: too much familiarity, not enough recognition that this was no longer the Democratic National Committee (DNC) or the presidential campaign. Each of these new, young additions to the staff wanted to "act on Ron's behalf" without understanding that they were now part of the federal government. These young "Turks" 20 – 30 somethings (Blacks, whites, and several Hispanics) were politically ambitious and connected to Secretary Brown from a variety of organizations and people who had served as boosters to Ron's rapid rise in the DNC and other related political circles. I mention African-American not simply because of Secretary Brown's race. Historically, there had not been many young Black political appointees in any administration since the Carter era in 1976. While I admired and welcomed their enthusiasm, a modicum of decorum and protocol had to exist. As I began to point this out, I became the visitor whose last day could not come soon enough. Ray agreed with me and insisted upon more structure and more orientation for new staff. As we made progress on this front, the real problem became Ron. He could not say "no" to the disappointed staffer who wanted a "senior position" (at least deputy assistant secretary) without a hint of qualifying experience.

Daily, a torrent of recommendations for senior positions flowed over the transom from the White House, influential members of Congress, and from industry. Unlike his counterparts at State, Defense, Justice, and Treasury, Ron was secretary of the one agency (within the top 5) that historically exercised the least control over senior appointments. Ron could not pick his senior team. When he realized this, he chafed at first; he made his case and lost. Then, during one of our many conversations on precisely this subject, he said: "To hell with it; I'm going to do what I have to do!" From that day forward, Ron became less involved in the appointment's process and more focussed on his role as commerce secretary. "Why pick fights I can't win?" he said in frustration. Ray assumed control of appointments, at least the dialogue with the White House Office of Personnel. Ron increasingly felt the most effective use of his time would be to define his role and establish himself as the new commerce secretary.

John Singleton, deputy chief of staff, and the most ambitious of the senior staff, was enraged by my direct access to Ron; by Ron's interest in developing the executive secretariat as a management tool; by Ron's directive to consolidate the public affairs function within commerce; and by Ron's growing independence. The "book" on Singleton was that he had political connections to the First Lady. What I did not know was whether his push for influence was personal ambition, or came at the behest of his political benefactors. Ray's blind spot was his early reliance on John as his principal deputy and alter ego; the man in charge of daily operations. John aspired to be the power behind the throne, the one with the vision to develop Ron as secretary. To do so he would need to become the "Bob Haldeman" of commerce. John's ambition was raw, unbridled, and publicly known. It also became a subject of corridor gossip. Several of the staff who were devoted to the secretary approached me one day. "George," they said, "you have got to tell the secretary what's going on. You are the only one here not looking for a job and Ron trusts you." My plate was full and this was the kind of situation I had hoped to avoid but, in this instance, I could not. I did a test run with Ray without going into detail but, he, too, was grappling with the enormity of his growing responsibilities and was convinced he could not survive without John Singleton. Oddly enough, at that time, Ron would have shrunk from firing anyone, even as dangerous an adversary as Singleton. He was very conscious of his every move and did not want to be perceived early on as authoritarian. This posture would appear to be at variance with his earlier statement about doing what he had to do. Although Ron did trust me, I was still the "outsider" and I felt the need to tread lightly. Therefore, I decided to wait for a more opportune moment not knowing it would arrive as quickly as it did. More on that later.

I was on the list of those who received the secretary's daily schedule. This gave me the flexibility to choose the meetings I attended. John Singleton was a ubiquitous presence, particularly in those areas important to the secretary, and it was in those areas he wished to exert his influence. I, too, adapted to meet the threat because he was bright, quick, and intimidating to others on the staff. I could envision the structure and functions of the secretariat so I arranged for Kim Hartstein to visit the Executive Secretariat of the State Department. An old friend there, Chase Hankins, agreed to show her around. It was important to me that she understand the model I was developing for Ron. I met with Nelson Dougherty, a press assistant, to talk about the press and media function at the cabinet level, media operations and procedures, and the differences between the press function at the DNC and within the federal system. Nelson wanted to learn and welcomed my interest, ideas, and support. Ron, meanwhile, was besieged with requests for interviews and Dougherty recognized he needed my help. Dougherty would go on to remain one of the secretary's most loyal and competent aides.

Market Access: Knocking The Doors Down

I now turned my attention toward the third area of concern to Ron: international exposure. My intent was to observe the deliberations of Thackery's group planning Secretary Brown's first international trip to Mexico. A career senior civil servant, Thomas Thackery was Acting Under Secretary for International Trade. Mexico and NAFTA in 1993 were important and President Clinton felt that the agreement needed shoring up. He tapped Ron for that role. NAFTA was the first major international bill pushed by the Clinton administration and it was experiencing some early difficulties. A key problem was it did not have organized labor support because labor saw the bill as a major 180-degree shift from a Clinton campaign promise.

Dwight Morris, a personal aide to Ron, was in severe discomfort over Thackery's intrusion into an area he felt was exclusively his responsibility. Dwight had different ideas about where Secretary Brown should travel and who should be involved in the planning process. Morris failed early on to appreciate that Ron Brown was no longer the peripatetic chairman of the Democratic National committee, accountable only to himself and not subject to the intrusion of an inquiring press, industry, and the White House. Ron was now the most visible member of the Clinton cabinet and Dwight could not accept that what may have been his modus operandi at the DNC regarding Ron's travel was not acceptable in the federal government. His total frame of reference was his most recent DNC experience and, to him, that model had to fit. Gently, I tried to insert myself as a neutral observer. I wanted to bring Dwight along, but he literally stormed out of one planning meeting on the planned Mexico trip in a fit of pique. Early the next morning, I met with Ray and the Secretary to talk about Dwight and his role at commerce. "You are in charge," Ray said. "Dwight is loyal and handled my travel at the DNC" Ron said. "This, however, is another level and Dwight needs to recognize that. Try to bring him along, but you are in charge!"

Later, I called Dwight at home and asked him to meet me in my temporary office in the main commerce building. The meeting was private, as a courtesy to him. I shared with him my conversation with Ron; talked about my background doing international advance for the White House Press Office, congressional delegations, and cabinet-level officials. I walked him through the differences, explained the level of accountability required by federal statute and the role of our embassies and diplomatic missions abroad. "There is a lot to learn," I said. "I do not want this role for myself; my sole objective is to ensure that you and others are able to do the job and do it well for Secretary Brown." I stressed the point that I, too, had to learn from others. To my surprise, Dwight was having none of it; nothing I had said registered with him. To salvage something from our meeting, I asked him to develop a plan, his plan, for the advance function by February 16th. It was now February 12th. Dwight disappeared for a week, much to everyone's disappointment. Thomas Thackery was relieved when it appeared he could relinquish the direction of the group. I now wanted operational control of planning for all international travel under these circumstances because time was of the essence, and I wanted to establish a model for how advance travel work should be handled for Secretary Brown and all commerce principals. Before relinquishing my duties at the Department of Commerce, I did author the first ever manual for advancing travel by the Secretary of Commerce. I doubt they ever used it.

My daily schedule began to reflect the range of activities I was long accustomed to: early morning senior staff meeting; meet with scheduling, correspondence review, and speech writers; meet with Nelson Dougherty and press officers from other public affairs' offices; meet with Ray Steinhouse and policy staff; work on secretariat proposal, and plan for the Secretary's first international travel. And my day was not yet complete. There were usually many more things to do, but I thrived on the pace and it became obvious that both Ron and Ray appreciated my effort. The pace at commerce was unyielding, even for someone with my experience. The solution was to bring the Office of the Secretary to complement as quickly as possible with competent people in all of the critical areas he would rely upon for advice, counsel, strategy, liaison to public and private entities, and relations with the media. We also needed a more seasoned manager to direct the operations of a reorganized executive secretariat. Tony Darwin, the candidate I had in mind, had worked for me at the State Department. Tony was a career member of the Senior Executive Service (SES) with all of the requisite qualifications: maturity, clarity of thought and purpose, able to set deadlines, and meet important goals. He was an effective leader and in his element juggling myriad, complex tasks while retaining the loyalty and support of his staff. Moreover, Tony had the stature and experience to work with high profile executives at the cabinet level of government. While developing the proposal for the secretariat, I impressed upon Ray Steinhouse the importance of selecting someone with the skills and attributes of a Tony Darwin. In the near term, my plan was to get Tony and Ray in the same room. Tony was ready for a change from the

Department of State and we looked forward to working together again, albeit briefly.

In the midst of clamor and madness, life had its pleasant rewards. Toward the latter part of February, life became easier for me. I was granted approval to hire Charlene Haskins as the new deputy press secretary. I had been acting press secretary and I was pleased to pass the baton. Charlene was a natural for this position. A product of the rough and tumble of mayoral politics in New York City and dealing with its press, she understood the rhythm of local and national press and how they functioned. In her, I felt Secretary Brown would have someone who could convey his activities and his achievements through strategically placed stories that would enhance his agency and build public support for Ron's vision as the Secretary of Commerce. On the personal side, Charlene had an infectious laugh and a zest for life. She sought challenges that stretched her talents and broadened her horizons. Her resume revealed that about her. At a memorial service for her following her tragic death with Secretary Brown, Nelson Dougherty eulogized her with a simple, but elegant statement: "Charlene did not move through life; she dominated it."

Charlene's arrival as an addition to the senior team meant I could then detach myself, although not totally, from public affairs to focus on Ron's March 1993 trip to Mexico. Dwight Morris was still smarting over self-perceived slights and generally unavailable. Marianna Martinez, the most senior, experienced Hispanic on Ron's staff, was not interested in doing any of the advance work for the Mexico trip. Ron, Ray, and I decided that I would organize, manage and lead advance activities for Secretary Brown until I could train a replacement. If Dwight Morris would not cooperate, then I would train someone else. Marianna recommended a young Hispanic male, Ignacio Rodriguez, who was looking for just such an opportunity.

Ignacio was a Godsend, a quick study, a vigorous appetite for learning, and high energy – exactly what I needed. He quickly grasped that scheduling and advance travel work were essential activities, but not rocket science. Both functions do require meticulous attention to detail, even minutiae. Everything is important when dealing with cabinet officials, the White House, and with members of Congress. Patricia Estrada, press assistant to Charlene Haskins, was the third member of my Mexico traveling team. Patricia was young with a good work ethic and wanted the experience. She was also Mexican-American with a reasonable command of Spanish - a real plus in dealing with the Mexican press corps. Press and media are a prime component of all travel by cabinet officials, particularly when someone of Ron Brown's stature is a major media attraction. A prime objective of this trip was to establish press and media as a central component in any international advance for Secretary Brown. If my hunch was correct, Ron was going to attract considerable media attention, more than is customary for a visiting American secretary of commerce.

Secretary Brown and his Mexican counterpart, Jaime Serra Puche had met in February during Secretary Puche's visit to Washington. Plans for Ron's visit were laid during this visit. The March 16 – 18 visit they agreed upon was propitious for both countries and for Ron as the new Secretary of Commerce. As the first Clinton administration cabinet official to visit Mexico, the new commerce secretary would use his visit to initiate trilateral (Mexico, Canada, and the U.S.) discussions about the North American Free Trade Agreement (NAFTA) supplemental agreements on labor, the environment, and import surges. During the discussions with our Mexican neighbors, he would also explain the fundamentals of President Clinton's economic program to strengthen the American economy. This broader issue would provide a strategically timely moment for Ron to establish himself as a credible spokesman for the new administration on issues of major importance to both countries: economic growth, trade, and bi-lateral relations. The secretary's Mexican counterpart was anxious to have Ron join him at the Second Annual Conference and Exhibition of Trilateral Chambers of Commerce in the Mexican city of Monterrey. A desirable outcome of this visit would be a mutually shared goal to increase the flow of bilateral commerce. After all, Mexico was our second largest market for manufactured goods in 1992. This was the concept, the scope for the visit; now I had to travel to Mexico to make it happen.

There were many young, enthusiastic, former DNC staff at commerce, most of whom had their sights set on participating in international travel advance preparation. Therefore, volunteers for foreign trips were three deep on an average day. Embassy cooperation and logistical and administrative support are the key to success for any visit at the cabinet level. I felt strongly from prior experience that an inexperienced and demanding advance team would not be well received by my embassy colleagues in Mexico City and at the consulate in Monterrey. My approach to "trip preparation" was simple. Limit the number of personnel in the advance party to three maximum and become an unobtrusive presence at the receiving embassy. This obviously was not well-received by many of these young, hard chargers anxious to travel with me to Mexico City. Once in country, I would outline our requirements and then work with our embassy colleagues to ensure that we work within the limits of available resources to meet them; and, most importantly, recognize the value of good will. This latter point can not be overemphasized. Our colleagues at the embassy should see our success as shared success, the most desirable outcome. That formula has produced more positive results than any other approach I was aware of; it had worked for me on countless visits throughout my career and I saw no reason to try and improve on success. More often than not, I was on the receiving end of official visits and the most effective advance directors always demonstrated that they considered embassy personnel partners in a shared enterprise.

Once Ignacio and Patricia understood our approach to this visit, we flew to Mexico City to meet with Ambassador Lawson and his team. The commerce representative there was Jackson Wheaton, reputed to be one of the best officers in the Foreign and Commercial Service (FCS). He did live up to his reputation and following my return to Washington, I lobbied vigorously to have Secretary Brown reappoint him to the position in Mexico City. Jackson, to his misfortune, was a "holdover" from the first Bush administration, whose tour of duty ended after the visit by Secretary Brown. Jackson commanded deep respect within the business community and the Mexican trade ministry in Mexico City. On that first day, before meeting with the ambassador, Jackson and I met in his office to talk about the pending visit. In addition to a review of the trip, I explained what distinguished Secretary Brown from his predecessors and why the "standard commerce reception package" would not suffice for him. Ron was not aware of this; this was personal. I will tell you why.

Secretaries of commerce customarily are the principal fundraiser for the President's successful election campaign. They occupy a prominent place within the cabinet, but, too often, defer to the U.S. Trade Representative (the President's principal trade advisor), or to the State Department in areas in which they rightfully should assume leadership – domestically and internationally. The arrival of a secretary of commerce in most major capitols abroad is generally a low-key, minimum effort event. I wanted to change the paradigm here for a simple reason: throughout my career, I have helped many white cabinet officers project a dynamic image of the United States. They were men of accomplishment, well respected by their peers, and politically well-connected. That is, after all, why they were appointed to the cabinet. Ron Brown was the first African-American to whom I could offer the full extent of my experience and ability and I was determined that he would be accorded the courtesies, respect, and media treatment accorded an American secretary of state. As I said, this was personal. I will use

Secretary Kissinger as a reference point.

Mexico – Up To The Task

Ambassador Lawson had already scheduled a Country Team meeting to introduce me and to review the embassy's approach to the visit. Chester Twining, the Economic Minister, was a trusted colleague from previous tours in the Philippines and in South Korea. Chester and his staff well understood the important role the embassy had to play to further NAFTA implementation in Mexico. Jackson Wheaton and I made three brief, but important, points in that meeting. First, that Secretary Brown takes seriously the responsibility of his commerce department to implement trade agreements; that he wants to ensure that American companies in Mexico receive all of the rights and privileges NAFTA accords them. Second, the embassy and its constituent posts are the front-line for American investors in Mexico, that their reporting on Mexican laws, regulations, and their impact on NAFTA would be invaluable to Secretary Brown and his advisors. Finally, the Secretary encourages the embassy to broaden its contacts beyond Mexico's trade bureaucracy to paint as complete a picture as possible of the Mexican federal response to NAFTA because the agreement is so broad in its impact. After the meeting, Arthur Webb, the ambassador's African-American deputy chief of mission, pulled me into his office. Arthur and I had served together in Paris just a few years earlier. We spent a few minutes catching up with each other, and he assured me that Jackson Wheaton had impressed upon them the importance of the Secretary's visit; that I only need let them know what I required. This is what I mean by "embassy buy-in" to an official visit – a true partnership.

For the next several days, working with elements of Jackson's staff, the embassy press officer, and Chester Twining's team, all under the watchful eye of Arthur Webb, the contours and the core elements of the visit took shape. This was going to be a highly successful visit. I listened intently to Mexican officials from both the public and private sectors discuss the visit from a more personal perspective. I heard comments like "Secretary Brown's visit has historical importance." "NAFTA is our future and we take seriously President Clinton's commitment to it" was repeated by almost everyone who would take part in the visit. As the highest-ranking member of the new administration to visit Mexico, the new secretary would find a receptive, even enthusiastic, reception for the message he would bring. Mexicans were not only excited about Clinton's election, but they had also been following Ron Brown's success as chairman of the Democratic National Committee. What I found striking was the degree of identification Mexicans felt with Ron Brown's success as an African-American man in American politics.

They seemed to understand the degree of difficulty he overcame to achieve the success he had, the kind of pride one sibling takes in the success of another. What I was hearing was more personal than official. Several ministry officials referred to the new secretary as a "builder." The executive vice president of the Chamber of Commerce used the term "architect" at a dinner hosted by Ambassador Lawson in describing Ron's achievements. Rising to the occasion, the same vice president went on to say that "Ron Brown recreated the Democratic Party, forged a consensus among party elements and orchestrated its recapture of the White House."

In a summary memorandum I forwarded to Ron describing the "political atmospherics" of his trip, I told him "Mexicans believe you represent new ideas, hence the future. They look forward to a new relationship with the U.S. and NAFTA is a cornerstone of that relationship." I pointed out that the role he played in advancing the NAFTA bill did not go unnoticed by our southern neighbor. (In the fall of 1994, NAFTA was signed into law.) By the third day of our team's visit, enthusiasm was very high; this was not going to be a standard reception for a visiting American secretary of commerce. Every major news organization including CNN and ABC News, trade publications, dailies, wire services, and widely read journals requested an interview. I knew early on that the schedule could not accommodate the volume of requests, although I wish we could have. The only practical solution was a press conference at the airport upon arrival. That, in itself, was an extremely rare occurrence for a secretary of commerce, but one I heartily endorsed. Over 50 journalists and media representatives would be on hand when Ron stepped off the plane. I saw this conference as the appropriate venue to lay out the purpose, the scope, and the atmospherics surrounding his visit to Mexico. He would have the tool at his disposal to reach the largest number of Mexicans short of a presidential visit. In my summary, or trip notes, I outlined some of the sentiment he would hear and specific point that he should be prepared to address.

American businessmen in Mexico had felt "locked out" for the past 12 years. The Department of Commerce office at the embassy (FCS) before the arrival of Jackson Wheaton was largely ineffective, according to businessmen; it had no access of value to them. The resident American business community felt Ron understood their concerns and they would be willing to listen to him. Moreover, they were prepared to believe that the new Clinton administration was serious about creating a partnership with the private sector, and that it would work hard to enhance America's competitive position via-a-vis its trading partners, but not through protectionist measures. Furthermore, they were still reeling from the indifference of the Reagan-Bush Department of Commerce. What they wanted was a commerce secretary willing to listen, represent their interests, and willing to be an honest broker. Mexicans, I wrote, are feeling the sting of the protectionist rhetoric heard recently in Washington. The office of the U.S. Trade Representative was sending confusing signals that suggested to them it did not understand its role. If NAFTA fails, Mexicans were prepared to invite the Japanese and the European Union as investment partners. The fault, their reasoning went, would be laid at the doorstep of their northern neighbor as an unreliable partner unable to deliver. Perhaps this was the opening gambit to lay down a marker with the new secretary and Ron needed to know that.

My last act before catching a return flight to Washington was to draft my trip notes to Ron. I could now contemplate my departure because I was confident the visit would go well. The final schedule had the full concurrence of the ambassador, the Mexican government, and Secretary Brown. Jackson's secretary, meanwhile, had learned that the eastern seaboard of the U.S. was blanketed with snow and ice; airports were closed and flights east had been cancelled. I was now stranded. The only option I had was a possible flight to Miami and then wait for a weather clearance to Washington, D.C. I called Ray Steinhouse to let him know why I would be unable to return prior to Secretary Brown's March 16th departure; that I would be on hand to greet the official party upon arrival. Apart from the air quality, Mexico City was a pleasant break from Washington, although I would not consider it among the world's iconic capitols. I had a free weekend, so what to do? Sampling the gustatory delights of Mexico had less appeal, having been a victim of "Montezuma's revenge" from eating hotel food earlier in the week. On Saturday and Sunday, I toured the city and its environs with one of my USIS colleagues. For the first time in a week, I was not preoccupied with some aspect of the visit. I relaxed knowing everything was in place.

American Airlines Flight no. 1593 arrived in Mexico City at 13:54 p.m. on Tuesday, March 16, 1993. Ambassador Lawson, myself, Cathy Austin, advisor to Secretary Serra, and an airport public relations official greeted Secretary Brown at plane side. Ron was in a great mood and eager to get started. We proceeded immediately to the pressroom for a briefing with the largest group of journalists ever assembled there for the arrival of an American secretary of commerce. Ron rose to the occasion. He outlined the purpose of his visit, emphasized the importance of NAFTA to both economies, and reiterated the new administration's commitment to strengthening the North American economy. By mid-afternoon, following a meeting with the ambassador and his senior aides, the Secretary was preparing for the 6:00 p.m. meeting with his Mexican counterpart, Jaime Serra Puche. That evening at the American ambassador's residence, Ron was briefed by Jeffrey Gannon, Chairman of the Board of General Electric Mexico, regarding a contract it was recently awarded by the Federal Electricity Commission (CFE) to construct a $675 million, 700 megawatt power plant for the CFE. The importance of this project for a visiting commerce secretary is that it would create 1,000 jobs in New York and South Carolina and generate $225 million in American exports. In response, Ron applauded Mexico's commitment to modernizing its infrastructure and their willingness to be open to private financing when public funding limitations result in underinvestment. That evening, we shared dinner with 40 CEOs of the leading American firms in Mexico.

The first day of his first foreign trip as the American secretary of commerce had gone very well; the press coverage for each event had been extraordinary and Ron was clearly excited. I felt enormous pride because this first African-American commerce secretary was destined for greatness and he had sought my assistance. That was compensation enough. We began the second day with breakfast at the presidential palace and a well attended joint press conference with President Carlos Salinas de Gortari. I had worked with many previous commerce secretaries and it was a rare pleasure to work with one so clearly qualified to represent America as Ron Brown was. His reputation as "builder of political parties" and "architect of a successful presidential campaign" transcended national boundaries. Mexicans were embracing him as if he were their own national son. The press coverage at each event was heavy, even while we were trying to reach our motorcade. On one particular occasion, I became concerned about Secretary Brown's security; nothing serious but, in their desire for more contact, journalists breached my personal security perimeter of four feet around the Secretary. The schedule had been exhausting that second day. A meeting with Mexico City Mayor Manual Comacho Solis, lunch with the American Chamber of Commerce (the largest American Chamber of Commerce outside the United States in 1993); live interviews with CNN, Univision, and CBS; and, dinner with his Mexican counterpart, were among the day's highlights. Ron had worked his famous magic on his hosts, and they had enjoyed the experience. What I saw during this visit was only a harbinger of more and better to come and I looked forward to it.

The Mexican President had placed one of his aircraft at our disposal for the flight to Monterrey the next morning. The flight was pleasant and provided the interlude I needed for phase two of this historic trip. In Monterrey, Ron addressed the Trilateral Chamber along with his host and counterpart, Secretary Serra. Around mid-afternoon, we bid our hosts farewell and headed for the airport. Ron had not known what to expect from the visit since this was my first opportunity to advance and arrange a foreign trip for him. While waiting to board our aircraft, he expressed his appreciation for a job "superbly well done." I appreciated the vote of confidence and in the spirit of the moment, I congratulated him for having acquitted himself so well in his first time at bat with a major trading partner. His supporters took great satisfaction from the success of Mexico observing, "We knew he was up to the challenge." His growing legion of detractors, even within the administration he, himself, was part of, only intensified their effort to paint larger, even brighter, targets on him.

Once back in Washington, I, again turned my attention to completing my proposal to establish an executive secretariat. My approach to completely restructure the secretariat had resonated well among several senior-level career employees who wanted to improve efficiency and coordination between and among the disparate elements of the empire that was the Department of Commerce. Weekly, I would receive encouraging memoranda from career staff with practical suggestions, encouragement, and resumes. Yes, even resumes! I had sought input from myriad sources within the department and many of those who communicated with me expressed interest in being assigned to the new secretariat were it to become a reality. As I reviewed the flip charts and rehearsed my 45 – 60-minute presentation, I felt confident Secretary Brown would approve it. However, before meeting with him, I had to make sure Ray Steinhouse, his chief of staff, was on board. The meeting with Ray would also include John Singleton, his deputy, who by now was determined to defeat any functional reorganization of the secretariat from its current structure. During our meeting, Ray had a number of technical and organizational questions, none of which challenged the need for a new approach. John proceeded cautiously at first and, unable to contain his disdain, unleashed a torrent of sarcasm declaring the concept "counterintuitive." I stuck to my game plan, refusing to be drawn into a debate over his objections. I explained the proven success of the approach I recommended and why I was convinced that the model would work within commerce. Ray, to my surprise, took issue with John and argued the technical and administrative merits of the concept. Ultimately, Ray agreed to schedule a meeting with Secretary Brown.

On a Wednesday night, my assistant Kim and I met Secretary Brown in his large, ornate office. He was in a good mood, jocular almost, saying: "Ray tells me you have the solution to one of my problems." With that as my cue, I explained that the central purpose of a strengthened executive secretariat is to serve as a management tool for the Secretary, the deputy secretary, and the chief of staff in their collective effort to strengthen leadership and direction; to improve policy development and coordination; and to bring greater efficiency to the decision-making process. The four principal functions of the proposed secretarial – as I explained it – would be: information and correspondence management; secretariat staff responsible for substantive policy/program review and rapid response; the executive office/administration with responsibility for personnel, budget, logistics, travel and protocol; and scheduling and advance. The secretariat's principal constituents would be the officials charged with directing those activities directly supporting the Secretary, his deputy, John Rollwagon, and Ray, the Secretary's chief of staff. Primary oversight areas would be public affairs, policy and strategic planning, business liaison, legislative and intergovernmental affairs, the executive director of the executive secretariat, the general counsel, and the inspector general of the department. Anticipating the most obvious question at that juncture, I went on to reiterate the principal functions of the new secretariat: first, manage and coordinate the paper flow to the secretary and his management team; second, to promote clear, concise memoranda to all of the principals (managers, department and independent agency heads) in commerce; and, third, to provide each bureau with adequate and consistent feedback and guidance on requests of commerce principals and feedback on their views and decisions.

By now, Secretary Brown was leaning forward in his chair, his gaze fixed on my charts, but he was not commenting, just looking intently. In a logical, methodical presentation, I walked him through each office and its functions while providing statistics where they strengthened key points I sought to make. He was surprised to learn how many categories of official correspondence there actually were and that there were timetables for responding to each of them. He also seemed more intrigued as I outlined the value of a professionally trained, experienced secretariat staff and that the expertise required was within his department. Moreover, that there were career civil servants eager to work with him. The missing element was a new approach to organizing and utilizing existing personnel and resources. John Singleton sat through the presentation, grim-faced, but he had the presence of mind to contain himself. Ray sat back with the smug look of the cat that swallowed the canary. After all, he would be one of the prime beneficiaries of this new office. As I concluded my presentation, all eyes shifted to Secretary Brown. He smiled, rose from his chair saying, "Thank you, George. That was a strong presentation. I like your approach; it makes good sense, and we will act on it." Later, as we all converged at the elevator to go down to the parking lot, the Secretary, again, thanked me for my ideas and for my support.

There is an interesting and ironic twist to this story. In private discussions with Secretary Brown shortly after my arrival there, he mentioned the grudging admiration and respect he and others within the Clinton administration held for James A. Baker, Secretary of State, White House Chief of Staff, and re-election campaign director for Bush 1. Baker's organizational and managerial skills were extraordinary, particularly the manner in which he managed the State Department. His was the model to emulate. The Executive Secretariat at State is hyper-efficient and effective as a management tool in the hands of a capable executive, as Baker was. Ron knew that I understood the system at State and was a product of it. He also knew my intent was to design a system that would improve his ability to unify his agency in a coherent manner, improve internal communication, and streamline the process by which policy is formulated, debated, and implemented within one of the most maligned agencies in the Executive Branch. This was my original task and it was now complete. Ray would coordinate the internal processes by which a new function within a federal agency is packaged and presented for approval to its congressional oversight committee. He would further assign a working group under the direction of the executive director of the secretariat (now Tony Darwin) to develop the plan to house, staff, and write operational procedures for each function within this new entity.

The day following my presentation to the Secretary, I learned from John Singleton's secretary that he was so enraged by Secretary Brown's positive reaction to the secretariat proposal that he shut his door shouting obscenities and throwing things at the wall. I was now the "nigger in the woodpile" causing him major distress. Little did he realize that the "coup de grace" was on the drawing boards. Weighing heavily on my mind was John's memorandum questioning Ron Brown's fitness to serve as the Secretary of Commerce. He was even more dangerous now and I feared his malevolent and narrowly directed intentions. It was still true that Ray was disinclined to take action against him, their disagreement over the secretariat notwithstanding. Daily, staff would implore me to "do something about Singleton." Ron had agreed to attend a meeting in Japan that would be followed by a trip to Jeddah and Riyadh in Saudi Arabia. In addition, there were rumors about him attending the Annual OECD Ministerial in Paris. The staff made the point that I would be "leaving this spring and there is no one else we can discuss our concerns with."

Secretary Brown had scored well in his international debut, much to the chagrin of his cabinet colleagues at State and at USTR. His press was positive and Ron was in high spirits and on a roll. It did not hurt that President Clinton was one of his most ardent supporters. John Singleton could retire to fight another day, or face the reality of Secretary Brown rising to meet the challenges inherent in his role as a highly visible member of the Clinton cabinet. The former choice seemed most probable and I therefore decided to arrange a visit with Michael Brown, the Secretary's son. The visit would be brief. When we met at Michael's office, I explained my concerns, the fears of the staff most loyal to Michael's father, and then I shared with him John's memorandum. His expression confirmed that our meeting would be short. "Shit!" he exclaimed. "That arrogant S.O.B. actually wrote this bullshit." Michael shook his head in disbelief. "Thank you, I will share this with my father today!" I could do no more. Within weeks, I heard that Singleton had been appointed to a spot on the First Lady's Task Force on Healthcare.

It was now late March, midpoint of my 150-day temporary assignment to commerce; an assignment I thought would not exceed 30-days. Although Toronto was my immediate future, the intensity of my involvement with Secretary Brown relegated all thoughts of Toronto to an afterthought. On several occasions, I actually considered approaching Ron about a permanent appointment with him and his team. We were laying the foundation of a legacy I very much wanted to be a part of. Mitchell Manson, my predecessor in Toronto, called once to arrange a meeting while in Washington on consultations. We met in my office. His principal purpose was to inform me that his next assignment necessitated that he curtail in Toronto and he wanted to know if a corresponding curtailment on my part was possible. In other words, since he would be departing Toronto in late spring, could I arrive at that time to ensure a seamless transition? My plan was to arrive in late July. When I explained the difficulty that would present for Secretary Brown, Manson then assured me the post was secure in the capable hands of my soon-to-become deputy, Dwight Maraniss. "Dwight" he said, "would probably be in touch soon, perhaps he will make a trip to Washington to ensure continuity of post operations." He also wanted me to be aware of several pending personnel actions that had "ugly" written all over them. I let him know I was comfortable with the arrangement he proposed. Manson and I never crossed paths after that meeting.

Japan and The Middle East – Building on Success
Secretary Brown would meet his Japanese counterpart, Yoshiro Mori, Minister of Trade and Industry (MITI) at Dulles International

Airport on March 26, hence a likely trip to Tokyo in late April. We were also talking about a presidentially-designated trip to Saudi Arabia in very early May. I was fortunate by this time to have Tony Darwin directing the executive secretariat and Charlene Haskins in public affairs. Filling these two key slots meant I could now concentrate on working with Secretary Brown to define his international role within the new Clinton administration. Friends at State had told me that Ron's success in Mexico had generated ripples of concern within Secretary Christopher's team; the deep-rooted concern that is born of professional envy. It was important to Secretary Brown that he establish his bona-fides among his international counterparts and, the sooner, the better. After all, he did not come from their world of international diplomacy and commerce. He was, however, comfortable in the business world. Should the Japan visit produce similar results, he would be on more firm footing with the Clinton administration and among his counterparts abroad. Success in Japan would also have the effect of increasing tensions between a newly activist Department of Commerce and his colleagues down the other end of Constitution Avenue at the Department of State. It also did not escape Secretary Brown that Saudi Arabia was vital to sustaining our geostrategic posture in the Middle East.

Thomas Thackery, still acting as the Undersecretary of the International Trade Administration (ITA), and his team had completed a draft of a scope paper for the Tokyo trip. I needed that paper to understand our purposes and the policy objectives the new administration sought to achieve with our most important ally in the Pacific region. President Clinton had asked Secretary Brown to represent him at the 2nd West-East Conference of Ministers of Economics, Industry and Trade in Tokyo on April 24-25, 1993. The official host would be MITI Minister Mori, and his invitees would include representatives from the G-7 countries, representatives from the states of the former eastern bloc and Russia, and from the OECD, the European Bank for Reconstruction and Development (EBRD), the European Commission (EC) and Denmark. Mexico had been a warm up; Japan was center stage. Secretary Brown would be meeting with his counterpart from the world's leading industrialized nations and from some of the important emerging economies. This conference would be a sequel to one involving the same participants convened by the German Economic Minister at Muenster, Germany in May 1992. The purpose of "Muenster 11," as the Tokyo meeting was named, would be to "stimulate action to increase the business orientation and attractiveness of the eastern countries' economic climates."

Secretary Brown's mission, as outlined in the scope paper, was very clear: express President Clinton's appreciation for the conference initiative, but state our preference that "conference-inspired activities not duplicate the work of existing multilateral organizations"; "support the conference's goal of focusing on microeconomic issues and providing a channel for fostering business-to-business contacts"; and, "propose that actual implementation of suggestions for action growing out of the conference process be accomplished through the work programs of existing international organizations, particularly the OECD." The rationale for this message was simple: The Clinton administration rightly sought to foster a climate within the economies of eastern Europe conducive to private enterprise e.g., structural reforms, restructuring of enterprise sector, including anti-monopoly privatization, environmental protection, and the development of small and medium enterprises. The OECD in our view was the better focus to advance the goals of structural reform, the promotion of international trade, foreign investment, and the development of industrial technology. It helped that most of our major European allies agreed with the Clinton administration's approach.

A skeptic could question the policy significance of a commerce secretary representing a new administration at a conference with such a narrow, almost technical focus. Is that not what commerce secretaries do, one might ask? Fair enough. The larger strategy behind the Japan visit was to take advantage of an excellent opportunity to build on the probable results of the President's summit meeting with Prime Minister Miyazawa on April 16th, and to pave the way for the forthcoming G-7 Summit meeting in July 1993. The broad policy objective for Secretary Brown's trip would be to provide the bridge between the April 16th meeting and the G-7 Summit. The first day of his Japan trip, April 23rd, would be devoted to bilateral discussions with our Japanese hosts. At that time, Secretary Brown would lay out an agenda to reinforce President Clinton's message about the need for Japan to take meaningful steps to open its markets. A positive response from the Japanese would create momentum toward ensuring a successful G-7 Summit.

The new commerce secretary was carrying the right policy message. Historically, what is significant is that for the first time, the messenger, the man of the hour, would be African-American. Foreign Service officers are generally the invisible, silent partners at historical events. That was nothing new. What I savored as a senior Foreign Service officer was helping the first African-American secretary of commerce to make political and diplomatic history. That simple fact motivated me beyond description. Over a three-day period, the Secretary would meet with the Japanese Prime Minister, his Foreign Minister and Minister of Trade and Industry, his counterparts from the OECD, the

European Community, and the former eastern bloc states; huddle with a large group of CEOs to learn about the ways and problems of doing business with eastern countries, do several live network interviews, and participate in at least two press conferences. As Thomas Thackery, his team, and I wrapped up the planning for the Japan trip, we launched into the planning for the trip to Saudi Arabia, now set for May 2nd – 5th, 1993. My team of Ignacio Rodriguez and Charlene Haskins would accompany me to Tokyo a week before the Secretary's arrival to lay the groundwork, meet Secretary Brown and his party upon arrival and, once the Secretary was "wheels up," redirect and fly to Jeddah and Riyadh in Saudi Arabia. For us, there would be no time to return to Washington between the Tokyo and Saudi Arabia visits.

Before we get into the details of the Japan visit, I will lay out the context, the scope of the visit to Saudi Arabia. Secretary Brown's visit there would be the first by a commerce secretary in over ten years. The trip's designation as a presidential mission highlighted the importance President Clinton attached to Saudi Arabia as a strategic and commercial partner. The consistent theme in each visit abroad was its emphasis on market opening measures by our trading partners. In this instance, Secretary Brown would support American firms bidding on nearly $10 billion worth of contracts in that country's civil aviation and telecommunication sectors; corporations that included Boeing, McDonnell Douglas, General Electric, Pratt & Whitney, and AT&T. The stakes in this trip were high and the American business community held its collective breath. The unsettled question in their minds was, was this new secretary of commerce up to squaring off against his sophisticated competitors representing AIRBUS and Europe's telecommunications giants - Siemens of Germany, Northern Telecomm (Canada), Ericsson (Sweden), Alcatel (France), GPT (Great Britain), and NEC (Japan)? Secretary Brown would have to effectively counter the intense efforts of high-level European government officials like Michael Heseltine, a member of British Prime Minister Major's cabinet, who were providing substantial support for our European competitors in Saudi Arabia. James Unkefer, Acting Assistant Secretary for International Economic Policy at Commerce, told Thomas Thackery and me, "with the exception of a late 1991 presidential letter, the United States has exerted scant influence on behalf of the American firms bidding on the Saudi sale." Previous administrations were "hands off" when it involved supporting U.S. business abroad. American firms were on their own in competing against foreign companies supported by their respective governments. The new commerce secretary had to get us back into the game; again, the stakes were high. Sometimes during a light moment, Ron would say, "Ron Brown is my name and commercial advocacy is my game."

To those who did not know him, or feared his intrusion into an exclusive domain, Ron was in his element; he was a "closer" with a deft touch, who kept his eye on the prize.

Although Secretary of State Warren Christopher had visited Saudi Arabia in February 1993, the Saudi Government remained uncertain about President Clinton's policies in the Middle East. Secretary Brown's second major task on the Saudi trip would be to use the local media to allay any fears the Saudis may harbor about the willingness of the Clinton administration to strengthen and expand a mutually-beneficial commercial relationship with Saudi Arabia. I told Charlene to establish contact with the embassy press officer in Riyadh and begin developing press events providing opportunities for Secretary Brown to reassure the Saudis that the U.S. values their country as an important ally, trading partner, and friend. I was surprised to one day to receive a telegram from our Commercial Counselor in Riyadh, Rockwell Frazier, advising me that Charlene would not be well received by a conservative Muslim media establishment and, that her presence is ill-advised. I had already raised that question within commerce and was told it would not be a problem. To err on the side of prudence, I called the Saudi Desk at State and, again, was told that it would not be a problem. In my response to Rockwell's message, I assured him that Charlene's presence would not be disruptive and that she would be traveling with me. Later, I learned that his motivation to exclude Charlene was more personal than any professional concern for her effectiveness. So, here was the backdrop for the Saudi trip. For the moment, however, we had to focus on Japan.

In mid-April, Leo, Charlene, and I arrived in Tokyo. Well, here I was in Japan, the land of my brother Michael. For a moment, I thought how momentous this trip would be with him as my guide. What would we do? Where would he take me? I wanted to know his Japan, the society that had captivated his heart for ten years.

Walter Chan, the Commercial Counselor in Japan, was the most senior member of the Foreign and Commercial Service and a delight to work with. We had spoken several times by phone and I knew what to expect from him and his staff. Walter had assigned to us the most proficient American linguist on his staff; an officer of truly extraordinary proficiency who astounded even the Japanese with his ability to conduct complex technical negotiations in Japanese. Ignacio was now a veteran having worked the Mexico trip. He knew the drill and would assume responsibility for introducing Charlene to the press office, coordinating with the Japanese nationals on the commerce staff there at the embassy, and developing a preliminary draft of the detailed schedule I would prepare for each trip. Meanwhile, Walter Chan had arranged a meeting with Ambassador Michael Armacost. The ambassador was an Asian scholar and comfortable in his surroundings. He also understood the frustrations inherent in advancing an aggressive market opening strategy with the Japanese. To the extent that this new commerce secretary could help him advance the glacial pace of the Japanese toward economic and trade policies they did not embrace, he welcomed Secretary Brown's visit. Following the meeting with the ambassador, Walter and I reviewed the scope of the visit over coffee in the embassy cafeteria. "The Japanese have done their homework, too," he said. "They are excited about meeting with Secretary Brown"

Several of the journalists here actually covered parts of the Clinton campaign, so they are somewhat familiar with his role as the former Chairman of the Democratic National Committee...Overall, I expect a very good visit," he said. "Secretary Brown is under no illusion about the tenacity of the Japanese," I said in response, but "he is looking forward to working with Minister Mori." I shared with Walter some personal impressions from working with Ron and, with a slight touch of humor, told him something to the effect that the Japanese had never dealt with a Ron Brown before. Therefore, the interplay of two unknowns would be well worth observing.

My team and I worked full fourteen-hour days, but for two nights we did find the time to explore the area around our hotel, the only modestly-priced hotel in the vicinity of the embassy. All meals, with the exception of hospitality extended by our embassy colleagues, were taken at the embassy cafeteria. Once, we found a noodle shop we could actually afford. By April 21st, we had completed all of the site visits, met with embassy and Japanese security officials, arranged times and locations for press interviews, and familiarized ourselves with all motorcade movements. Satisfied that every detail had been covered on our end, I called Thomas Thackery and Ray Steinhouse to brief them on our progress.

The Secretary and his delegation arrived early afternoon of Thursday, April 22nd and spent the balance of the day trying to overcome the effects of jet lag. Japan was 12-hours ahead of Washington. On Friday, April 23rd, we shifted into high gear. Secretary Brown had breakfast with and spoke to the American Chamber of Commerce at the American Club. The 200 American business executives in attendance were anxious to learn what they could expect from the new Clinton administration and Ron Brown in particular. Following the American Chamber event, we returned to the embassy for exclusive print and television interviews. "Why are you in Japan and what specifically do you hope to accomplish?" was the general thrust of most of the questions. Secretary Brown had just delivered a speech addressing those very questions, therefore everything was fresh in his head. An hour later, it was lunch at the American ambassador's historic residence with approximately 20 senior Japanese business executives representing the automobile industry, the high technology sector, trading companies, financial services, and business organizations. After lunch, we had 30-minutes to be on time for an hour-long 2:30 pm press conference at Japan's National Press Club. That afternoon, at 4:45 pm, we had a private meeting with Japanese Prime Minister Kiichi Miyazawa to talk briefly about U.S. - Japan relations and to reinforce the importance the U.S. attaches to increased market access in Japan for all American companies. Meetings of limited duration (30-minutes) at this level of diplomacy are more perfunctory, governed more by protocol, but useful to lay an agenda on the table. Details would come later. Within 20-minutes, we were meeting with the Japanese Foreign Minister Kabun Muto. Again, the message from our side was market access for American companies doing business in Japan.

We arrived back at our hotel with barely enough time to catch our breath, have a quick shower and meet with MITI Minister Mori for dinner at Restaurant Kitcho, one of Tokyo's famously discreet dining spots for senior government and corporate officials. Minister Mori and Secretary Brown reminded me of two candidates on the campaign trail: in their comfort zones, uninhibited, and enjoying each other's company. The menu was sumptuous and the conversation was good. It was obvious why American diplomats could never reciprocate the hospitality for which the Japanese are well noted. The budget allocation to do so would have to be a line item in our national budget. I am not exaggerating. That night back at the hotel, we spent some time trying to estimate the cost of that evening's dinner complete with drinks and gifts. We settled on an unscientific estimate of $500 to $600 for each of ten invited guests.

Saturday was round-robbin meetings with the Chairman of the Board and CEO of McDermott International (McDermott was participating in the $10 billion Russian Sakhalin oil and gas project); the economic and trade ministers of Germany, Italy, Poland, and Russia; a luncheon hosted by MITI; and the opening of the Muenster 11 Conference - a business-government roundtable discussion, followed immediately by a welcome dinner for all conferees. I gave Secretary Brown credit: he maintained this torrid pace without a hint of fatigue. In fact, he was energized by it. The Sunday schedule was equally as demanding. A late night dinner concluded the Japan visit.

Secretary Brown had been very much in command of his broader international debut. I had been through this on many occasions with other new-to-cabinet personalities, but this was different. The Secretary was charismatic; people wanted to be with him and in his orbit, government officials included. He knew his brief and, in meetings, did not concede a point without a reciprocal concession from his interlocutor. Secretary Brown was the consummate negotiator and dealmaker having honed his skills working the back-rooms of Democratic National Committee politics and managing the presidential campaign of Jesse Jackson. At the end of the day, the balance of success had to be his. What a delight to work with someone like this. On Monday, April 26th, it was "wheels up" for the Secretary returning to Washington. My team and I caught our breath and spent time thanking our embassy colleagues for their support and the success of our visit. My last stop was Preston Jackson, the Commercial Attache. He and I had been having serious discussions about African-Americans in Japan because I had shared with him personal impressions derived from my brother's experience during his ten years there. I wanted to know if my brother's experience had been an anomaly. That led to several illuminating discussions, I being the one educated, in this instance. Preston gave me something I keep to this day: a documentary video regarding the personal experiences of African-American entrepreneurs in Japan, their reception by the Japanese, and the success each of them had achieved. The key to their success, each of them pointed out, is to learn the Japanese language, as difficult as it is. That is a valued and respected indication of your respect for them and their culture. I reviewed the final draft of a telegram to Ray Steinhouse and headed for our bus. It was a three-hour ride to Narita Airport for our flight to Jeddah. Secretary Brown's visit to Japan and my role in facilitating that visit were now history. My focus shifted to Saudi Arabia, the next stop on this new commerce secretary's international agenda.

Years later, my most vivid memory of the flight from Japan to Saudi Arabia was the length of it; I thought we would never arrive. Even the comfort and amenities of an upgrade to business class did not diminish my desire to get out and walk. I just could not find a comfort zone to relax and sleep during that flight. The day following our departure from Japan, we arrived in Jeddah. Surprisingly enough, the heat was not oppressive. I attribute that pleasant condition to the relative lack of humidity. From Jeddah, we connected with our flight to Riyadh arriving close to mid-day. The embassy had arranged lodging for the advance party and the Secretary's delegation at the Riyadh Conference Palace. The general manager there, Mr. Hamad Al-Rajhi, was very gracious, but could not confirm our reservations, even though I was able to present the documentation provided to us by the embassy. I called the embassy and spoke to the Charge' A. Chester Hartwick regarding lodging for the night. It was mid-day and we were travel weary. The ambassador had departed country and Chester authorized our use of Quincy House, the ambassador's residence, pending confirmation of our reservations at the Conference Palace. I fully expected a call the next day, which I did receive. An embassy driver took us to the residence, whereupon I dropped my luggage and crashed. I slept the balance of the afternoon. Later, I took a shower and met briefly with my team. That night, we were guests for a light supper.

Early the next morning, I met with A. Chester Hartwick. Chester and I were colleagues from my stint in the Bureau of Public Affairs at State. At that time, he was the right hand man to Jack Trimble, Under Secretary for Political Affairs. Again, on trips like this, it is always reassuring to encounter colleagues with whom you have worked productively in the past. While going over the major appointments in the Secretary's schedule, I digressed for a moment and asked him about Rockwell Frazier, the embassy's senior commercial officer. Chester was aware of Rockwell's attempt to eliminate Charlene Haskins from the advance team. "Rockwell," Chester said, "is a difficult officer with strong opinions about everything; he is not comfortable working with female officers and he is a real pain in the ass! His pretentiousness does not sit well with either his own staff or his colleagues here at the embassy. You will just have to deal with him where necessary, but he won't be a problem." Chester went on to say, "we are looking forward to Secretary Brown's visit." At that point, I was reassured simply because I had plenty of experience with officers like Rockwell. As Chester and I concluded our meeting, his secretary told him the general manager at the Riyadh Conference Palace had called to confirm our reservations, and that we could move in immediately.

The Riyadh Conference Palace is the official guest quarters for all official visitors of the royal family. I had enjoyed the hospitality of several of Europe's finest hotels, but here was a different standard: a multi-storied, sumptuous palace constructed around an atrium with a six-story crystal chandelier unmatched in its brilliance, beauty, and size. We were the only guests at that time with full access to the staff and all amenities. International telephone calls, laundry, dry cleaning, the business center, and the restaurant were without charge. An unnamed embassy colleague told me the logic behind the hospitality was simple: concentrate your official guests in one place, provide full service in a secure environment, and keep an eye on them. Obviously, all outgoing calls were monitored. That aspect concerned me less than having an ideal, secure location with the ability to make instant connections to any addressee with whom Secretary Brown might wish to communicate. What I did not expect was a severe reaction to the ubiquitous, fine-grained desert sand. My allergy condition kicked into high gear with severe congestion and major discomfort, particularly at night. The heat was less of a problem. One night, my physical distress prompted me to call a friend in Washington familiar with my allergy condition. I prevailed upon her to take my medicine to Tony Darwin at the Commerce Department. He would ask Jack Turner to bring it with him when he arrives with Secretary Brown on May 3rd. The medicine was strong and habit-forming, but I was desperate and afraid to sleep.

While Charlene worked on press and media events with Brendan Wozniak, the Public Affairs Counselor at USIS, Ignacio met with embassy security to review arrangements for the Secretary and all motorcade movements. Rockwell, Chester, and I worked through appointments and discussed probable outcomes of certain meetings scheduled with the Crown Prince, and the Saudi Defense and Commerce Ministers.

Riyadh by day would have to be nirvana for the serious student of architecture. The most striking architectural designs were of those federal ministries headed by a member of the royal family. I recall asking someone if individual ministers were competing with each other to design the most unique building to grace Riyadh's skyline. Cameras were not permitted therefore I could not record for posterity the images I would find difficult to describe to friends back at home. The Saudis, I was told, are very sensitive to misperceptions by the casual foreign observer or visitor. What others, or we, might consider ostentatious flaunting of wealth or profligacy, they would consider "different," or a "reflection of a different standard." On the fourth day, we did have time to shop. Charlene had been badgering us about a gift she had to buy. She said it had to be a gold chain. Ignacio and I naturally agreed to accompany her on the street because she had refused to wear the customary garb for women in public. The real reason we agreed to accompany her was her discernible fear of the religious police and the probability, if encountered, she would be attacked with a switch. Ignacio and I agreed to accompany her on the condition that she buy something for us, otherwise, we would abandon her to the first religious policeman we saw. We teased her incessantly and Charlene was never more than inches from us whenever we appeared together publicly. While negotiating the price of a particular chain, a religious cleric came in and the proprietor positioned Ignacio and me behind Charlene to obscure the view of her exposed legs. Charlene became visibly concerned until the cleric left the shop. The religious police recently had attacked an embassy spouse on the street and we were anxious to avoid another incident.

Riyadh was a new city, ultramodern, with traces of its early desert heritage – Musmak Fort. The diplomatic and expatriate community lived within the confines of an enclave some distance from the city to avoid offending the sensitivities of Saudi men.

For this visit, the pace was less demanding and we were able to explore the city by car. One location was famous for public executions. However, none were scheduled the day we visited. Evenings were pleasant and relaxing, so we caught up on our sleep. At 7:40 pm (12:40 am EST), Secretary Brown and his party arrived aboard a Special Air Mission (SAM) flight (C-20 Gulfstream, tail number 60206) at the royal terminal in Riyadh. The royal terminal is for the exclusive use of the King and members of his family and is constructed entirely of pink marble. It has a separate mosque for the King and one for his wife. The terminal is accessible by its own exit off the freeway. In a country where status symbols abound, there are two that surpass others: your own private exit off the freeway and a living organ donor who travels with you.

The Secretary's counterpart, Commerce Minister Al-Solaim, A. Chester Hartwick, the Charge', Rockwell Frazier, and I met Secretary Brown upon arrival. Earlier in the week, we had delicately advised Minister Al-Solaim that it would be impolitic for the American Commerce Secretary to be seen riding in a Mercedes limousine. We offered the use of the embassy's Cadillac. Minister Al-Solaim politely refused, suggesting he understood but felt it was his responsibility to receive his guest. For the occasion of the Secretary's visit, he obtained a new Cadillac STS.

Presidential flights are in a league by themselves, so the delegation had not suffered excessive fatigue. The aircraft used on presidential missions are housed at Andrews Air Force Base in the Washington, DC suburbs and are maintained by the same personnel who service the other aircraft in the presidential fleet, including the legendary Air Force One. Secretary Brown met with the press corps, took a few questions and accompanied Minister Al-Solaim to the Riyadh Conference Palace.

Saudi Arabia – Advancing Strategic Interests
The next morning, we met with representatives of the aerospace

and telecommunications industries: Boeing Middle East, McDonnell Douglas Middle East, AT&T Network Systems International and AT&T Saudi Arabia, for a brief industry overview. Secretary Brown let this group of anxious businessmen know he was prepared to fly anywhere in the world where he could make a difference for an American industry. They were somewhat anxious because the Secretary was an unknown to them. Heads nodded around the room. This was a new message, one that resonated well. The first Saudi Government official to receive an American secretary of commerce since 1982 was Secretary Brown's counterpart, Minister Solaim. In that meeting, the Secretary pressed his case on the aircraft replacement contract and the telecommunications expansion and modernization program. Other items on the Secretary Brown's agenda were the Arab boycott of Israel and its effect on some American firms, American businessmen denied Saudi visas on the basis of their names, and the reactivation of the U.S.-Gulf Cooperation Council economic dialogue. His meeting with the Saudi Foreign Minister was important because of the Foreign Minister's insider role in decisions awarding major commercial contracts. Moving ever closer to the royal family, Secretary Brown reiterated to the Defense and Aviation Ministers the Clinton administration's interest in the decisions to upgrade Saudi Airlines and the royal family aircraft fleets, and the planned telecommunications expansion. Defense Minister Sultan was a member of the royal family, chairman of the Saudi Board, and another key player in the decision to award the Saudi contract. The importance the U.S. attaches to the bids of U.S. firms in Saudi Arabia was the subject for brief comments by Secretary Brown at a luncheon hosted by his counterpart, Minister Al-Solaim. Local press covered the event and it was important that the substance of the Secretary's remarks regarding U.S.-Saudi relations be brought before the Saudi public. The Secretary was back on message that evening at a dinner hosted by the Charge' at Quincy House for approximately 36 people that included members of the Secretary's delegation, embassy personnel, leaders from the American business community, the Saudi Government, and the Saudi business community.

When we returned to the Royal Conference Center later that evening, the Secretary asked "has the meeting with King Fahd" scheduled for the following day "been confirmed?" "No, it hasn't" I replied. "I am told by Chester Hartwick that the King normally does not receive guests until after 10 pm, but that could change." "Each of his ministers is aware that you might be called out of a meeting, so we can only wait." "The delegation, however, will be restricted in size to perhaps you and Chester." The Petroleum and Mineral Resources Minister and his counterpart at Posts, Telephone and Telegraph (PTT) occupied the Secretary until noon of the second day. In both meetings, I made sure I was near a telephone to receive word regarding the meeting with King Fahd. An afternoon luncheon hosted by the American Businessmen's Group of Riyadh (ABGR) offered the best forum for press coverage throughout the visit. Saudi TV and print media covered Secretary Brown's remarks live. By 8 pm, there was still no word from the King's press officer as we headed out to a private dinner hosted by a leading Saudi CEO, Soleiman Olayan. Dinner was relaxed, the food was outstanding, and there was time to actually engage our Saudi hosts in pleasant conversation around his indoor pool. I would also have been content to continue the conversation in the pool. This was my first, and perhaps last, visit to Saudi Arabia and by this time, several things had aroused my interests and I welcomed an opportunity to raise a few issues with our guests. Secretary Brown concluded his visit and the dinner on a positive note by thanking his hosts for their gracious hospitality emphasizing the importance the Clinton administration attaches to the U.S.-Saudi relationship, and reiterating to the American business community his support for their efforts to expand trade and create jobs.

We returned to the Royal Conference Center close to 11 pm. Around midnight, we received word that the King would see the Secretary. Chester Hartwick and Secretary Brown literally jumped back into the car and sped off into the night for a late night meeting. The invitation was restricted to the two of them. Rockwell Frazier commandeered a car and followed the Secretary's car to the King's Palace. He, then, literally followed Secretary Brown and the Charge' into the meeting. Both the Secretary and Chester were surprised to see him but, at that moment, it would have been awkward to eject him. Chester was livid and Secretary Brown was embarrassed. This was a "Rockwell Frazier moment" that I was not prepared to accept unchallenged. I contacted Thackery for a private meeting when I returned to share with him the substance of my concerns and those of the Charge' about his senior commercial officer. The question was his suitability as our senior representative in Riyadh.

Leo, Charlene, and I had been pre-approved to accompany the Secretary on his return flight to Washington. Bags were packed and loaded onto the bus. Secretary Brown returned close to 1 a.m. and we headed for the airport. We thanked Chester and his team for their great support and for a successful visit. Two hours later, we landed briefly in Cairo for an airport meeting between Secretary Brown and our ambassador there. The next leg of our journey took us to Ramstein Air Base in Germany for a change of aircraft and crew. I should note that service on a SAM flight is impeccable and the food is outstanding.

The seats are large, comfortable, and recline almost an astonishing 180 degrees. I actually slept aboard an aircraft in flight for the first time in memory. When we arrived in Gander, Newfoundland, we took several photographs with the Secretary to capture the trip and the moment for posterity. I have warm and indelible memories of working with Charlene. I can still hear her on the street that day: "Don't you guys leave me!" She really was afraid of the religious police, especially after Ignacio and I shielded her when they entered the shop where we were the day we were out shopping.

During the return flight, I noticed Jack Turner would often occupy the engineer's seat between the pilot and the co-pilot. I asked and was granted permission to occupy that seat when we landed at Andrews Air Force Base. How often would I have that privilege in life? Since I lived across the street from Andrews, and many SAM flights, including arrivals of Air Force One (AF-1), are visible from my bedroom, I recognized my own home as we prepared to land. Before others in our party had cleared the base, I was practically pulling up to my driveway. Including the trip to Japan, I had been in travel status for almost four weeks and it felt good to be home again.

Back On The Ground – Washington, D.C.

The next morning, I did pursue the matter of Rockwell Frazier with Thomas Thackery, if for no other reason than to eliminate the possibility he would embarrass Secretary Brown should he return to Saudi Arabia, as he undoubtedly would. I was not made aware of the outcome of any discussion between Thackery and Frazier but I felt compelled to register my concern at the embarrassment Frazier had caused the Secretary. A $10 billion contract and a complex bilateral relationship require nurturing. Secretary Brown would indeed be returning to Saudi Arabia; I just would not be with him.

I recall sitting in my office several days after the Saudi trip feeling somewhat reflective. While the past three weeks had been exhausting, I felt immensely gratified. Perhaps I was still in transition psychologically from the demands of the road and the order of my immediate existence. Tony Darwin dropped by and we began to talk about Secretary Brown's trip and how it was "playing" locally. Tony had an extensive network of contacts within Washington's media establishment that made him a veritable fount of reliable information. I depended on this when we worked together at the State Department. According to Tony, the word on the street was that Secretary Brown was an emerging force within the Clinton administration and a new face of credibility within the larger business community. The new commerce secretary had not fallen on his face. In fact, many in the corporate community well appreciated Secretary Brown's willingness to get on a plane and fly anywhere to promote the interests of American business. As Tony talked, I felt a powerful sense of identification with this new face of change. Obviously, I had reached a critical juncture in my brief relationship with commerce and its new secretary. My relationship with Secretary Brown and several of his principal advisors was quite strong. Tony made the point that the senior staff was functioning more as a team than had previously been the case. That was good news because one of my earlier concerns was about the need to protect the Secretary's back. Senior-level appointees were arriving almost daily to fill important slots, a measure of relief for a cabinet official anxious to set his program in motion. Several of them I would encounter later during trade missions to Toronto. More cohesion and teamwork within Secretary Brown's inner circle, plus the support of new arrivals afforded him the degree of protection he would need in the days ahead. Something else was happening there that gave me heart: a spirit of optimism, confidence, and certainty about the future for commerce itself. Moreover, the positive "spirit" of Secretary Brown was becoming pervasive, contagious. I was part of something new and exciting. The challenges I could foresee were surmountable and I was spoiling to help the Secretary deal with his detractors in a Republican-led Congress determined to eliminate his department. Each success abroad strengthened the bulwark against the force of Newt Gingrich and his legions. Man, I was pumped!

Secretary Brown knew of and appreciated my interest in remaining on his team, but I also recall his memorable words during a private conversation in Japan on this subject: "If you don't return to State, they will cut you off at the knees. You will no longer have a future there." He also said that he "looked forward to our collaborating in the future." I knew what he meant. Secretary Brown had his eyes set on assuming the helm of the Department of State; it should have been his but President Clinton did not have the courage to step off the brink on that one. That personal opinion aside, the Secretary was right on his larger point. White officers similarly positioned in the past were rewarded for their ability to transfer skills to another Executive Branch agency, particularly at the level of senior advisor to an important member of the cabinet - as Secretary Brown most assuredly was. Talking to Tony helped me achieve clarity regarding my continued involvement with commerce, at least for the balance of my temporary assignment. With little more than a month remaining, my first priority would be to complete the proposal to integrate the 14 public affairs' offices at commerce. Ray had hired Jillian Casemyer as Secretary Brown's new press secretary and I wanted to get the proposal in her hands before

I became immersed in anything else. Charlene Haskins became her deputy.

Ignacio Rodriguez had emerged as the most qualified person to direct the advance team by dint of his hard work and successes in Mexico, Japan, and Saudi Arabia. I also knew Dwight Morris was biding his time until my June departure. Moreover, I knew he would be given the responsibility simply because of his relationship to the Secretary. Dwight was less petulant now than previously, but he was still untested at the international level. Ignacio also understood this dynamic and we began to discuss his future after my return to the State Department. What I came to admire about Ignacio was his willingness to continue working with me under the circumstances. To ensure that he would not be cast adrift, I met with Ray and with the Secretary and sought their commitment to take care of Ignacio. Assured that his future was secure there, I asked Ignacio to work with me on the upcoming Paris trips.

Commerce In Motion – Pushing The President's Business Agenda
Paris was the destination for Secretary Brown's fourth overseas mission as a member of the American Delegation to the June 2-3 Ministerial meeting of the Organization for Economic Cooperation and Development (OECD). The American Delegation, headed by the Treasury Secretary, would include his cabinet colleagues from Agriculture, Labor, Energy, USTR, and the chairwoman of the President's Council of Economic Advisers. The Paris meeting was the annual gathering of the trade, finance, and foreign affairs ministers of the-then 24 member countries of the OECD. The agenda of the 1993 Ministerial – economic growth and employment, the world trading system, and relations with non-members, including the eastern European countries, and the Newly Independent States (NIS) – offered yet another forum for Secretary Brown to burnish his credentials as a principal spokesman for the Clinton administration on economic growth, trade expansion, and job creation policies – issues of great import to Ron Brown personally.

Now a veteran of three highly successful overseas missions and many bilateral meetings in Washington, Secretary Brown was a known quantity to many of his OECD minister-level counterparts and therefore he would be among friends. During the second day of the two-day meeting, with the departure of the Treasury Secretary, Ron would serve as the Chair of the U.S. Delegation. Chairing the delegation was important to him because he would approve the OECD Communique issued at the end of the meeting that helped set the stage for discussions at the July G-7 Economic Summit in Tokyo. American participation in the OECD

Ministerial is a "set-piece operation" coordinated by a capable team of professionals at the U.S. Mission in Paris (of which I am an alumnus). My advance team for this trip had the complex task of arranging more than two-dozen bilateral meetings with other developed countries trade ministers, media interviews, working luncheons with Secretary Brown's French hosts, and working group discussions at the American Mission. Scheduling and logistics would be complicated and I would need the full assistance of the commerce representatives at both of our embassies in Paris. To steal a march on coordinating the numerous requests for interviews from European-based American media organizations, and the European media, we dispatched press assistant Patricia Estrada to Paris in mid-May, a full ten-days prior to my early morning arrival on May 24th. Rachel Lashton, the commerce officer at our Mission to the OECD, had arranged comfortable accommodations within walking distance of the mission, not far from my old apartment across the street from the former Russian embassy in the 16th Arrondissement. Frederic Mansfield, our ambassador to the OECD, was the consummate senior Foreign Service professional, an economic policy expert, and someone with whom I had worked previously. I had one meeting with him and then Rachel, Ignacio, Patricia, and I went to work.

Rachel Lashton was my kind of officer and reminded me of my former executive assistant Saundra Parkinson. She knew how to anticipate, paid meticulous attention to detail, knew her principals and her terrain, and what was achievable from both. More often than not, I agreed with her and she would already have drafted the appropriate memorandum for signature. This meant I could entrust a large measure of the planning for Secretary Brown's participation in the ministerial to her while I became more involved in planning the Secretary's visit to the Paris Air Show from June 9th to the 13th. For that event, Secretary Brown was to be President Clinton's representative. Already there was controversy being generated by several in the media and on Capitol Hill who alleged that the Air Show was merely a "junket." To further complicate the planning process, Ambassador Paulene Stockwell, our ambassador-designate to France, had offered Secretary Brown the use of her beautiful and historical residence during his stay in Paris. She told Secretary Brown she was still vacationing in the U.S. and would not be there to greet him. I should note that Paulene Stockwell was a personal friend of Ron and Alma Brown and thus her absence was perfectly acceptable. She had been a powerful political ally who supported Ron during the early days of his quest to become Chairman of the Democratic National Committee (DNC).

With the OECD planning in good hands, my team and I headed

over to our bilateral embassy (to France) to meet with Jamie Lee, the senior commercial officer. Jamie, as it turns out, was from the old commercial officer's school: delighted to be in Paris, content to take his direction from the deputy chief of mission rather than from his parent agency, and inclined to dismiss Secretary Brown's objectives for his Paris trip in favor of a more benign role advocated by the ambassador's deputy. Secretary Brown had already generated a level of political and media interest traditionally reserved for secretaries of state and, truth be told, there was professional envy. I reminded Jamie Lee that both he and I worked for the Secretary of Commerce and that our primary, in fact only, responsibility was to ensure a successful visit; that there could be no ambiguity surrounding that. Furthermore, that the deputy chief of mission could not unilaterally decide which French officials Secretary Brown would be allowed to meet with. Here was a perfect example of the kind of commerce officer American businessmen complained about i.e., lacking independent judgment, excessively bureaucratic, and wallowing happily in mediocre splendor in complete deference to his state department "betters." I, again, reviewed the scope, purpose, and objectives of Secretary Brown's participation in the OECD Ministerial and at the forthcoming Paris Air Show. To conclude, I said "if we are unclear about any aspect of the Secretary's visit, I am prepared to call Under Secretary Thackery for further clarification." For a split second, our eyes locked and he blinked. One Rockwell Frazier was already one too many.

The Big Show – Paris

For a week, I shuttled among our Mission to the OECD, our embassy to France, and ambassador Paulene Stockwell's residence at 41, due du Faubourg St. Honore. On May 31st, I faxed the final schedule to Ray Steinhouse and Thomas Thackery. On Tuesday, June 1, 1993, at 10:40 am, Secretary Brown and the American delegation arrived by U.S. military aircraft at Villacoublay Airport (French Military Airport). Mrs. Brown and Jack Turner arrived the following morning on United Airline's overnight flight 914 from Dulles. Secretary Brown plunged immediately into two full days of plenary sessions, working discussions with his counterparts, media interviews, and luncheons. When possible, I occupied one of the seats allocated to the American delegation. The more I observed Secretary Brown in action, the more I understood the ability of the man. He, and only he, would be the architect of his future greatness or downfall. The choice would be his, not that of his detractors. Therefore, my personal objective for the ministerial was to help him establish a leadership position vis-a-vis his foreign counterparts. I think we succeeded.

OECD Ministerials are time-consuming, almost deadening to the senses. You have to have an interest in the stuff they talk about. By the end of that second day, even Secretary Brown needed a break. Alma's presence established the imperative to create a pleasant diversion for them. The Secretary extended his stay in-country over Friday and Saturday and took Alma by train to Beaune in France's fabled wine country. Alexander Gilbrey, a friend, would host them in quiet and comfortable seclusion from noon on Friday until their return to Paris at 10:00 am on Saturday. With them out of town, Rachel, Ignacio, Patricia, and I went to dinner. Rachel said she would take care of the wrap-up reporting on Monday. Otherwise, I would have worked on it over the weekend. I was exhausted as were my colleagues. The Secretary and Alma returned to Paris on Saturday and headed straight for the airport to catch their flight to Washington. We took off the rest of the weekend. There were just two workdays before Secretary Brown returned on June 9th.

Sunday evening, I had dinner with a friend and former colleague at our mission to the OECD. During dinner, I must have appeared detached because at one point, I heard her say, "George, where are you?" Apologizing for not being my usual charming and witty self, I told her that I had been feeling pensive and perhaps my mind had drifted for a moment. I then shared with her highlights of the past four months and how profoundly affected I had been by the experience; that having the opportunity to work with Secretary Brown represented one of the most memorable chapters in a life I felt was already quite rewarding. In fewer than 10-days, I mentioned to her, I've got to leave the Secretary and pick up the threads of my life. A very large thread is my assignment to Toronto. And then my friend said something that summarized my state of mind more succinctly than I could have at the moment. She said, "George, look at your experience with Secretary Brown as a gratifying anomaly and the assignment to Toronto as the continuation of your reality." Well, there it was, the splash of cold water; momentary jarring, and, necessary, nonetheless.

Transition – Hand Off
I knew from Tony Darwin and others back in Washington that Secretary Brown was taking a scorching in the press about the Paris Air Show trip, even though he would be the president's personal representative. I suppose that the Secretary being the first Secretary of Commerce to serve as the president's personal representative rankled some on Capitol Hill and their ideological allies in the media.

While this trip may have been a junket in the past, it certainly would not be on Secretary Brown's watch. Economic conditions had changed. The Paris Air Show – held every two years – was the premier international trade event for the world aerospace industry. The U.S. aerospace industry with its 220,000 jobs was our number one net exporter. Moreover, the Air Show provided an important forum for American companies to showcase their products and extend their penetration into other markets.

On June 9, 1993, undaunted by the bleatings of his critics, Secretary Brown arrived in Paris with a delegation of 25 U.S. industry representatives, trade press, and U.S. Government officials. Also among this group was Dwight Morris, who hours later, ignoring instructions, almost caused the Secretary major public embarrassment. When I showed him a graphic example of the embarrassment quite literally at the Secretary's doorstep, his horrified expression told me that maybe he finally "got it." I was too preoccupied with other matters to follow up with him at a more opportune moment, and I would be departing Paris before Secretary Brown. Dwight was now in charge and I could only wish him well. I had prepared a very detailed handbook for the advance function and I don't recall seeing it in his possession.

Unlike his predecessors, Secretary Brown had a real agenda as the president's Personal Representative and that agenda was linked to an economic reality. Worldwide defense restructuring, a weak global economy, increased international competition, and a depressed airline industry had resulted in severe downward pressure on the aerospace industry: lay-offs among large aircraft manufacturers, defense-related aerospace manufacturers and their suppliers. True to form, Secretary Brown was in Paris again to support American industry. He was there to fulfill his public pledge to "travel where the markets are to help American businesses compete." On his agenda, apart from the protocol events, were a meeting with French President Mitterrand and his Defense Minister; bilaterals with the Russians, Ukrainians, the Saudis (as follow up to his May trip to Riyadh), the Malaysians, the Israelis, and the Indonesians. Also on his crowded schedule were meetings with the General Dynamics Corporation and 15 executives from the approximately 110 American exhibitors.

For three days, Secretary Brown was in motion; a blend of business, charm, and diplomacy. He knew what had worked for him in Mexico, Japan, Saudi Arabia, and his recent trip to the OECD. Before leaving Paris, Jack Turner and I had a private dinner. I would be participating in a two-week senior leadership seminar at the State Department on Monday, June 14th and this was the last time we would have to talk, an informal post mortem on the first five months of commerce under Secretary Brown's leadership. Jack thanked me for my support over the past several months saying "we could not have done it without you...We understand why you have to leave, even though our preference is for you to remain with us." He also wanted my candid assessment of the people around the Secretary, particularly staff. "Talk about operations and any suggestions you might have to improve how we do what we do." Jack and I had worked out the basis for a strong, productive relationship therefore I was comfortable offering unvarnished impressions. He was host for dinner and I chose to hold my comments until dessert and coffee. I wanted to savor my last meal in Paris. My strongest recommendation was that he strengthen his role as a confidant and key advisor to the Secretary; that there needed to be more counterbalance to Ray Steinhouse to protect the Secretary. "Secretary Brown is destined for the pantheon of greats as a public official" I said "and you have to take a more active role in shaping and protecting his pubic image." There are still too many people swirling in his orbit in a supporting role who will let him down because of their inexperience, egos, and desire to be with the hottest property in Washington." I continued, "somebody has to mind the store; somebody has to be willing to say no, perhaps even to the Secretary on occasion... do not let the advance function get out of hand. Sometimes, it is an embassy's first contact with the Secretary and impressions are formed. As you can see, we accomplished a great deal with only three people." Turner agreed with me and promised to give more thought to his own role. I don't know that he ever did. The next day, Friday, June 12th, at 12:25 pm, I caught United Airlines flight 915 to Washington. Although this chapter had come to a close, I hoped that the Secretary and I would again have an opportunity to combine energies. I thought we made a good team.

My experience with Secretary Brown was less about learning and more about applying lessons learned: exhibiting confidence in my competence, projecting a shrewd, vital image on behalf of an important member of the President's team, understanding well the responsibility I accepted and then ensuring that resources sufficed to achieve my objectives; improvising when required and, above all, getting the job done. My team and I maintained a torrid pace that last five months that did not permit the luxury of prolonged reflection or self-doubt. The pace we maintained under the conditions we did was my natural element. And while I did not know what my next assignment would bring, I instinctively felt it would not rise to the level of intensity I experienced during my interlude at the Department of Commerce.

The President's Representatives to the Paris Air Show Between 1967 and 1991

1991 Senator Malcolm Wallop

1989 Congressman William L. Dickerson

1987 Senator Strom Thurmond

1985 Senator Ted Stevens

1983 Senator John G. Tower

1981 Senator Barry Goldwater

1979 Senator Howard Cannon

1977 Secretary of Transportation Brock Adams

1975 Congressman William L. Dickerson

1973 Senator Barry Goldwater

1971 Senator Barry Goldwater

1969 Vice President Hubert H. Humphrey

1967 None, although Secretary of Commerce-Designate Trowbridge attended as a "senior official"

CHAPTER 17

MOMENT OF TRUTH – AT THE HELM

To the casual observer or newcomer that I was, Toronto in July 1993 had the outward appearance of a major mid-western city, like Chicago, for example: warm, vibrant, with a pace considerably less frantic than that of Washington, D.C. or other cities of comparable size. However, I knew from policy briefings and discussions with my colleagues on the Canadian desk at the Department of Commerce and at the State Department that beneath this veneer of tranquility was a large segment of the Canadian population increasingly suspicious and resentful of a national government in Ottawa they alleged had sold out their country to the hated Americans.

For perspective on this, we need only consider recent political history of the 1980s and 1990s. The United States and Canada were almost mid-way through the ten-year implementation phase of the U.S.-Canada Free Trade Agreement (CFTA). The year preceding my arrival had been the most difficult. Canadians, meanwhile, were unhappy over the requirements of a new single integrated market while suffering at home from a deep and prolonged recession. To exacerbate the sense of foreboding felt by many, Canadian critics saw a direct link between the recession and the free trade provisions of the Agreement (CFTA). An already contentious bilateral relationship was roiled further by the successful conclusion of the North American Free Trade Agreement (NAFTA) negotiations.

Coincident, therefore, with my arrival in Toronto were heightened fears by Canada's nationalists that Ottawa had sold out; as I said, capitulated to the Americans. The political delicacy of this situation reminded me of a similar period in our relations with the Philippines during the 1960s. As Consul General, Lawson Glasgow worked with his ambassador, then Justin C. Tracewell, to manage a delicate relationship with Filipino politicians almost 30 years earlier during the

American buildup to the Vietnam War. In an identical capacity, I now bore the responsibility for carefully managing our bilateral relationship in Ontario, Canada's largest, most populous province. My early goals would be to build Canadian confidence in the U.S. as an economic and strategic partner; to avoid new disputes, and to resolve outstanding ones in ways that kept new tensions off the table. New disputes and unresolved old ones would only fuel critics on either side of the border while both governments went through their respective CFTA/NAFTA ratification processes. The politics of this assignment were delicate, intricate and I intended to tread lightly – at least early on. This is the thumbnail sketch of the political/psychological climate the day I arrived. The historical analogy was helpful to me as a reminder that I had been in similar circumstances earlier in my career. The difference is, it was now my turn at bat.

Well, here I was in Toronto. The American Consulate General in Toronto at that time was the largest constituent post in Canada and one of the most important in the World. There were small constituent posts in Montreal, Quebec, Calgary, Halifax, and Vancouver. As the Principal Officer and Consul General, I was now responsible for a staff of 22 Americans and 52 Canadian national employees, including elements of the U.S. Information Service (USIS) and the Department of Commerce. In addition, there were 100 officers from the Immigration and Naturalization Service (Department of Justice) and U.S. Customs (Department of the Treasury) at Toronto's Pearson International Airport. Although I was not an ambassador, the size of my staff, the importance of the Canadian relationship, and the scope and complexity of my responsibilities did exceed that of many ambassadors at smaller missions. My point is, this assignment was preferable to many that came to mind, even at the ambassadorial level. Here is another way to look at this assignment. I well understood that consulates historically have been, and continue to be, an extremely important platform for American interests, and to apply all the tools of a diplomatic presence.

The physical dimensions of my consular district were impressive: an area 50 percent larger than Texas with over nine million of Canada's total population of 26 million in 1993, including some 100,000 American citizens. The Province of Ontario, one of nine plus two territories, accounted for 40 percent of Canada's Gross National Product (GNP) and $100 billion dollars of trade with the United States. Toronto, Ontario's largest city, seat of the provincial government, was, and remains, the commercial, cultural, and financial center of Canada. This was center stage in career terms. Toronto was the culmination of a career's quest to head an important mission abroad. This was the serious responsibility that fueled my dreams, that was the content of my broadest aspirations.

It was high summer in Toronto; warm with bearable humidity and a pace to my liking. It was also the perfect time to plan for the fall quarter and become acquainted with my new surroundings e.g., residence, neighbors, staff, and essential consulate operations. The official residence I was to occupy was an unimposing three-story brick colonial in the upscale Forrest Hills section of Toronto approximately three miles from the consulate. The grounds around the house were spacious and neatly manicured. Two full-time Filipino household staff were on hand to help me maintain the house and to assist me with my many representational duties. I was a bachelor at that time and they subsequently became my family. The house was old but very comfortable with larger representational space than the residences of my former ambassadors in Brussels and Paris. Posted outside my front door standing a 24-hour vigil (more accurately sitting in an unmarked vehicle) was a member of the protective division of Canada's famed Royal Canadian Mounted Police. My immediate neighbor to my right (of the prominent Labatt Beer family) told me that he and the other neighbors rested well at night secure in the knowledge that my security protected them as well. The consulate's offices occupied a prominent three-story building designated by city officials as a historical landmark on Toronto's University Boulevard. I was literally minutes from the financial center of the city, the University of Toronto, Queens Park, seat of the provincial government; the Mayor's Office, the theater district, and Skydome, the most famous sport's facility of its type in the world. And then, there was CN Tower. My friend and mentor, Joseph Manning, had advised me to "put together a good speech and make good and appropriate use of it." "That's what good Consuls General do," he said. That would come in good time but, for my initial round of introductions to local and provincial leaders, I chose to be more spontaneous. Spontaneity was one of my strengths, thus one of the most effective tools I had at my disposal. I resolved to be different than my predecessors, more inclusive. I also felt I and my message would be well received; I just did.

In all of my early conversations during the fall of 1993, NAFTA ratification was the "flavor" of the day and everyone, politicians, civic leaders, businessmen and women alike, wanted to know "will NAFTA be ratified?" Confidently, I predicted NAFTA would be ratified because President Clinton has said, "turning away from the deal is not an option." While my audience of several or many digested the confidence of my assertion, I would then launch into a vigorous affirmation of the benefits

NAFTA offered to North America, the world's largest market. By linking NAFTA to Canada's future, I could speak of hope for the unemployed, for medium size industries, and for young people on both sides of our common border, and all through increased trade. "Imagine," I said, "370 million people growing and prospering together." Paraphrasing President Clinton, I would share a view that had deep personal meaning for me: "that when you live in a time of change, the only way to recover your horizons is to adapt to the change, to embrace it, to move forward." That had been the story of my life. "NAFTA," I continued, "offers us this unique opportunity."

For years, Toronto was the center of finance and commerce in Canada yet it was accustomed to a benign presence of the American consul general. As I began to reach out in the city, I heard frequently that "we saw your predecessors upon arrival, at the appropriate civic events, on July 4th sometimes at the residence, and upon their departure." Well I wanted to change this; I wanted to be part of the city's social fabric, part of the dialogue that shaped Canadian attitudes about the United States. The one thing Americans and Canadians did share was a firm belief that each understood the other better than was actually the case. The reality, I learned, is that each side is a captive of stereotypes and bias. Also, I wanted to understand the reality of American business in Canada, and I wanted to be perceived as someone businessmen and others could trust to convey that reality to the American ambassador in Ottawa, former Michigan governor and Member of Congress, Norville Chamberlin, someone many Canadians did trust. Norville Chamberlin had grown up on the American side of the border, knew his way around Canada and had many friends there. I was the unknown quantity. It was not easy; I had to earn their trust. Here is a good example. Whenever I would arrange a visit to a resident American company, the management would politely receive me; after all, I was the American Consul General. Inevitably during the introductions or, when I was awaiting a response to a statement I had made, the question arose, "Mr. Kennedy, why are you here? What can we do for you? None of your predecessors ever visited with us." Wanting precisely that very reaction, I described to them my role as a conduit and source of information for the resident American business community; my effort to secure greater market access for their products, and the varied services we could offer them. Gradually, I would earn their trust and their respect because their concerns were my concerns and I was willing to meet them where they were, literally, if it helped me to help them.

Within the consulate, I solicited the support of my staff early on for this change in emphasis. I told them that I was not going to just pay lip service to something each of my predecessors had; and that I would not ignore the consular function that was central to the consulate's raison d'être. Staff utilization deserved my full attention. I had a sizable staff that issued visas and rendered services to Canada's large resident American community. Nevertheless, I pointed out that this was the perfect place and the perfect time in the history of our relations with Canada to demonstrate a real commitment to promoting American interests and to supporting American businesses in Ontario. Therefore, we would make a concerted effort to reach out to and establish contact with a broad and high-level circle of opinion leaders in government, civil society, and the business community. My early goal as the senior American representative within my consular district was to establish myself as spokesman for the United States in Toronto. My highly competent staff was enthusiastic about this shift in program direction and, before long, my officers and I were in demand at business roundtables, policy forums, strategy meetings, and as keynote speakers before the most influential academic, business, and civic organizations in the Province of Ontario. Drawing on my experience with Secretary Brown, I instituted a series of business outlook dinner discussions at my home shortly after my arrival to explore the oft-perceived divergent interests between the business sector and the city's political leadership. Included among my dinner guests were the president and/or CEO of Proctor and Gamble, Canada; the Bank of America, General Electric Canada, Shoppers Drug, and a partner of one of Toronto's largest and most prominent law firms. This was a first for an American consul general. To me, it was the natural thing to do. At that first dinner, I took the plunge. I wanted each of my guests to know that it would not be enough for us to meet periodically over dinner and cigars. "If we are serious about developing a real partnership to advance our mutual interests," I said, "then we are going to have to trust each other, avoid public recriminations, and reduce the level of tension between our two societies." I met several of my dinner guests at other functions during the following week and each of them said my message of cooperation had been well received.

When the ambassador's deputy, Jasper Hubbell, visited Toronto in January 1994, he asked Danville Huddelston, the senior commerce officer at the consulate, what he thought of me as the new consul general. He responded that "no other consul general has come anywhere near the success of George Kennedy." Hell, I was naturally suited to the role and this environment and I knew it! Ambassador Chamberlin and I had met in Washington before either of us arrived to assume our official duties. This was customary if the ambassador was in Washington. Since we were unknown to each other, I asked about his goals as the new ambassador, the role he envisioned for the constituent posts, including his views regarding the rivalry between the consulate in Toronto and the embassy in Ottawa. That broke the ice and we found we had much in common regarding our approach to public diplomacy. We also shared the personal goal of becoming the most successful ever in our respective roles. I think we both realized at the end of that meeting that ours was to become a productive relationship.

My years of experience in academia, public diplomacy, media relations, and business outreach had taught me the value of being able to bridge the most important part of communication – the last six inches between yourself and your interlocutor. Bridge that gap and you have understanding, not always agreement; you have laid the foundation for mutual respect and a relationship built around honesty and candor. It all came together for me in Toronto, as it had for Cheston Clifton before me, Albert Zucca in Rome, Lawson Glasgow in Manila; ambassadors Parsons and Larry Manning in Washington, at the United Nations and elsewhere; and for Secretary Brown at Commerce.

If I owe a debt of gratitude to anyone for the success I am reputed to have achieved in Toronto, it is to David Fassbinder, a partner in one of Toronto's most prominent law firms: Smith, Lyons, Torrance, Stevenson & Mayer. David is one of those valuable resources resident in most major cities around the world that you want to meet early in your tour rather than later: a friend of the United States, politically well-connected, and willing to extend himself on your behalf to ensure your success. A Canadian advisor to the Mexican government I met while in Mexico City with Commerce Secretary Brown a few months earlier introduced me to David. I had met this valuable contact, herself a member of one of Toronto's most prominent business families, through Jackson Wheaton, our Commercial Counselor in Mexico City. Jackson's words rang in my ears. "George, this lady knows everyone you will need to know in Toronto. She helped me here in Mexico City." The contact was Kim Samuel, the daughter of Ernest Samuel of Samuel, Son & Co., one of Ontario's preeminent businessmen who, as it turned out, befriended my son and me on many occasions during my three years there. Between Kim and David, there was literally no one they did not know. I hit the ground in full stride, thanks to both of them.

The timing, venue, and audience for your debut as the principal American representative anywhere abroad are significant. You get it right on all three and you hit an early home run rather than field a base hit, to use a baseball analogy. My debut was as luncheon speaker before the prestigious Toronto Board of Trade on September 21, 1993, another first for an American consul general. I had the right audience and as David and Kim put it, "the membership of the Board of Trade is comprised of those who shape attitudes and behavior in Ontario about NAFTA and our economic relationship with the U.S. Reach them and you will succeed here." The membership included the CEOs of all the principal Canadian and American enterprises in Ontario plus those representing many medium-sized companies; civic officials, and their local government counterparts. I made several points in my speech I thought would be well received, or that would stimulate questions: "It was my firm belief that we South of the 49th Parallel (the border between the United States and Canada) need to do a better job of explaining our positions particularly in the economic, business, and commercial area." They could not take issue with that point. Second, that "no other country is more important to the security and well-being of the United States than Canada...Canada is not only our largest trading partner, doing substantially more trade with us than Japan, but that the Province of Ontario does more trade with us than Japan." I continued: "NAFTA is our future and it deserves your full support." It bears remembering that Canadians are polite to a fault and perhaps that inhibited the discussion I expected given the level of public criticism about the NAFTA Agreement. I recall there were a few perfunctory questions but nothing to challenge the foundation of my logic about NAFTA.

Several days later, I called David to join me for lunch at home; I wanted the unvarnished truth regarding my remarks. What had been the impact? David told me that all of the calls he had received, the conversations he had, were positive. "They liked your message but, George, they liked you...They liked your approach, your style, your interest in them as the businesses community...They saw in you someone very different than your predecessors," as some of them put it. David's words were gratifying and I thanked him for his support and his friendship. I then shared with him a more private thought. What I was soliciting was his reaction to an idea. The idea simply was to project myself as a catalyst, an intellectual provocateur to stimulate debate about the differences we perceive exist between Americans and Canadians beyond those that are legitimate differences. "Many Canadians are naturally reticent but I am not...My plan is to raise my visibility to talk about some issues that people might take more seriously than if I took refuge in the comfortable niche reserved for American consul's general... Over the next few months (into 1994)" I said, "I will explore various mechanisms to bring together select Canadian opinion leaders from the academic, cultural, scientific, and business communities on issues that seemingly divide us and that are central to our bilateral relationship." I then asked David if he would join me in this enterprise. "Yes, I will," he responded, and "enthusiastically so!...We need this kind of initiative now given the unease over NAFTA and our relationship in general, and you are the person to launch it." When David left that day, I was feeling energized and confident; I had the support of a pillar of the Conservative political establishment and someone who was admired and respected by practically everyone I had met. The introduction of the kid from Mizpah had gone well. My purpose now was to sustain the momentum.

Concurrent with my goal to extend our outreach program to each of the four corners of the Province of Ontario was the equally important goal to allocate a fair amount of my time to several prime management issues. The first of them was to do what I could to heal the rift between the consular staff and the administrative staff. My early intervention became necessary because my predecessor had given his administrative officer an unprecedented degree of authority over daily operations. A little context might be helpful here. The consular staff included a large contingent of American officers and locally-hired Canadians to provide the myriad services required by visitors to the United States and the huge resident American community (several hundred thousand) in the City of Toronto and the Province of Ontario. The demand for consular services was the core function and raison d'etre for the size and scope of our presence in Ontario's largest city. Perhaps the administrative officer felt the pendulum had swung too far in favor of the consular staff e.g., awards, other forms of recognition, and promotions. The administrative officer's staff, slightly fewer in number, provided the capability to sustain a large physical presence, support for the consul general, security budgeting, and other essential operations. His remedy did not achieve balance or parity in any of these areas essential to staff cohesion and morale. Morale plummeted to the extent that it came to the attention of the Canadian desk in Washington. Sanford Bloomington, the director of the Canadian desk asked me during my pre-departure briefing to "look into that situation when you get to Toronto." That is State Department parlance for "solve this problem; we would prefer not to get involved." Well, I got involved much to the chagrin of my administrative officer, himself a recent arrival at the consulate. He looked forward to becoming "the new mayor" as his predecessor saw himself. I sternly disabused him of that notion. There was only one principal officer and I had been tagged.

I was mobile. Daily, I would visit every office and, on a regular basis, I talked to each member of the staff until I had a clear understanding of each staff member's concerns. I called a meeting one day in August that summer to thank the staff for their honesty and candid assessments of issues that affected morale, efficiency, and staff performance. I also talked about some administrative changes I planned to make that I hoped would move us toward resolving the most egregious problems. This had to be done because I needed their combined support to pave the way for a multi-million dollar physical restructuring of our building. This complex project, still under discussion after ten years, was a millstone around the neck of several of my predecessors, and now I had to wear it. Although a renovated facility would have improved staff morale, mine included, and improve the delivery of services to our demanding public, the project never achieved "lift off" because several key officers in the embassy saw it as a rival to their goal of building a new chancery in Ottawa. One major project for Canada was enough. Personalities, egos, and bureaucratic politics combined to delay major improvements in Toronto, but the Office of Foreign Buildings (FBO) within the State Department never tired of requesting more data, more studies, hosting conferences, and sending architects to Toronto for yet more measurements. And then, there was the informal dialogue between the General Services Officer (GSO) at the embassy and the Canadian desk on embassy priorities. This is commonly referred to among Foreign Service officers as the "back channel." This dialogue conspired against Toronto's interests because the GSO's husband, the Minister-Counselor for Economic Affairs in Ottawa, coveted my job since it had been on his short list of preferred assignments. The deck was stacked against us on this one but I had to play the hand I was dealt: going through the motions. What a waste of time and energy. We accomplished little toward this goal during my three years in Toronto. My predecessor had warmed me of just this probable outcome.

I did, however, achieve success with the second of my management challenges: work with my embassy colleagues to develop a contingency plan for the possible consolidation of the Canada-wide immigrant visa function in Toronto. In conjunction with this plan, we proposed to offer a "900 number" consular information service in response to the thousand of queries we handled on a weekly basis. By strengthening the management role of my deputy – also the Chief of Consular Operations at the consulate - I was able to direct post operations through him and devote more time to my other management challenge of reducing the rivalry between Toronto and our embassy. Closer coordination between my office and those of the economic and political staffs in Ottawa reduced some of the friction. I knew I could not eliminate the rivalry because Ottawa could not compete with Toronto in areas of prime importance to an embassy: finance, economics, commerce, the arts, and culture. What I could do was extend an open invitation to the director of each principal office at the embassy to visit Toronto whenever they felt the need to consult with me or with any local officials in my district. All I would require was the courtesy of advance notice that they would be in Toronto. My larger strategy was to develop a strong relationship with ambassador Chamberlin. Chamberlin was a skilled politician who thrived on the energy, the intrigue, and the social diversity of a large city, something Ottawa was not. Most of his friends and corporate contacts also lived in Toronto. Not surprisingly, he was in Toronto frequently, to my satisfaction but to the dismay of his staff that wanted him in Ottawa, who tried mightily to make their concerns his daily priorities. In Toronto, Chamberlin and I could talk without the embassy filter. On several occasions, he commented, "my staff does not know how to use me." There was more than an element of truth in that statement. Many Foreign Service officers derive considerable gratification from reading telegrams, attending meetings, drafting endless memoranda, and debating the merits of each other's policy perspectives. That was not Chamberlin. Their more parochial concerns often did not resonate with him. Chamberlin and I worked well together because we had similar goals, our styles were complementary, and we wanted to make things happen in the three years allotted to us. (Executive-level assignments as ambassador, deputy chief of mission, and consul general are limited to three years unless extended by the Secretary of State or the President.) My preferred approach to working with the ambassador utilized his political talents, knowledge of Canada, and the ease with which he forged important relationships in Toronto. Ambassador Chamberlin opened doors for me that may have proved more difficult were I completely on my own to do so. My approach, therefore, did not endear me to my embassy colleagues, but that was a price I was prepared to play.

Within six months of my arrival, I had built significant bridges to many of the "movers" in town and around Ontario. I am not overstating my accomplishment; this was the view of Chamberlin's corporate friends and the leadership of Ontario during his private meetings with each of them. At the end of my first year, ambassador Chamberlin had this to say in an assessment about my performance as the American Consul General in Toronto: "a strong viable presence in Toronto and the Province of Ontario is vital if I am to accomplish my mission here and if we are to gain greater market access for potential American investors here. George embodies that presence." He also gave me credit as a "strong, effective manager in confident command of his post, a seasoned senior officer who well understands the practical political realities of managing a delicate, complex bilateral relationship – our largest." As the anniversary of my arrival in Toronto approached, I realized I was positioned exactly where I wanted to be.

As I began to chart my own course, I made a number of important friends along the way. One of them was Andrew Brandt, Chair of the Liquor Control Board of Ontario (LCBO), the most profitable Canadian enterprise in Ontario: in excess of $4 billion dollars annually during my tenure there. The LCBO is important to the U.S. because it controls all imports of wines and distilled liquors in the Province of Ontario. Canadians consume millions of gallons of wine annually and exporters from New York State, California, Oregon, and Washington State were aggressively trying to increase their market share of the wine market in Canada's largest, most populous province. In the mid-90s, French wines occupied the lion's share of shelf space in the LCBO's outlets and American exports were a distant second. I cannot recount the number of times I attended wine tastings by the principal American wineries as they launched new products in Ontario. They wanted a larger share of the Canadian market and my role was to assist them in whatever fashion I could. Andy Brandt and I saw each other so frequently that he – half in jest – offered me a desk in his office. "George," he would begin, "you Americans are doing very well in Canada. American wines are very competitive and Canadians' tastes are changing slowly. But, for a long time, French wines did not have serious competition here."   I knew that to be true but my purpose was to remind him regularly that we intended to keep up the pressure. Imports of wines for wine tastings were not subject to duties and therefore could not be sold commercially. All wines including partially full bottles not consumed at these events were turned over to the American Consul General to be used at his discretion – in this instance, my discretion. I had a wine cellar full of the finest wines America had to offer which I used for representational events. Often, the embassy would ask if I could share my largesse with ambassador Chamberlin for use at his official functions. Andrew Brandt had been a provincial cabinet minister when the Conservative Party was in power. Moreover, he was a personal friend of David Fassbinder, an admirer of the United States and, through him, I strengthened budding relationships with Ontario's Conservative political establishment and built new ones through his vast network of business and social contacts.

America's Independence Day, July 4th, is probably noted on the personal calendars of government officials and leaders in the local business community around the world. On that day, many are guests of the resident American ambassador, or an American consul general at his or her residence. As July 4, 1994 approached, I looked forward to renewing ties and showing my appreciation to my many supporters in provincial government, Toronto's City Hall, and the business community for making my first year the success it was. I arrived after July 4th in 1993, so this would be my first Independence Day event at my home. In late spring 1994, I approached business leaders for donations, or in-kind support for an old-fashioned western bar-be-que I planned at the residence. My representation funds were inadequate for such an event. With embassy approval, I was allowed to approach the business community for additional financial support. The response was overwhelming considering that ambassador Chamberlin had approached the same business leaders to support a picnic he planned to host on that same day. Generally an invitation to an event at the ambassador's residence is more coveted but my attendees declined the ambassador's invitation in favor of the event I planned to host. The President of the Bank of America expressed sentiment I heard from many that day when he said, "many of us prefer a smaller event at your home with people we know and see regularly than having to travel to Ottawa for a picnic with a cast of thousands. There is also the small matter that we appreciate your interest in our community and the support you have demonstrated about our concerns." Throughout the day, I heard similar expressions from other provincial and local officials who seemed to genuinely enjoy themselves. Although it was a luncheon event, most of the invitees did not return to their offices that afternoon. Neither did I. It was a beautiful day – in many respects.

While assembling the materials for this memoir, I looked for a copy of the program for the July 4th event at the house. The names and corporate affiliation of each co-sponsor was listed on the back page. Although I could not find the program, I do recall some of the names: Ford Canada, GE Canada, the Bank of America Canada, Proctor & Gamble, Sun Microsystems of Canada, the Royal Canadian Mounted Police, the Bank of Montreal, IBM Canada, Ltd.; K-Mart Canada, Ltd., Campbell Soup Company Ltd., The Bitove Corporation, Pratt & Whitney Canada, Inc., Shopper's Drug Mart, Chemical Bank of Canada, The O'Keefe Center for the Performing Arts, The Liquor Control Board of Canada, Salomon Brothers Canada, Inc., Westinghouse Canada, Merrill Lynch Canada, Inc., Purolator Courier Ltd., and Coca Cola Beverages Ltd.

My guests also included the Premier of Ontario, the Honorable Bob Rae; the mayors of Toronto, Oakville, Markham, North York, and Mississauga. I had put in the time this past year and I felt I was in a position to reap dividends. My game plan for the second year included several elements, the first of which was to maintain an extensive and well-targeted program of political and economic reporting regarding the effects of NAFTA implementation and the political environment in which the effects are judged. In Ottawa and on the Canadian desk in Washington, I was given high praise for my reporting. In an institution like the Foreign Service, good reporting is the coin of the realm. My officers and I stuck our necks out and attempted some predictive analyses in the run-up to the provincial elections during the summer of 1995. The Conservative Party in Ontario under Bob Harris were poised to capture the reigns of provincial government from Bob Rae's Liberal Party and Ontarians were schizophrenic about the choice.

The second element of my plan was to develop a formal approach to managing the cumulative effect of numerous niggling trade disputes (dispute settlement process, steel imports, softwood lumber, beer imports, and salmon and herring) and their potential to erode the public's perception of a large, healthy relationship. In addition to my "Business Outlook" discussions that targeted the government and business sectors in both countries, I also launched my "Consul General's Forum." A third initiative I planned to launch was designed to bring mayors and their city councils together with manufacturers to create a dialogue between those who govern and those who challenge government to create a positive environment for economic growth and for competitiveness to flourish. The Consul General's Forum would bring together select Canadian opinion leaders from the academic, cultural, scientific, and business communities on issues central to U.S.-Canada relations. Moreover, I would continue an active schedule of public appearances, interviews, and visits with municipal leaders, directors of economic and business development, university presidents, CEOs, and plant managers in every major city in Ontario. We had already identified the cities I needed to visit, the people I needed to consult and the issues I should be prepared to discuss. Weekly, sometimes, I would shove off to spend a day or more in one of the principal cities in my district.

The ledger, however, was balanced with enough other challenges to make life less enjoyable. It went with the territory. It was my misfortune in 1994 to undergo another formal inspection by State's Inspector General. In the case of Canada, a country with six constituent posts, the inspection would be of each post, plus the embassy in Ottawa. Earlier, I described the effect an inspection can have on a program, the daily rhythm of an organization, and the staff. This would be my first overseas inspection since Pusan in the late 1970s. There were several areas I felt the involvement of the inspectors would be beneficial e.g., staffing, more control over representation funds, and the process and the pace of the proposed renovation of my building. Apart from these areas, I felt we were in good shape and that nothing major would emerge from this intrusion into our lives. Was I ever mistaken! The day I received the inspectors' draft report, I was scheduled to visit with the mayor of Sudbury. To reiterate, I expected no major surprises so, I threw the report into my briefcase to read during the several hours' drive. In fact, there were no surprises until I saw a formal recommendation to transfer the immigrant visa processing operation from Toronto to Montreal. Confident that this was a simple error in transposition, I called my deputy, Dwight Maraniss, to confirm before I placed a call to Jasper Hubbell, Chamberlin's deputy in Ottawa. Dwight confirmed that he, too, was unaware of such a radical change. I called Jasper Hubbell on my mobile telephone, again, to report a simple error. He was slightly irritated by my call and from his tone, he was aware of this recommendation. "It was in the draft, George; I don't understand why you are surprised" he said. I had not seen any language to this effect prior to the report in my hand and I strove to make that point. I also reminded him that Toronto had the most efficient immigrant visa processing operation in Canada. This he acknowledged. I further reminded him that at Washington's request, we, in conjunction with his staff in Ottawa, had developed a contingency plan to consolidate the Canada-wide immigrant visa function in Toronto, not Montreal. "Jasper," I asked, "why would I assume the transfer of this function to Montreal?...From what I know, they do not want the responsibility." It was obvious he knew more than he was revealing during our conversation and my query apparently highlighted a very delicate decision he had made without consulting either Dwight or me. At a minimum, as chief of consular operations in Toronto, Dwight should have been made aware of a decision of this magnitude.

As in most situations of this type, details eventually emerge. During the inspection of our consulate in Montreal, the inspectors concluded that the facility was too large and too costly for that post's limited operations; that Ottawa should consider a less costly location. Jasper Hubbell decided to transfer the immigrant visa function to Montreal to avoid losing a desirable property. Although there were well established inefficiencies in the immigrant visa program in Montreal, Jasper made a tactical and administrative decision that ultimately destroyed morale in Toronto and severely weakened the immigrant visa program in Canada. The human consequences of this were considerable for me. I was never able to convince my staff that I was not part of that fateful decision. My Canadian staff complement was reduced by eight positions. Several American officer positions were not filled once the incumbent had transferred. The eight Canadian nationals were discharged with a very generous severance package, a package both Dwight and I would have accepted if it had been offered. For the remaining 19 months of my tour, the issue never died. It took a return trip to Canada by the inspectors to follow up on the transfer of this function, repeated conversations between my staff and their Canadian national colleagues in Montreal and Ottawa, and even further explanation from my successor to finally convince my former staff that I had not betrayed them.

On a personal level, I was disappointed in Jasper Hubbell because, to that point, we had a good, strong relationship founded on honesty and trust. At the end of the day, I could only register strong dissent with the inspectors, ambassador Chamberlin, and the Director of the Office of Canadian Affairs. Jasper's decision was his to make, but it could have been handled more forthrightly without destroying the lives of eight people on my team and without fragmenting an already fragile staff. Change was in the wind and that wind blew in my direction. My relations with embassy Ottawa were permanently altered. It is standard operating procedure (SOP) in these situations to hope for your day in court; make your case, and then move on. I was reminded briefly of Ron Brown when he could not control appointments to his senior team. Were I a drinking man, I would have had a stiff one or two or three, slept on it and put it behind me. My recourse was to press forward with my larger outreach agenda.

Canadians will often assert that they must be forever vigilant to guard against the contamination of their society by developments in the United States. Truth be told, however, they are profoundly affected by social, cultural, and educational trends across their southern border. I always met with the president of a local university during a visit to a university town to balance insights and a perspective gained from meeting business people, civic leaders, and politicians. Besides, I enjoyed academia. The provincial government funds universities in Ontario. Thus, political change at the provincial level affects all university administrators, and I thought their views would greatly enhance my understanding of the social climate in Ontario. Adopting as my theme "How Should Colleges and Universities Be Adapting to Change?" I hosted several discussions at home with the presidents of McMaster University, York University, and the University of Toronto. Trends in American higher education were very much on their minds. Many of their students were highly mobile and keenly attuned to the differences in curriculum offerings between American and Canadian institutions. Student enrollments fluctuated at each of their universities because of the attractiveness of course offerings across the border and, therefore, opportunities for careers. "Brain drain" at both the student and faculty levels also was a constant area of concern for them. As administrators, they were prohibited from engaging in fundraising activities to augment inadequate budgets. The bureaucrats at the provincial level, concerned about maintaining control, discouraged innovation by university administrators. Moreover, as administrators, they felt hamstrung in their effort to create the intellectually stimulating, competitive environments that made American institutions the most desired in the world, even for an increasing number of Canadian students.

My options or, more accurately, recommendations here were more limited. I did encourage more U.S.-Canadian student and faculty exchanges. Although more politically delicate, I also encouraged them to lobby individually and collectively for more autonomy to raise funds for specific programs and to attract faculty of international repute; in addition, to build a case for more synergy between universities and the business community to foster additional research and technological development. This was the early-to-mid-90s. Perhaps there have been significant changes since that time.

Exchanges with university administrators always stimulated ideas and one of them regarded how to launch my Consul General's Forum discussions. The idea was to blend change, education, responsibility, and opportunity as themes with a group most affected by all of them: young people. I took seriously my responsibility as a mentor to the five junior officers on my staff and, working with them, I decided to include all of them in my inaugural forum discussion with eight legislative interns from the Ontario Legislature. As moderator and guest, I invited a distinguished professor of History from York University, Dr. Jack Granastein. Legislative interns were not accustomed to this level of attention by an American consul general, but they were interested enough and curious enough to participate. Somewhat reticent initially, they warmed up to the idea that we were interested in their opinions on these themes and the larger theme of the individual and civic responsibility. While the differences between Americans and Canadians of the same generation with comparable levels of education are vast regarding, for example, the role of government in civil society and the individual's responsibility for shaping his or her own life, we started something that night in late November 1994 that my junior officers and I were able to build on in the months ahead: goodwill and a mutual interest to learn more about each other. For my purposes, that was an acceptable result.

My second forum discussion a few months later took a broad look at "Canada, Ontario and the New World Order" with a mixed group of university administrators, members of Ontario's Provincial Parliament, a prominent banker, several law professors, and the vice president of the Canadian Federation of Independent Business. That evening, I had one of the most intellectually stimulating conversations I could recall. Concerns over NAFTA ignited a spirited discussion which highlighted the frequent "perceptions and misperceptions" at the heart of our bilateral relationship. It was all good-natured, serious, and a little humorous at times. The value for each of us was an awareness of how easily we assume a level of understanding exists on issues of mutual concern because of our proximity as neighbors when, in fact, it often does not.

The third forum discussion centered on education with the presidents of Brock University, Ryerson Polytechnic University, the University of Toronto, and the president of the Ontario Teachers' Association. A fourth meeting on health care in Ontario rounded out the series in the spring of 1995.

Meanwhile, my visits with mayors and their directors of economic and business development had heightened my visibility while igniting interest in a dialogue with my office. As executives of cities affected by trade with the United States, thus the larger economic relationship, we had mutual concerns. I was surprised to learn however that as mayors, they did not communicate with each other in any formal way as their American counterparts would. Under the general rubric of examining mutual perspectives on U.S.-Canadian issues, I invited a large group of mayors to the residence for a half-day of discussion and lunch. Seven mayors accepted including the irascible mayor of Mississauga. To avoid an open-ended discussion that most likely would degenerate into America-bashing, I raised questions that addressed issues they each had raised with me during my visit to their respective locales. My larger purpose was to force them to recognize that they had common problems and that they might be able to help each other. The important beneficiary of any fruitful dialogue, and positive outcome, I pointed out, would be the U.S.-Canada relationship. For four hours, they grappled with the kinds of obstacles firms faced in their cities in conducting cross-border business. I wanted to know if they had heard any complaints. What areas of cross-border trade should harmonization of regulations be a top priority? An interesting debate ensued when I asked about additional efforts they would like to see from the provincial government to facilitate trade. Did they see value in Sister Cities and Twinning? What other political tools can cities use to attract and retain employers? Most of them told me they felt powerless to do much here because of political constraints. What about other mechanisms available to create jobs I asked? To those mayors close to Pearson International Airport, I asked about the impact of the new Open Skies Agreement. The 1995 Open Skies Agreement was a bilateral aviation agreement to improve and expand transportation links between the United States and Canada.

The provincial mayors assembled around my table were

effective barometers of public sentiment particularly on those issues that defined Canada's relationship with the United States. Many of their constituents worked in subsidiaries of American corporations. On this day, they expressed genuine gratitude that an American consul general had taken the initiative to do what they should have been doing themselves. Repeatedly, they spoke about the importance of cooperation in establishing better trade and economic relationships.

I had well-established ties with most of the business and economic development directors throughout Ontario, all of whom were more intimately linked to the business community than were their mayors. As economic development officials, they saw room to maneuver, to be proactive in their business environments, but each of them needed the active support of their mayor. This, for a variety of reasons, was not always possible. They, then, exhorted me to reach out to their political leadership because as a "neutral" third party, I had the greater political leverage to raise questions and advance ideas than they apparently felt they could. Each director recognized that to be able to speak truth to power (their mayor), they each had to be willing to walk out the door if they crossed a threshold. On that basis, I achieved a measure of success in establishing a policy-focussed relationship with each of the principal municipal mayors, a new constituency, in Ontario.

I suppose a logical question could be, why is any of this important? Well, bear in mind, the genesis of my journey, the stops and detours enroute to Toronto, or my center stage, as I call it; the career goals I set to position myself for greater and senior responsibility, and my accomplishments within the context of history. By July 1995, I had reached the zenith of my Foreign Service career as consul general. I will elaborate. During my journey, it was important to live the role, to embody the values, to be guided by the counsel I offered others – usually at their request. Thirty years of experience fortified me with a focused point of view and an anchor of ideas and beliefs about how to accomplish our mission in Canada because my assignment was to Canada. It could have been anywhere. I trusted my instincts and I trusted my knowledge of the economic and business factors at the heart of an important bilateral relationship. Viewed through a global prism, I knew that my actions supported the Clinton administration's commercial diplomacy campaign to boost American business abroad. That is the macro view. On a micro level, my insights contributed substantially to the formulation of U.S. policies in Canada and to the advancement of our policy objectives in the Province of Ontario. One of ambassador Chamberlin's primary goals during our second year was to dial down the temperature of our various trade disputes with Canada. We did so. "George contributed to that success" he said in my second annual performance assessment "because of his unprecedented effort to reach out to those who could mold opinion not only in Ontario, but in Canada at large." My interlocutors did not always agree with me, but they did understand well American economic and trade policy and they were generally supportive of our policy initiatives. In many regions of Ontario by this time, there was much less anxiety about Canada's relations with its powerful and dominant southern neighbor. I contributed to this turn of events. This is the role I envisioned for myself that memorable day in Bonn thirty years earlier when ambassador Cheston Clifton expressed his confidence in my ability to rise to the senior levels of the Foreign Service. With a year remaining on this assignment, mine had been an extraordinarily challenging and interesting personal experience.

I could have dialed back the intensity of my own efforts that third and final year, but several things happened to sustain an already intense level of engagement. The first was the tragedy in Oklahoma. Within 36 hours of that horrific event, I lost a cherished level of personal freedom I had come to take for granted. Early intelligence reports indicated that the perpetrators of the bombing were headed to Canada. Between Washington, the embassy in Ottawa, and the Canadian Government, I was provided with an additional security team from the Canadian Secret Service. I literally could not go to the laundry without them in tow. They insisted that I not drive my own vehicle because I was a prospective target. It took a few days to sort out how I felt about this sudden change in my status. In an instant, the fact that the world was still a hostile place became personally real. I could not take anything for granted, even in one of the world's most desired places to live.

The second thing that happened was the provincial elections. Bob Rae, the Premier in 1995, and his Liberal Party were in a race for their political lives. Mike Harris and the Conservatives threatened to bring a level of change that would topple the structure of government generosity many Ontarians had been accustomed to and that fueled a monumental sense of entitlement. Publicly, the view was Harris was too radical; his proposed brand of austerity and fiscal discipline would be the wrong medicine for Ontario's ills. Privately, many Ontarians recognized the benefits of the bitter pill they would be forced to swallow. While polls gave the Liberals a better than even chance to remain in power, my contacts were increasingly confident of Mike Harris's success. I called his campaign manager to extend an invitation for dinner and private conversation. To my delight, Mike Harris accepted. Over dinner and drinks, Mike Harris described the "Harris Revolution," all neatly detailed in his famous red book. "What I offer the people of Ontario is in my red book," he said; "nothing more, no surprises." "Would a Harris Administration significantly alter the business and investment climate in Ontario?" I asked. For several hours thereafter, he told me that the health of Ontario's economy, the staggering provincial debt, and their importance to U.S.-Canadian relations were a source of motivation to become his party's candidate. "Our debt is destroying us, the investment climate in Ontario, and the stability of Canada." He continued: "We cannot afford the profligacy of current policy and the example it sets for our young people. A healthy Ontario means a healthy Canada. A healthy Canada strengthens the most important relationship we have." When Mike Harris left that evening, I called ambassador Chamberlin and suggested that we prepare ourself for a change in leadership.

The timing and policy thrust of Mike Harris and his Conservative movement in Ontario was coincident with the emergence of the Gingrich Revolution in the United States. In Mike Harris, House Speaker Gingrich saw an ideological soul mate that also advocated a balanced (provincial) budget. The U.S. Federal Deficit Reduction Movement (1994-1995) was not only gaining adherents among Republicans and the Clinton "Centrist Movement," but also among concerned Ontarians across the border seeking change. Following a meeting with the Speaker of the House in Washington, Mike Harris, however drew the line at adopting the policy prescriptions of the "Contract With America." Mike Harris won in November and was subsequently reelected to a second term. Canadians stepped up, took the bitter pill and complained all the way to the ballot box.

The third thing that happened in early 1966 was my decision to retire from the Foreign Service. I had been actively considering the idea since my arrival in Paris eight years earlier. There was nothing complicated about my decision. My old friend and mentor Al Zucca always said, "know when to go!" I had had a remarkable career with opportunities to learn four languages (Italian, French, German, and Korean); to live in seven countries (Italy twice, Germany, France, Belgium, Korea, the Philippines, and Canada); and to travel to a dozen other countries. I had been a participant in or an official witness to significant events, several of which defined and shaped the latter half of the twentieth century: the erection of the Berlin Wall in 1961 while on military duty in northern Italy; the 1963 assassination of President Kennedy while assigned to the American Embassy in Bonn, Germany; the build-up to America's involvement in the Vietnam War in 1965 during my tour in the Philippines; a witness to Secretary Kissinger's shuttle diplomacy that frequently brought him to Rome while he negotiated the end of the Vietnam War in 1973; President Reagan's historic visit to the European Parliament in Strasbourg, France in 1985 while assigned to the American Mission to the European Communities; the French Bicentennial in 1989 while assigned to our Mission to the OECD in Paris; the dissolution of the Soviet Union, the fall of Communism, the dismantling of the Berlin Wall in 1989; Nelson Mandela's history making visit to the Department of State in 1990; and serving as a senior advisor to the first African-American Secretary of Commerce in our nation's history.

Major events during my tenure as Deputy Assistant Secretary of State included several noted above and representing the Department of State during the White House planning sessions leading to the Gulf War in 1991, and the implementation of the North American Free Trade Agreement in 1994 while serving as American Consul General in Ontario. Each of these events, and myriad others, had great personal significance for me. My career spanned three decades for a total of 35 years, the maximum number of years for which an officer can be compensated upon retirement. It was time to go and I was comfortable with the prospect of reclaiming the balance of my life.

On April 4, 1996, a friend and commerce colleague and future business partner, Howie Hodges, called me from Washington and asked if I had heard the news. "What news?" I asked. "About Secretary Brown." I expected to hear almost anything except news of his violent and untimely death on a fog-shrouded mountainside near Dubrovnik, Croatia, while on a presidential mission. I was immediately engulfed by a cascade of emotion and unsure how to react or what to think. Incredibly enough, I was able to reach Secretary Brown's home and to leave a message of condolence for Alma, his wife. All that evening, I could only retreat to my study and the privacy of my memory about a rewarding experience I had had with a true American patriot, a man of extraordinary talent, humanity, and compassion, who in the course of his travels across the globe, touched the lives of people great and small as no American had since President Kennedy. Ron Brown belonged to the ages and I mourned his loss.

My last official act was to say farewell to friends and supporters in Toronto and Ontario. Whatever emotional fortitude I could muster was going to be necessary to get through this last official, yet personal act. The most wrenching of numerous farewells was for a yard full of my closest friends and I did lose it. I repeat here the text of my farewell:

"The warmth and generosity of you and others who welcomed me and my son to Toronto three years ago has sustained me on many

an occasion. The opportunity to direct one of our largest and most important consulates comes very infrequently. The successes I achieved could not have been possible without your friendship, cooperation, and support. Together, we have contributed to managing the largest and most successful bilateral relationship in the world. Ours' has been a momentous journey. When I arrived in July 1993, NAFTA was yet to become reality and a new civil aviation agreement linking Toronto and Washington was still on the drawing boards.

Today, because of NAFTA, we have witnessed a tremendous increase in bilateral trade and Open Skies is a stunning success story. Despite the occasional dispute, the U.S.-Canada relationship remains vibrant, strong, and mutually profitable. We are good neighbors, good partners, and good friends."

And it was over. I brought to an end a rich and rewarding career. I also began an enduring love affair as a private citizen with Canada. As the doors closed on my Foreign Service career and my official duties in Canada, a parallel set of doors opened wide offering countless opportunities to extend some relationships and to enrich others.

While packing the last of my personal effects that last evening before the ten-hour drive to Washington the next day, I felt reflective. When this happens, I usually look for a yellow pad and pen to jot down my thoughts before they disappear into the nether reaches of a "senior moment." I was thinking beyond events I had observed in my career – and there were many. I was thinking beyond other events in which I had been a participant or had helped to create. I was looking at a larger topic: the government I represented for 35 years. The real question on my mind was: had my career experiences reshaped the prism through which I viewed my own government? After all, I had spent three decades selling the American story and the efficacy of our government and its policies to others. How did I still feel about that? I quickly concluded that the one indispensable element I look for from my government, as do millions of Americans and others around the world, is leadership. From leadership, I reasoned, comes judgments of fairness, balance or comprehensiveness, vision, strength, and ability. Often, this is how we characterize government. The highs and lows of 20th century history, particularly during my career from 1962 – 1996, evolved to a large extent around the quality of American leadership during crises and the consequences of our failure to act in a manner consistent with our values as a nation and our responsibilities as a global power. We are at our best when we act unselfishly; when we remember we cannot respond solely to our own narrowly construed self-interests.

The instinct to do so stems from a sense of entitlement as a superpower, a right we often express as divinely conferred. The respect my Foreign Service colleagues and I enjoyed at times abroad and fought to regain at other times stemmed from American actions whose consequences were global in their impact.

In each of my foreign assignments, it was very much the case that the resolution of conflict, the key to bilateral understanding, the bridge to reconciliation of most issues on our bilateral issues' agenda was our willingness to lead. While America's allies, and certainly its detractors, would not and could not always agree with us, there was the expectation that American leadership was up to the task. When we were perceived as weak, others took the initiative and it was America who had to contain, neutralize, or defeat adventurism that threatened peace, order, and stability. When we were perceived as strong, enlightened, and focused, others accepted our lead, not always willingly. The simple immutable fact is there was no universally accepted alternative to firm, patient, American leadership. In the unipolar world that characterized the final seven years of my career (1989 – 1996), I knew that the world we are destined to live in and to inherit will be shaped largely by the creativity of America leadership to fashion practical solutions to problems that have the potential to metastasize across national borders and engulf whole communities, and to create further conflict and more enmity.

It might be unrealistic to expect American leadership to assume responsibility for the aspirations of two-thirds of the world's populations, but only we embody the values the world's dispossessed hold dear. Only we hold out the promise of hope to realize the dreams many die in pursuit of; and, lastly, only we purport to have the solutions many seek to the problems that seem to plague their very existence. When we don't act in a manner that recognizes our unique role and the unique responsibilities only we can shoulder, it is also America that pays. We pay in national treasure and often with the lives of a new generation of Americans that have stepped forward. This was apparent in 1963 when I joined the Foreign Service and it was no less true as I ended my career three decades later. Although I did not always agree with my leadership, I was proud to represent my country.

As I brought my tenure in Toronto to a close, the arc of my Foreign Service career was at its zenith. And, as I looked down, I expressed gratitude to all those upon whose shoulders I stood. Were they alive, I think their only requirement of me would be that I make my shoulders available to others. The scope of my successes was in direct proportion to the friendship they offered, the wisdom they unselfishly imparted, and the direction I sorely needed. Each of my giants treated me not as I was, but as they each thought I could become. I grew into the shoes they felt confident I could wear. Along the way, I sometimes missed a step or two wearing shoes that were initially too large but, eventually, I grew comfortable with the larger size. I never forgot an essential quality of Cheston Clifton's approach to life that I tried to bring to my own: He thought it was futile to spend too much time trying to predict the future to gain advantage. "Create your own future," he would say. "There is greater value added." There were no shortcuts, just hard work, many sleepless nights, no time for "pity parties," and, if you were lucky as I was, you learned a lesson, acquired a skill and maybe a new friend. Remember, nothing ventured, nothing gained.

And so it was that during that final drive back to Washington, no longer an active senior Foreign Service officer, I came to a proper appreciation of my own insignificance. I could not have developed this earlier in my career. It was only in retrospect that my vision reached that level of clarity. I had always been in pursuit of the dream, the life by design.

A final thought. I will pay eternal tribute to those who made my path easier, smoothed out a few of the bends in the roads I trod, and helped me overcome instincts that required greater maturity. However, of all those I encountered on my journey to my moment of truth in Toronto, it was Ronald Harmon Brown who truly embodied a consequence of creating your future. The hard reality is that the success each of us may achieve just may come at great personal sacrifice. By the time I crossed paths with him, I understood that well. At the end of the journey though, the only remaining question you must answer before exiting is, have you enjoyed the trip? I have.

DEDICATION

I enjoyed writing this book because I had the time to reflect on a personal journey that spanned practically the second half of the twentieth century.

The encouragement I received from others to complete this project combined with their support made it more than fun. I take considerable pride in dedicating it to my son JiYub and a generation of beloved nieces and nephews who, together, best represent that generation of the family intellectually curious about their universe, willing to stretch their wings, and are the best and brightest hope to continue this journey.

Personally, I could never forget those family members who loved me unconditionally and who nurtured the boy into the man. To my older brother, Bernard, who was my greatest supporter, role model and early sherpa who died too soon; before I could tell him how valuable his early advice had been. To my maternal grandfather, George W. Elam, who most embodied the man I always wanted to become. I hope I made him proud. To his wife, Gladys V. Elam, my maternal grandmother, who provided the key to unlock the door to my future. To my uncle George ("Brother") Elam, whose myriad exploits fed the dreams of the dreamer. And, to my mother, Emma Eleanor Kennedy, without whose firm hand, moral guidance, iron will, and willingness to sacrifice for her children, the journey would have died, consigned to life's countless afterthoughts.

To my younger brother, Michael, an important early collaborator on this project, a giant of a man whose life, career aspirations, dreams, and experiences paralleled my own. He had begun to chronicle his journey until it was interrupted by an unfortunate, but fatal, motorcycle accident on June 27, 2004. To my lifelong friend, Vincent Cream, our friendship was a masterpiece, painstakingly crafted over time to endure as it did. You were my friend, my brother, and you live in my memory. To Elsie J. Kent, whose faith in me never wavered and whose early financial support fueled big dreams when desire was not enough. And, to my friend and fellow Foreign Service traveler, Csaba Chikes, whose critical pen and eye for clarity and structure helped to bring coherence to the story I now share.

Also beyond the family, I am forever indebted to Frederick L. Adams, Ambassador Chester C. Carter, Congressman James W. Symington, Dr. Rafael L. Cortada, Ruby G. Smith, Dr. Arthur Pearl, Albert L. Zucca, James E. Nance, Kwang-ji Lee, U.S. Consul General

422

Lewis E. Gleeck, Alexander Bernitz, Ambassador Denis Lamb, Ambassador Paul Bamela Engo, Dee Daniels, Susan Povenmire, C. Howie Hodges, 111, and former Commerce Secretary Ronald H. Brown for their love, wise counsel, inspiration and whose collective broad shoulders were always there for me when a bend in my road appeared to be an end of the road.

To protect the anonymity of former colleagues and personal friends, I took some creative license with actual identities. My purpose was to shield identities while permitting their humanity, or lack thereof, to speak. It was important to me that the reader understand those whose influence shaped the man I sought to become to endure the rigors they knew I would encounter on my journey.

GLOSSARY

SETAF – Southern European Task Force (1959 – 1962). Major U.S. Army Military Command in Italy during the 1950s and 1960s. Southern command of US Army Europe – USAREUR

Charge' d'affaires – Diplomatic title for Deputy Ambassador
DCM – Functional title for Deputy Ambassador

MAAG – U.S. Military Assistance Advisory Group, American Embassy Bonn, Germany (1963 – 1965). Although I was not a member of the U.S. military at this time, readers should be familiar with the term.

The FCC – The Federal City College, Washington, D.C. (1968 - 1971) predecessor institution to the current University of the District of Columbia

ECMIN – Economic and Commercial Minister, U.S. Embassy Rome (1972 – 1976)

CPAO/PAC/PAO – Country Public Affairs Officer/Public Affairs Counselor/Public Affairs Officer. Senior representative at American diplomatic missions for the former U.S. Information Agency/U.S. International Communication Agency.

USIA/USICA – The U.S. Information Agency, predecessor institution to the U.S. International Communication Agency. Renamed USICA under President Carter in April 1978. In August 1982, President Reagan changed the name back to the U.S. Information Agency (USIA) with Public Law 97-241.

UNDP (South Korea) – The United Nations Development Program. Works to eradicate poverty and reduce inequalities in countries around the world (1977 - 1979)

USIS – U.S. Information Service (USIA as it was known in U.S. missions around the world)

EC – European Communities, headquartered in Brussels, Belgium

USEC – U.S. Mission to the European Communities

GATT – General Agreement on Tariffs and Trade

USIS/USEC – United States Information Service at the U.S. Mission to the European Communities (1983 - 1988)

OECD – Organization for Economic Cooperation and Development, headquartered in Paris

CEMA – Council for Mutual Economic Assistance – the old Soviet and East European Counterpart to the European Communities

USIS/USOECD – United States Information Service at the U.S. Mission to the Organization for Economic Cooperation and Development (1988 – 1989)

G-7 Group – In 1989, this group of the world's most industrialized nations (the United States, Canada, the United Kingdom, France, the Federal Republic of Germany, Italy, Japan and the President of the European Commission) held their annual summit in Paris in conjunction with the French Bicentennial to celebrate 200 years of the rights of man. In 2016 it is the G-20.

PRINCIPAL OFFICER/CONSUL GENERAL – Principal representative of the resident American Ambassador at U.S. diplomatic and consular missions outside the capital city (1993 - 1996)

NAFTA – North American Free Trade Agreement

CFTA – U.S. - Canada Free Trade Agreement

CPSIA information can be obtained
at www.ICGtesting.com
Printed in the USA
FSOW01n0102121017
39623FS

9 780998 905907